The Hollywood Film
Music Reader

The Hollywood Film Music Reader

Edited by

MERVYN COOKE

UNIVERSITY PRESS

2010

OXFORD
UNIVERSITY PRESS

Oxford University Press, Inc., publishes works that further
Oxford University's objective of excellence
in research, scholarship, and education.

Oxford   New York
Auckland   Cape Town   Dar es Salaam   Hong Kong   Karachi
Kuala Lumpur   Madrid   Melbourne   Mexico City   Nairobi
New Delhi   Shanghai   Taipei   Toronto

With offices in
Argentina   Austria   Brazil   Chile   Czech Republic   France   Greece
Guatemala   Hungary   Italy   Japan   Poland   Portugal   Singapore
South Korea   Switzerland   Thailand   Turkey   Ukraine   Vietnam

Published by Oxford University Press, Inc.
198 Madison Avenue, New York, New York 10016

www.oup.com

Oxford is a registered trademark of Oxford University Press

Library of Congress Cataloging-in-Publication Data
The Hollywood film music reader / edited by Mervyn Cooke.
    p.   cm.
ISBN 978-0-19-533118-9; 978-0-19-533119-6 (pbk.)
1. Motion picture music—United States—History and criticism.
2. Film composers—Interviews. I. Cooke, Mervyn.
ML2075.H64 2010
781.5'420973—dc22   2010007437

Printed in the United States of America
on acid-free paper

Contents

Introduction

As the academic discipline of film-music studies continues to flourish, with theoretical analyses of film soundtracks growing ever more sophisticated and increasingly straying into exciting intellectual territories in which various formerly discrete scholarly disciplines now fruitfully interact—and this at a time when popular and journalistic interest in film music has reached an all-time high—it seems timely to offer enthusiasts for the subject a vivid reminder of the altogether more down-to-earth experiences of those whose hard work laid the foundations for the rich legacy of film-scoring practices from which movie-goers benefit today. The present volume therefore aims to provide a comprehensive collection of (often firsthand) accounts of working practices in the American film industry from the silent era to the modern blockbuster age, supplemented by a selection of historically significant items of film-music criticism. The sheer amount of vital source material pertaining to Hollywood film music that at the time of writing has long been out of print is truly remarkable, and it is to be hoped that the extracts from seminal writings reproduced here will pave the way for complete reprints of some of the more substantial testimonies from which it has only been feasible to offer relatively short extracts.

A large part of the book is devoted to the personal reminiscences of some of the leading film composers who helped change the face(s) of Hollywood scoring as it branched out from its classically influenced origins to embrace modernism, nationalism, jazz, and popular music. (The last two are each worthy of their own dedicated anthologies, as are musically rich filmic genres such as the screen musical, and it is to be hoped that this volume will prove to be merely the first in a series of similar books exploring in greater depth the fascinating source materials relating to various other facets of international film music.) The pioneering working practices of silent-film music directors, arrangers, and accompanists—some of whom worked on the East Coast—are here recounted by Max Winkler, Ernö Rapée, Hugo Riesenfeld, and Gaylord Carter. The experiences of the first generation of European-born sound-film composers, echoes of whose groundbreaking achievements are still frequently to be heard in modern film scores, are reflected in accounts penned by Max Steiner, Dimitri Tiomkin, Franz Waxman, Miklós Rózsa, and Adolph Deutsch. Their American contemporaries are represented by George Antheil, Aaron Copland, Bernard Herrmann, and David Raksin, all of whom made significant contributions not only to film scoring but also to the fledgling art of film-music criticism. Gail Kubik, Ingolf Dahl, Scott Bradley, and Carl Stalling offer telling insights into the scoring of the specialized genres of documentary and comic animation, while the attitudes of a new generation of younger and more stylistically adventurous Hollywood composers are reflected by the recollections of Elmer Bernstein and Jerry Goldsmith. Henry Mancini and André Previn provide colorful accounts of the changing shape of film music as it came under jazz and other popular influences during the 1950s, just as the future of the legendary Hollywood studios began to look distinctly precarious. Finally, the best of contemporary film scoring is represented by interviews with John Williams and Thomas Newman, the former continuing the Golden Age tradition of substantial orchestral scoring and the latter exploring fresh and evocatively minimalist soundworlds.

Three considerations emerge with striking consistency in the words of all of these composers, no matter what their individual temperaments or the historical period in which they were working: the sheer hard labor they were routinely forced to endure in order to meet punishing production schedules; their pragmatism and lack of aesthetic pretentiousness; and, above all, a wonderfully refreshing sense of humor—no doubt serving, in time-honored fashion, as a cathartic defense mechanism in the face of adversities beyond their control. Another salient feature of the composers' own accounts of life in Hollywood music departments is their innate understanding of the absolute necessity of effective teamwork and collaboration (though this consideration is often tacitly downplayed by those composers hailing from the classical arena who felt they were in danger of compromising their artistic integrity by entering the film studio). Many tributes are paid in these pages to the skill and dedication of some of the most highly regarded orchestrators and arrangers in the business, and several of our texts testify to the sometimes visionary and occasionally intransigent leadership provided by formidable studio music directors. The roster of musically sensitive film directors whose work is discussed is impressive: they include Frank Capra, Charlie Chaplin, Cecil B. DeMille, Blake Edwards, John Ford, Howard Hawks, Alfred Hitchcock, George Lucas, Lewis Milestone, Vincente Minnelli, Franklin Schaffner, Steven Spielberg, Orson Welles, and William Wyler, with Sidney Lumet contributing a sympathetic essay about his own creative relationships with a wide variety of musicians of differing temperaments. There are also glimpses of composers' notoriously unpredictable dealings with powerful producers and studio bosses, some of whom were famously hotheaded and/or musically ignorant.

In addition to the views of composers Antheil, Bernstein, Copland, Herrmann, and Raksin—and a few amusingly brutal swipes at the film industry from those luminary modernists resident in Los Angeles, Arnold Schoenberg and Igor Stravinsky—this selection of critical commentary on film music draws attention to the growth of intelligent writings on the subject begun by Leonid Sabaneev, Ingolf Dahl, and Lawrence Morton, and continued with sometimes forbidding rigor (and with fluctuating relevance to the actual craft and functions of film composition, as opposed to its intellectual interest or otherwise) by Theodor Adorno, Hanns Eisler, and F. W. Sternfeld; these and other authors laid the basic foundations for the fertile ground of present-day interdisciplinary film-music scholarship.

Here, then, are some lively and often entertaining insights into a commercially oriented and internationally enjoyed musical product, now of indestructibly long standing, that has been variously described by its practitioners as "the connecting link between the screen and the audience" (Max Winkler), a "psychological resonator of the screen" (Leonid Sabaneev), "a small flame put under the screen to warm it" (Aaron Copland), or simply regarded as a uniquely pleasurable creative phenomenon that "just perfumes the air with music" (Gaylord Carter).

I

From "Silents" to Sound

As unlikely as it may seem today, when lucrative Hollywood films have dominated the world market without interruption for so many decades, the legendary
film industry of the West Coast was not always at the forefront of global production and consumption. After their tentative beginnings in the 1890s as show-
booth and vaudeville attractions, moving pictures became more sophisticated
largely through the efforts of pioneering filmmakers in Europe and on the East
Coast of the United States. Edison Pictures employee Edwin S. Porter discovered
the importance of continuity editing in the early years of the twentieth century,
and the burgeoning film industries of France and Italy later strove to produce
substantial feature films that both made the new medium artistically respectable
and demonstrated its international commercial potential. The success of the
French school of *film d'art* (for which Camille Saint-Saëns wrote one of the first
original film scores in 1908) and the commercial drive of the powerful Pathé
and Gaumont companies lay behind the establishment in Paris of the world's
first luxurious picture palaces, the first of which opened in 1906, when the U.S.
film industry was still a fledgling. Even as American film production blossomed
in the 1910s, Italian historical epics were the equivalent of today's Hollywood
blockbusters, commanding huge budgets and massive audiences abroad. European dominance was finally checked by the First World War, by which time U.S.
filmmakers had shifted their center of production squarely to what had, only a
few years before, been an insignificant village near Los Angeles.

The ascendancy of the Hollywood film companies resulted from the sustained determination of independent producers who rebelled against the
strictures of the Motion Pictures Patents Company, which had attempted to

control the industry from 1908 onward; these forward-thinkers realized the commercial potential inherent in the multireel feature film (in contrast to relatively insubstantial single-reel productions favored by the MPPC), and forever changed the nature of both film production and distribution. The leading figures behind this initiative included William Fox (whose Film Corporation of 1915 would two decades later merge with Twentieth Century), Carl Laemmle (who founded Universal Pictures in 1912), Samuel Goldwyn and Louis B. Mayer (whose companies merged to form MGM in 1924), the Warner brothers (whose company was incorporated in 1923), and Adolph Zukor (whose Famous Players–Lasky Corporation, founded in 1916, became Paramount Pictures in 1935). The output of their highly industrious studios increased rapidly: by 1915, approximately 60 percent of U.S. motion pictures were being made in Hollywood; and by 1919, when the flourishing former village officially became part of greater Los Angeles, no fewer than 90 percent of all films shown in Europe were now being imported from the States.

The West Coast film companies remained to some extent dependent on the East Coast, not only because of the need for substantial financial investments from Wall Street but also in their desire to disseminate appropriate music to accompany their products. Powerful companies such as Famous Players–Lasky had their own distribution arms (in their case, Paramount, which by 1915 was consistently releasing three or four features each week), which enforced block bookings of their films across the nation's theatrical outlets. Previously, the nature and extent of a motion picture's musical accompaniment had been left almost entirely to the whim of individual exhibitors. At precisely the time when Hollywood was establishing itself as a major center of film production, the industry began its attempt to standardize what had formerly been haphazard musical provision in the nation's nickelodeons. Instead of rambling keyboard playing and irrelevant musical selections, film companies now demanded a reliable and formulaic mode of musical accompaniment for their products. Unless gramophone recordings were used for this purpose, as they rarely were until the short-lived boom in disc-recorded soundtracks in the late 1920s, such music had to be performed live by the venues' resident musicians, and the only way to control what they played was through the influence of the leading East Coast music publishers. Max Winkler's reminiscences of his seminal role in the launching of musical cue sheets for films are given below, alongside accounts of the high-profile careers of renowned East Coast music directors Ernö Rapée and Hugo Riesenfeld, whose work at major Broadway theaters lent the finest Hollywood silent films a sense of audiovisual coherence and artistic respectability approaching that of the popular operas, ballets, and melodramas from which much early film music took its direct inspiration.

Recorded musical accompaniments to silent films were generally felt to be inferior to the attractiveness of live music, which had long been a vital part of the cinemagoing experience, but this view disappeared almost overnight once the novelty value of better-quality and more substantial disc-recorded sound-tracks caught the public imagination. Disc-recorded sound, played back in synchronization with the moving images via a mechanical coupling between gramophone and projector, was at first geared toward the reproduction of short musical performances that were designed to fit naturally into the vaudeville-like miscellany on offer at most provincial projection venues. The spectacular but short-lived success of Western Electric's Vitaphone technology (purchased by Warner Bros. in 1925) also showed how a continuous orchestral accompaniment in the silent-film manner could now be enshrined on disc and—provided theaters could afford the relevant equipment—conveniently distributed with a film, thereby both obviating the need for venues to employ their own performers and ensuring a uniformly high performance standard. It was the sudden irruption of synchronized dialogue, thanks to Al Jolson's on-screen

Cartoonist H. F. Hoffman draws attention to the haphazard nature of early silent-film accompaniment in the journal *Moving Picture World* (June 21, 1911, p. 124). The drummer has abandoned his post (note, in addition to the traps, a revolver and anvil for providing crude sound effects), and the pianist is adjusting her hair in a mirror while a climactic action scene takes place on the screen in complete silence.

antics in Warner Bros.' *Jazz Singer* (dir. Alan Crosland, 1927), which quickly put paid to any suggestion that the old-fashioned method of saturated film scoring would continue unchecked.

As sound-on-film technology rapidly began to replace the cumbersome disc system, music now not only had to contend with the greater importance of dialogue but also had to find a way of tackling what many commentators found to be a depressing return to stage-bound theatricality in the new talking pictures: the fantastic elements and bold structural experimentation that had distinguished the finest silent films were for a few years almost entirely abandoned, thus offering severely reduced opportunities for creative scoring. Many influential filmmakers and theorists in the 1920s, especially those working in Europe, were deeply skeptical about the aesthetic value of synchronized naturalistic sound. And the introduction of synchronized soundtracks was controversial not only for artistic reasons: almost overnight, in both the United States and Europe, musicians who had formerly enjoyed steady employment in movie-theater bands found themselves out of work—and this on the eve of the Great Depression, which brought its own major slump in the industry's fortunes at a difficult time when the novelty value of talking pictures was in any case beginning to wear thin. Vociferous protests by several musicians' unions at the wholesale redundancies of their members came to naught, and the prerecorded synchronized film score continued to enjoy an unassailed position in the industry until the 1970s saw the gradual revival of live performances of the classics of silent cinema.

I

Max Winkler: "The Origin of Film Music" (1951)

The standardization of film music in the 1910s was aided by the introduction of systematic methods for disseminating approved musical selections to accompany individual motion pictures. The simplest of these was the cue sheet, a development from the listings of musical suggestions that had already appeared in the film industry's trade press, which now took the form of a separate publication tied directly in to a specific release: the musical items suggested for the principal scenes were to be extracted either from preexisting classical scores or from the relevant publisher's rapidly expanding libraries of music compiled or freshly composed for this purpose. The credit for the cue sheet's invention was taken by Max Winkler (1888–1965), whose lively—and not altogether reliable—account of what quickly became a publishing phenomenon is reproduced below. His recollections also include a vivid snapshot of the anxiety in the music business engendered by the coming of the sound film in 1927.

Winkler worked as a clerk for the New York publishing house of Carl Fischer, Inc., and his cue-sheet idea secured him business links with Universal Pictures and other production companies in Hollywood; his initiative therefore demonstrates the close link between West Coast movie production and East Coast music-publishing interests that was crucial to the success of the film industry at this early stage in its history. Winkler later left Fischer's and went into partnership with rival cue-sheet compiler S. M. Berg. Similar links were

Source: *Films in Review*, 2/34 (December 1951); reprinted in James L. Limbacher, ed., *Film Music: From Violins to Video* (Metuchen, N.J.: Scarecrow Press, 1974): 15–24.

established between other film companies and publishers—for example, between Famous Players–Lasky (through their distributor, Paramount) and G. Schirmer, Inc. In 1915, Schirmer's employee George W. Beynon began compiling complete film scores based on preexisting music, the publisher's advertisements for its Paramount tie-ins declaring that "Music is the Power Behind the Screen" and that "the 'right music' must be put in proper form or it is not of practical use in picture-playing . . . PRINTED MUSIC SCORES SAVE TIME, TROUBLE, MONEY."

The year 1912 was the beginning of the greatest and most prosperous era in the history of the American amusement industry. Scores of theaters played on Broadway. Victor Herbert was at the peak of his fame. Irving Berlin had begun the ascent to his. Vaudeville prospered throughout the country and the big movie chains, such as Fox and Loew's, had begun to hire vaudeville acts with guarantees that ran to as much as 104 weeks of continuous employment.

All this had tremendous repercussions on the world of music publishing, and soon the exciting waves of prosperity reached the band and orchestra counter in the Carl Fischer store. We began to sell unheard-of amounts of waltzes and songs, of potpourris and marches, of overtures and interludes. Orchestra arrangements of the popular songs of the day arrived from the printers in staggering quantities and were disposed of quickly.

Nothing that happened in the rapidly expanding world of musical comedies, operettas and vaudeville was comparable, however, to the breath-taking development of the silent movies. The men who became the giants of the film industry were beginning to produce films on a large scale in Hollywood. Big movie theatres were being erected, not only in New York but in every town and village. This was of tremendous consequence to the music business. The silent film needed music to bring it to life.

"On the silent screen music must take the place of the spoken word" had become one of the credos of the film industry. Huge theatre orchestras were hired to play in the movie palaces of the big cities, and smaller ensembles, trios, or simply an organist or a pianist, were employed in thousands of towns and villages.

Only in a few isolated theatres in big cities was any effort made to coordinate the goings-on on the screen with the sounds in the musical pit. Thousands of musicians never had a chance to see a picture before they were called upon to play music for it! There they were sitting in the dark, watching the screen, trying to follow the rapidly unfolding events with their music: sad music, funny music, slow music—sinister, agitated, stormy, dramatic, funereal, pursuit, and amorous music. They had to improvise, playing whatever repertoire came to their worried minds, or whatever they made up themselves on the spur of a short moment. It was a terrible predicament—and so, usually, was the music.

One day in the spring of 1912 [*recte*: 1916] I went to one of the small movie houses that had so quickly sprung up all over town, to see one of the superb spectacles of the day. It was called *War Brides* and featured the exotic Nazimova in the role of a pregnant peasant woman. The king of the mythical country where Nazimova was living passed through her village. Nazimova threw herself in front of him, her hands raised to heaven. She said—no, she didn't say anything but the title on the screen announced: "If you will not give us women the right to vote for or against war I shall not bear a child for such a country."

The king just moved on. Nazimova drew a dagger and killed herself.

The pianist so far had done all right. But I scarcely believed my ears when, just as Nazimova exhaled her last breath, to the heart-breaking sobs of her family, he began to play the old, frivolous favorite, "You Made Me What I Am Today."

The pianist was one of my customers and I just could not resist going backstage afterwards and asking him why he had chosen this particular tune at that particular moment. "Why," he said, "I thought that was perfectly clear. Wasn't it the king's fault that she killed herself?"

More and more musical mishaps began to turn drama and tragedy on the screen into farce and disaster. Exhibitors and theatre managers made frantic efforts to avoid the musical *faux pas* that made their films appear ridiculous. Carl Fischer's was probably the most famous and certainly the most successful house in the field of orchestra music. I began to understand their problems. We gave advice, we helped some of them, and when they described to us a particular scene in a film, we usually would know of a piece that would fit the mood.

All this had, of course, a very stimulating effect on the volume of business transacted by Carl Fischer's orchestra department, and as the orders came in I had visions of an even more magnificent future.

One day after I had gone home from work I could not fall asleep. The hundreds and thousands of titles, the mountains of music that Fischer's had stored and cataloged, kept going through my mind. There was music, surely to fit *any* given situation in *any* picture. If we could only think of a way to let all these orchestra leaders and pianists and organists know what we had! If we could use our knowledge and experience not when it was too late, but much earlier, before they ever had to sit down and play, we would be able to sell them music not by the ton but by the train-load!

The thought suddenly electrified me. It was not a problem of getting the music. We had the music, plenty of it, any conceivable kind, more than anybody could ever want. It was a problem of promoting, timing, and organization. I pulled back the blanket, turned on the light and went over to my little table, took a sheet of paper and began writing feverishly.

Here is what I wrote:

MUSIC CUE SHEET
for
The Magic Valley
Selected and compiled by M. Winkler

Cue

1 Opening—play Minuet No. 2 in G by Beethoven for ninety seconds until title on screen "Follow me dear."

2 Play—"Dramatic Andante" by Vely for two minutes and ten seconds. Note: Play soft during scene where mother enters. Play Cue No. 2. until scene "hero leaving room."

3 Play—"Love Theme" by Lorenze–for one minute and twenty seconds. Note: Play soft and slow during conversations until title on screen "There they go."

4 Play—"Stampede" by Simon for fifty-five seconds. Note: Play fast and decrease or increase speed of gallop in accordance with action on the screen.

I kept on writing for hours. *The Magic Valley* was just an imaginary picture with imaginary scenes, situations and moods, but the music was real music. It was music I knew. The years of close contact with it, of carrying it around, of sorting it out, of hearing it, listing it, handling it, living with it, now began to bear unexpected fruit. I went to bed exhausted, and when I woke up the next morning it took me a little time to remember how these densely covered sheets of paper had come into my room.

The next day I copied them cleanly and wrote a letter to the New York office of the Universal Film Company.

"If you would give me a chance to see your pictures *before* they are released I could prepare such a cue sheet for each one of them," I wrote. "You could send them out before you release the prints of your films. It would give the local theatre time to prepare adequate musical accompaniment. It will help everybody, the industry, the musicians, and the public." It would also, of course, help the orchestra department of Carl Fischer's, and there was still another party I was hoping the scheme might be able to help, but I didn't mention him in my letter.

Two days later I found myself in the office of Mr. Paul Gulick, publicity director of Universal, in the Mecca Building, 1600 Broadway. It was late in the day. I had not dared to leave my job at the store, not even for so exciting an appointment. Gulick had my letter and the cue sheet for *The Magic Valley* before him on his desk. He began asking questions. What was I doing? What made me think that I would be the man to fit music to pictures? It wasn't just an occasional picture, he explained, there might be ten, fifteen, twenty every week— I wouldn't have time to go home and think and consult catalogs or listen to a lot of tunes till I found the right one.

"Just give me a chance," I said. "Let me try. I'll show you."

"All right, come up tomorrow night. Be here at seven. We'll see."

Between seven o'clock and a half hour past midnight the next night I was shown sixteen different subjects—slap-stick comedies, newsreels, a trip through the Sahara, a Western. I had been provided with a little desk, a stop watch, a stack of paper, a little mountain of pencils. I looked and stopped my watch and wrote. As the pictures flashed by, the bins in the Fischer store appeared before my eyes. I not only *heard* the music that would fit perfectly to the camels slowly swaying through the sand, I *saw* the bin that stored Tchaikovsky's "Dance Arabe," and the title I had printed on the card over the bin, and while the camels trotted across the screen I wrote it down on the cue sheet without a moment's hesitation.

Gulick sat there, watched me, and never said a word. When I had finished at last, everything was going in circles before my exhausted eyes. Gulick took my notes.

"We'll let you know," he said, yawning. "Good night."

The next day—it was 3:30 in the afternoon and I will never forget it—a messenger boy strolled into the Fischer store. He came over to the orchestra counter. He didn't have to ask for me. Before he could say a word I took the letter he held in his hand, signed a receipt with a trembling scrawl. I tore open the envelope. It contained a letter signed by a live vice-president of Universal, engaging me for a four-week period to preview "the films made by this company in advance of actual release date and to prepare music cue sheets for said films, regardless of character or length, such cue sheets to contain only musical compositions published and easily available to our distributors and exhibitors. The films will be shown to you every Tuesday night at Projection Room C in our offices at 1600 Broadway. Your remuneration for said services will be $30 per session. If this meets with your approval please sign the enclosed copy and return same for our files."

During the following weeks I saw more silly comedies, blood-curdling murders and tear-milking melodramas than any other human being has ever been condemned to see. But nobody ever enjoyed them more! Each night Universal rushed my feverishly scribbled notes to the printer and the next day thousands of copies went out to every theatre manager, pianist, organist and orchestra director in every theatre in America.

The response was overwhelming. Everybody was delighted. It seemed as simple as Columbus' egg—why had nobody thought of it before? Soon Universal was swamped with requests for cue sheets for films which had been released prior to my appearance on the scene, and Gulick asked me to work an extra night on his old pictures. For the two evening sessions he offered me a salary of forty dollars a week. . . .

Soon we went places. Berg and I had, in the past, been the real stars in the cue sheet world and now that we had become united, we established a virtual monopoly. We supplied the musical cue sheets for Universal, Triangle Films, Douglas Fairbanks, Sr. (then, of course, very much Jr.), William S. Hart, Fox Films, Vitagraph and Goldwyn, and the Great M stars: Mabel Normand, Mary Garden and Mae Marsh.

Every scene, situation, character, action, emotion, every nationality, emergency, wind storm, rain storm and brain storm, every dancer, vamp, cowboy, thief and gigolo, eskimo and zulu, emperor and streetwalker, colibri and elephant—plus every printed title that flickered in the faces of the five-cent to twenty-five-cent audiences—had to be expressed in music, and we soon realized that our catalog of so-called Dramatic and Incidental Music was quite insufficient to furnish the simply colossal amounts of music needed by an ever-expanding industry.

We searched for composers who would supply what we needed and we found them. They were fine musicians, but they were specialists in just one phase of music, film music, and most of them are forgotten today. Who still knows the compositions of Walter Simon, Herman Froml, Gaston Borch, Charles Herbert, Irene Berge, Leo Kempinski, Maurice Baron, Hugo Riesenfeld? Very few, if any, still remember them and yet, in those days, gone only a few decades, their music was heard by more people in this country than was the music of all the great masters combined.

In those days of the silent film these men created the connecting link between the screen and the audience, and the film companies and large theatres which employed orchestras clamored for more and more music. Their instructions to us were: "Once we play a piece of music we don't want it duplicated for at least three months."

This, of course, made our task even more difficult. Our composers were writing film music by the mile, and in order to augment their unceasing efforts we began to import music from Europe, where a whole battery of writers were busy turning their talents to picture music. Among them were: A. W. Ketelbey, world-famous composer of "In a Persian Market"; Ricardo Drigo, whose Serenade from "Les Millions d'Arlequin" is still being played throughout the world; Giuseppe Becce; Patou; and even some of the works of the great Sibelius. Our catalog of Agitatos, Animal Cartoons, Church Music, and such sub-divisions as Sinister, Chase, Sad, Happy, Gypsy, Mysterious, Furious and Majestic, grew and grew.

But no matter how hard we pushed our composers, they had only twenty-four hours a day to put music on paper and that just wasn't enough. We were not only working for the film companies in New York, we had arrangements with some seventy theatres all over the country to view the pictures they booked and to make special musical cue sheets for their orchestras. The cue sheets plus the actual music were to be in their possession a week before the picture went on. The demands upon us grew into staggering dimensions.

In desperation we turned to crime. We began to dismember the great masters. We began to murder the works of Beethoven, Mozart, Grieg, J. S. Bach, Verdi, Bizet, Tchaikovsky and Wagner—everything that wasn't protected by copyright from our pilfering.

The immortal chorales of J. S. Bach became an "Adagio Lamentoso for sad scenes." Extracts from great symphonies and operas were hacked down to emerge again as "Sinister Misterioso" by Beethoven, or "Weird Moderato" by Tchaikovsky. Wagner's and Mendelssohn's wedding marches were used for marriages, fights between husbands and wives, and divorce scenes: we just had them played out of tune, a treatment known in the profession as "souring up the aisle." If they were to be used for happy endings we jazzed them up mercilessly. Finales from famous overtures, with "William Tell" and "Orpheus" the favorites, became galops. Meyerbeer's "Coronation March" was slowed down to a majestic pomposo to give proper background to the inhabitants of Sing Sing's deathhouse. The "Blue Danube" was watered down to a minuet by a cruel change in tempo. Delibes' "Pizzicato Polka" made an excellent ac-companiment to a sneaky night scene by counting "one-two" between each pizzicato. Any piece using a trombone prominently would infallibly announce the home-coming of a drunk: no other instrument could hiccup with such virtuosity.

Today I look in shame and awe at the printed copies of these mutilated masterpieces. I hope this belated confession will grant me forgiveness for what I have done. But in those days these pieces saved our lives; no composer could ever catch up with me, blue-pencilling and re-creating with scissors and paste a section of Beethoven's "Pastoral Symphony." Soon we produced these "works" at a breath-taking speed and our list of Dramatic and Incidental music covered almost any situation the most extravagant film writer could think of.

Our firm had grown with the movie industry, for music had become one of the big features of the tremendous movie palaces which had been built all over the country. Hundred-thousand-dollar organs and 60-piece orchestras were advertised in screaming letters everywhere. Also, it was an era of prosperity and a publisher who specialized, as I did, in music for films, and stayed away from other adventures, was bound to prosper. And then, suddenly, it was all over. Completely, with terrifying speed, and with absolute, crushing finality.

There had been rumors about an invention that could make pictures talk. We had shrugged them off. But after attending the grand opening [in 1927] of the first sound film, *The Jazz Singer*, we couldn't shrug anymore. A few weeks later I had to realize that what had been an industry, what I had made my own and very special business, music for the silent films, would within a short time be a thing of the past. I went home dazed. Again I was faced with the fact that there is no such thing as security. What I had thought was a solid foundation for my life was crumbling.

Within a few months 15,000 film theatres throughout the U. S. were clamoring for sound equipment. If one theatre in a town was able to obtain it, every other house immediately turned into a morgue. Nearly 100,000 musicians found themselves without jobs. It was a grim, sweeping, disastrous collapse.

My tremendous stock of music became worthless overnight. There was nothing to do but to face facts. I sold no less than 70 tons of printed music to a paper mill for 15 cents a hundred pounds. $210 for the entire lot! But two days before it was to pay the $210, the mill went bankrupt, after having been in business for over 90 years. I never received a penny for my entire stock, the fruit of ten years of toil.

For a little while there was just nothing to do but to sit and wait and think. I did not despair. I had seen too many of these changes, and I had acquired enough hope and confidence to take what was coming and to make the best of it.

And then the talkies, which had dealt me so crushing a blow, helped me to catch my breath. The film companies soon realized that nobody could better help them with their new, uncharted task of fitting music to the sound track of pictures, than the men who had done the same type of work for silent pictures. Soon fabulous prices were offered for the services of such men as Hugo Riesenfeld, conductor of the Rivoli Theatre in New York, Erno Rapee of the Roxy, and Nat Finston of the New York Rialto. Within a short time these men found themselves in Hollywood preparing musical scores for sound film. And what was more logical than for them to fall back on the material they had used in the past and knew so well—the mood music, dramatic and incidental, that would fit the situation in sound pictures as it had fitted the situation in silent ones?

The men who were selecting and recording music in Hollywood were all my friends. They knew every piece in my catalog. It was a life-saver for them and for me. I didn't sell sheet music any more. I now sold film companies the right to use my music on sound tracks. This soon became a general practice. I was in business again.

But I knew it couldn't last long. The film companies were paying millions of dollars to publishers and composers for the use of published music. They soon found it more profitable to hire composers to write original music and to organize their own publishing houses. When Warner Brothers spent a million dollars to acquire the old established catalog of M. Witmark and Sons [in 1929], with thousands of valuable copyrights, the rush was on. Soon most of the major film companies were in the music publishing business and were not interested in outside publications any more. My catalog was again heading for the junk pile, this time for good. I knew that if I wanted to survive I had to draw a final line under the past and find an entirely new field of activity.

2

T. Scott Buhrman: "Photoplays De Luxe" (1920)

The most ambitious musical accompaniments for silent films were those offered by the huge picture palaces in major cities, of which perhaps the most famous was New York's Strand on Broadway, which opened in 1914 and could seat 3,500 spectators; its music, overseen by the legendary Samuel L. Rothapfel (popularly known as "Roxy"), was supplied by a thirty-piece resident orchestra and a gargantuan Wurlitzer organ. The provision of more extravagant musical resources coincided with a boom in the production of film epics, not only those made in America but also those imported from France and Italy. The most celebrated indigenous example was D. W. Griffith's enormously influential *The Birth of a Nation*, which received its East Coast premiere at New York's Liberty Theater in March 1915 with a three-hour compilation score by Joseph Carl Breil, replacing the classical selections prepared by Carli Elinor for the Los Angeles premiere exactly one month before. On the date of the West Coast launch (8 February) the *Los Angeles Times* had excitedly reported that Breil's efforts for the upcoming New York screening were

> no less than the adapting of grand-opera methods to motion pictures!
> Each character playing has a distinct type of music, a distinct theme
> as in opera. A more difficult matter in pictures than in opera,
> however, inasmuch as any one character seldom holds the screen
> long at a time. In cases where there are many characters, the music is
> adapted to the dominant note or character in the scene.

Source: American Organist, 3/5 (1920): 157–75, 171–73.

> From now on special music is to be written in this manner for all
> the big Griffith productions.

Soon well known on both sides of the Atlantic, Breil's achievement was pro-
phetic of later film scores in combining operatic grandeur with commercial
success, its love theme ("The Perfect Song") selling well in sheet-music form
when subsequently furnished with lyrics.

Two of the best-known music directors at the most sumptuous theatrical
venues on the East Coast, many of them appointed by and answering to Roxy
as part of his Broadway empire, were Ernö Rapée at the Capitol (see Chapter 3),
and Hugo Riesenfeld (1879–1939) at the Rialto, Rivoli, and Criterion theaters—
among the largest in New York after the First World War. In Los Angeles, Roxy's
counterpart was Sid Grauman, whose movie palaces included Hollywood's
Chinese and Egyptian theaters. Riesenfeld had been concertmaster of the
Vienna Opera before his emigration to the States to take up the same post with
the Metropolitan Opera in 1907, and, not surprisingly, in his film-exhibition
work he had an inbuilt tendency to privilege musical quality over the visual
image. This was strikingly shown by his unusual habit of editing segments of
film himself or requiring the projector to be run at variable speeds so that the
images might fit better with his musical selections. The following account of
his working practices was written by the editor of *American Organist* in 1920,
the year in which it began publishing a regular column devoted to film music.

A person visiting a photoplay for the first time would not know much about
either picture or music, but the Rialto and Rivoli programs are planned not for
such patrons but for those who visit the theaters as regularly as the latter-day
saints go to church—at least once a week. And with a process of education such
as this the patron soon begins to know as much about the proper way to present
a picture as he does the proper way to comb his hair; if a theater is to hold its
patrons it must hold its standards.

Usually a program of films is engaged a week or two in advance and then
when a new program starts its run on the first day of the week the director
begins his arduous task of setting music to the program of the coming week's
production. To visit a projection room during the musical scoring of a film is an
interesting experience. At one end of a twelve by thirty-foot room is a screen
possibly six feet square; in the wall at the opposite end are two holes for the
machines and two for the operators to peep through or stick their heads through

for an occasional conference with the director: directly under these holes are half a dozen comfortable wicker chairs with a long table-like bench conveniently in front and a swinging phone within grabbing distance; to the right is an upright piano; around the walls are cabinets of piano scores and violin scores all carefully assorted under proper heads, "love scenes," "home scenes," "waltzes," "Russian," "Overtures," "suites," "military marches," etc., ad infinitum; and in the ceiling is an electric light of excellent power which keeps going full force through the entire operation.

"There are millions of ways," says Hugo Riesenfeld, who scores all the pictures of the Rialto, Rivoli, and Criterion programs, "of selecting music to serve as accompaniment for a picture, but there are only two ways that a good musician would choose. One is to select beautiful music that is appropriate for the scenes of the picture, and the good musician, inexperienced in motion picture presentation would undoubtedly follow this course. The second course, and the one that requires the hardest work, is to select music such as would be chosen in the first mentioned way, but with an ear to its subjugation. There may be half a hundred waltzes that would go prettily with certain scenes, but the experienced scorer of motion pictures will, after listening to the piece, know whether it is too striking—or even too beautiful." And all through the few hours when I had the privilege of observing the scoring process under Mr. Riesenfeld's magic hand, I witnessed this "subjugation" in actual fact. "Not so fast," "Slower, please," "Oh, not so fast," "Take it this way," and the director would hum the tune or whistle it or beat it out on the table with his thumb; in every case the music was "toned down," "subjugated" to the picture. Had it not been done I imagine the effect would have been one of frivolity, if not completely grotesque; but subjugated in this way, and ultimately in many other ways of which only Hugo Riesenfeld can give the clue, music of the most attractive kind—attractive to musicians—lends itself admirably to the screen.

The success of the Riesenfeld productions is not only a matter of the films selected; I question if the films have even fifty per cent of the credit. In fact I know of one case where Mr. Riesenfeld scored a picture, after cutting up the film and showing it as he wanted instead of as the producers photographed it, with success, while the same picture in its original form under the management of other producers in other houses fell a failure.

At half after ten on a Monday night, when most people were beginning to seal up their day as well done and turn their thoughts to hot or cold showers according to taste, and feather pillows, I got safely by the guards (an iron gate that works with difficulty) and climbed two flights of stairs at Broadway and 42nd Street. In the director's private projection room were already gathered the operators, conductors, pianist, and librarian, with Mr. Riesenfeld seated in his comfortable chair ready to "make" another Riesenfeld production. Mr. Riesenfeld had already seen the picture once, of course, so he began his search for music of a certain well defined type. Piece after piece (only a little of each, of course) was played on the piano as this or that conductor would pick out one as a suggestion, and all that could be gotten out of Mr. Riesenfeld was "No," "Not that," "No," "No, that won't do," "Oh, no, not that"—and all the while the cameras were waiting to click their first inch of the film, not a picture as yet having gone to the screen; the director had his head stuck deep in a folio of possibly two hundred selections of a given type, every one of which he glanced through in his search for the "right" one. Finally it was found; and what a relief. "Slower; oh, not so fast," then "Ah, that's it, that's it," and the ready amanuensis jotted down a few abbreviations to show that when the picture was ready to begin the music would be this piece, and that so much of it would be used. A mark was put lightly on the score. All that work for about sixty seconds' worth of music! To the question, "What is Hugo Riesenfeld?" we might answer, "Infinite capacity for taking pains." The piece, before being laid aside, was again played on the piano at proper tempo, that is at Mr. Riesenfeld's own tempo, the director pushed the button, the picture announcement began, and I almost thought I was going to see a free picture show this time. But no, I read some words announcing the title of the picture, and some other words telling who photographed it, and still more words advising me all about the people who acted in it; and then the fatal button was pressed and the "show" stopped. Then the search for music began all over again. Soon something was tried which pleased Director Riesenfeld and as the pianist started to play it again the button was pressed and the picture resumed its course just where it left off. That is, resumed it for another two seconds till the emotions of the screen drama changed and with it changed the emotions of this highly-strung bit of human machinery who controlled the fatal button—and the picture went dead again till some new bit of music could be found to suit the new emotions.

And so it went. George G. Shor said of a certain film, "In the picture you saw, the orchestra played the following movements for the feature film; six one-steps, four fox-trots"—and let us recall that the fox-trot or gallop or agitato in the middle of a Beethoven symphony is given in Mr. Shor's parlance under the name of its matter-of-fact content and not under its classic title—"one gallop, three agitatos, four waltzes, one two-step, one march, two songs, eight intermezzi, one operatic movement, one symphonic selection, one mysterioso, one suite movement, and one tarantelle." And this only tells a small part of the story; it forgets all about the cuts, the arrangements, the slides and glides and skips and hops through all musicdom in order to make these things go together in a proper sequence of keys as one piece.

After little snatches of the film are thus projected and music fitted intimately with the moods of each, with proper record made of each separate bit of film and the music corresponding with it, Mr. Riesenfeld takes the music under his wing and spends laborious hours over it, marking, timing, cutting, trimming, fitting, and preparing it to time rightly with the film. When this is done and the librarians and orchestrators have arranged and written such things as are needed for the film, the film itself is taken in hand for revision. Projection machines can be made to run at variable speeds to suit the occasion, and these speeds can be arbitrarily set by a projector without interfering in any way with the picture; I doubt if any but a very skilled man would be able to detect the many changes Mr. Riesenfeld must get from his operators. Many times the titles and joints in the film are deleted to just the right amount to make the film time exactly with the music, while at other times, the speed accomplishes the result. Thus after the music is first fitted to the picture, the picture is then fitted exactly to the music. Ordinarily pictures hit the screens at the rate of from eight to sixteen per second, while the fanciful rushes are said to fly as fast as one hundred and twenty-eight per second, at which rate I am told the novel extremely slow pictures are actually photographed in the original in order to be projected ultimately as the normal rate and produce the slow picture.

Hugo Riesenfeld was born in Vienna in 1879 and graduated with honors from the Vienna Conservatory; he came to America in 1907 and has since conducted himself as a loyal and distinguished fellow citizen of whom we may be proud. His first American engagement was with Oscar Hammerstein as concertmeister and conductor; confining his activities to light opera; during the Century Theatre's second season he was conductor of the serious opera given there in English. When the Rialto and Rivoli were opened Mr. Riesenfeld was engaged as conductor, and in January, 1919, he took the managing directorship into his own hands, adding the Criterion in April of the present year. Personally he is a man of medium height and weight, soft spoken and mild in manner with nothing of the hustle and bustle of his active life appearing in his manner, but with his artistic temperament cropping out all over; one would never take him for a manager, only an artist. That's why the music of the Rialto and Rivoli is being written about in these columns. There is never anything theatrical in his productions; they are always artistic. . . .

3

Ernö Rapée: "Musical Accompaniment to the Feature Picture" (1925)

In 1925, on the eve of the demise of the silent film, Ernö Rapée (1891–1945) here summarizes the basic principles of its music, demonstrating in the process how the scoring methods emerging since the early 1910s had by this late stage become codified and formulaic, and ready to form the basis for the orchestral accompaniment to the Hollywood sound film with surprisingly little need of modification. Among the devices recommended by Rapée and already commonplace are the use of specific themes associated with individual characters (after the Wagnerian principle of leitmotif, for more about which see pp. 88 and 290–91), the desirability of including a prominent love theme, the use of locational music appropriate to a film's geographical setting, and the exploitation of contrasting instrumentation to vary a single melodic idea. Rapée also offers practical advice on how a music director should deal with contingencies such as a sudden break in the film or a fire in the projection booth (a common enough problem with the highly combustible film stock in use at the time), and how a working music library should be maintained. All of these observations serve as a vivid reminder that silent-film music was a live and sometimes unpredictable performance activity, fundamentally different in spirit and audience impact from the set-in-stone quality of later soundtracks. Yet Rapée's firm belief that an audience need not be consciously aware of film music in order to be psychologically influenced by it was echoed by many later commentators on the role of music in the sound film.

Source: *Encyclopaedia of Music for Pictures* (New York: Belwin Inc., 1925; reprinted by Arno Press Inc., 1970): 13–16, 19–20.

Born in Hungary, Rapée possessed a wide experience of musical direction in movie theaters both in Europe and the United States, and published *Motion Picture Moods for Pianists and Organists* (New York, 1924) in addition to the *Encyclopaedia of Music for Pictures,* from which the following text is taken—and of which the bulk is devoted to an alphabetical listing of dramatic situations (e.g. "Aeroplane," "Gruesome," "Shopping Stores," "Skeleton"), each containing suggestions of appropriate music culled from the light classics and from original cues specially written by American composers. Rapée well knew the power of the hit theme tune, and went on to achieve million-copy sales of the sheet music to his songs "Charmaine" and "Diane," featured in *What Price Glory?* (dir. Raoul Walsh, 1926) and *Seventh Heaven* (dir. Frank Borzage, 1927) respectively, the former starring Dolores Del Rio. Both films were silent productions to which mechanically synchronized recorded scores were added in the wake of the success of the disc-recorded music in *The Jazz Singer*. But Rapée could on occasion experiment in a bolder fashion than his formulaic practical manuals would suggest. In collaboration with Roxy, for example, he was responsible for accompanying a 1921 New York screening of the German expressionist classic *Das Cabinet des Dr Caligari* (dir. Robert Wiene, 1919) with a selection of relatively avant-garde music by a range of challenging modern composers, including Prokofiev, Schoenberg, and Stravinsky.

A great deal has been written on how to arrange music to feature pictures. Experience and observation have taught me that the simplest procedure is as follows:—Firstly—determine the geographic and national atmosphere of your picture,—Secondly—embody everyone of your important characters with a theme. Undoubtedly there will be a Love Theme and most likely there will be a theme for the Villain. If there is a humorous character who makes repeated appearances he will also have to be characterized by a theme of his own.

It will happen quite often that two characters, each having a theme will appear together in which case it will be necessary to write original music for that particular scene treating the two themes according to the rules of counterpoint.—After your atmosphere is established and your characters are endowed with their respective themes determine if either the playing of atmosphere music or the individual theme will suffice in portraying happenings on the screen or if the psychologic conditions are such that the emotional part will have to be portrayed in preference to atmospheric or characteristic situations. Now you can start setting each scene: if you have a picture playing, for instance, in China, you will have to find all your accompaniment material in existing Chinese music, both to cover atmospheric situations as well as to endow your characters. If there happens to be two Chinese characters and one English you will of course cover your English character, by English music for the sake of contrast.

The choice of the Love Theme is a very important part of the scoring as it is a constantly recurring theme in the average run of pictures and as a rule will impress your audience more than any other theme. Special care should be taken in choosing the Love Theme from various angles. If you have a Western picture dealing with a farm-hand and a country girl you should choose a musically simple and sweet ballad. If your Love Theme is to cover a relationship between society people, usually portrayed as sophisticated and blasé, choose a number of the type represented by the compositions of such composers as Victor Herbert or Chaminade.

It will often happen that the situations on the screen require the Love Theme being used for an extraordinary length of time in which case you may have to play four or five choruses. This situation should be handled by varying your orchestrations, play one chorus as a violin solo, then have all the strings play it; the next one can be played on the Oboe or Cello and so forth. If you have exhausted all variations and particularly if the situation is of a dramatic sort have your men play that same chorus 1/2 a tone higher or lower.

As long as you vary your instrumentation or your tonality it will not get tiresome. The danger of monotony is often encountered playing an oriental picture, as the playing of oriental music for an hour or longer will naturally get on the nerves of almost any listener, more so as oriental music is of very specific type. In that case grasp every opportunity the picture will afford and play some English, French, Italian or American music to break the monotony.

The Villain ordinarily can easily be represented by any Agitato of which there are thousands. Distinction should be made between sneaky, boisterous, crafty, powerful and evil-minded villains. A crafty villain who does not exhibit any physical villainy in the course of the picture can be easily described by a dissonant chord being held tremolo and very soft. If the Villain happens to be of the brute type who indulges in lots of physical activities, a fast moving number would be more apt. Sometimes you have a villain whose power to do evil is mighty but he achieves his evil deeds without any physical activities in which case chords slow and heavy should be a proper synchronization.

The portrayal of humorous characters seems to be rather hard as there is very little music written which in itself sounds humorous and you very often will have to fall back upon your own ingenuity for the creation of such themes. Emotional and dramatic characters and situations are the hardest to fit, firstly because it requires that the music should swell and diminish in accord with the emotional moods portrayed on the screen and it is a rare good luck to find a piece of dramatic music which will rise and fall simultaneously with the action; secondly because that very dramatic music we have reference to ought to play around the themes which are identified with the characters and within whom the emotional or dramatic situation exists. This also very often necessitates the writing of original music. The use of Silence will prove very often highly effective in situations like the appearing of an unexpected person, committing a crime, in fact all unexpected happenings which are followed, as a rule, by stillness. The recitativo, to be effective, should also be built on the theme or themes of the characters. Very often the arranger of the music for the picture will not have time to cover every little detail in the manner here suggested, but he can help a great deal by shaping the orchestra's playing. A good musician can take an ordinary 4/4 Andante and as readily make it into a misterioso as into a recitativo. This is purely a case of ingenuity and adaptability on the part of the leader.

The flash-backs seem to be a continuous source of trouble to the inexperienced leader. If the flash-back is not of extreme length and the scene preceding the flash-back is of such character that it will hold attention even during the flash-back, I would not advise changing the music but would advise bringing it down to "PPP." Another source of trouble I found is the making of musical endings. The brutal procedure of breaking your music no matter where you are just because the cue for the next number is flashed on the screen is an antiquated procedure not in use any more in first-class theatres. If you train your orchestra sufficiently and arrange for some kind of a signal for your men, you will not have to go more than 8 or 10 bars in most compositions before you can come to a tonic close. The finishing of most numbers during a feature picture should not be in a decisive cut-off manner but more of a dying-away effect. The more segues you can arrange between your numbers the more symphonic the accompaniment will sound.

The turning of pages in the orchestra is a comparatively easy matter, if you have more than one man to each instrument. It is important that the out-side men religiously stick to playing only and have the turning done by the inside-men. In theatres where you have time to prepare a score most of your numbers will not start at the beginning, but with certain passages which you think will fit particular scenes. The number on your music and the place where it should start should be marked very plainly by an arrow so that the eye can grasp it in a second. If you have more than one theme it will be an easy matter if you will carry out the following suggestions:—If theme No. 1 is also 7—13—18 and 24 put all these numbers on top of the page and have the music sticking out in the center of your stand above your other music; if theme No. 2 is also 3—14—29 and 34 put that number also on top of your music and have that piece sticking out of the right or left side of your stand. If you will then mark on the bottom of No. 6 that the next number is Theme No. 1 I think you will find no difficulty in handling two or more themes. If your film breaks, which nowadays is a rare happening, I advise keeping on playing the number and if necessary make a D.C. If you were playing your number soft and with strings only, bring in your brass and wood-wind and play the number in concert form. Fortunately these breaks never last more than 10 or 15 seconds. Should there be a fire in the booth, which may necessitate a wait of several minutes, I advise bringing up the house lights and having the men play any popular hit of the day which they may know by heart. It is advisable to keep in mind some such selection for use in case of emergency. The main object is to prevent the audience from getting nervous and to keep them entertained.

The effects in the percussion section and back stage can be made very effective if used judiciously. I only advise the use of effects if they are humorous or if they can be made very realistic. The shooting of the villain, unless a real shot can be fired back stage and can be timed absolutely, will be much better handled by stopping your orchestra abruptly and keeping silent for a few seconds than if the attempt of a shot is made with a snare drum. In one of the foremost theatres in New York City, I saw a picture in the course of which the villain jumped through the window and immediately after was slapped on the face by the heroine. The effect-man back stage was supposed to drop some glass at the proper moment to imitate the breaking of the window. As it happened the man was asleep on the job and the dropping of the glass occurred when the heroine slapped the villain, so what would have been a tolerably descriptive effect turned out to be the cause of hilarious laughter on the audience's part.

Effects which can be worked most satisfactorily are storm effects, obtained by the use of batteries of large square head drums and wind machines back stage.

In theatres where singers are available, vocal selections back stage will occasionally prove very effective. The most effective incident of such type I remember was applied in the Capitol Theatre in New York City during the presentation of the "Passion" where during the scene of the funeral of the French King a mixed chorus chanted the Funeral March from [Giordano's] *Madame Sans-Gene*. The effect was almost uncanny as outside the death chamber there were a multitude of people assembled.

It is the Vaudeville theatres throughout the country which commit the grossest insults to feature pictures for reasons I was never able to quite understand. If the musicians are too tired after having played the vaudeville to play music to the feature picture, then there should be an organist who is alive to the possibilities. If it is ignorance on the leader's part it is up to the management to see that the accompaniment to the feature picture is placed in proper hands. Happenings like one I witnessed where Dvorak's "Largo" was played from beginning to end with frightful tuning and wrong tempo during a reel of snappy events depicting dancing cannibals, Italian Army, Streets of New York, etc. indicated a condition which ought to be remedied if for nothing else but for the sake of music and its masters.

In choosing your orchestrations I would advise the use of arrangements which are so cued that if necessary they can be played with strings alone and will sound full, for in three quarters of the average feature picture music of very soft quality is required. The "Over-playing" by which is meant playing so loud that it attracts the ear more than the picture attracts the eye, has killed many a good picture. Careful study of the various headings and the numbers contained therein of Chapter 16 will prove a very useful asset to the person arranging music for the feature picture. . . .

In installing a library in a theatre particular care should be taken that the selections representing various moods should be represented numerically in accordance with their importance. Andantes, Marches and Agitatos will need most consideration as they are most in demand. If you are in a position to install a first-class library, I would advise the 16th Chapter of this book as a guide. If your library is only of medium size, it is not necessary to go into the many classifications which are represented in Chapter No. 16. Happy and Neutral Andantes could be put in one book and if the library is very small even the Pathetics could be placed in the same collection with the Andantes. In short the five hundred odd classifications which are noted in the 16th Chapter could be condensed according to the size of the library. For quick reference work in the library I found a double index system the most efficient. On one set of cards I would arrange Composers alphabetically and list on their respective cards all of their compositions indicating also their classification and library number. On the other set of cards I would put the various moods in alphabetical order and put on each card all compositions classified under that mood. The use of wooden shelves or steel cabinets is largely a question of expenditure. Wooden shelves can be built by your carpenter to fill all vacant wall space in your library, but it will have the disadvantage of necessitating climbing and besides that these shelves cannot very well be dust proofed. Steel cabinets are somewhat more expensive but are absolutely dust proof and will indicate on the outside card very readily how many hundred numbers you have in each cabinet. When much music is composed on the premises, I would suggest a book containing nothing but manuscripts, regardless of their classification as in future uses you will easily recall that a certain number you are looking for was written by you or by your staff and as such is easily traceable through the manuscript folio.

The erasing of marks on your music after the orchestra is through with it is an important factor; if the proper methods are not used the music will be ruined after having been used only three or four times. In marking the music a soft pencil should be used with as little pressure as possible as an eraser will remove any slight marking as long as there are no grooves. An erasing machine with a small dynamo, very much on the principle of an electric vibrator, will prove a great time saver. It means a small investment and can be made by your house electrician.

Although the classification of music is a Musical Director's job it is the work of the Librarian to keep it under correct headings and properly indexed. If you classify each Movement of a suite or selection separately, it will be necessary to buy additional piano parts, but it will prove a satisfactory investment since you will put one piece of music to 3 or 4 different uses. Overtures containing Hurries, Agitatos, or Misterioso Movements should each, after being classified as Overtures, also be classified under above mentioned respective headings, and marked just where those classifications begin in the composition. The saving up of old time popular hits is of great importance as they can always be used. If your orchestra only consists of Violin, Piano or Cello I, nevertheless, would advise the buying of a small orchestration because not only does it cost just as much as three or four parts, but should you increase your orchestra you will have the extra parts in readiness and will not have to go to the trouble of buying one 2nd violin or one flute or trombone part.

I would advise every Leader to lay aside a certain amount of money every month for buying new music, particularly of the descriptive type, since it is just as necessary to offer your patrons new music as it is to offer them new pictures. The type of new music to be purchased will have to be determined mainly by the type of picture you play. If you play mostly Western pictures you will have to buy Hurries, Agitatos, and Mysteriosos. If your house plays more society dramas, the replenishing of your Intermezzos and Andante Folios will be more necessary. The offering of new picture music from time to time will not only please your audiences but will instill a new interest in the members of your orchestra.

4

An Interview with Gaylord Carter, "Dean of Theater Organists" (1989)

In 1986–87, film historian and television director Rudy Behlmer conducted two substantial interviews with a living legend: the doyen of cinema organists, Gaylord Carter (1905–2000), who was then in his eighties but still engaged in recording his own music for the rerelease of seven of Paramount's 1920s silent films on home video. Most of Carter's reminiscences focus on his early work in movie theaters in Los Angeles at the time these films were originally made, a career he began as a teenager at the Sunshine Theatre at Fifty-fourth and Park Avenue before establishing himself in the summer of 1926 at the Publix chain's premier projection venue, the Million Dollar Theatre.

Adept at handling both the mighty Wurlitzer, king of cinema organs, and other less familiar keyboard contraptions, Carter provides a fascinating account of the diversity of film music on the West Coast in the heyday of the silent film. Alongside his memories of the various techniques used by keyboard players and small instrumental ensembles are revealing insights into rehearsal patterns, the practical problems of synchronization with the on-screen images, the pressures exerted on theaters by the production companies, and sketches of his encounters with influential figures as diverse as silent-film comedian Harold Lloyd, arranger Carli Elinor, and music director Leo Forbstein.

Source: Rudy Behlmer, " 'Tumult, Battle and Blaze': Looking Back on the 1920s—and Since—with Gaylord Carter, the Dean of Theater Organists," in Clifford McCarty, ed., Film Music I (New York: Garland, 1989): 22–28, 38–39, 42–43, 48–51.

BEHLMER: Was that a regular piano at the Sunshine?

CARTER: It was more than a piano. It was a Wurlitzer unit orchestra, which consisted of a piano keyboard, two little sets of pipes—one a flute sound and one a kind of string sound—and then various handles that you'd pull down if you wanted a crash, or a whistle, or a toot, or a bang or something. And it also had rolls. There were two places to play player rolls. So you could score. You could set up maybe a "hurry" in one of these things and a love theme on the other, and you'd go back and forth on these things. I played the feature picture, and I'd play the rolls during the serial and sometimes during the comedies. You could put on the little mandolin effect that would give you the plinky piano sound, which I used to use a lot and still do. I like that music. Along about the middle of the second show at night, the manager, who was a very nice guy, came down and relieved me and said, "Well, there's hardly anybody left; I think I'll play rolls until the end of the picture and you can go home."

BEHLMER: After you had gotten your experience there, how did you manage to segue into the big houses?

CARTER: That was interesting. After I'd been there about a year, the manager got a chance to buy a little theater organ. It was a two-manual Robert Morton. It had drums and xylophones and bells and tambourines and castanets and the whole *schmeer.* Not very many pipes, but enough. And I learned to play theater organ with that little two-manual. I was getting $16 a week; then they raised my pay to $25 a week, with the organ. And then they sold the house. And I didn't like the new owners; they didn't appreciate what I was trying to do. So I quit and started going to UCLA. I had an organist friend—in fact, I took organ lessons from him—and he occasionally substituted at a little theater in Inglewood called the Seville. It was on West Boulevard. And he said, "Why don't you go down there and play one night a week, and keep your finger in by substituting for this gal?" So I remember I had a little Model-T Ford; and after I'd come home from UCLA I'd rattle out to this place on West Boulevard, and they had a very nice theater organ there—a little Estey. The organist wasn't much of a musician, and she didn't know quite what to do. When great events would take place on the screen like the crashing of the chandelier in *The Phantom of the Opera* [1925], she wouldn't do anything. So I went down and said, "Honey, you've got to make a crash there!" She said, "How do you do that?" [*Laughs.*] Well, it wasn't long until the management decided that she wasn't quite filling the bill and they gave the job to me, and I hated to take her place but I did.

BEHLMER: Where are we in time, now?

CARTER: We're in 1926, because one of the big drawing cards in those days for silent movies in little theaters like that was Harold Lloyd. He always had his pictures on a percentage, and he would send a representative out to see that they were getting the proper percentage. The representative would buy the first ticket when the box office opened, and then would either buy the last one or get the number of the last one. Then they could claim their proper percentage. Nobody trusted anybody. And this guy had nothing to do while he was there, so he'd come in and sit down and listen to the picture. Later he went to Harold and said, "There's a kid out here in Inglewood who's really kicking the heck out of the score to this picture, and he's helping the movie by what he's doing." So Lloyd apparently came out and listened. While I didn't meet him at the time, he recommended me to the management of the Publix Theatres in downtown Los Angeles. They had at that time the Million Dollar, the Metropolitan—later on called the Paramount—and the Rialto, all in downtown L.A. And they had brought me down to be at the Million Dollar Theatre, which was the main presentation house! When I went there about the end of August in '26, the feature picture was *The Temptress* with Greta Garbo. There was a small symphony orchestra playing the music for the feature, and I would spell the orchestra. We'd share most of the films, and then I'd play the last one at night.

BEHLMER: When you say you'd "share," you wouldn't play along *with* the orchestra?

CARTER: No, I wouldn't play with them.

BEHLMER: It would be either the orchestra or you.

CARTER: They would play about 30 minutes, and then we'd find a place where there was, let's say, an oboe solo, and I'd start playing the oboe solo on the organ and the oboe would drop out and then gradually everybody else would drop out and I would bring in the full organ, and we would do that in such a way that people wouldn't realize that the orchestra had stopped playing.

BEHLMER: Then the orchestra could take a break.

CARTER: They'd take a break for about 20 minutes. They'd quietly take off from the orchestra pit and fade.

BEHLMER: Was that more or less the pattern all over?

CARTER: Yes. What they wanted to do was find somebody who could play in an orchestral manner. And there were some who could and some who couldn't. The minute the organ started, you suddenly went from the opera house into the cathedral or [*laughs*] a very small church.

BEHLMER: What size orchestra?

CARTER: Thirty-six people, and the director was Leo Forbstein, who later on became Music Director for Warner Bros. In addition to the feature picture, which we shared, there was an orchestral overture always and I would usually come in on the finale for that. Then there would be a stage show. When I first went there, Paul Whiteman, with his great orchestra, was on the stage. He introduced the *Rhapsody in Blue*, and I want to tell you, that was an experience. It was.

BEHLMER: They were on the stage versus the pit.

CARTER: They were on the stage and there was the regular orchestra in the pit, so you can imagine how many musicians there were. Whiteman had an orchestra with close to 30 people on the stage, and there were 36 in the pit. They didn't play together, but there they were. The orchestra played the news-reel and I would play the cartoon. Then for the last show at night the orchestra would start and play for about ten minutes and then I would play the rest of the last show. And when we did *Ben-Hur* [1925] at the Million Dollar Theatre the manager gave me a little description of what he wanted that I've been using ever since. He said, "Now Gaylord, while the people are coming in we want you to keep some music going, but don't assault them with a lot of frantic organ. Just 'perfume the air with music'."

BEHLMER: [*Laughs.*] And you nodded knowingly.

CARTER: People were always late getting there, and I played for about an hour. *Ben-Hur* ran six months at the Million Dollar Theatre. I still have the score. I carried it home with me, and I still refer to it.

BEHLMER: When you were playing during this period, did the theater always use the score provided or did you use an alternate score?

CARTER: Well, Forbstein had a scorer—we also called him a synchronizer—and usually the score that we did there was his compilation. C.P. LanFranchi was his name. He was a very nice little Italian guy who liked to use a lot of Verdi and Puccini in his scores.

BEHLMER: How did he function, exactly?

CARTER: He had to get the music together and see that it fit, make proper cuts and arrange for the segues and do it so that when the orchestra got a hold of it, it all made sense.

BEHLMER: And, usually, the big theaters would all have their own synchro-nizer?

CARTER: Yeah, yeah. In *The Scarlet Letter* [1926] with Lillian Gish, which we premiered there, here is Lillian walking down the street with a crowd of vil-lagers following her with nasty comments, throwing things, and she had on the scarlet letter, and for this LanFranchi introduced the "Via Appia" from [Respighi's] *The Pines of Rome*. And I was so impressed with that piece that I've used it in my compilation score to *The King of Kings* [1927] ever since.

BEHLMER: This was not the *Scarlet Letter* score that was sent out?

CARTER: No. In this particular case, LanFranchi scored *The Scarlet Letter*.

BEHLMER: He would do it for just that theater?

CARTER: For just that theater, yes.

BEHLMER: Based on your knowledge of other places, did this go on a lot? In all the major theaters?

CARTER: In all the major theaters, I would say. Now the *Ben-Hur* score was by David Mendoza and William Axt. They were at the Capitol Theatre in New York and they did most of the scores for MGM's big pictures at that time.

BEHLMER: But the theaters did not necessarily use their scores?

CARTER: They were available if you wanted.

BEHLMER: What percentage, would you say, used the scores that were supplied?

CARTER: I wouldn't even be able to hazard a guess. I would think that in the major cities they would use them. Maybe in places like Woodstock, Kansas, where they didn't have orchestras in the theaters, the organist would be invited to use it if he wanted to. But you know, we all had cue sheets in those days. When I was playing at the Seville and at the Sunshine Theatre, when the manager would book the shows the film exchanges would give him a cue sheet and he would hand me eight or ten cue sheets at a time. In this way you'd know what you were up against—whether it was a drama or a comedy, whether it was an Indian picture or frozen north or tropical picture or what—and you'd also know if there was going to be a bugle call or a chime, or bells, or steamboat whistles; you'd know in advance, so you didn't get caught. When you're looking at a picture and you suddenly see a train whistle and you're not ready for it, it's gone.

I remember one time we did a picture with Gilda Gray called *The Devil Dancer* [1927]. It was a Goldwyn picture, and Goldwyn, instead of having Leo Forbstein and his scorer LanFranchi do a score for that, hired Carli Elinor, who was musical director at the Carthay Circle Theatre, to compile and arrange it. Well, Forbstein was so annoyed—they're all dead now, so I can tell you this—Forbstein said, "Now Gaylord, you play Elinor's score, but don't play it too good." [*Both laugh.*] Now another case, when we did *Beau Geste* [1926] with Ronald Colman, there was a score that was provided. I don't remember whether this was Hugo . . .

BEHLMER: . . . Riesenfeld. Yes, it was.

CARTER: We got the score from the Forum Theatre. It was just full of wonderful music, including the music that was written for the score—"Brother Theme" and the "Legion March." I remember that score. I went out and borrowed the music and still have it.

BEHLMER: Was it a compilation score?

CARTER: Right. Some original material . . . just very few things.

BEHLMER: What was the determining factor in this instance?

CARTER: It was Paramount. They insisted that we use the score that they had at the Forum.

BEHLMER: Would they "insist" a lot? Did different studios . . .

CARTER: Mostly it was recommended. I'll tell you another example of studio pressure. *The Student Prince* [1926] with Ramon Novarro premiered at the Million Dollar. Now, the studio wanted to avoid any royalties, so they told us they wouldn't let us use the Romberg score. They wanted us to use the score to Luders' *The Prince of Pilsen* [1926], which didn't fit it *at all*. But there was so much fuss made. They previewed the picture out in Glendale. A friend of mine, Frank Lanterman, played the picture. They didn't want him to play the Romberg score and he said, "Well, I'm going to do it because everybody will expect it, and the other doesn't fit." Well, the studio was adamant in refusing to pay for the Romberg score. But by the time we got it, they had compromised. And we played the picture with the Romberg score. I couldn't conceive of doing it without it; it would have been pure corn. So we just took the Romberg music and LanFranchi adapted it to the orchestra we had, made the orchestrations, and the studio went along with it . . .

BEHLMER: What would be a pattern for rehearsing, since obviously the theater was going all the time? When the new picture was coming up, when *did* you rehearse?

CARTER: Well, Forbstein, when we'd start scoring a new picture, would tell me how much the orchestra was going to do and how much I was going to do, and then he would hand me his score, his guide. LanFranchi would hand me the main themes, and I would incorporate them into my organ music for that part of the picture that I would do. Now, in the case of *Ben-Hur*, of course, I played the score as written for my part. When we would have a picture like *Ben-Hur*, about three days in advance of the opening we would have rehearsals in the morning, and the orchestra would be all splendid musicians. They could read all this at sight.

BEHLMER: This would be rehearsal with the film?

CARTER: No, there would not be a rehearsal with the film. It would be just a rehearsal of the orchestra parts. Maybe there was a rehearsal with the film. I don't really remember. But I would have a rehearsal with the film, usually, because the operators would run the film the night before to be sure they had a good print, and I would just stay over, after my last thing, and I'd work on the score we had put together—with the film on that occasion.

BEHLMER: Would there be more than one or two rehearsals?

CARTER: On a major picture like *Ben-Hur*, we would rehearse for two mornings. On a smaller picture, like maybe *Chang* [1927] or whatever, one rehearsal.

BEHLMER: We're talking about three hours?

CARTER: About three hours for each rehearsal. Then the first performance in the afternoon of the opening day would be the rehearsal with the film. And that was kind of tricky. They would have a speedometer on the musical director's stand to be sure that the film was going at the speed that the scoring was done to.

BEHLMER: The speed of silent film varies.

CARTER: It really did. It started at about 18 frames a second and then I think it went to 19, and then to 20, and sound, of course, is 24 frames.

BEHLMER: Would there be an annotation on the score, saying it was to be projected at . . .

CARTER: *Ben-Hur* was designated, I think, at 20 frames. Now, of course, when we do it, we run it at 24 frames. I had an argument with a guy about that once. I was playing a concert version of the Galley Slave theme, and somebody said, "No galley slave could possibly keep up with that tempo." [*Laughs.*] And I said, "Well, we're running the film now at 24 frames, and it does go a little faster than the original. But if we ran *Ben-Hur* at 20 frames, we'd be there all night." I remember a few years ago we were running *The Thief of Bagdad* [1924] in San Francisco. It is a long, long movie—over two hours at 24 frames. And some projectionist up there said, "Well, this is a silent picture. Let's do it at silent speed (18 frames)." I was just dragging out this stuff unmercifully. And I didn't understand what was the matter. A buddy of mine with the theater realized it was going at the wrong speed and had the projectionist increase it.

BEHLMER: Unfortunately, that's a common mistake. People somehow feel that silent films should run at 16 or 18 frames, which, of course, is not, with rare exception, the case. If you don't have a rheostat, they're better off running at 24. . . .

BEHLMER: In those days, in some of the theaters, did you have the elevator, with the organ coming up?

CARTER: Well, not at the Million Dollar. It just sat on the floor of the orchestra pit. But when I went to the United Artists, they had it there. They had it at the Paramount. You'd come up to what was called "picture level." That would mean the top of the organ console would be about even with the stage. And most of the control boards had the picture level on them—if you were coming from the depths down below. But at the Million Dollar, we just walked down the aisle and through a little sliding door onto the organ. The one in the

Chicago Theatre—I was so surprised to discover that the organ elevator, the one that Jesse Crawford made famous, rose only four feet.

BEHLMER: Were there any other players at the time with whom you were particularly impressed—I mean organists who were doing motion picture music?

CARTER: Oh, sure. Most of the ones that were my predecessors at the Million Dollar—Jesse Crawford had played there, of course. We all listened to him because he was the kingpin. I used to think that his arrangements were oversimplified. "When the Organ Played at Twilight" was one of his big numbers. Milton Charles had played at the Million Dollar, and Henry B. Murtagh. But the best of all during that period were Albert Hay Malotte, who wrote "The Lord's Prayer" music, and Alexander Schreiner, the chief organist of the Tabernacle in Salt Lake City. He was organist at the Paramount Theatre at one time.

BEHLMER: In Los Angeles?

CARTER: Los Angeles, uh-huh. It was called the Metropolitan when he was there. I would go and hear him play these dazzling solos. He would do something like [Wagner's] "The Ride of the Valkyries," which would make your hair stand right up. Then they wanted something on a more popular style and they hired a man by the name of Herb Kern. And he came in and played "Isle of Capri" and that kind of thing. It wasn't very stimulating. Both Schreiner and Malotte were magnificent organists. An awful lot of other organists who were in this particular field got by with a minimum of scholarship, so that when you found somebody who really knew something about the organ and was in addition a profound student of music, it was a great thing. Then the scores took life and soared and did great credit to what was going on on the screen.

BEHLMER: I imagine some of the others were rather mechanical.

CARTER: Yeah, well they relied on the cue sheet, and it said to play some piece for 3/4 of a minute and that's what they'd do. They watched their clock instead of watching the screen. It was a period, like anything else, where you had every conceivable combination of talent and experience. I kind of had my own ideas about things through the organ being a part of my family setup, and so I used to think that most of the organists in the theaters didn't have any actual classical background in organ playing. They didn't make it sound like an organ. Did you know when sound arrived, the Los Angeles Times came out with a story, and the headline said, "Sound Films Drive Organists From Theatres. Managers Rejoice." [Laughs.] . . .

BEHLMER: What was this one machine that we were talking about earlier . . . the Fotoplayer?

CARTER: The Fotoplayer. That was a piano with two sets of pipes. A kind of a little flute sound, and a little . . .

BEHLMER: You mean it was a piano with partial organ . . .

CARTER: Yes, partially organ. You'd press a key and if you put down the stop that said flute, it would not only play the piano, it would play the flute too. They were kind of funny little things. They hooted, and . . .

BEHLMER: Were they popular?

CARTER: Oh, the smaller theaters that couldn't afford pipe organs had them. The first that I ever played was in the Kansas Theatre in Wichita.

BEHLMER: Would you say that most theaters had live accompaniment or automatic instruments—automatic pianos and automatic orchestras?

CARTER: I don't remember any automatic in Los Angeles. Now in Wichita, where I was, they had the Fotoplayers there. They would have two slots where you would put in piano rolls, and so you could put one in here and run it for a little while and then put one in here, and when you wanted to change the scene you'd bring in the second one. And they'd go back and forth, so you could score that way. I never heard of any theater in L.A. doing it.

BEHLMER: Forgetting L.A., would you say that in general throughout the country there would be considerable use of this or . . .

CARTER: I don't think so. I mean, they either had a piano player or an organist, or a small combo.

BEHLMER: How small a combo?

CARTER: I think maybe five or six people was the smallest. Because the music was arranged for at least one trumpet and one clarinet and maybe one trombone, and then strings. So, you take a place like the Mission Theatre in downtown Los Angeles, where they had the premiere of *The White Sister* [1923] with Ronald Colman and Lillian Gish . . .

BEHLMER: They didn't have a full orchestra?

CARTER: They had six pieces. A drum, a trumpet, trombone, clarinet, violin, and a cello, I think. Something like that. You wouldn't have a string quartet in a pit doing these things because they don't provide the kind of sound that's expected. The first thing you had to have, if you had any kind of a combo, was the drummer. So you could get the punches and rifle shots and cataclysmic things like an earthquake. You'd need a trumpet for bugle calls. And it would be nice to have a clarinet. You didn't have to have it. You had to have usually one violin and a second violin. You wouldn't have a viola, but you'd have a cello and maybe a bass. And you could make a lot of music with these. I'll never forget, while I was between the matinee and the evening shift, I dropped in to see *The White Sister*. And they did something that I had never heard before. There were some very dynamic scenes. And they always started with a tremendous tympani roll. It would just raise you out of your seat. We never did this at the Million Dollar. It was very startling. And another thing, it introduced me to "The Swan" from *Carnival of the Animals* by Saint-Saëns. That was the theme for *The White Sister*. [*Hums.*]

BEHLMER: For *Wings* in 1927, didn't they, at least at the road show performances, have some percussionists backstage or in the wings?

CARTER: Oh, I believe they did, yeah.

BEHLMER: So this would be in addition to the pit.

CARTER: For the battle scenes.

BEHLMER: The booms and the crashes and bombs and so forth were being done with the augmented tympani.

CARTER: The supplied Zamecnik score for *Wings* in the opening aerial battles indicated the Mendelssohn *Midsummer Night's Dream* scherzo, which I didn't think quite fit an aerial battle. And so I wrote another little thing for it. Of course, everybody said, "Gaylord, do you think you're better than Mendelssohn?" I would say to that, "Well, Mendelssohn was one of the world's greats, but he didn't write that for a movie."

BEHLMER: In the 1920s the assumption was that there were not many movie-going people who would be that familiar with the standard repertoire, so you could do a lot of things that you wouldn't dare do now—certain musical clichés as we now regard them.

CARTER: Oh, definitely! It was desirable to use [Rossini's] *William Tell* Overture for a chase, for example. Of course, that was before *The Lone Ranger*. It was acceptable.

BEHLMER: Would the Mission Theatre be considered a middle-of-the-range theater?

CARTER: Well, it was a first-run house.

BEHLMER: So a lot of first-run houses would have a six-piece . . .

CARTER: Oh, yeah.

BEHLMER: In Los Angeles during the '20s—we're talking about what? Maybe three or four houses that would have a 38-piece orchestra?

CARTER: Yes, there was a house—the California Theatre—I believe it was on Main Street. That's where Carli Elinor had his orchestra. They had a big orchestra, maybe 24 to 26 to 30 pieces.

BEHLMER: Did you know Carli Elinor?

CARTER: Yes, I did. He was a little bit imperious.

BEHLMER: What about the Egyptian and the Chinese?

CARTER: They had about 24 to 30 pieces.

BEHLMER: What you'd call a large orchestra then would be 38?

CARTER: Oh, yes, that would be large. The Million Dollar had 38. Also the Paramount and maybe the Carthay Circle. That would be about it.

5

Leonid Sabaneev: *Music for the Films* (1935)

Two of the earliest substantial texts on the general aesthetic and practical issues of film music in the formative years of the sound film were both published in London during the 1930s. Kurt London's *Film Music: A Summary of the Characteristic Features of Its History, Aesthetics, Technique; and Possible Developments* (Faber and Faber, 1936), originally written in German, devoted nearly three hundred pages to its subject but dismissed American film music altogether by declaring that "hitherto the artistic level of the American super-films (technically of such first-rate workmanship) has remained, apart from jazz, far more notable for its visual than for its musical achievements. The Americans are masters of compilation, even today. The originality that we find in their pictures, and occasionally also in their sound-construction, deserts them when it comes to music" (212). The author admitted in passing that exceptions were to be made in the case of Max Steiner, Alfred Newman, and Leo Forbstein, but devoted the remainder of his text exclusively to European and Soviet film music. In contrast, Leonid Sabaneev's *Music for the Films*, originally written in Russian, scrupulously avoided naming even a single director or composer, preferring to offer in strictly general terms both an account of the technicalities of film composition and sound recording in the mid-1930s and sage practical advice to the budding film composer.

Sabaneev (1881–1968) was well attuned to the limitations of soundtrack recording methods at the time, devoting a major part of his text to advice on

Source: *Music for the Films: A Handbook for Composers and Conductors*, trans. S. W. Pring (London: Isaac Pitman and Sons, 1935): 4–10, 18–24.

which instruments and combinations of instruments worked best with the primitive microphone and amplification technology then available. The sections from his book reproduced here provide a concise technical explanation of how the optical soundtrack functions, describing two different methods of recording, one using a lamp and the other a mirror; he also offers an assessment of the relative importance of the various sound components as they were generally deployed in soundtrack dubbing in the 1930s. Elsewhere in his book he touches on two perennial challenges confronting the film composer both then and now: how to avoid direct competition between dialogue and background music, and how to locate music cues strategically (a process referred to in the film industry as "spotting"). In offering advice on the desirability of composing "extensile" music that can be modified at short notice should the editing process require it, he specifies two techniques evident in the work of renowned Hollywood composers: an inbuilt flexibility of timing that can be adjusted through spontaneous interpretation (Erich Wolfgang Korngold was a notable exponent of this approach), and the use of sequential or repetitive material as simple building blocks through which cues can be shortened or extended at will (a simple technique which Bernard Herrmann later favored and for which he was beloved by music editors and recording engineers).

In the sound cinema we have to deal with two technical processes: the systems of recording and the system of reproduction.

1. The system of recording by the variable density method is as follows—

The sounds which make the record on the film are produced in front of a microphone (Plate I, Fig. I*a*), which converts the sound vibrations into a system of electric currents. These are not of constant strength, but vary in exact accordance with the vibrations of the microphone diaphragm, which, in its turn, repeats the vibrations of the resonant body (the violin, the orchestra, the human voice, etc.). We learn from physics that every sound complexus has a definite figure of vibration which exactly corresponds to it, and this figure is as exactly transmitted in the vibrations of the strength of the current.

The electric currents thus received are very feeble, and have to be intensified by an amplifier (Plate I, Fig. I*b*), whereby a greater amplitude is imparted to the vibrations without altering their figure.

The amplified currents pass through an oscillating electric lamp (Plate I, Fig. I*c*), and affect the strength of the light; the lamp begins to twinkle rapidly, and again the figure of the twinkling corresponds accurately to the vibrations of

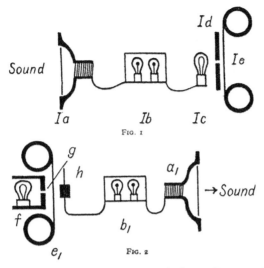

Fig. 1

Fig. 2

PLATE I. The variable-density method of recording sound on film stock. (Leonid Sabaneev, *Music for the Films* [1935], p. 5)

the resonant body. The light from this lamp falls on a small and narrow slit (Plate I, Fig. Id), before which passes the edge of a moving sensitized film (Plate I, Fig. Ie); on it a photograph is produced, in the form of a series of bars, which are lighter or darker in proportion to the intensity of the light emitted by the lamp at any given moment, and which, again, exactly correspond to the vibrations of the resonant body. A negative of the film is thus obtained, and from it any number of positives can be printed.

2. The system of reproduction is as follows—

The film with the bars (the sound track) photographed on it (Plate I, Fig. 2e_1) is run through the projecting apparatus. A small lamp, known as the exciter lamp (Plate I, Fig. 2f) with the help of a condenser throws a beam of light through a narrow slit (Plate I, Fig. 2g). The beam is thereby reduced to a fine pencil of light, which passes through the sound track and emerges as a series of variable vibrations in exact correspondence with the vibrations of the resonant body. It then falls on a photo-electric cell (Plate I, Fig. 2h) in which is incorporated a piece of selenium. This non-metallic element has the property of altering its electrical resistance in accordance with the amount of light it receives, and consequently the electric current passing through it varies in intensity, and its vibrations once more prove to be exactly similar to those of the resonant body. These vibrations are now transmitted through an amplifier to the diaphragm of the loudspeaker (Plate I, Fig. 2a_1) which converts them into sound.

Thus in the process of cinematograph photography sound undergoes a series of transformations, in the course of which its timbre is generally more or less distorted and some of its qualities are lost or altered. Furthermore, very intricate vibrations set up by complex noises or complex sequences of sounds run the risk of being somewhat blurred, and this explains why they are always less satisfactorily reproduced than clear and simple sounds.

Persons experienced in the *montage* of films can form a fair idea of the character of the sound merely by examining the sound track. For the musician it is important to be able to find the silent spots (in them there is no undulatory shading), and the spaces in which the resonances are stable, i.e. in which they remain unchanged for a comparatively long period; in the latter case the figure of the waves remains constant for several decimetres, but it is much more difficult of detection by the eye (Plate II, Fig. 2).

Usually the sound and the picture are photographed on separate films and in separate studios. The *montage* of each is carried out independently, after which they are combined into one for which purpose they must be made to correspond as closely as possible.

The other system of recording is known as the variable width method. The only distinction between it and the variable density method is that in the former the currents, differing in intensity, which issue from the microphone fall on a galvanometer and deflect to a varying extent a microscopic mirror; the rays on reaching the mirror are deviated more or less, in proportion to the strength of the current, with the result that the sound track shows a jagged line of a constant intensity, instead of a series of darker or lighter bars.

While the shades of tone are not so accurately transmitted by this method as by the variable density method, they are more easily distinguishable from the external appearance of the sound track, the jagged profile being more characteristic than the shaded bars (Plate II, Fig. 1).

As the movement of the sound film must be perfectly steady, and the picture film passing in front of the lens travels, as everyone knows, by leaps, it is impossible to print the sound on the same part of the film as the scene to which it corresponds. This must therefore be done either before or after the loops which the film forms before and after passing in front of the slit of the projecting apparatus. Nowadays the sound film is printed at a distance of nineteen frames (36.2 cm.) from the picture film; the sound slit is nineteen frames below the slit of the latter, where it once more moves evenly, but as the pictures on the film are reversed, it is necessary to look for this place on the sound film (positive or negative) nineteen frames above the corresponding points of the picture film. Thus, if we were to have a sound track with the pictures, the sound corresponding to a given frame of the picture film would

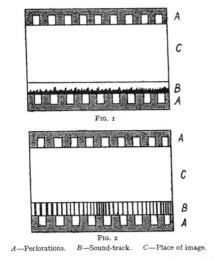

Fɪɢ. 1

Fɪɢ. 2

A—Perforations.   *B*—Sound-track.   *C*—Place of image.

PLATE II. A variable-width soundtrack (above) and variable-density soundtrack (below) as they appear on the celluloid strip. (Leonid Sabaneev, *Music for the Films* [1935], p. 8)

never be found in that frame, but would have to be sought higher up the film, at a distance of nineteen frames. These remarks have an important bearing on the *montage* of a film and on the understanding of its technique and methods. . . .

Here we are interested only in the question of music for the film, and the aesthetics of that music. It was associated with the cinema from the very beginning, when its aesthetic function was, *inter alia*, to fill up the tonal void which was an inherent feature of the silent film. Here aesthetics played a real part; aesthetic custom, too, had always required that a spectacle should be accompanied by sound. Independently of this, music, in its illustrative capacity, supplied the poetry and emotion which the captions, necessarily brief and of an informatory nature, could not give. Music provided rhythm for the happenings on the screen and, as it were, interpreted the emotions of the characters and of the screen in general.

With the arrival of the sound film the rôle of music was altered. First and foremost, for technical reasons, it ceased to be mere improvisation and developed into strict and solid composition. Previously it had been possible to play anything one chose for the screen, but that is no longer permissible. On the other hand, whereas music was once the sole provider of sound for the cinema, it now has to share its functions with dramatic speech and various naturalistic noises. But its position has remained. Speech, pictures, and noises constitute the purely photographic section of the cinema; music, whether with the silent or the sound films, supplies the romantic, irrational element illustrating emotion.

As we have said, the sounds connected with the sound film are divisible into three categories: music, speech, and noises, and to understand the aesthetics of music in the new cinema it is very important that we should know how the boundaries of their spheres of action are delimited. It is, of course, evident that when two or three varieties of sound are proceeding simultaneously, the attention can with difficulty be concentrated on any one of them. The dialogue, which has replaced the caption, naturally occupies the first place, if only from the fact that it explains the meaning of the picture on the screen and music should therefore give way to it. The filling of the silences of the cinema was formerly entrusted to music, but speech is now employed instead. As everyone knows, it is difficult to listen to music and speech at the same time; usually one of them is lost—either the music, or the meaning and beauty of the words. On the one hand it is felt that someone is preventing us from enjoying the dialogue, on the other that someone is talking during a musical performance. Both are aesthetically distressing.

It should always be remembered, as a first principle of the aesthetics of music in the cinema, that logic requires music to give way to dialogue. Even if the former is relegated entirely to the background and is barely audible, it still interferes to some extent with the dialogue, and, as it becomes vague and can hardly be heard, its aesthetic value is only second-rate.

The same remarks apply to music in connexion with photographic sounds—noises, shouts, etcetera—which usually drown it and deprive it of any aesthetic significance.

Thus we naturally come to the following conclusions: music should cease or retire into the background when dialogues and noises are taking place. Except in rare instances it blends but poorly with them. When combined with dialogue we get a kind of melodeclamation, and then both dialogue and music are faced with the demands generally presented to melodeclamation, that is to say, coincidence of rhythm, and their artistic symbiosis, which, as we know, is usually difficult to achieve. When we have noises and music simultaneously, the former become part of the musical whole and have the effect of percussion instruments of a sort; in this case they require to be reduced to order; their rhythm must be coincident, and they must be incorporated in the musical composition and not be a mere disorderly din, drowning the music and making it meaningless.

Normally, the musical background should be suppressed on the entry of dialogue or noises—they are incompatible planes. There is a good aesthetic reason for stopping the music on such occasions, but the precise method to be adopted is one of the most difficult problems of the sound cinema. Music has its inertia; it forms a certain background in the subconsciousness of the listening spectator, and its sudden cessation gives rise to a feeling of aesthetic perplexity, even though the music be kept entirely in the background. The substitution of dialogue and noises for music, on the contrary, does not cause perplexity. The music itself may not be noticed, but if it is stopped without being replaced by other sounds the gap becomes perceptible, as a false note and a cinematographic dissonance.

Of course it must not be imagined that the existing films always corroborate what has been said, but that signifies nothing: these aesthetic principles are gradually penetrating the consciousness of cultured directors.

Music in the cinema, occupying the position of a separate and unreal, non-photographic, plane, preserves a large measure of its individuality and its independent nature. It should possess a musical form of its own, in some way subordinated to the rhythm of the screen, but not destroyed by them. Indeed music often dictates its rhythms and tempi to the screen, and this state of affairs, recognized by all directors, even appears to be normal. The rhythm of the screen is regulated by the music, and this is particularly noticeable when there is no noise or dialogue. Music in the cinema cannot sacrifice the principles governing its form: no matter what is happening on the screen, the music must have its melodic structure, its phrases and cadences, and it must not be asked to suffer dilution by the rhythms and occurrences of the picture. It expresses the general mood of the scene on the stage, and should not be required, except in a few instances mentioned below, to follow the events in detail, otherwise it is untrue to its nature and becomes anti-musical.

Sometimes, to produce an aesthetic impression, it is sufficient that the musical background should not be at variance with the mood of the screen. Very characteristic of the cinema is the use of neutral music, which fills the tonal spaces and annihilates the silences without attracting special attention to itself. In general, music should understand that in the cinema it should nearly always remain in the background: it is, so to speak, a tonal figuration, the "left hand" to the melody of the screen, and it is a bad business when this left hand begins to creep into the foreground and obscure the melody. On the comparatively rare occasions when the interest is concentrated on the music, the latter may emerge from its subordinate position for a time, but as a rule it should be subdued and should make its presence felt without effort, nor should it attract attention to itself at the expense of the screen.

This musical background serves as a sort of psychological resonator of the screen, enhancing its effect and augmenting its emotional passages. Hence it is as important that the music and the picture should synchronize and that their rhythms should coincide. If these precautions are observed, the aesthetic effect of the stage action will be strengthened. A procession gains enormously if accompanied by music with a well-marked and coincident rhythm, just as the impression will be lessened if the music and the screen do not synchronize. This applies equally to the non-coincidence of the emotional tempo and rhythm. So long as this harmony is observed the music is not noticed of itself—it merely forms part of the general effect—but in the contrary case the audience becomes aware of it as a dissonance, a disturbing element.

Music may exercise a powerful influence on the rhythm of the screen, may act as a kind of throttle-valve. Unfortunately this attribute of music has not been fully exploited by film directors, who have not yet realized that, though occupying a secondary place, it is important and indispensable. They look upon it as of no consequence, forgetting that, if the cinema wants to become and remain an art, the background should be carefully thought out and thoroughly well done; in art nothing is unimportant. The rhythmizing and resonating function of music is particularly evident in comic films and animated cartoons. The congruence of the movements with the musical rhythm is always very effective and enormously emphasizes their significance. Furthermore, it may be said that music in general best and most naturally illustrates movements and gestures. The importation of a certain portion of Dalcroze's theory into the cinema would be by no means unprofitable. Then, and only then, would music be aesthetically bound up with the screen, creating an artistic amalgam, and not an amateurish improvisation round about the screen. . . .

The cinema has a public of its own, which differs from that of the theatre. In the mass the former is aesthetically backward: its aesthetic psychology is infantile, its tastes undeveloped, its comprehension of, and ability to distinguish, musical details and texture limited. All this must be borne in mind. The cinema audience regards as vital those forms which, in the eyes of advanced art, bear the impress of banality, and on the whole its tastes are more antiquated than those characterizing the main tendencies in art. Effects long since relegated to the museum still bring tears to the eyes of the cinema-goer, and sentimentality and naïve methods of exciting him have not yet lost their sway. Hence melodeclamation, to which any dialogue to music is reduced in the cinema, offers a wide field for development. By way of comfort, however, it should be noted that, while the aesthetic tastes of the cinema audience may be primitive, they are nevertheless more refined and more elevated than is supposed by many cinema promotors, and even directors, who ascribe their own lack of artistic development to "the demands of the crowd." In the final reckoning this public appreciates anything that is genuinely good, and is presented in such a manner as to be within everybody's grasp; and it rejects all that is coarse in form and anti-artistic. This public has been badly educated: its aesthetic conceptions have not been artistically developed and it has been fed on trash, as being cheaper and more profitable. The cinema, of course, is run on commercial, and not on artistic, lines, to a far greater extent than is the case with any other branch of art.

II

Film Composers in Their Own Words

As the texts in this section demonstrate, the technical, practical, and aesthetic challenges facing Hollywood film composers have changed remarkably little since cinema was revolutionized by the introduction of synchronized and pre-recorded optical soundtracks in the late 1920s.

The first generation of composers working for sound films, who were responsible for developing an essentially formulaic manner of accompaniment that owed much to the operatic and melodramatic elements of orchestral music for silent films (notably in a reliance on leitmotifs and a romantic-cum-impressionistic harmonic palette), are represented here by Max Steiner, Dimitri Tiomkin, and Franz Waxman. These three composers were members of an important group of European immigrants whose exceptional facility won them ready acceptance in the highly pressurized West Coast entertainment industry during the 1930s, and they hailed from backgrounds typical of many early film composers: Steiner had worked both in Vienna (with its strong tradition of operetta) and on Broadway, Tiomkin was steeped in Russian silent film and ballet, and in his years in Germany Waxman had straddled parallel interests in jazz and modern concert music. Apart from Alfred Newman, who also hailed from Broadway and became best known for his work at Twentieth Century-Fox from the later 1930s onward, American-born talents made their names a little later than their immigrant counterparts: among the ablest was David Raksin, whose vivid accounts of his fluctuating working environments form an important body of source material for any student of Hollywood's musical fortunes between the 1930s and the end of the twentieth century.

With rare exceptions, the composers who were most successful in the specialized discipline of composition for feature films were those who understood their role as part of a closely knit collaborative team. The ruthless efficiency of the Hollywood studio system, which took no prisoners in attempting to meet punishing release schedules, is vividly recounted in a number of the texts presented here: hard-pressed composers found their work by turns exhilarating and frustrating, and at times detrimental to their physical and psychological health. Their accounts include behind-the-scenes glimpses of the work of the music departments of several studios that flourished between the 1930s and late 1950s, including Columbia, MGM (Metro-Goldwyn-Mayer), Paramount, RKO (Radio-Keith-Orpheum), Warner Bros., United Artists, and Universal. Clearly evident from these accounts is the sterling work undertaken by skilled orchestrators such as Leo Arnaud, Bob Franklyn, Arthur Morton, Eddie Powell, and the long-serving Herbert Spencer, without whom composers would never have come even close to meeting their punitive deadlines; studio music directors like Alfred Newman and Leo Forbstein, whose administrative and conducting skills were often far more crucial to a studio's efficient operation than their compositional abilities were; and the extraordinary rods of power wielded by legendary producers such as Harry Cohn, Sam Goldwyn, Dore Schary, Irving Thalberg, and David O. Selznick, whose musical input into their films could range from inspired creative suggestions to truculent ignorance or sheer ineptitude.

An essential prerequisite for film composers contracted to the Hollywood studios was a willingness to allow their music to fulfill a strictly secondary role when other sonic elements crucial to the clear presentation of a film's narrative needed to predominate in the final audio mix. Many of the composers featured here demonstrate understandable frustration when witnessing their music deliberately hushed in order to make way for dialogue or sound effects, and the most pragmatic of them habitually underscored dialogue scenes with great economy so that the problem was largely circumvented. Also evident is the wide range of genres in which composers were expected to work, including film noir, melodrama, historical epics, horror, literary adaptations, science fiction, fantasy, swashbuckling action adventures, westerns, musicals, documentaries, propaganda films, and animation. Some composers were destined to become typecast in particular genres, but the angst-ridden nature of their darker assignments spurred some to explore modernist devices that might not otherwise have seemed appropriate in the generally conservative stylistic climate of mainstream film music.

Music for cartoons acquired a stunning virtuosity (and also reflected modernist influences to a sometimes surprising degree) in the 1940s in the ebullient shorts produced by Warner Bros. and MGM. Many of these featured the slapstick antics of such famous anthropomorphic creations as Bugs Bunny (Warner) and the violent cat-and-mouse duo Tom and Jerry (MGM), and they relied on witty music not only to catch their physical actions with spirited Mickey Mousing but also to aid the audience's suspension of disbelief—something very necessary in a world inhabited entirely by two-dimensional stylized drawings. The reminiscences below include an early article on the subject by Ingolf Dahl and vivid firsthand accounts of the cartoon composer's typical working practices by the two leading composers in the genre: Carl Stalling, whose work was a direct extension of his earlier musical experiences at Disney and elsewhere and involved tapping Warner Bros.' rich catalogue of popular tunes; and Scott Bradley, whose sophisticated scores for the Tom and Jerry series drew on elements from jazz and modernist concert music.

The heyday of the documentary film came in the 1930s and 1940s. An early highlight was the work of the General Post Office Film Unit in the United Kingdom, where, under the strong influence of Soviet realist cinema in both their filming and montage techniques, directors benefited from the involvement of creative talents of the stature of Benjamin Britten and W. H. Auden during the mid-1930s. Also in the 1930s, the sometimes experimental music of Hanns Eisler enhanced politically aware documentary films made in Europe, and his inventive work in the genre continued after his emigration to the United States. Virgil Thomson had at the same time helped forge a distinctively nationalistic, folk-oriented style of American film music in his scores for the seminal documentaries *The Plow That Broke the Plains* (1936) and *The River* (1937), both directed by Pare Lorentz, a musical initiative subsequently taken up by Aaron Copland in his score for *The City* (1939). The U.S. government's funding for documentary productions that highlighted the achievements and aspirations of the Roosevelt administration (an initiative much disliked by the Hollywood studios, which felt that state backing for these surprisingly popular films was threatening their commercial livelihood) was withdrawn in 1940, but with the country's entry into the Second World War in the following year came a new opportunity to produce, on a regular basis, factual (or purportedly factual) films in the national interest. One of the most highly regarded composers of wartime documentary scores was Gail Kubik, who collaborated memorably with director William Wyler and whose views on the subject are reproduced below.

After Copland made a sporadic but distinctive contribution to the art of film scoring in 1939–40, and again in 1949, Hollywood film composers began to widen their medium's stylistic horizons by espousing overtly nationalistic elements that moved somewhat away from Eurocentric stylistic stereotypes and found a particularly appropriate home in the homegrown genre of the western. As Copland shows in the extracts from his writings reproduced here, he was one of the few "serious" composers in America to be attracted to film music and to appreciate its fundamental difference from compositional genres intended for the concert hall or opera house. Nevertheless, it was the growing popularity of Copland's and others' film scores in the shape of concert suites that did much to draw wider public attention to the possibilities of the medium. A side effect of this initiative was a tendency for audiences and critics to view film music as self-sufficient when divorced from the visual images for which it had originally been conceived; this encouraged a sense, particularly deeply rooted in musicians from a classical background, that autonomous musical structures were preferable to the piecemeal subservience to visual and narrative details evident in the majority of film soundtracks. The tension between these two apparently mutually exclusive types of accompanimental music was to remain endemic in film-music appreciation.

Occasionally a composer emerged with such a forceful personality and sharply defined musical idiom that he (and the pronoun is used advisedly, since until the 1980s virtually all successful U.S. film composers were male) could constantly command from hard-nosed directors and producers an unusual measure of respect—though it was sometimes granted only grudgingly. The outstanding example is Bernardm Herrmann, some of whose trenchant views are reproduced here. Herrmann was one of several composers who developed a more modernistic and less theme-based manner of film scoring in the 1950s; another comparably innovative figure whose reminiscences are included is Jerry Goldsmith, who, like his contemporary Elmer Bernstein (see pp. 341–46), managed to negotiate the transition from the stable studio-based contracts of the so-called Golden Age (c. 1930–55) to the freelance basis on which film composers were forced to work after the collapse of the studio system in the late 1950s. This dip in Hollywood's fortunes coincided not only with the lucrative boom of the television industry, but also with the decimation of the film studios' creative personnel by egregious anticommunist purges and the blighting of its musicians' livelihoods by industrial action that killed off the concept of permanent studio orchestras. One way in which Hollywood producers attempted to lure television viewers back into movie theaters in the later 1950s and early 1960s was by making extravagant star-driven historical epics, luxuriating in their novel stereophonic sound and expansive widescreen cinematography, a genre with which Miklós Rózsa became inextricably associated on account of his innovative attempts to make music for such period films historically "authentic."

The supremacy of traditional orchestral scoring was challenged by more popular idioms from the 1950s onward, first in the shape of jazz, and then more pervasively by pop music. Henry Mancini and the young André Previn were two of the versatile composers making their names in the 1950s who, as their accounts below attest, evidently throve on the challenge of keeping pace with these developments on the eve of the studio system's collapse. Traditional scoring was enduringly revived in the 1970s by the blockbusters of the "New Hollywood," most indelibly associated in the popular imagination with the long-standing and fertile collaboration between director Steven Spielberg and composer John Williams. Williams cannily updated the lush romantic musical language of Golden Age film composers such as Erich Wolfgang Korngold (who was in the 1930s that exceptional rarity: a celebrity film composer with an impeccable classical pedigree) and produced—and at the time of writing continues to produce—a steady stream of memorable film scores that consistently top the soundtrack record charts internationally.

If the structural and technical challenges tackled by Williams are essentially similar to those familiar to Steiner, Waxman, and Herrmann, younger composers have since the 1980s tapped elements of pop, folk, and jazz to create less emotionally explicit scoring methods that owe a great deal to the hypnotic minimalism introduced to the concert hall and opera house in the 1970s by composers such as Steve Reich and Philip Glass. Our selection ends with an interview with perhaps the most interesting and original of the filmic minimalists, Thomas Newman. No matter whether traditional or fashionable in style, modern film scores require their freelance composers to be resourceful entrepreneurs, often surrounding themselves with sizable teams of trusted assistants, arrangers, and technicians, and fully prepared for their studio recordings—which in a former age all took place within a few square miles on the West Coast—now to be outsourced to ensembles and studios as far-flung as the United Kingdom, Spain, Italy, Eastern Europe, and New Zealand.

6

Max Steiner: "Scoring the Film" (1937)

The founding father of an indestructible lingua franca of orchestral film music in the early years of sound cinema was the Vienna-born composer Max Steiner (1888–1971), one of a clutch of immigrant musicians from Europe who shaped the Hollywood film score with sturdy but largely old-fashioned compositional techniques borrowed from opera, operetta, and stage melodrama. His career had begun in Europe as a musical director of stage shows, and it was in this capacity that he began work on Broadway following his emigration to New York at the beginning of the First World War. After the Wall Street crash in 1929, theatrical productions were affected by the harsh economic realities of the depression and a number of experienced musicians (among them Alfred Newman, soon to become a major musical and administrative force in Hollywood) left Broadway for the new opportunities offered by the film industry on the West Coast. When Steiner began work for RKO Radio Pictures in 1929, he was already skilled as a composer, arranger, and director of both classical and popular musical styles, and therefore (again like Newman) proved equally adept at scoring dramas and arranging musicals.

Steiner's breakthrough film-scoring assignments were *King Kong* (dir. Merian C. Cooper and Ernest B. Schoedsack, 1933) and *The Informer* (dir. John Ford, 1935), his score for the latter winning one of the film's four Academy Awards for RKO. (The music award had been instituted in 1934,

Source: Nancy Naumburg, ed., *We Make the Movies* (New York: W. W. Norton, 1937; London: Faber and Faber, 1938): 216–39.

Max Steiner conducting his score to RKO's landmark monster movie *King Kong* (dir. Merian C. Cooper and Ernest B. Schoedsack) in 1933. The projection screen for the benefit of the conductor is clearly visible at the rear of the studio, and the suitably outlandish orchestration includes a sousaphone (far left). (Photofest; © RKO)

and until 1938 was given to the studio's music department as a whole and not to individual composers.) After moving to Warner Bros. in 1936, Steiner became one of the most prolific of all Hollywood composers, scoring massive assignments like *Gone With the Wind* (dir. Victor Fleming, George Cukor, and Sam Wood, 1939) with the aid of a team of brilliant orchestrators and copious quantities of Benzedrine. His musico-dramatic methods were somewhat literal-minded, with a heavy reliance on leitmotifs, quotations of immediately recognizable preexisting melodies (for example, national anthems appropriate to a film's geographical setting), and graphic Mickey Mousing. The last technique, also known as "catching the action" and gaining its popular label from its habitual use in cartoons, involved musical gestures directly imitating the physical actions to which they were synchronized, and Steiner's sometimes slavish adherence to this approach occasionally met with harsh criticism.

In her comprehensive symposium on the mechanics of film production in the later 1930s, independent documentary filmmaker Nancy Naumburg

(1911–88) included chapters devoted to producers, story editing, scriptwriting, directing, set designing, casting, acting, photography, sound recording, editing, composing, color design, and animation. One of the two chapters on acting was contributed by rising star Bette Davis, who (like many of the book's contributors) was then under contract at Warner Bros., and for many of whose films Steiner composed the music, winning an Academy Award for his score accompanying her fine performance in Irving Rapper's *Now, Voyager* in 1942. Steiner's contribution to the volume provides revealing insights into his daily work as a busy film composer and includes an account of his role as musical director for RKO's *Gay Divorcee* (dir. Mark Sandrich, 1934), one of several musicals made by the studio to showcase the talents of Fred Astaire and Ginger Rogers, and the first winner of the newly instituted Academy Award for Best Song (Con Conrad and Herb Magidson's "The Continental").

Steiner begins by describing how background music gradually made its way onto film soundtracks at the start of the 1930s in reaction to the general avoidance of such descriptive music in the early years of the sound film (1927–30), when it was widely believed that audiences would be confused by the ghostly presence of invisible musicians and needed a clear visual justification for each music cue.

In the spring of 1931, due to the rapid development of sound technique, producers and directors began to realize that an art which had existed for thousands of years could not be ruled out by "the stroke of a pen." They began to add a little music here and there to support love scenes or silent sequences. But they felt it necessary to explain the music pictorially. For example, if they wanted music for a street scene, an organ grinder was shown. It was easy to use music in night club, ballroom or theater scenes, as here the orchestras played a necessary part in the picture.

Many strange devices were used to introduce the music. For instance, a love scene might take place in the woods, and in order to justify the music thought necessary to accompany it, a wandering violinist would be brought in for no reason at all. Or, again, a shepherd would be seen herding his sheep and playing his flute, to the accompaniment of a fifty-piece symphony orchestra.

Half of this music was still recorded on the set, causing a great deal of inconvenience and expense. Whenever the director, after the completion of his picture, made any changes, or recut his film, the score was usually ruined as it was obviously impossible to cut the sound track without harming the under-lying continuity of the music. Occasionally we were able to make cuts that were not too noticeable.

At this time the process of re-recording was slowly being perfected, and we soon learned to score music *after* the completion of a picture. This had two ad-vantages. It left the director free to cue his picture any way he pleased without hurting our work, and we were able to control the respective levels between dialogue and music, thereby clearing the dialogue.

To go back to 1931: With re-recording being rapidly improved, every stu-dio again began to import conductors and musicians. At the time, I was gen-eral musical director for RKO Studios. I wrote *Symphony of Six Million*, and *Bird of Paradise* soon after, the first of which had about 40 per cent, and the latter 100 per cent musical scoring. Both pictures had been shot for music. The directors and producers wanted music to run throughout, and this gradual change of policy resulted in giving music its rightful chance. One-third to one-half of the success of these pictures was attributed to the extensive use of music.

After that many pictures were completely scored, one of which was *King Kong* [1933]. This score I wrote in two weeks and the music recording cost was around fifty thousand dollars. The picture was successful and the studio again attributed at least 25 per cent of its success to the music, which made the artifi-cially animated animals more life-like, the battle and pursuit scenes more vivid. After this other studios followed suit and began to score their pictures. At this time I wrote the music for *The Lost Patrol* [1934], directed by John Ford. Mr. Ford also directed *The Informer* [1935], and he and I conferred on the use of music for this picture before it was shot. This was not the case with *The Lost Patrol*. At first it was not intended to have any music, but after the picture was finished the producer decided that, because of the long silent scenes, it was necessary to underscore the entire production.

In order to explain the modern technique and procedure of composing, directing, and recording music for the screen, I will outline my way of scoring which may differ to some extent from the systems adopted by composers and directors in other studios: but the fundamentals are the same.

When a picture is finished and finally edited, it is turned over to me. Then I time it: not by stop watch, however, as many do. I have the film put through a special measuring machine and then a cue sheet created which gives me the exact time, to a split second, in which an action takes place, or a word is spoken, as in the following example:

Excerpt from cue sheet of Reel III, Part I, of *The Informer*:

		MIN.	SEC.	FEET	FRAMES
CUE:	The captain throws money on table		0	0	
1.	Gypo grabs money and exits		20	30	
2.	Door slams		26	39	
3.	CUT to blind man		33	49	5
4.	Gypo grabs blind man's throat		41	61	6
5.	Gypo leaves him		58	87	
6.	The blind man's step is heard	I	5½	97	7

By comparing the respective timing, the reader will be able to discern the method of underscoring. The music for each cue is timed exactly by the number of feet and extra frames and by the number of minutes and seconds each cue runs.

While these cue sheets are being made, I begin to work on themes for the different characters and scenes, but without regard to the required timing. During this period I also digest what I have seen, and try to plan the music for this picture. There may be a scene that is played a shade too slowly which I might be able to quicken with a little animated music; or, to a scene that is too fast, I may be able to give a little more feeling by using slower music. Or perhaps the music can clarify a character's emotion, such as intense suffering, which is not demanded or fully revealed by a silent close-up, as, for instance, the scene in *The Charge of the Light Brigade* [1936], where Errol Flynn forges the order sending six hundred to their death.

After my themes are set and my timing is completed, I begin to work. I run the picture reel by reel again, to refresh my memory. Then I put my stop watch on the piano, and try to compose the music that is necessary for the picture within the limits allowed by this timing. For instance: For fifteen seconds of soldiers marching, I may write martial music lasting fifteen seconds. Then the picture might cut to a scene at a railroad track, which lasts for six seconds, when I would change my music accordingly or let it end at the cut. Once all my themes are set I am apt to discard them and compose others, because frequently, after I have worked on a picture for a little while, my feeling towards it changes.

Having finally set my themes I begin the actual and tedious work of composing according to my cue sheets, endeavoring to help the mood and dramatic intent of the story as much as possible. The great difficulty lies in the many *cuts* (sections; different locations) which make up a modern motion picture. For example: The first two minutes on my imaginary cue sheet consist of the arrival of a train in some little town. I would use music that conforms with the pounding of the locomotive, a train whistle or the screeching of the brakes, and perhaps some gay music to cover the greetings of people getting on and off the train. After these two minutes, the picture cuts directly to the death bed of the father in a little attic in an outlying farmhouse, the scene lasting three minutes in all. I must, therefore, devise some method of modulating quickly and smoothly from the gay music in the station to the silence and tragedy in the death room. These two scenes would consume five minutes of the ten-minute reel, and at the point of the father's death we might cut directly to a cabaret in New York where the daughter is singing, not knowing that her father is dead. Here is a transition which I would not modulate at all. Instead, it would be very effective to let a hot jazz band bang right in as soon as the cut, or *short fade*, to the cabaret was completed.

There is nothing more effective in motion-picture music than sudden changes of mood cleverly handled, providing, of course, they are consistent with the story. During this cabaret scene, while the jazz orchestra is playing, if the daughter is notified of her father's death, it would be absolutely wrong to change from the hot tune in progress to music appropriate to her mood. We must consider the jazz orchestra as actual music, not as underscoring; and, in order to make this sequence realistic, we should contrive to make the music as happy and noisy as possible. For, in the first place, the orchestra leader does not know what has happened, and would, therefore, have no reason to change his music; and, second, no greater counterpoint has ever been found than gay music underlying a tragic scene, or vice versa. The latter, of course, applies only if the audience is aware of tragedy taking place unknown to the players.

Standard symphonic music, such as Beethoven's *Eroica*, should not be used in its entirety for the same reasons stated in my last paragraph. The change of locale and cutting back and forth make it almost impossible. For example, if I were to use a funeral march from the *Eroica*, however well it might fit the scene and mood, if the picture cut on the twelfth bar to a cabaret in the Bronx, what would I do with the funeral march by Beethoven? I would have to rewrite, discontinue or break it up in some way, and I, for one, am loath to recompose the old masters.

Furthermore, it is my conviction that familiar music, however popular, does not aid the underlying score of a dramatic picture. I believe that, while the American people are more musically minded than any other nation in the world, they are still not entirely familiar with all the old and new masters' works. I am, therefore, opposed to the use of thematic material that might cause an audience to wonder and whisper and try to recall the title of a particular composition, thereby missing the gist and significance of a whole scene which might be the key to the entire story. Of course there are many in our industry who disagree with my viewpoint.

In composing a score there are certain facts which I have found important to consider. For instance, it pays to watch the particular pitch in which a person talks. A high voice often becomes "muddy," with high-pitched musical accompaniment, and the same is true of the low pitch. I rarely combine these except when I want to attain a special effect, such as matching voice and orchestra so that one is indistinguishable from the other.

The speed of the dialogue is also of great importance to the modern motion-picture composer. Fast music, over a slow dialogue scene, may help to speed up the action, but it may also ruin the mood, whereas slow music, over a slow scene, may either fit admirably or retard the action to an unprecedented extent. I rarely use fast music over fast dialogue. Instead I try to punctuate a fast-moving dramatic scene with music which seems to be slower, but which, in reality, approximates the same speed.

Pronounced high solo instruments or very low ones, or sharp or strident effects (oboe, piccolo, muted trumpets, screaming violins, xylophone, bells, high clarinets, and muted horns fortissimo) are taboo with me, because we should be able to hear the entire combination of instruments behind the average dialogue. But I have found muted strings, harp, celeste and low woodwind effects to be successful. Of course, there are exceptions to this rule, and in many of my pictures I have broken it entirely.

In fact, by now, the reader may well ask: What's the matter with Steiner? In one paragraph he gives advice and sets down a rigid rule, and in the next he reverses it. That is true . . . there are no rules, and there won't be as long as music continues to assume more and more importance in pictures, and the development of sound continues to make such rapid strides.

When the music has been composed and orchestrated, the orchestra assembles on a sound stage, especially treated for acoustics. The modern music-recording stage has soft and hard *flats* (panels) which can be moved around the stage on rollers at will to accommodate the different orchestral and vocal sounds produced. The reason for the flexibility of these flats is the varying sizes of orchestras and choruses required to score a motion picture. Naturally, inside a theater an orchestra has a different tone quality than it would have out-of-doors; and, by the same token, a singer in a fairly small room would sound entirely different than the same singer in a large concert hall. In order to reproduce these tone qualities as closely as possible, these flats are moved around either to reduce or enlarge the size of the tone space required. Often these flats are not used at all, particularly when the orchestra or chorus is very large.

The monitor booth is usually located on the first floor, out of everyone's way. That is the room in which the recordist sits and manipulates the various dials (channels) which combine the different microphones and thereby produce the final orchestra sound track. This recordist, in most instances, is himself a former musician, or at least a person who has great interest in music. His work is tedious and of great responsibility, because of the enormous expense incurred during the recording of the picture, involving musicians' salaries and film expense.

If one considers that the orchestra may have to do ten to twenty takes of the same number in order to get one good recording, one can imagine the time involved, not to speak of the thousands of feet of film needed.

A good take can easily be spoiled by the noise of an overhead airplane. Many times mail planes pursuing their duty swoop a little too low over the recording stage during a very tender violin solo; and, of course, this recording cannot be used, as the most modern microphones are extraordinarily sensitive. Also accidents occur, such as the scraping of a chair, the dropping of a mute or a bow, or even the scraping of a shirt button on a stand, the swish of music sheets being turned over, or an unavoidable cough. It is not always a wrong note or a conductor's mistake which causes a take to go wrong. Sometimes the projection machine *freezes* (gets out of order) and it may take fifteen or twenty minutes to repair. With a fifty-piece orchestra the expense is about two hundred and fifty dollars in unused salaries for this twenty-minute delay, as the musician gets paid from the time he is called until he leaves, whether he plays or not.

To get back to our first rehearsal of a new picture: The orchestra is rehearsed a little more thoroughly than other orchestras, for the better an orchestra plays, the less takes will be required and the less money spent on salaries and film. During this rehearsal the recordist places his microphones according to the wishes of the conductor, who indicates what instruments or orchestra sections shall be specially emphasized or *miked*. Then, when this is accomplished, while someone else conducts, the conductor goes upstairs to the booth to determine whether everything is to his liking. If it is, we then record our first take. Of course long association between recordists and conductors results in tremendous speed in balancing. I work with recordists whom I trust so implicitly that I rarely go up into the booth unless the recordist asks for advice, such as in the case of a special orchestral effect I wanted for the money theme in *The Informer*.

After our first take, we play it back. That means a loud speaker plays back the record that has been made on a separate recording machine, but which reproduces exactly the same result as on the film itself. It stands to reason that we cannot replay an undeveloped film; for, first of all, the negative would be spoiled, and, second, we would need a dark room for unloading, loading and re-winding. Should this playback be satisfactory, we go into our next sequence; rehearsal again, and we proceed exactly as before. We make as many takes as necessary until we get a perfect recording.

Each film is divided into sections of a thousand feet, and one such section is called a reel. A modern feature film consists of approximately nine to ten thousand feet. The latest projection machines in the theaters are able to run films of two thousand feet each, which are simply the first and second thousand-foot reel spliced together. However, the laboratories only develop thousand-foot reels. In recording music we divide a reel into as many sections as possible, for it is much easier for musicians and conductor to remember a two-minute scene than a ten-minute one.

In writing the music and recording it, great care must be taken by orchestra and conductor that the overlaps are properly handled, so that when the film is finally completed the listener is not conscious of the "breaks."

With our first day's recording over, we await the next morning with great expectation, or, shall I say . . . anxiety . . . when the laboratory sends the developed and printed recordings back to the studio for us to hear and pick takes. We sometimes print two or three recordings of the same number to be on the safe side, and in some instances intercut from one to the other. For instance, in a composition of one hundred and twenty bars' duration, the first ninety bars may be perfect whereas the last thirty may have been spoiled by any one of the aforementioned factors.

Our profession is not always "a bed of roses," and looks much easier to the layman than it really is. The work is hard and exacting, and when the dreaded "release date" is upon us, sleep is a thing unknown. I have had stretches of work for fifty-six consecutive hours without sleep, in order to complete a picture for the booking date. The reason for this is the fact that the major film companies sell their pictures for a certain date before they have even been produced; and, if the film's final editing has been delayed through some unforeseen happening, the music and re-recording departments have to pitch in to make up for lost time.

After we have picked our developed takes which have been returned by the laboratory, and providing everything is satisfactory, these takes are turned over to the music cutter and he synchronizes them to the film and dialogue track. When these tracks have finally been set up the entire film is taken up to the re-recording room. There both dialogue and music are mixed and regulated; again numerous takes are made; and impurities of the film and sound tracks are ironed out. These re-recording sessions are every bit as tedious and painstaking as the original recordings, since they constitute the final product. The next day, when these re-recorded takes come back from the laboratory, the same procedure of picking the best takes is followed. This time, of course, more attention is paid to the ratio between dialogue, music and sound effects.

Then, some evening, the picture is given a *sneak* preview at some obscure theater, where only the highest executives are allowed to witness its initial showing. The studio management thereby wishes to prevent any unfavorable opinion from penetrating the papers before the final editing. Should the projection equipment have been in mediocre or very bad condition, the sound and music departments would be the butt of unfavorable criticism. Happily for us, all picture theaters, including the small neighborhood houses, are gradually buying or renting new first-class standard equipment. I think most of our troubles in that respect will be over in another year or so.

I have often been asked: What are the requirements that make for a competent film composer-conductor? I would answer: ability, good disposition, PATIENCE. A thousand and one things can happen to a music sound track from the time it leaves the composer's brain until it is heard by the audience. I have had pictures which did not require any music whatsoever, according to the producers. Some of these turned out to be 100 per cent underscoring jobs. On other pictures I was told that a certain film could not be released without an entire underscoring job, and I would work for weeks, day and night. When the finished product left the studio to go to the exchanges, only 60 per cent of all the music written remained. Many factors cause this: a bad preview reaction, very bad sound, the unfortunate presence of a director or producer, who might still be opposed to the use of music throughout, or dialogue that may have been recorded too softly at the outset, so that no music could be heard at the low level required to keep this dialogue intelligible.

In some instances a composer or musical director himself may feel that music did not help a particular scene. This is not always easy to recognize in the studio projection room because of the absence of any audience reaction. Besides, one who works close to a film is apt to get so used to the dialogue that he knows it by heart, and, therefore, does not miss any part of it during the multitude of runnings which are required to complete the job.

Underscoring of musical pictures, apart from the actual performed songs, dances, or orchestral selections, is handled precisely like background music in dramatic pictures. But as far as the songs or dances are concerned, musical directors in the industry follow different methods.

I will endeavor to explain my method of handling a musical picture by using as a specific illustration *The Gay Divorcee* [1934], for which I directed, orchestrated and composed some of the music.

Unlike dramatic pictures, songs to be used in a musical picture must, of course, be composed either while the script is being written or immediately upon its completion. All songs that Fred Astaire and Ginger Rogers sang were recorded on the set with the entire crew present: director, cameramen, make-up experts, chorus girls, electricians, extras, etc., and some of them were accompanied by the orchestra I conducted—a very difficult procedure when one considers that because of the camera set-ups my orchestra and I were sometimes as far as a hundred feet away from the soloists. On a big stage where sound might have traveled at the rate of about ¾ sec., I had to be a little ahead of Mr. Astaire's taps, or voice, to offset this so-called sound lag. Singers often became uneasy because they could not see me, and because of the lag that they sensed due to the great distance between the orchestra and themselves.

Some of the songs were recorded with soft piano, i.e., a piano with a muffler on it, which was used to keep the principals in tempo and on pitch. This was to be covered later by the proper orchestra accompaniment, the conductor listening through earphones to both voice and soft piano. Naturally, with both the first and second channels working in perfect synchronization, it was possible to join the loud piano track obtained by this second channel to the voice and soft piano, thereby giving the conductor a loud accompaniment, which was somewhat easier to follow.

By way of explanation: This sound microphone was placed so close to the soft piano's sounding-board that it naturally picked up only the sound of the piano, and could easily be eliminated when the orchestra accompaniment was recorded. This method is still in vogue and is used almost universally when either the set-ups during the filming of a song change frequently or when the director or dance director is shooting *off the cuff*; i.e., when it is impossible to determine in advance what is to be done with the song or how much of it is to be used when the tempo is so rubato that a pre-recording is out of the question.

Pre-recording means pre-scoring, pre-playing with an orchestra, piano, or whatever is required of the song or dance number to be used in the picture. This sound track is usually pre-recorded before the picture has even gone into production, and then re-recorded the same way as the soft piano would have been. What little sound has been picked up from these *low-loud* speakers (to which I shall hereafter refer as "horns"), if handled properly, should not be noticeable.

I have always insisted on my music cutter syncing (matching) these tracks by the modulations visible on the film and not by sync marks. This is because sometimes even that very faint morsel of tone that has seeped through gives the regular pre-played orchestra sound track a phonograph-like quality which is disturbing. However, if put in sync properly, this seems to disappear. For example: the singer sets his key with the musical director, and the routine is discussed with the director, or dance director; it is orchestrated and recorded on the proper music-recording stage with the respective soloists present. But—he does not sing. Only the orchestra accompaniment is played, and I usually have the soloists go through the motions, or go up to the monitor booth and actually sing the song while I am playing it downstairs, simply to be sure that everything is satisfactory. It is obvious that were the performers to sing along with the orchestra on the same sound stage, the microphones would pick up the voices as well, and this would make the pre-recording track useless. This pre-scoring improvement was brought about through necessity. The soft piano and standard recording were cumbersome and unsatisfactory. A clever engineer invented a loud speaker that could be played so low that the new directional ribbon microphones could not pick up enough tone to spoil the track. These horns are placed as close as possible to the principals and they sing freely. The sound track can be stopped at will, and is played back either by special records (discs) to save time, or off the actual film on a special film playback machine. This low-loud speaker method has its points; but, like everything else in our world, it is not perfect. Any singer lacking excellent pitch is always in danger of singing flat or sharp, as the case may be, through his inability to hear the accompaniment distinctly. Also it seems rather hard to get an artist to give his best, and really let loose, with the music at a whisper when it should be lively and loud. However, I consider this method most advisable until something better turns up.

There is one other way which is used extensively in musical pictures of a more operatic character. Here the pre-scoring is done with singer, chorus and orchestra together. The singer then can sing with all the abandon necessary without fear of the camera and, in the case of more serious music, I believe, this gives the best result.

When this kind of pre-scoring is used, the track is played back also by horns, but at full power. The picture is then photographed silently, the singer following his or her own voice as closely as possible.

In many instances the singer will again sing his or her part while being photographed, while taking care to imitate as closely as possible his or her original rendition.

With dancing the procedure is similar, but only necessary when the particular dance steps are audible, as in tap dancing, for example. This is also recorded by the low-loud speaker system, as in the case of Fred Astaire, because it later facilitates the clearing of the taps, and the lag between orchestra and dancer is likewise removed. This is unavoidable when standard recording is used. Sometimes, however, loud playbacks are utilized and the picture is shot silently just as in the aforementioned procedure when voices are to be recorded.

As to composition: It is similar to musical comedy procedure, or comic opera. There is no difference. For underscoring we naturally paraphrase the actual songs used in the picture, and try to mold them neatly together to avoid the intrusion of music as much as possible. It is amazing what can be done in putting together long dance routines, such as the "Carioca," "The Continental" and "The Piccolino." Each one of these dance routines was shot in short pieces, some of them not even eight bars long; then put together like a mosaic and freshly underscored, re-orchestrated, improved upon, then taps, sound, and vocal effects added.

A very important requisite is the *click* or tempo track. These click tracks, as they are commonly called, are used universally in cartoon series such as *Mickey Mouse, Silly Symphony,* and *Looney Tunes.* These tempo tracks are filmed with every possible metronome tempo recorded on them. Conductor, orchestra and singer, while recording music for a cartoon, all wear earphones, usually only one, in order to leave one ear free to play on pitch. These tempo tracks even keep the players in exact time with the animation of the cartoon. These animations are drawn in frames to correspond with the exact bars of music to be used. I sometimes use this click track to guide me in long sequences, when the tempo is more or less unvarying, such as storm, train, racing, or battle sequences. Like the cartoon people, I simply decide on a tempo and then compute the frames into which the desired effects must enter, and write my music accordingly.

It might not be amiss to mention the music-clearing procedure. All music is divided into two classifications: copyrighted and public domain. Public domain means music of unknown origin, unknown authorship, or music on which the copyright has expired. Music on which the copyright is still enforced must be purchased either directly from the composer, or from his publisher. In order to facilitate this there is one central agency that has been set up in New York City, called the Music Publishers' Protective Association. This constitutes the clearing house for all music publishers and composers.

There are certain compositions that are not available at all, such as the Gilbert and Sullivan operas. Up to this writing the Gilbert and Sullivan Estates have absolutely refused to perform their works on the screen for reasons best known to themselves, and there are many composers of the same mind. Then there are highly restricted compositions, usually some number from a stage production which the producer, as co-owner of the copyright, is loath to release for film use. He may still have hopes of being able to sell the entire "works" to some major film company, and, therefore, does not wish to break up the complete score.

Economic necessity is one of the principal reasons why a major picture company brings well-known composers out to Hollywood, as well as the desire to procure original music for new films. It stands to reason that if only published and copyrighted music were used, the cost of one hour's scoring would be prohibitive, as its usage must be paid for whether it lasts fifteen seconds or ten minutes. A circular inquiry was sent to all musical directors, asking for an opinion as to what time limit should be placed on one complete usage. Three minutes were suggested, and anything over this amount would constitute another usage. Therefore, should a number, song or orchestral selection, for instance, cost five hundred dollars for three minutes, three minutes and ten seconds would cost a thousand dollars. Because of this, almost all major picture concerns have direct affiliations with, or own, their own publishing house. The copyrights to the contract-composers' music are, of course, owned by the respective studios. An exception of prior rights is made and already listed by the American Society of Composers, Authors and Publishers, if the composer is a member.

The new wide range and ultra-violet recording has made it possible to reproduce faultlessly the entire range of the human voice from coloratura to basso profundo. Also, the orchestra range has been widened to such an extent that almost no limitations are placed upon the orchestrator or composer. (Very different from a few years ago when the low G on the double bass caused the most unpleasant consequences.) What is true of vocal reproduction is also true of orchestral color. It is becoming more and more "high-fidelity" (true to life) every day. I agree with Mr. Leopold Stokowski that the ultimate perfection is in sight. More than that, I believe, as he does, that the recorded music of the future will be made to sound, both in volume and quality, far better than is conceivable today. I further believe that the limit of music in pictures has not been reached and that, finally, opera and the symphonic field will find their rightful place in this great medium.

7

David Raksin: "Life with Charlie" (1983)

David Raksin (1912–2004) was one of the most innovative and outspoken U.S. composers working in Hollywood, where he first arrived in 1935 in response to an invitation to assist former silent-film star Charlie Chaplin with the scoring of his sound film *Modern Times* at United Artists. Raksin recounts the circumstances of this momentous occasion in his career in the characteristically humorous text below, which also provides an illuminating description of the older U.S. composer who would become his mentor: Alfred Newman (1900–1970), who was then on the verge of becoming one of the most powerful and influential music directors in Hollywood, and for whom Raksin was later to work at Twentieth Century-Fox. Between them, Raksin and Newman came to typify the strengths of the best American musicians working alongside their many European colleagues: in Raksin's case, an interest in both jazz and modern concert music and a willingness to experiment, and in Newman's a formidable blend of effective managerial and conducting skills.

Chaplin had since 1915 directed all the films in which he starred, and had also taken control of their musical accompaniment: he genuinely believed himself to be a composer, though he was entirely untutored, could not read music, and was heavily dependent on a succession of hard-pressed arrangers (most of whose work was contractually obliged to remain uncredited). As an early auteur director with overly controlling tendencies, he welcomed the advent of the sound film because it allowed him to create a permanent soundtrack, in contrast

Source: Quarterly Journal of the Library of Congress, 40/3 (1983): 234–53; reprinted in Iris Newsom, ed., Wonderful Inventions: Motion Pictures, Broadcasting, and Recorded Sound at the Library of Congress (Washington, D.C.: The Library, 1985): 159–71.

Modern Times (1936), Charlie Chaplin's delicious satire of contemporaneous industrial mechanization, had a score "composed" (as in many of his films) by Chaplin himself. In reality, the music was the result of considerable hard work by an accomplished team of arrangers, orchestrators, and conductors that included the young David Raksin, Edward Powell, Bernhard Kaun, and the great Alfred Newman.

to the vagaries of musical provision in the silent era, and he also believed that good film music served an educational purpose for the masses. His sound films included *City Lights* (1931; music prepared by Arthur Johnston), *The Great Dictator* (1940; music prepared by Meredith Willson), and *Limelight* (1952; music prepared by Raymond Rasch and Larry Russell), which in 1973 received a belated Academy Award for Best Score on its rerelease. Despite his succession of different collaborators, Chaplin's musical idiom remained remarkably consistent. But it was unashamedly old-fashioned, and this led to a serious contretemps when the music for *Modern Times* was prepared: when Raksin attempted to dissuade Chaplin from using a style that in his opinion was vulgar, Raksin was (temporarily) sacked.

Raksin's first significant solo assignment came at Fox in 1944, when he supplied Otto Preminger's mystery *Laura* with a score distinguished not only by its technical sophistication but also by the memorability of its lush main theme, with which (at Newman's suggestion, and for compelling dramatic reasons) a good deal of the film is saturated; this melody became a hit song when lyricized after the film's release, and was later widely adopted as a jazz standard.

Among the better-known of Raksin's later scores are those to Preminger's *Forever Amber* (1947) and Abraham Polonsky's *Force of Evil* (1948). Later in his career he became noted as a film-music educator, teaching at the University of Southern California from 1956.

The new adventure began on August 8, 1935, four days after my twenty-third birthday, with a telegram from Eddie Powell, addressed to me "care Harms Inc." in New York City. Since I was in Boston, arranging and orchestrating Music for *At Home Abroad,* a show that was in its pre-Broadway tryout, the people at Harms forwarded the wire to me. It said:

> HAVE WONDERFUL OPPORTUNITY FOR YOU IF INTERESTED IN HAVING
> SHOT AT HOLLYWOOD STOP CHAPLIN COMPOSES ALMOST ALL HIS OWN
> SCORE BUT CANT WRITE DOWN A NOTE YOUR JOB TO WORK WITH HIM
> TAKE DOWN MUSIC STRAIGHTEN IT OUT HARMONICALLY DEVELOP HERE
> AND THERE IN CHARACTER OF HIS THEME PLAY IT OVER WITH PICTURE
> FOR CUES WE WILL ORCHESTRATE TOGETHER NEWMAN CONDUCT STOP
> BEST CHANCE YOU COULD EVER HAVE TO BREAK IN HERE CHAPLIN
> FASCINATING PERSON ALTHOUGH MUSIC VERY SIMPLE AM SURE
> NEWMAN WILL LIKE YOU AND KEEP YOU HERE YOU SPENCER AND I CAN
> HAVE GRAND TIME WORKING TOGETHER STOP THIS OFFER TWO HUN-
> DRED PER WEEK MINIMUM OF SIX TRANSPORTATION BOTH WAYS STOP
> YOU CAN STUDY WITH SCHOENBERG WHILE HERE I HAVE SOLD YOU TO
> NEWMAN BECAUSE COMPOSER AND ORCHESTRATOR CAN ALSO GET YOU
> IN WITH MAX STEINER AT END OF THIS JOB IF YOU WISH ANSWER
> IMMEDIATELY BY WESTERN UNION REGARDS.

That yellow page, with its strips of uppercase letters pasted on, has reposed in my abandoned scrapbook for quite a while, and I will bet this is the first time I have looked at it—really looked—since I put it there so long ago. It is not likely that I shall ever get to ride one of those magnificent rockets to the moon; but I doubt that the moment that followed "We have ignition . . . we have lift-off!" could have been more thrilling to the fellows in the *Columbia* than the one after "ANSWER IMMEDIATELY" was to me.

There I was, fresh from the University of Pennsylvania, survivor of a harrowing year in New York City that included plenty of supperless evenings—to remind me that not every young composer has it as easy as Felix Mendelssohn did. When the society dance band with which I had come to New York from my home in Philadelphia developed a case of chronic underemployment, the leader elected to withdraw to safer ground on the Main Line, and the band followed.

I was the only one who stayed in the big town, and I only managed that because our first saxophone player gave me what was left of a due bill as a farewell gift. . . .

I arrived at the Pasadena station, to be met by two of the great masters of the orchestra whom our country has produced. Herb Spencer (who is mentioned in the telegram) is a brilliant musician who came to the United States from his native Chile to study and remained to make a great name for himself in our profession. Today he is the admired orchestrator of John Williams's scores for such films as *Star Wars* and *Close Encounters of the Third Kind*. Eddie Powell is renowned for his elegant and fastidious work as orchestrator of Alfred Newman's film scores. What was, however, more important in August of 1935 was that he and Herb turned up to meet me in Eddie's new LaSalle convertible—which is an ideal way of impressing upon a traveler that he has made it to Hollywood. And indeed, when we glided down Sunset Boulevard into what seemed a veritable parade of convertibles filled with beautiful girls, I knew that I had come to the right place.

Paradise found, some might say—but not quite yet. I am not sure whether what happened next would have surprised the inhabitants of sixth-century Sybaris; but it came as a rude awakening when at dinner Powell and Spencer informed me that our next stop would be the United Artists studio, where I would be pressed into service to help them make up the time they had expended on the welcoming festivities. It seemed that a recording had been scheduled for the next morning; Alfred Newman would be conducting the score of a new Goldwyn picture, *Barbary Coast*, and Eddie and Herb still had a mountain of sketches to orchestrate before the copyists came in at 3:00 A.M. To be called upon so soon to lend one's talent in an enterprise for which one has no experience is quite a compliment. It is also unnerving.

Since Powell and Spencer were using the only two music studios on the United Artists lot, they took me over to a sound stage where there was a piano. Eddie gave me a list of the instruments that would be available at the recording and several very sparse sketches of film sequences written in a hand with which I was to become extremely familiar in time, the musical script of Al Newman. I had met him earlier that day—a small, intense, and dapper man who exuded power and strong cologne. He had asked a question, seemingly innocuous, about the way in which I viewed the assignment, the challenge of the project itself, and the prospect of working with one of the great film artists. It was soon obvious that my reply had left him wondering what his two associates could have been thinking when they recommended me; he appeared to be put off by my enthusiasm. This was not my first experience with the chill of disapproval but, had I been in his place, I would have judged any young man not inspired to rhapsodies by such good fortune to be temperamentally unfit for the job. Still, the encounter left me wondering what kind of man could have considered my response some kind of social gaffe.

And that disconcerting thought kept me company as I worked alone in the vast emptiness built to accommodate film scenery and production equipment. Eddie and Herb had generously started me out with the relatively easy task of making several string arrangements of a Stephen Foster melody that Newman was interpolating in the score of *Barbary Coast*. The sequences had already been timed to synchronize with the film footage and my job was to make elaborate settings of the tune for a large group of strings. I was well prepared for that; but when from time to time the memory of Newman's raised eyebrow materialized I knew for sure that if my work turned out to be in any way below the standard which he set I would be on the train back to New York the next afternoon.

Fortunately, in such cases the work itself becomes the indicated therapy. I got lost in the intricacies of the task at hand, and when my two friends showed up near midnight, ostensibly to bring me coffee but actually to see how I was doing, it was evident from their expressions of approval that I had not disappointed them. Newman's chief copyist, Fred Combattente, arrived as I was finishing the last of the sequences and seemed relieved to find my manuscript legible.

After a few hours of sleep, Eddie, Herb, and I went together to the recording session on stage 7, where I witnessed for the first time Al Newman's virtuosity with an orchestra. The sound he got from his hand-picked ensemble was nothing less than gorgeous, and his ability to elicit beautiful and impeccable playing at extremely slow tempi was a revelation to me. For some reason, I failed to anticipate what this style of conducting would do for the notes I had set down during the long night, so that when he turned his attention to one of those sequences I did not immediately connect the glowing sounds that emerged from the orchestra with the monochromatic symbols I had written on the score pages. When he had read through the first of my arrangements, Newman put down his baton and summoned me to the podium, where he introduced me to his musicians in a manner that left me blushing.

Newman and I were to go through a relationship during the years when we worked together that was almost familial in its intensity; but at that moment a bond was established that survived serious differences of purpose between us. Many years later, after Al died, his son Tommy entered my class in composition at the University of Southern California. And one day, trying to explain to him why it meant so much to me to find the son of my old mentor in my class, I told him that I had at one time been another son of his father's.

I think it was on the day after the *Barbary Coast* recording that I went to Chaplin's headquarters, near the corner of Sunset Boulevard and La Brea, to meet the great man. The studio had a facade of one-story brick buildings with Tudor-style timbers inset; behind these were several moderate-sized film stages. In his projection room, a small theatre, Chaplin awaited me. For some reason, it often seems to surprise me to find that great artists are really people. I have met perhaps more than my share of them, because so many have spent time in Hollywood, and I am always amazed that they somehow lack the wings, or the X-ray vision, or the noble proportions to which (some misconceived synapse keeps telling me) their genius entitles them. The man who stood before me was certainly exotic enough—from his abundant white hair to his anachronistic shoes with their high suede tops and mother-of-pearl buttons—and urbane to match. But he was neither twelve feet tall nor two-dimensional; yet, so charming and gracious that I was immediately captivated.

In the years since that meeting, it has never occurred to me to wonder how I appeared to Chaplin. But this article has sent me searching through my souvenirs for photographs and other memorabilia; and among the curiosities that surfaced was a page of yellow foolscap on which I copied down his very words, as related to me by the playwright, Bayard Veiller, to whom Chaplin introduced me one day at the Beverly Hills Brown Derby. According to Veiller, Charlie said, "They tell you, 'I've got just the man for you—brilliant, experienced, a composer, orchestrator, and arranger with several big shows in his arranging cap'— and this infant turns up!"

Since this happened before the decades during which it was revealed that talent is the exclusive province of the young, Charlie may indeed have had misgivings. If so, he overcame them sufficiently to show me the new film. *Modern Times* was then in a first-final edit, meaning that substantial changes were now unlikely, although fine tuning could, and would, continue beyond production deadlines and right down to the wire; a measure of Chaplin's hard won independence from the stranglehold of studio policy.

I loved the picture at once, and I laughed so hard at some of the scenes (particularly the feeding machine sequence) that some time later Charlie told me he had wondered whether I was exaggerating for his benefit. By the time that came up, however, he knew better; for after about a week and a half of working together a serious difference of opinion as to the precise nature of my job arose between us, and I was summarily fired.

Like many self-made autocrats, Chaplin demanded unquestioning obedience from his associates; years of instant deference to his point of view had persuaded him that it was the only one that mattered. And he seemed unable, or unwilling, to understand the paradox that his imposition of will over his studio had been achieved in a manner akin to that which he professed to deplore in *Modern Times*. I, on the other hand, have never accepted the notion that it is my job merely to echo the ideas of those who employ me; and I had no fear of opposing him when necessary because I believed he would recognize the value of an independent mind close at hand.

When I think of it now, it strikes me as appallingly arrogant to argue with a man like Chaplin about the appropriateness of the thematic material he proposed to use in his own picture. But the problem was real. There is a specific kind of genius that traces its ancestry back to the magpie family, and Charlie was one of those. He had accumulated a veritable attic full of memories and scraps of ideas, which he converted to his own purposes with great style and individuality. This can be perceived in the subject matter, as well as the execution, of his story lines and sequences. In the area of music, the influence of the English music hall was very strong, and since I felt that nothing but the best would do for this remarkable film, when I thought his approach was a bit vulgar I would say, "I think we can do better than that." To Charlie this was insubordination pure and simple—and the culprit had to go.

The task of informing me was given to Eddie Powell, in whose studio I was living at the time; and although he relayed the unhappy news as gently as possible it just about broke my heart. The next evening, Eddie and his wife, Kay, and Herb Spencer took me to a favorite Hollywood hangout, Don the Beachcomber's, for dinner. At one point I was so overcome with unhappiness that I walked to the doorway quickly and stood there struggling for control. Just then, someone tapped me on the shoulder, and when I turned around I saw it was Al Newman. "I've been looking at your sketches," he said, "and they're marvelous—what you're doing with Charlie's little tunes. He'd be crazy to fire you."

I was packing the next day when there was a phone call from Alf Reeves, an endearing old gentleman who had worked with Chaplin years before in the Fred Karno troupe and was now general manager of the studio. I went to see him, and he said that they wanted to hire me again. I replied that I would like nothing more, but that before I could give him an answer I wanted to talk to Charlie—alone—otherwise the same thing would happen again. So Charlie and I met in his projection room and had it out.

I explained that if it was a musical secretary he wanted he could hire one for peanuts; if he wanted more "yes" men, well, he was already up to his ears in them. But if he needed someone who loved his picture and was prepared to risk getting fired every day to make sure that the music was as good as it could possibly be, then I would love to work with him again. We shook hands, and he gave me a sharp tap on the shoulder—and that was it, the beginning of four and a half months of work and some of the happiest days of my life.

Charlie would usually arrive at the studio in midmorning, at which point the staff, which had been notified that he was en route, would spring into activity; Carter de Haven, Jr., the son of one of Chaplin's cronies (and now a film producer), would alert me. I would put aside the sketches of the previous day or so, on which I was working, and join Charlie in the projection room. Our equipment included a small grand piano, a phonograph, a portable tape recorder, a large screen for the 35 mm projectors, and a smaller one for the "Goldberg," a projection movieola that could also back up in sync.

When he appeared, Charlie was generally armed with a couple of musical phrases; in the beginning, apparently because he thought of me as an innocent, he seemed to enjoy telling me that he got some of his best ideas "while meditating [raising of eyebrow]—on the throne, you know." Innocent or not, few composers can afford to be squeamish about the loci of the muse, so unless one of us had some other idea that could not wait we would first review the music leading to the sequence at hand and then go on to the new ideas. First, I would write them down; then we would run the footage over and over, discussing the scenes and the music. Sometimes we would use his tune, or we would alter it, or one of us might invent another melody. I should say that I always began by wanting to defer to him; not only was it his picture, but I was working from the common attitude that since I was ostensibly the arranger the musical ideas were his prerogative.

Here it may be valuable to discuss the nature of the collaboration which Chaplin found necessary, and which has invariably been misinterpreted. For example, in an article by one of Chaplin's biographers, Theodore Huff, in the very first paragraph we read, "When *City Lights* first appeared with the credit title 'Music composed by Charles Chaplin'. . . [people] assumed that Chaplin was stretching it a bit in order that the public be certain that from him came everything in the film." The fact is that in *City Lights,* as in all of his films, Chaplin was assisted by another composer; in that instance it was Arthur Johnston ("Cocktails for Two," "Pennies from Heaven"). I do not know how large a part Johnston played in that score, but I did discuss the music for *The Great Dictator* with the man who assisted Chaplin on that film.

The Great Dictator was Charlie's first real talkie; although he had used a sound track in *City Lights* and *Modern Times,* he had only been heard in the "Titina" sequence of the latter film. The composer who worked with Chaplin on *The Great Dictator* was Meredith Willson (*The Music Man*), an old friend who authorized me to quote him: "I know you will want to make it clear that Charlie was a very brilliant man, a very creative man. He would come into the studio they had given me to work in, and he would have ideas to suggest—melodies. After that, he would leave me alone. When he came in to see me again I would show him what I was doing, and often he would have very good suggestions to make. He liked to act as though he knew more music than he actually did, but his ideas were very good." (It is interesting to note that in James Limbacher's book *Film Music,* p. 333, Chaplin and Willson are listed as cocomposers of the score for *The Great Dictator.*)

From Meredith's account of his experience, it seems clear that he had more to do with the score for *The Great Dictator* than I had with *Modern Times.* Charlie and I worked hand in hand. Sometimes the initial phrases were several phrases long, and sometimes they consisted of only a few notes, which Charlie would whistle, or hum, or pick out on the piano. Thus far, it does not seem too different from what Willson has recounted. But here the differences begin. Whereas Meredith went on to write alone in his studio, I remained in the projection room, where Charlie and I worked together to extend and develop the musical ideas to fit what was on the screen. When you have only a few notes or a short phrase with which to cover a scene of some length, there must ensue considerable development and variation—what is called for is the application of the techniques of composition to shape and extend the themes to the desired proportions. (That so few people under-stand this, even those who may otherwise be well informed, makes possible the common delusion that composing consists of getting some kind of micro-flash of an idea, and that the rest of it is mere artisanry; it is this mis-conception that has enabled a whole generation of hummers and strummers to masquerade as composers.)

Theodore Huff and others to the contrary, no informed person has claimed that Charlie had any of the essential techniques. But neither did he feed me a little tune and say, "You take it from there." On the contrary; we spent hours, days, months in that projection room, running scenes and bits of action over and over, and we had a marvelous time shaping the music until it was exactly the way we wanted it. By the time we were through with a sequence we had run it so often that we were certain the music was in perfect sync. Very few film composers work this way (Erich Korngold did work in a projection room, and a few others—Aaron Copland, Leonard Bernstein and Jerry Goldsmith come to mind—used movieolas); the usual procedure is to work from timing sheets, with a stop clock, to coordinate image and music. But *Modern Times* was my first job in Hollywood, and I did not learn the sophisticated system of visual cueing until I took my sketches to Al Newman's assistant, Charles Dunworth, who devised the "Newman" system. Dunworth took my timing and sync marks and transferred them to the film, so that during the recording sessions they would appear on the screen as *streamers* (white lines moving across the screen to indicate sync points) and *punches* (mathematically calculated holes punched in specific film frames).

Chaplin had picked up an assortment of tricks of our trade and some of the jargon and took pleasure in telling me that some phrase should be played "vru-bato," which I embraced as a real improvement upon the intended Italian word, which was much the poorer for having been deprived of the *v*. Yet, very little escaped his eye or ear, and he had suggestions not only about themes and their appropriateness but also about the way in which the music should develop, whether the melodies should develop, whether the melodies should move "up" or "down," whether the accompaniment should be tranquil or "busy." I recall an earnest discussion about a certain melody (or countermelody). I had sug-gested that we had already used the tune in the middle and upper registers and that it was time we played it in the lower register; by the time Charlie and I explored the possibilities, we eliminated the French horn as having too soft an edge, the trombone as being too declamatory, the bassoon as a bit too mild, and I think we wound up using a tenor saxophone there.

The result of this process was a series of sketches, quite specific as to prin-cipal musical lines and cueing to the action on the screen, but far from com-plete as to harmonies, subsidiary lines and voice leading, and instrumentation. While we were working at full momentum, it would have been foolish for me to keep Charlie standing there while I meticulously filled in all of the parts. So this first set of sketches was rather sparse, except that when an idea was clearly revealed I felt it worthwhile to speed write the whole thing immediately. Some-times Charlie would attend to other matters while this was going on, or do his improvisations; more often than not he just stood around and kibitzed while I scribbled away. But most of the time I would settle for the shorthand sketch, and would either clean it up or rewrite it legibly in the mornings before he ar-rived at the studio or, if we had not worked after dinner, I would clear up my sketches at home; I often worked on weekends. (I still have a set of the rather primitive first sketches; but what has become of the more complete set from which Eddie Powell and I would later orchestrate the score for recording I do not know. I am afraid they may have been lost in the fire that destroyed the Powells' house in Beverly Hills.)

Sometimes in the course of our work, when the need for a new piece of thematic material arose, Charlie might say, "A bit of 'Gershwin' might be nice there." He meant that the Gershwin style would be appropriate for that scene. And indeed there is one phrase that makes a very clear genuflection toward one of the themes in *Rhapsody in Blue*. Another instance would be the tune that later became a pop song called "Smile." Here, Charlie said something like, "What we need here is one of those 'Puccini' melodies." Listen to the result, and you will hear that, although the notes are not Puccini's, the style and feeling are. . . .

Chaplin was actually an admirer of fine concert music. In our projection room there was a pretty good phonograph, and he had brought some of his recordings in from home. These included a Symphony in D by Mozart (I cannot remember whether it was the *Paris*, K. 297, or the *Haffner*, K. 385, but I think the conductor was Thomas Beecham); also, *Prometheus*, by Scriabin (Stokowski's recording); Stravinsky's *Symphony of Psalms* (with the composer conducting, I believe); the First Symphony of "Szostakowicz" (I think I copied that spelling from the label of the album, and that the recording was probably the one by Stokowski with the Philadelphia Orchestra); a Balinese gamelan recording; and finally, a recording of Prokofiev's Third Piano Concerto (with Piero Coppola conducting the London Symphony and the composer as soloist). This last piece figured in a practical joke that says something disconcerting about the brashness with which I sometimes behaved, as well as the almost fatherly tolerance with which Charlie put up with my peccadillos.

Charlie had a portable tape recorder. (I believe it is the same one visible in some of the photographs taken when the two of us were reminiscing about the work on *Modern Times* on the day in 1952 before he left to live in Europe.) Occasionally he would play something back for me that he had hummed into the machine, and he liked to tell his guests that he used it so as not to lose some good idea that might come to him when I was not around to write it down. I think that this irritated me because the way in which he said it was outside the scope of our bargain—it seemed to reduce me to the flunky I had no intention of being. One morning, when he was late getting to the studio and I had no sketches to clean up, I put some bits and pieces of the recorded works on tape by recording them from the phonograph. Naturally, this would have to be the day that Charlie turned up with his wife Paulette [Goddard] and their guest— H. G. Wells, no less. As expected, at one point he delivered his little spiel about the magic machine and ended by saying, "Let's see what's on the tape," and turning it on at full volume. With which, out blasted the second theme of the first movement of the Prokofiev Third Piano Concerto—and for a moment I thought that this was going to be the end of me. But everybody else thought it was funny, which seemed to help Charlie past a bad moment. (Today, I think I deserved a swift kick, but I am just as happy that I never got it.)

If I do not have my events mixed up, that was also the day we took Wells over to the recording session after lunch. As we were leaving the projection room, Wells, who had apparently been hearing about me from Charlie, turned and said, "Red. . .very red, I'm told." While I stood there agape over the idea that this futurist should find my politics other than quaint, that beautiful young woman, Paulette, said in her best eager voice, "Oh, yes!" And Wells, in the manner of a farceur delivering an exit line, said, "Ah . . . a nice, old-fashioned color," and swept out the doorway.

The recording sessions were a unique combination of working time and social event. Charlie was at his best, in his most elegant finery, sitting near the podium, listening and carrying on, sometimes conducting a bit, and generally charming everyone with his antics. He was delighted with the way the score was turning out, and his euphoria was contagious. Al Newman liked to record at night, when the rest of the United Artists studio was shut down. Since the stage was soundproof, this could not have been because of a need to avoid the distraction of daytime activities. After a while, I realized that there is a quality of isolation which those of us who work at night experience, a psychological remoteness that provides blessed relief from the clamor of everyday banality, and that this was what Newman was after. And when, after three or four hours of intense concentration, an intermission was called, the entire orchestra of about sixty-five, the sound crew, and the rest of us would adjourn to an adjacent stage where tables had been set up and a supper was served in grand style by the staff of the best caterers in town, the Vendome. This period of congeniality must have been very expensive—supper for about eighty-five, five nights a week for several weeks—but it was surely worth it, for it helped to sustain the feeling that something special was afoot, something elegant, and worth the effort.

Eddie Powell and I shared a problem which the others were spared. When the recording sessions were over, the musicians and the sound crew went off to get some rest, to be ready for the next evening's work. But Eddie and I had to keep one jump ahead of the copyists and the orchestra, so we would usually resume work on the next round of orchestrations when everyone else had gone home. Since this went on and on, after a while we were both ready to be carted away from sheer exhaustion. One day Al Newman said to me, "You look sick. Why don't you take the night off—skip the recording." I must have been pretty well worn out to agree to miss the session, but it was either that or collapse. So I went off to dinner with a friend and then back to my apartment to listen to some music—and embarrassed myself by falling asleep.

When I arrived at the studio next morning, I learned that Al and Charlie had had a fierce argument at the session; they too were operating on ragged nerves, and after one bad take Charlie had accused the players of "dogging it"— lying down on the job. At this, Newman, who at the best of times had a hair-trigger temper, had broken his baton and stalked off the stage, and was now refusing to work with Chaplin. This was put to me in a way that reveals a sleazy side of studio politics. Several of Sam Goldwyn's younger executives, who knew all the gossip, told me that I would be expected to take over and conduct the remaining sessions. I realized later that they would have enjoyed watching me struggle with the temptation offered by such an opportunity, believing that it was certain to supersede whatever loyalty I might feel toward Newman. But I said that if what they had told me was true, then Charlie was at fault and owed Al and the orchestra an apology, and that I could not agree to anything that would hurt Al or weaken his position. As it turned out, the United Artists people invoked Powell's contract with them and had him complete the sessions. With Eddie conducting, I did most of the remaining orchestration, and the recordings concluded in a rather sad and indeterminate spirit. Eddie and I thought that this was not the way to end things, so we gave a big party for the orchestra, complete with the best that the Vendome had to offer. But nothing could quite compensate for the fact that, as a result of my stiff-necked adherence to what I thought was right, Charlie and I became estranged, and we would not become friends again until many years later.

When, during the final recording session, we came at last to the ending of *Modern Times*—the scene in which Charlie and the gamine (Paulette Goddard), once again dispossessed and having had to escape from the detectives, find themselves on the road at sunrise—I remembered something that Charlie had said when we were working to get the music just right. We had a guest that day, Boris Shumiatsky, the head of the Russian film industry. (I do not know whether I could have managed to be civil to him if I had known that he was the Soviet bureaucrat who had gone to such lengths to make Sergei Eisenstein's life miserable, to censure him, and to thwart his plans.) A note I wrote to myself that day contains no reference to Shumiatsky except to say that he was present. But it does juxtapose my own naiveté with Charlie's more worldly outlook:

> So now the film ends on a beautiful note of hope, with conquerable worlds on the horizon, and we spent much time deliberating [as to] how the music should soar—but Charlie is a bit cynical about the future of his . . . hero and his gamine. "They'll probably get kicked in the pants again," he says (as we watch them on the screen, trudging hopefully away into the dawn). And they probably will, and it will probably happen in his next film.

Charlie's next film was *The Great Dictator*, in which he played a dual role: he was Hynkel, dictator of Tomania (a satiric figure modeled on Adolf Hitler), and also a Jewish barber. Paulette played Hannah, and in the story they all had their share of troubles. Meredith Willson worked with Charlie on the score. Busy with my own thriving career—I was now composing film scores on my own—I would still have a long way to go before Charlie and I would resume our friendship; but that is another story. . . .

8

Aaron Copland: *Our New Music* (1941)

Along with Virgil Thomson, who wrote a number of fine scores for documentary films in the 1930s, Aaron Copland (1900–1990) was one of very few established U.S. concert composers to make a significant contribution to the art of film scoring during the Golden Age of Hollywood. Both composers turned deliberately away from the overblown and outdated romantic clichés under which film scores had long labored, preferring to cultivate clear textures, diatonic harmonies, and folk-inspired elements that combined to create a fresh and immediately recognizable "American" sound. The style of Copland's mature concert and ballet music—particularly the cowboy idiom of *Billy the Kid* (1938), the limpid economy of *Appalachian Spring* (1944), and the dignified nationalistic overtones of *Lincoln Portrait* (1942) and *Fanfare for the Common Man* (1943)—exerted a powerful influence on younger film composers, and its characteristics still resonate in many modern film scores, especially those with patriotic scenarios.

Copland first worked for Hollywood in 1939–40 when he scored film versions of John Steinbeck's *Of Mice and Men* (dir. Lewis Milestone) and Thornton Wilder's *Our Town* (dir. Sam Wood). On the whole he found the experience congenial, and, like the British composer Ralph Vaughan Williams, he celebrated the fact that in film work modern composers could find a ready outlet for instant (and high-quality) performances of their latest music. Copland was sufficiently stirred by the potential inherent in the medium to devote a chapter

Source: *Our New Music: Leading Composers in Europe and America* (New York and London: Whi⊦˙ House/McGraw-Hill, 1941): 260–75.

Lewis Milestone's film of John Steinbeck's *Of Mice and Men* (1939) was one of a number of screen adaptations of U.S. literary classics that made Aaron Copland's name as an innovative film composer with strong nationalistic leanings. Copland recalled that he found it straightforward to write graphically illustrative music cues, such as the sustained dissonance illustrating the hand-crushing incident pictured here, but rather harder to provide background music intended to have a dramatically neutral quality.

of his 1941 book *Our New Music* to the subject of music and film. Copland's account of the positive and negative factors of film scoring, reproduced here, and his description of the film composer's working practices have remained remarkably relevant and suggest that little fundamental has changed in the film industry's attitude toward music since his remarks were penned.

While working on his book, Copland provocatively discussed the theme of film music in the pages of the *New York Times*. In his article "The Aims of Music for Films" (March 10, 1940), he made a plea for the medium to be taken seriously—by composers, critics, and the general public alike—and emphasized the importance of independent producers and musically sensitive directors in allowing composers a degree of free rein. Noting that films with clearly defined period or geographical settings perversely continued to employ music in an ersatz nineteenth-century Viennese style, Copland identified a particular weakness of film scoring that would be thoroughly addressed only by Miklós Rózsa, in his concerted crusade in the 1950s to supply historical epics with more stylistically appropriate accompaniment (see pp. 165–71). The specific instance Copland cited of a film set in medieval Europe with anachronistic music was in all probability *The Adventures of Robin Hood* (dir. William Keighley and Michael Curtiz, 1938), for which Erich Wolfgang Korngold won an Academy Award with a score that accompanies scenes of ribald banqueting with a lush waltz idiom reminiscent of Richard Strauss's opera *Der Rosenkavalier* (1911).

When Copland revised and enlarged his book *Our New Music* under the title *The New Music, 1900–1960* (New York: W. W. Norton; London: Macdonald and Co., 1968), he wrote by way of preface: "The final three chapters of the original edition were concerned with such matters as the radio, the phonograph, and film music; these discussions are now superannuated and have been removed. In their place is a new third section, which deals with the preoccupations of the younger men: serialism, aleatory matters, and the new electronic media" (12). Clearly, by this stage in his career his interests had shifted well away from the potential he once identified in popular media. Even in his 1941 text, however, he unwittingly reveals the classical composer's tendency to harbor a somewhat elitist attitude toward the craft of composition as a strictly individual activity, tacitly downplaying the value of collaborative creative work by failing to mention the fine orchestrators who had helped him to meet his tight Hollywood deadlines.

For more on Copland's views on film music, see pp. 317–26.

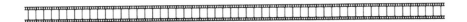

With the radio and the phonograph, the music track of the sound film must be set down as a revolutionizing force in today's music. The medium is so new, and the possibilities so vast, that this brief chapter can hardly do more than introduce the subject. Even so, it treats of little more than the Hollywood aspect of film music. Though artistically of a low order, historically the music of the West Coast is certain to loom large in any stocktaking of filmdom's musical achievements.

Everyone is so prepared to hear the worst about Hollywood that it is a pleasure to be able to start these observations on a cheerful note. The best one can say about Hollywood is that it is a place where composers are actually needed. The accent is entirely on the living composer. Day after day and year after year there are copyists, instrumentalists, and conductors who do nothing but copy, perform, and conduct the music of contemporary composers. Theoretically, at any rate, the town is a composer's Eldorado.

For the movies do need music and need it badly. By itself the screen is a pretty cold proposition. In Hollywood I looked at long stretches of film before the music had been added, and I got the impression that music is like a small flame put under the screen to help warm it.

It is this very function, however, which so often gives the composer a minor role. There is no sense in denying the subordinate position the composer fills. After all, film music makes sense only if it helps the film; no matter how good, distinguished, or successful, the music must be secondary in importance to the story being told on the screen. Essentially there is nothing about the movie medium to rule out any composer with a dramatic imagination. But the man who insists on complete self-expression had better stay home and write symphonies. He will never be happy in Hollywood.

Whether you are happy or not largely depends on two factors: the producer you work for and the amount of time allotted for completing the score. (I am assuming that the film itself is an intelligent one.) The producer is a kind of dictator, responsible only to the studio executives for every phase of the picture's production. This naturally includes the musical score. The trouble is not so much that these producers consider themselves musical connoisseurs but that they claim to be accurate barometers of public taste. "If I can't understand it, the public won't." As a result of this the typical Hollywood composer is concerned not with the reaction of the public, as you might think, but with that of the producer. It isn't surprising therefore, that all film music originating in Hollywood tends to be very much the same. The score of one picture adds up to about the score of any other. You seldom hear anything fresh or distinctive partly because everyone is so intent on playing safe. A pleased producer means more jobs. That alone is sufficient to explain the Hollywood stereotype of music.

The demand for speed from the composer is familiar to anyone who has ever worked "in pictures." The composer may sit around no end of time, waiting for the picture to be done; as soon as it's finished the director, the producer, the script writer—everybody—is in a frightful hurry; valuable time is passing, and the studio has visions of the money it is losing each day that the film is not in a theater. It is difficult to make studio executives realize that no one has yet discovered how to write notes any faster than it was done circa A.D. 400. The average movie score is approximately forty minutes long. The usual time allotted for composing it is about two weeks. For *Of Mice and Men* I had about six weeks, and I believe that other composers insist on that much time for writing an elaborate score.

The purpose of the film score is to make the film more effective; that's clear enough. But I don't think anyone has as yet formulated the perfect solution for this problem. In fact, I came away with a sense of the mysterious nature of all film music. In retrospect, I can see three important ways in which music helps a picture. The first is by intensifying the emotional impact of any given scene, the second by creating an illusion of continuity, and the third by providing a kind of neutral background music. Of these three, the last presents the most mysterious problem—how to supply the right sort of music behind dialogue.

Intensification of emotion at crucial moments is, of course, an old tradition of theater music. True, it is no more than the hearts-and-flowers tradition, but still, perfectly legitimate. The one difficulty here is to get the music started without suddenly making the audience aware of its entrance. To use a favorite Hollywood term, you must "steal the music in."

Obvious, too, is the continuity function of music. Pictures, jumping from episode to episode, from exterior to interior, have a tendency to fall apart. Music, an art that exists in time, can subtly hold disparate scenes together. In exciting montage sequences where the film moves violently from shot to shot, music, by developing one particular theme or one type of rhythmical material or some other unifying musical element, supplies the necessary continuous understructure.

But "background" music is something very special. It is also the most ungrateful kind of music for a composer to write. Since it's music behind, or underneath, the word, the audience is really not going to hear it, possibly won't even be aware of its existence; yet it undoubtedly works on the subconscious mind. The need here is for a kind of music that will give off a "neutral" color or atmosphere. (This is what creates the indefinable warmth that the screen itself lacks.) To write music that must be inexpressive is not easy for composers who normally tend to be as expressive as possible. To add to the difficulty, there's the impossibility of knowing in advance just what will work in any given scene. If one could only test the music by adding it to the scene before it is shot or have the music performed while the actors speak their lines! But this is utopian. Once the scene is done and the music is added, the result is fairly problematical. Even dubbing it down almost below the listening level will not always prove satisfactory.

If Hollywood has its problems it has also its well-known solutions. Most scores, as everybody knows, are written in the late nineteenth century symphonic style, a style now so generally accepted as to be considered inevitable. But why need movie music be symphonic? And why, oh, why, the nineteenth century? Should the rich harmonies of Tschaikovsky, Franck, and Strauss be spread over every type of story, regardless of time, place, or treatment? For *Wuthering Heights* [1939; music by Alfred Newman], perhaps yes. But why for *Golden Boy* [1939; music by Victor Young], a hard-boiled, modern piece? What screen music badly needs is more differentiation, more feeling for the exact quality of each picture. That does not necessarily mean a more literal musical description of time and place. Certainly very few Hollywood films give a realistic impression of period. Still, it should be possible, without learned displays of historical research and without the hack conventions of symphonic music, for a composer to reflect the emotion and reality of the individual picture he is scoring.

Another pet Hollywood formula, this one borrowed from nineteenth-century opera, is the use of the leitmotiv. I haven't made up my mind whether the public is conscious of this device or completely oblivious to it, but I can't see how it is appropriate to the movies. It may help the spectator sitting in the last row of the opera house to identify the singer who appears from the wings for the orchestra to announce her motif. But that's hardly necessary on the screen. No doubt the leitmotiv system is a help to the composer in a hurry, perhaps doing two or three scores simultaneously. It is always an easy solution mechanically to pin a motif on every character. In a high-class horse opera I saw this method was reduced to its final absurdity. One theme announced the Indians, another the hero. In the inevitable chase, every time the scene switched from Indians to hero the themes did, too, sometimes so fast that the music seemed to hop back and forth before any part of it had time to breathe. If there must be thematic description, I think it would serve better if it were connected with the underlying ideas of a picture. If, for example, a film has to do with loneliness, a theme might be developed to induce sympathy with the idea of being lonely, something broader in feeling than the mere tagging of characters.

A third device, and one very peculiar to Hollywood, is known as "Mickey-Mousing" a film. In this system the music, wherever possible, is made to mimic everything that happens on the screen. An actor can't lift an eyebrow without the music helping him do it. What is amusing when applied to a Disney fantasy becomes disastrous in its effect upon a straight or serious drama. Max Steiner has a special weakness for this device. In *Of Human Bondage* [1934] he had the unfortunate idea of making his music limp whenever the clubfooted hero walked across the scene, with a very obvious and, it seemed to me, vulgarizing effect. Recently Mr. Steiner has shown a fondness for a new device. This is the mixing of realistic music with background music. Joe may be walking around the room quietly humming a tune to himself (realistic use of music). Watch for the moment when Joe steps out into the storm, for it is then that Mr. Steiner pounces upon Joe's little tune and gives us the works with an orchestra of seventy. The trouble with this procedure is that it stresses not so much the dramatic moment as the ingenuity of the composer. All narrative illusion is lost the instant we are conscious of the music as such.

It may not be without interest to retrace some of the steps by which music is added to a film. After the picture is completed, it is shown in the studio projection room before the producer, the director, the studio's musical director (if any), the composer and his various henchmen, the conductor, the orchestrator, the cue-sheet assistants, the copyists—anybody, in fact, who has anything to do with the preparation of the score. At this showing the decision is reached as to where to add music, where it should start in each separate sequence, and where it should end. The film is then turned over to a cue-sheet assistant whose job it is to prepare a listing of every separate moment in each musical sequence. These listings, with the accompanying timing in film footage and in seconds, is all that the composer needs for complete security in synchronizing his music with the film. The practiced Hollywood composer is said never to look at a picture more than once. With a good memory, a stop watch, and a cue sheet, he is ready to go to work. Others prefer to work in the music projection room where there are a piano, a screen, and an operator who can turn the film on and off. I myself used a movieola, which permits every composer to be his own operator. This is a small machine that shows the film positive through a magnifying glass. Using the movieola, I could see the picture whenever and as often as I pleased.

While the music is being written, the film itself is prepared for recording. Each important musical cue must be marked on the film by some prearranged signal system that varies in every studio. These "signals" show the conductor where he is. If he wants to hit a certain musical cue that, according to the cue sheet, occurs at the forty-ninth second, the film must be marked in such a way as to indicate that spot (always with sufficient warning signals), and if the conductor is competent he can nearly always "hit it on the nose." In Hollywood this knack for hitting cues properly is considered even more important in a conductor than his ability to read an orchestral score. Another method, much more mechanical but used a good deal for Westerns and quickies, is to synchronize by means of a so-called "click track." In this case, the film is measured off not according to seconds but according to regular musical beats. There is no surer method for hitting cues "on the nose." But only the experienced composer can ignore the regularity of the beat and write his music freely within and around it.

For the composer the day of recording is perhaps the high point. He has worked hard and long and is anxious to test his work. He hears his music sounded for the first time while the film is being shown. Everything comes off just as it would in a concert hall. But if he wishes to remain happy he had better stay away from the sound-recording booth. For here all the music is being recorded at about the same medium dynamic level so that later on the loudness and softness may be regulated when the moment comes for rerecording.

Rerecording takes place in the dubbing room. This is a kind of composer's purgatory. It is here that the music track is mixed with other sound tracks—the dialogue, the "effects" track, and so forth. It is at this point that the composer sees his music begin to disappear. A passage once so clear and satisfying seems now to move farther and farther off. The instant a character opens his mouth, the music must recede to the near vanishing point. This is the place that calls out all a composer's self-control; it's a moment for philosophy.

From the composer's standpoint, the important person in the dubbing room is the man who sits at the controls. It is he who decides how loud or soft the music will be at any given moment, and therefore it is he who can make or ruin everything by the merest touch of the dials. But surprisingly, in every studio these controls are in the hands of a sound engineer. What I don't understand is why a musician has not been called in for this purpose. It would never occur to me to call in an engineer to tune my piano. Surely only a musician can be sensitive to the subtle effects of musical sound, particularly when mixed with other sounds. A Toscanini would be none too good for such a job— certainly a sound expert is not qualified.

While on the subject of sound levels, I might as well mention the unsatisfactory way in which sound is controlled in the picture theater. The tonal volume of a picture is not set for all time; no mechanical contraption permanently fixes the loudness or softness of the music. The person who decides on the sound levels is not even the film operator but the individual theater manager, who is, of course, susceptible to advice from Tom, Dick, and Harry sitting anywhere in the house. People who love music tend to prefer it played loudly. Those who don't care for it especially want to hear it only at a low level. So no matter how much care is taken in the dubbing room to fix proper tonal levels, the situation will remain unsatisfactory until a method is found to control the casual and arbitrary way in which dials are set in the theater operator's booth.

Hollywood, like Vienna, can boast its own star roster of composers. Alfred Newman, Max Steiner, Victor Young, Anthony Collins are composers created by the film industry. It is easy enough to poke fun at the movie music they turn out as so much yardage, but it would at the same time be foolish not to profit by their great experience in writing for the films. Newman, for example, has discovered the value of the string orchestra as a background for emotional scenes. Better than the full orchestra, the strings can be depersonalized. This is important in a medium where the sound of a single instrument may sometimes be disturbing. Another secret of movie music that Steiner has exploited is the writing of atmosphere music almost without melodic content of any kind. A melody is by its nature distracting, since it calls attention to itself. For certain types of neutral music, a kind of melodyless music is needed. Steiner does not supply mere chords but superimposes a certain amount of melodic motion, just enough to make the music sound normal and yet not enough to compel attention.

Composers who come to Hollywood from the big world outside generally take some time to become expert in using the idiom. Erich Korngold still tends to get overcomplex in the development of a musical idea. This is not always true, however. When successful, he gives a sense of firm technique, a continuity of not only feeling but structure. Werner Janssen, whose score for *The General Died at Dawn* [1936] made movie history, is still looked upon as something of an outsider. He shows his pre-Hollywood training in the sophistication of his musical idiom and in his tendency to be overfussy in the treatment of even the simplest sequence. Ernst Toch, who belongs in the category with Korngold and Janssen, wrote an important score for *Peter Ibbetson* [1935] several years ago. On the strength of this job, Toch should be today one of the best known film composers. But unfortunately there aren't enough people in Hollywood who can tell a good score when they hear one. Today Toch is generally assigned to do "screwy music." (In Hollywood music is either "screwy" or "down to earth"—and most of it is down to earth.) Toch deserves better. The latest addition to Hollywood's roster of "outsiders" is Louis Gruenberg, who composed a distinguished score for *So Ends Our Night* [1941].

The men who write Hollywood's music seem strangely oblivious of their reputations outside the West Coast. I have often wondered, for instance, why no concerted effort has ever been made to draw the attention of music critics to their more ambitious scores. Why shouldn't the music critic cover important film *premières*? True, the audience that goes to the films doesn't think about the music and possibly shouldn't think about the music. Nevertheless, a large part of music heard by the American public is heard in the film theater. Unconsciously, the cultural level of music is certain to be raised if better music is written for films. This will come about more quickly, I think, if producers and directors know that scores are being heard and criticized. One of the ways they will find out what's good and what's bad is to read it in the papers. Let the press now take this important business in hand.

9

Ingolf Dahl: "Notes on Cartoon Music" (1949)

Among the pioneering publications of the composer, pianist, and musicologist Ingolf Dahl (1912–70) was this timely assessment of the art of scoring animation in the 1940s. (For his controversial interview with Stravinsky on the general subject of film music published a few years before, and for further information on Dahl, see pp. 273–80.) Dahl's essay on cartoon music appeared when MGM's Tom and Jerry shorts had already scooped no fewer than five Academy Awards for Best Cartoon (in 1943–46 and 1948), so not surprisingly MGM's celebrated cartoon composer Scott Bradley is given particular prominence in Dahl's coverage of the subject; Bradley's own views on his role in animation's unique blend of musical and visual rhythms are reproduced in the following chapter. Dahl describes a distinct historical shift from the simple style of symmetrical four-square scoring that early cartoons had inherited from vaudeville, circus, and silent-film antecedents to a more sophisticated manner of accompaniment that resulted in what he claims to be "the only completely creative combination of the aural and the plastic arts in movement." The audiovisual result, he argues, is a kind of choreography in which detailed Mickey Mousing of slapstick action is more important to suspension of disbelief than fully rounded musical structures, though in fact Bradley was remarkably adept at combining the best of both worlds.

Dahl describes a typical process of composition that moves from sketches on detail sheets to precise recording with the aid of a click track—a preset

Source: Film Music Notes, 8/5 (May/June 1949): 3–13; reprinted in James L. Limbacher, ed., *Film Music: From Violins to Video* (Metuchen, N.J.: Scarecrow Press, 1974): 183–89.

pattern of metronomic beats to aid synchronization common in all film scoring from the 1930s to the present day, but invented specifically for animation and first used in Disney's sound cartoon *The Skeleton Dance* (1929). Although he does not discuss Disney's work in detail, Dahl notes that the Disney studio was important for its use of preexisting classical music, principally in *Fantasia* (1940), which included a bold abstract picturization of J. S. Bach's Toccata and Fugue in D minor based on ideas by experimental animator Oskar Fischinger. Dahl also mentions abstract animators Norman McLaren and the brothers John and Jack Whitney, who experimented with animated sound (i.e., soundtracks created not by audio recording but by drawing or painting designs directly onto celluloid film stock, a process that creates unorthodox sounds when the filmstrip is played back through a projector's sound head). He singles out for special commendation two very different examples of audiovisual artistry, both released in 1947: the sociopolitical allegory *Boundary Lines* (dir. Philip Stapp for the International Film Foundation; music by Gene Forrell) and the Tom and Jerry classical-music caper *The Cat Concerto* (MGM; music adapted by Bradley from Liszt's Second Hungarian Rhapsody).

If film music, as far as critical attention goes, is the poor relation of concert music, then cartoon music must be the destitute nephew of the poor relation. Little has been said, written or thought about the subject and very rarely have the efforts of the makers of short cartoons received much critical interest, least of all those who supply it with music. At the same time be it remembered that it is their joint product which is the only part of the regular cinema fare that unfailingly receives advance applause by the audience, for better or for worse.

Seeing old cartoons again we realize how much the medium has changed. The procedure used to be one of fitting humorous story and action to cheerful, zippy, bouncy music which hovered in style between Gilbert & Sullivan and Zez Confrey. The music was rhythmically defined, symmetrically constructed in eight-bar phrases somewhat on the order of a dance tune, and its changes of mood ("chase," "danger," "villain," "heroism," etc.) were modified by the structural symmetry of popular music and its inherent simplicity. The cartoons presented in essence a kind of humorous "choreography" to catchy music. This analogy can even be carried into details: just as the dancer reserves his more spectacular tricks for the cadences at the end of musical phrases so the cartoonist, probably out of instinct, achieved some of his funniest effects by placing outstanding action (be it the bounce of a ball or the impact of a pie on a face) on the same cadential accents with which in popular music every eighth measure ends. This "cadence plus stylized action" has been changed in most of the newer cartoons to just the opposite approach: the action is determined purely from the story angle and developed independently of musical considerations. I am aware, of course, of the exceptions, such as the cartoons to pre-scored pieces of serious or popular music for which Disney is justly famous. But in the ordinary cartoon nowadays the music is added to a predetermined course of hectic events and is in many cases required to do nothing more than duplicate the action by synchronous illustration, taking the role of sound effect together with the role of musical characterization. It attests to the stubbornness of some few composers that in spite of this more or less mechanical application of their art they still try here and there, to invest their "sound tailoring" with some musical meaning. "Realism of action" (whatever that can be in drawn images) has become more important than rhythmic stylization. This is clearly reflected in the average present-day cartoon score: when we look at the music we see that it makes sense only if considered as "recitative accompaniment" to an action in pantomime.

This is not a new musical form. To quote just two of the most famous historical examples: Beckmesser's pantomime scene in the third act of [Wagner's] *Die Meistersinger*, as well as the opening scene of the third act of [Strauss's] *Fledermaus*. Both are accompanied by such a direct anticipation of cartoon music techniques that once more they give one cause to reflect: have technical advances of our new media called for and developed commensurate musical advances?

The change from the "composed" cartoon to the "realistic" action cartoon has brought with it an attendant confusion of styles which is just as noticeable in some of Disney's Technicolor excesses (one is tempted to quote Frederick Packard from the *New Yorker*: "Be quiet, Technicoloriot!") as in the cartoon concept of humor. Cartoons are funny, should be funny, but now we are forced to stretch our definition of what is funny in the forties to include continuous sadistic violence in which steam rollers and dynamite sticks constitute the more playful ingredients.

But cartoons, at the same time as they are the buffo intermezzi of modern dramatic entertainment, are also the only completely creative combination of the aural and the plastic arts in movement. As such they have hardly scratched the surface of their possibilities yet. Only comparatively few (such as *Boundary Lines*, to mention just one) seem to be aware of the possible directions. Considering the opportunities which such a combination offers both to the artists and to general entertainment it is to be hoped that continued critical examinations of the two arts and their common denominators be carried on in discussion and experiment. To be dealt with, among other things, should be the question of repetition (can or should the image repeat as pronouncedly as music must for the sake of its form?), the question of how much rhythmic coincidence is required and where, as well as the relation of variety and order in the pictorial elements to harmonic progression and structure in the music, etc. The experiments of Fischinger and Fischinger-Disney ("Toccata and Fugue"), of the brothers Whitney, Norman McLaren, and others, point to these problems, both through their shortcomings and their achievements.

Much cartoon music is being written in Hollywood as part of the regular schedules of the studios and a considerable amount of talent, thought and hard work goes into the composing and recording of it. To name just a few names of the most prominent composers in the field: Scott Bradley (MGM), Oliver Wallace (Disney), Paul Smith (Disney), Carl Stalling (Warner Brothers).

In order to give an example of the specific techniques of writing cartoon music, let me take you on a visit to Scott Bradley, composer at MGM. After asking him by mail for some information about himself I received a blue slip of paper which I am impelled to quote in toto:

METRO GOLDWYN MAYER. INTER-OFFICE COMMUNICATION TO: Dahl SUBJECT: Dis-a and dat-a FROM: Bradley. Born . . . Russelville, Arkansas (but not an "Arkie" I hasten to add) . . . Studied piano, private instruction . . . organ and harmony with the English organist Horton Corbet . . . Otherwise entirely self-taught in composition and orchestration . . . fed large doses of Bach, which I absorbed and asked for more. Conductor at KHJ and KNX in early thirties . . . entered the non-sacred realm of pictures in 1932 and started cartoon composing in 1934 with Harman-Ising Co. Joined MGM in 1937 . . . have so far been able to hide from them the fact that I'm not much of a composer. Personal: dislike bridge, slacks and mannish dress on women, all chromatic and diatonic scales, whether written by Beethoven or Bradley. Also, crowds and most people (and especially biographers). Favorite composers: Brahms, Stravinsky, Hindemith, Bartok. This will be boring to most everyone, so cut it as short as you wish. Signed: Scott.

Without comment, one would want to add to this that six Academy Awards have been given to cartoons to which Bradley has written scores (the famous *Cat Concerto* was one of them).

Bradley has his office in the MGM cartoon building which is separated from the main lot by a highway. As we enter his office we see him brooding over a half filled odd-looking sheet of music paper while an old-fashioned pyramidal metronome is clicking away in front of him. The music paper on which he is working is covered, in addition to the few finished measures of music, with all kinds of signs, figures, multi-colored words, directions and descriptions. This is a "detail sheet" for a new Tom and Jerry cartoon which has just been finished by the cartoonist and which is ready for scoring. The music that will have to go on the empty staves of the detail sheet must be composed, orchestrated and recorded within the next two weeks. In order to refresh his memory at any given point and in case the vivid prose on the detail sheet is insufficient to prod his muse into delivering the goods, Bradley has also been given a rough cut of the pencil reel (non-colored) which he can run at any speed, forwards or backwards, through a viewing machine (movieola). Before this he has not seen the cartoon and knows the script only in general outlines. However, if the particular cartoon contains any song-and-dance routines they would have been recorded in pre-scoring *before* the drawings were made to fit the timing of the music. The detail sheet contains a complete breakdown of all items of action. These are tabulated according to a regular number of frame units on which the animation was based. This unit, whether it be of 10 frames, 16 frames, or whatever number, indicates the smallest rhythmic denominator of the scene. Translated into music, it represents a beat that forms the regular, non-deviating time unit of a scene. The composer determines his metrical structure accordingly. Ten frames equal a metronome (MM) beat of 144, sixteen frames (a beat per foot) equal MM 88, etc. His bar lines will then be set according to the metric scheme in which he wants to group several beats, and only musical requirements plus his ingenuity will determine the meter.

Synchronization in post-scoring will be achieved by means of the "click track," a loop of sound track that is run through a reproducing unit and which is marked, or punched, at regular intervals (every 10, or 16, etc., frames), thereby producing an audible click in earphones that are worn by the playing musicians. Bradley records most of his music in post-scoring; i.e., like the average dramatic feature film, after the shooting and editing has been completed. The exceptions, as mentioned above, are songs, dances, the cartooning of set concert or popular pieces (right now Bradley is preparing to record the *Fledermaus* Overture for a future cartoon, without clicks).

The reason for his procedure is that most cartoon directors are not musical and would have difficulty in constructing their action to fit a musical pattern. Therefore the music will have to adjust to the fast shifting image (sometimes one could say "the convulsively shifting image") and the composer will try desperately to find ways of creating a semblance of musical coherence and structure. Expediency is the motto, and a wide variety of styles and techniques a requirement. Musical *illustration* is another requirement, and the degree to which illustration is lifted above the purely mechanical duplication of action depends again on the inventiveness of the composer. Another problem is the excessively short time in which music must make its points and within which it must accomplish changes of mood, of character, of expression. This calls for constant flexibility in the handling of thematic material and the ability of applying the variation technique to phrases of aphoristic brevity. One sustained melodic note on the violin may consume four feet of film, not to speak of the whole of such a melody. There is little chance for musical extension of any kind.

There are still other restrictions and hazards: the constant preoccupation with a metronomic beat from which the composer, at least subconsciously, cannot escape, tends to impart a certain rhythmic squareness to his phrases and it takes much conscious effort on his part to overcome this. Tied down, as he is by metronome and timing sheet, it is difficult for him to write music that has flow and overall continuity and that is written *across* the bar lines rather than shackled by them. But if, on the one hand, he has to fight the constraining influence of the squarely regular time unit he has to try, on the other hand, to create musical *symmetry* where the cartoon lacks it. The cartoon, being a very extrovert and direct form of entertainment, needs the reassuring directness of symmetrically constructed music. But how to supply this when the direction has crystallized the form of the film entirely outside of musical considerations?

The rigid discipline and regimentation that are imposed by the mechanics of cartoon composition are not the only factors which tie the composer down. The scope of musical expression is equally limited. For how long can a composer continue to restrict himself exclusively to the bright yellows and reds of the musical palette in painting whimsical, cute, hilarious pictures? Even men of genius like Rossini or Offenbach did not have an inexhaustible supply of humorous ideas and there comes a time when piccolo and bassoon in unison will sound rather threadbare. And if it is not whimsy it is violence. With an anguished expression on his usually cheerful face Scott Bradley sighs, "It's fights, fights, fights for me . . . and how I am getting tired of them! A beautiful, developed tune—alas, that's never the fate of Scott."

However, there are compensations. Bradley knows how much satisfaction there is in seeing how music can give definition to screen action and how it can invest the drawn characters with personality, from the jocose to the maudlin. At best, music can add charm and profile to the drawings. The good composers realize this and they are straining against the requirements of the "electric buzzer" kind of mickey mousing which is unaware of the richer musical possibilities.

In writing his music the composer will have to consider at all times the scope and the limitations of his orchestra. It is a small group, consisting of anywhere between 16 to 30 musicians. Bradley usually has at his disposal four violins, one viola, one cello, one bass, piano, one percussion player, one each of flute (doubling piccolo), oboe, bassoon, three clarinets (doubling saxophones) three trumpets, two trombones. Microphone placement and recording tricks (such as multi-channel recording of the screened-off sections of the orchestra, parts of which receive artificial reverberation in the dubbing) will have to overcome the inadequacies of balance and instrumental proportion. There is some flexibility in instrumentation and just recently Bradley recorded a whole cartoon (*Texas Tom*) which was scored for only a small woodwind and brass ensemble with very fresh and charming results.

It must be obvious to anyone who has ever seen and heard cartoons that even within the normal orchestral group there are instruments that stand out as cartoon specialists. The marionette quality of the characters and their action finds expression through the comparably "impersonalized" wind instruments, and the above mentioned piccolo and bassoon, as also the dry, jerky xylophone have become cartoon instruments par excellence.

The musically interested person must regret that instances of imaginative instrumentation (I am not talking of the orchestration here) are so rare in a field that actually demands it. It is equally strange that some of the newer devices of tone production have not found their way into a medium that is doubtlessly made for them. I am speaking of sounds like those marvelous chord structures, waves, rolls, strummings, whisperings, crashes, etc. that Henry Cowell gets out of a piano and also of the completely enchanting (as well as radio-genic) sound world of bells, chimes, drums, gongs, underwater xylophones, etc. into which John Cage can transform the piano. Some day a cartoon director is going to wake up to the fact that he is missing a sure-fire bet by not availing himself of the talents of Cage for the cartoon. His sense of sound as well as his remarkably developed rhythmic inventiveness make him (or his techniques) a natural for cartoon music.

10

Scott Bradley: "Personality on the Soundtrack" (1947)

Scott Bradley (1891–1977), whose working practices are vividly described in the preceding chapter, was arguably the most resourceful cartoon composer active in Hollywood in the 1940s and early 1950s and is best known for his virtuosic scores to MGM's highly successful Tom and Jerry shorts. The series was launched in 1941 by animators William Hanna and Joe Barbera, working under the guidance of producer Fred Quimby, and became notorious for its breathtaking slapstick and a high degree of what Ingolf Dahl termed "sadistic violence"—later to be affectionately (and gorily) parodied in the brutal "Itchy and Scratchy" inserts of the long-running animated TV sitcom *The Simpsons*. Unlike the competing animated shorts released by Warner Bros. (see chapter 11), the Tom and Jerry cartoons were almost entirely free of dialogue, and as a direct result Bradley's music was constantly foregrounded as the prime vehicle for promoting continuity, momentum, graphic illustration, and, above all, a mischievous sense of humor.

As Bradley revealed in his writings, the precise timings of the cartoons' complex patterns of Mickey Mousing were so carefully preordained on the detail sheets that when the scores came to be recorded it was not necessary for the film to be screened for the conductor's benefit (as was invariably the case in the scoring of narrative features): synchronization was instead achieved by strict adherence to click tracks. As an appendix to the published version of a talk entitled "Music in Cartoons," given at the Music Forum on 28 October

Source: "Personality on the Soundtrack: A Glimpse Behind the Scenes and Sequences in Filmland," *Music Educators Journal*, 33/3 (January 1947): 28–29.

1944 and published in *Film Music Notes* (4/3, December 1944), Bradley included a facsimile of a typical detail sheet, on which the music was sketched on three staves beneath lines indicating the corresponding physical action and sound effects. In both his talk and the text reproduced below—in which the specific cartoons discussed include MGM's *Milky Waif* (1946) and *Dr. Jekyll and Mr. Mouse* (1947)—Bradley mentions his surprising but highly apposite adoption of Schoenberg's atonal twelve-note compositional techniques alongside more traditional elements, a modernist leaning some years in advance of the use of such dissonant intellectualism in the scoring of live-action features. In his talk "Music in Cartoons," Bradley recounted how he hit upon Schoenberg's technique while working on an assignment in which he had found it problematic to come up with a musical illustration of a little mouse running round wearing a dog's mask:

> Finally, I tried the twelve-tone scale [i.e. a note row], and *there it was!* This scene was repeated five times within the next fifty seconds and I had only to use my scale—played by the piccolo, oboe and bassoon in unison. I hope Dr. Schoenberg will forgive me for using *his system* to produce funny music, but even the boys in the orchestra laughed when we were recording it.

In his autobiography *Double Life* (New York: Hippocrene Books, 1982, 141), Miklós Rózsa recounts an amusing incident when he invited Bradley to visit his film-music class at the University of Southern California in the late 1940s. During his illustrated talk, Bradley explained that music in animation "underlines the gags in a unique way" and showed a clip from a Tom and Jerry cartoon twice in order to demonstrate the point: the first showing was without music, and the second with. Unfortunately for Bradley, the students found the silent version so hilarious that "the class rocked with laughter" during the first clip, much to the composer's annoyance, but he doggedly proceeded to play the second clip with his music, saying: "you'll see immediately how much funnier it is." Rózsa continued: "A joke is funny only once. The music went wild—xylophones clattered, bass drums thumped as the characters fell about—and nobody laughed."

Beethoven started it. The great innovator of the orchestra, in his *Pastoral Symphony*, imitated the birds of the forest with instruments of the orchestra. However, the music of this beautiful symphony suggests rather than imitates the call of various birds. At least, Beethoven's quail sounds are unlike the ones which awaken me in our San Fernando Valley home. California quail simply give out a joyous, rapid "chup-chup-chup," which is indeed great music in the early morning stillness.

Richard Strauss was more realistic. His imitation of the sheep in the Second Variation of *Don Quixote* is clever enough to fool even the wariest sheep. Saint-Saëns (*Carnival of the Animals*) and Respighi (*The Birds*) are among the other famous composers who gave musical personality to the non-speaking animals.

The whole thing may well have stopped there, had it not been for the evolution of the sound film which gave auditory rather than abstract identity to them. Then came the animated cartoon, which added fantasy and, more often, slapstick. Finally, the film composer appeared—last, as always—but equipped with the devices and tone colors of the modern orchestra, and supplied the music which attempts to personalize the various birds and animals as they appear in cartoons and live-action pictures. We shall discuss in this paper examples of both, the first with live animals. The picture is MGM's *Courage of Lassie* [1946], for which I had the pleasure of composing the music for the forest and animal sequences. The musical treatment presents a special problem, since the first twenty-five minutes contains no dialogue, and music must carry the burden of the story by giving to each animal a certain identity and personality.

The picture opens with a lake scene, which dissolves into a series of short cut-backs to various animals and birds. There are two ways of scoring such a sequence: The first, and by far the easier, is to treat it simply as part of an overall scene, creating a general mood of wild life and nature; the second way is to give each a definite character through the medium of orchestration, with short musical phrases, all blending into a unified composition. The latter seemed the better way, so the scene opens with a tranquil melody in the oboe and solo violin, with harp and strings. Soon the scene cuts to three birds on a tree branch; a syncopated figure, first in flute, then oboe, then bassoon, gives identity to each. Now a beaver is seen drying his face with his hands; he draws two clarinets, playing an eccentric figure in minor seconds. Then a timid little rabbit emerges from a tree trunk, and the oboe hesitates right along with him. The scene cuts to a little quail hobbling along (a string is tied to his leg to keep him from running away), described by a jumpy little theme in the flute. No attempt is made to imitate his call (who am I to try to improve on Beethoven), but the music synchronizes his action. Here now is a nervous little chipmunk on a log; he gets two piccolos and two oboes in high register. A grumpy old porcupine was given the bassoon treatment, accompanied by glissando celli and low clarinets. The sequence is completed with repetition of the rabbit and bird fragments as the camera cuts back to them. All of this happens in just 121 seconds! How simple. Just be ready with the right music at the right time.

You have probably noted in the above analysis that, for the most part, only a few instruments are playing, chiefly wood-winds, which offer endless combinations in tone color. Why should the whole orchestra be playing (er—pardon me, Mr. Petrillo!) when only these naive and simple characters are having their brief moment in the spotlight? We hear too much "full swell, coupled to great" scoring in pictures, and the human ear gratefully accepts a little contrast.

Later in the picture Lassie, who is only a puppy at the time, meets a huge black bear, and they become good friends. Again, the wood-winds come to the rescue, the contra-bassoon playing a clumsy theme for the bear, while the upper clarinets and flutes play a counter theme for the puppy, playfully blending in complete accord to the friendly action, accompanied of course by the rest of the orchestra. Presently, a vicious eagle swoops down on the puppy; the eagle gets three horns, playing in consecutive fifths (pardon me, you purists, this is drama!). Later, as dialogue is now heard, the orchestra reduces to strings alone.

This is lesson number one in scoring pictures: If you want to hear your music, write for string quintet under dialogue or suffer the consequences. Just throw in a few muted trumpets or staccato wood-winds, and your brain child fades out in favor of the spoken word.

With animated cartoons, it is different story. Here the action is lusty and uninhibited, and music has a fighting chance to be heard above the sound effects. I stoutly maintain that any progress in creative contemporary film music will be made in this medium because endless experiments in modern harmony and orchestration are acceptable. Since it deals in pure (sometimes, alas, not too pure) fantasy, more freedom in composition is allowed. Established rules of orchestration are blandly ignored, since beauty in cartoons is rarely even skin deep, and we must employ "shock chords" which sometimes reach the outer limits of harmonic analysis.

In the cartoon The Milky Waif we find a scene near the beginning in which a basket is placed upon little Jerry Mouse's doorstep. Suddenly it begins to move, although no one knows what the basket contains nor what causes it to move. Here again music must tell the story, since neither Tom nor Jerry ever talk, thank goodness! No one knows what the music is either, for it is based on a modified form of the twelve-tone scale, quasi Schoenberg. Don't listen for tonic or dominant rest points, for the clarinets, muted trumpets, piano and oboe go their own way entirely independent of each other. Luckily for the audience the scene is brief, and soon the music relaxes into conventional diatonic progressions. Later in the cartoon, a scene definitely demands Shortenin' Bread. Although original music is usually better for all film scoring, we sometimes have to use well-known tunes as cues. Yes, from Schoenberg to Nelson Eddy all in one reel!

Both images are from *Dr. Jekyll and Mr. Mouse* (MGM, 1947). *Top*: Tom mixes his magic potion to mock-dramatic music by Scott Bradley (see p. 106). *Bottom*: Transformed by the potion, a muscular Jerry relentlessly pursues Tom to the accompaniment of a grim march incorporating the theme from "Superman," a popular 1940s series in both radio and cartoon form.

Again, in a recent MGM cartoon, *Dr. Jekyll and Mr. Mouse*, we find burlesque mystery melodrama, as Tom mixes the witches' brew while trying to exterminate Jerry Mouse. The music is mock-dramatic, with the horn motive in C-sharp against a four-octave tremolo in C-major in the strings. The dark colors of English horn, bass clarinet and viola add intensity to little Jerry's dilemma, as he unsuspectingly samples the potion. However, the tables are turned on Tom, as the poison, far from exterminating Jerry, makes a raging demon of him. As he stalks relentlessly after Tom, the full orchestra plays an *ostinato* march, the harmonic structure being based on parallel fourths in altered form, while the timpani and four horns blast out the Superman theme. Fun? Loads of it! I'd rather score a cartoon like this than a half-dozen ordinary live-action pictures. No noisy actors shouting at the top of their voices, drowning perfectly good music!

But whatever the situation, be it cartoon or live action, the orchestra is always ready to supply personality on the sound track—pointing up the high lights of one scene, emphasizing the intensity of another, and making possible long sequences of silent action which, but for the music, would be unbearable.

II

Conversations with Carl Stalling (1971)

The founding father of cartoon music, Carl Stalling (1891–1971), brought with him his solid experience of providing keyboard accompaniments to silent animations when he provided the music for a number of Walt Disney's early sound films starring Mickey Mouse. A significant turning point in Disney's work came with the Silly Symphonies series launched by *The Skeleton Dance* (1929), which, at Stalling's suggestion, foregrounded its precomposed score. In 1936, Stalling joined the music department of Warner Bros. and earned lasting fame as the studio's house composer for a huge number of animated shorts starring Bugs Bunny, Daffy Duck, and other vivid anthropomorphic creations dubbed by vocal talent Mel Blanc under the watchful eye of director Chuck Jones.

The soundtracks for the long-running Looney Tunes and Merry Melodies series found their definitive shape in the hands of Stalling, who drew on his experience as an improviser by inventively sequencing snatches of popular tunes (many derived from Warner's own publishing catalogue, an initiative which for economic reasons the studio contractually imposed on its composers), extracts from familiar classical music, and a more modern novelty idiom derived from the work of bandleader Raymond Scott—all at the same time as deftly catching the action of the on-screen antics as required. Stalling retired from his post as Warner Bros.' musical director for animation in 1958, by which time he had composed the music for more than six hundred cartoon shorts released by the studio. His departure was timely, coming as it did just two years

Source: "An Interview with Carl Stalling," *Funnyworld*, 13 (Spring 1971): 21–27; reprinted in Daniel Goldmark and Yuval Taylor, eds., *The Cartoon Music Book* (Chicago: ACappella, 2002): 37–60.

Cartoon composer Carl Stalling (left) poses with Walt Disney and friends as they participate in an NBC radio show in the late 1930s. (Photofest)

before Bugs Bunny established himself on the small screen: the Warner Bros. cartoon studio finally closed in 1962, MGM's having already shut down as both companies now transferred their attention to new series designed specifically for a younger television audience, and to the cheap repackaging of existing theatrical shorts for broadcast to the world's living rooms.

The interview material below was compiled in 1971 by animation historian Mike Barrier on the basis of two conversations with Stalling conducted by Barrier, Milton Gray, and Bill Spicer in Hollywood during June and November 1969.

MG: What did Walt [Disney] say when you brought up the idea for *The Skeleton Dance*? Did he like it right away?

CS: He was interested right away. After two or three of the Mickeys had been completed and were being run in theaters, Walt talked with me on getting started on the musical series that I had in mind. He thought I meant illustrated songs, but I didn't have that in mind at all. When I told him that I was thinking of inanimate figures, like skeletons, trees, flowers, etc., coming to life and dancing and doing other animated actions fitted to music more or less in a humorous and rhythmic mood, he became very much interested. I gave him the idea of using the four seasons, and he made a cartoon on each one of those. I scored one of them [*Springtime* (1930)] before I left.

For a name or title for the series, I suggested *not* using the word "music" or "musical," as it sounded too commonplace, but to use the word "Symphony" together with a humorous word. At the next gag meeting, I don't know who suggested it, but Walt asked me: "Carl, how would 'Silly Symphony' sound to you?" I said, "Perfect!" Then I suggested the first subject, *The Skeleton Dance*, because ever since I was a kid I had wanted to *see* real skeletons dancing and had always enjoyed seeing skeleton-dancing acts in vaudeville. As kids, we all like spooky pictures and stories, I think.

That's how the Silly Symphonies got started. Of course, everyone knows that if it had not been for Walt Disney, then in all probability there would never have been a Mickey Mouse. This makes me wonder sometimes, would there ever have been a Silly Symphony or who would have suggested *The Skeleton Dance*—if?

BS: What are your recollections of *The Skeleton Dance* preview?

CS: It was a late show at the Vista Theater down on Hillhurst and Sunset in Hollywood, a small theater. Walt was disappointed in it. There were very few people there, no house. We saw *Steamboat Willie* [1928] in New York at eight or nine o'clock, with a full house. But here in Hollywood, at eleven o'clock, there were only a few stragglers. There wasn't any reaction, and Walt didn't think it went over at all. He said, "What the hell's the matter with the damned thing?" But they did ship it that night, I think, by Air Express to New York. The next we heard it was running at the Roxy, for two weeks. They liked it so well they ran it for another two weeks, a return engagement.

MG: How was Walt as a boss? Was he demanding, or easy to work for?

CS: Well, he couldn't explain just what he wanted, at times. We'd go crazy trying to figure out what he wanted. But he inspired us that way. We wanted to help him, we wanted to do it, and we all worked together in that respect. That was his genius, I think, inspiring the people who worked for him to come up with new ideas.

MB: Did Walt tell you what he wanted in the way of music?

CS: He had definite ideas sometimes, and sometimes it'd be the other way around.

MG: Did you work in the same room with the animators at Disney's?

CS: Yes; everybody worked in one big room.

MB: Was that room the one called "the music room"?

CS: I only remember one big room, outside of the two business offices.

MB: You invented the "tick" system of recording music for animated cartoons, didn't you? Do you recall the circumstances that led to that?

CS: The "tick" system was not really an invention, since it was not patentable. Perfect synchronization of music for cartoons was a problem, since there were so many quick changes and actions that the music had to match. The thought struck me that if each member of the orchestra had a steady beat in his ear, from a telephone receiver, this would solve the problem. I had exposure sheets for the films, with the picture broken down frame by frame, sort of like a script, and twelve of the film frames went through the projector in a half second. That gave us a beat.

MG: . . . If you chose a twelve-frame beat. You had other beats, too.

CS: Six, eight, ten, etc., depending on the kind of music used. We made recordings of "tick" sounds at different beats—a tick every eight frames, or ten frames, or twelve frames—and played this on a phonograph connected to the recording machine and to earphones. Each member of the orchestra had a single earphone, and listened to the clicks through that. It wasn't necessary for the conductor to give a beat, but I did, because one or two of the musicians didn't like to use the earphones. We had a woman cello player at Warner's, and she didn't like to use the earphones because they hurt her head or something. She was a fine cellist, so we couldn't criticize her too much, and she didn't get off the beat much.

MG: Did you record before the animation was completed, or after?

CS: Both, but usually before. The animators and I all worked from that same exposure sheet, and I just recorded from our beat, without seeing the picture. By the time they had the picture ready, I had the recorded music ready.

MB: Did you pre-score much of your music at the Disney studio—did the animators fit their actions to your music, instead of the other way around? I was reading a Disney book by Bob Thomas called *The Art of Animation* [1958] again recently, and I came across this paragraph about how the early Disney cartoons were made: "The musician put the songs and tuneful bits together and handed the score to the animator [Thomas means the director]. The animator timed the music on his yellow exposure sheet and then fashioned the action to fit the music." That seems to contradict your statement that you composed your music after the exposure sheets were prepared, and not before. Is that what happened, or is *The Art of Animation* correct?

CS: Both statements are correct. Sometimes the director made the action fit a certain piece of music, and other times I wrote music to fit certain actions. Most of the time, the directors and animators were free to do what they thought best to make the action most effective.

MB: Do you mean that not even *The Skeleton Dance* and the other Silly Symphonies were pre-scored?

CS: No. I pre-scored the music only when it wasn't possible to animate without pre-scoring. At Iwerks' and Warner's, I worked almost entirely from exposure sheets.

MB: If you wrote most of your music at the Disney studio after the exposure sheets were prepared, did you confer with Walt about the beats *before* the sheets were prepared?

CS: Yes, usually, to prevent monotony. A change of beat would mean a change of tempo or rhythm, or both.

MG: When was your "tick" system first used?

CS: It must have been in 1929, at Disney's, on *The Skeleton Dance*.

MB: How did you record the music for cartoons before you started using the "tick" system?

CS: I had lines drawn on the prints of the cartoons that I used for recording. The lines would show on the screen so that the whole orchestra could see them, and that's how I got my beat when I was conducting.

When I was composing the music for *Gallopin' Gaucho* and *Plane Crazy* [both 1928], the two silent pictures, I had the cartoons shown at the theater where I worked, so that I could decide what music would be appropriate. I was having trouble figuring out how to get the music synchronized with the picture, then I hit on the idea of drawing 'half-moon' lines on the film that started on the left side of one frame, then moved to the right across the following frames, and then back toward the left, with the beat occurring when the line returned to the left side of the screen. That way, the beat didn't catch the musicians by surprise when we were recording. We also used these lines when we recorded the music for *The Barn Dance* [1928] in New York.

MB: I've read that Walt drew marks on the print of *Steamboat Willie* that they used for recording in New York, so that the conductor could watch the marks as they flashed on the screen and stay on the beat.

CS: I don't think he did that, because the pictures and the music seemed out of sync at times.

MB: Wilfred Jackson has said that there was another line system that Ub Iwerks worked out, based on your system. He said that Ub animated a horizontal line rising and failing, and that the line was photographed at different speeds so that the complete cycle of rising and falling took eight frames, or twelve frames, or whatever the beat happened to be. He said that these loops of film would then be projected on a screen that the orchestra could watch as they recorded the music.

CS: Yes, we did that for a while. We used the line moving up and down for the fifth and sixth Mickey Mouse cartoons, *The Op'ry House* and *When the Cat's*

Away [both 1929], and then we started using the "tick" system on *The Skeleton Dance.* . . .

MB: When you first came to Warner's, they had somebody else writing cartoon music, didn't they?

CS: They had a man who had had some trouble with Leon Schlesinger, who was making the cartoons at that time. I was hired to replace him, in 1936. I don't know what the trouble was about, but the inside of the music room desk was all cluttered with empty whiskey bottles.

MB: Schlesinger knew of your work already?

CS: Oh, yes. There was a director and story and gag man working for Schlesinger named Ben Hardaway—they called him "Bugs"—who had been a newspaper cartoonist back in Kansas City, and I knew him there. He was also at Ub's, when I was there, and then he went to Schlesinger's. He was there when my predecessor was laid off, and he recommended me very highly to Schlesinger.

MB: Now, after you went to work for Schlesinger, you were the only composer Warner's had until you retired?

CS: For the cartoons, yes, for twenty-two years. I retired in 1958.

MB: Did your music differ much at Warner's from what it had been at Disney's and Iwerks'?

CS: Yes, because at Warner's, I could use popular music. That opened up a new field so far as the kind of music we could use. At Disney's, we had to go back to the nineteenth century, to classical music, to "My Old Kentucky Home."

When I came out here, there was no law that cartoon music was copyrightable. That went into effect in the late forties. Then they started paying royalties retroactive from the day I started with Warner Bros. They're still paying, on the television reruns. Royalties are paid to composers whose music I used, and also to me for my original music.

MG: Apart from the increased use of popular songs, did you notice much of a change in your music over the years, as you composed it?

CS: It depended on the picture. When we had a very modern picture, I used as much music in the modern style as I could think up—augmented intervals, and so forth. But other than that, my style didn't change much.

MB: Of your music for cartoons, how much was other composers' music that you reworked and how much was original?

CS: Eighty to ninety per cent was original. It had to be, because you had to match the music to the action, unless it was singing or something like that.

MB: Were you ever ill, so that someone else had to be called in to do some cartoons for you?

CS: Yes, once. I had a brain operation in 1950. I bumped my head and a clot as big as my hand formed in between my skull and my brain. I was ill for four or five weeks. Gene Poddany, Chuck Jones' composer now, and Milt Franklyn filled in for me.

MG: They were making four cartoons every five weeks at Warner's back in the Forties, so you had to turn out almost one complete score every week. How did you turn out so much work?

CS: We had an arranger, of course. I would write the piano part—the basic, skeleton parts, you might say—and jot down all the cues and everything, then send it to the arranger, who worked at home. He arranged the music for orchestra, but whenever I wanted to feature an instrument or instruments in the orchestra, I'd make a notation. It took about a week, maybe eight days for me to prepare each score.

MB: Did you ever get really pressed for time?

CS: No, I had that schedule, and I stayed on time, although I sometimes had to do some homework in the evenings.

MB: Were there ever any cartoons that you had trouble writing music for, where the music didn't seem to suggest itself naturally?

CS: No. You see, I had played in theaters for about twenty years before sound came in. We improvised all the time, on the organ. I'd have to put music out for the orchestra, for features, but for comedies and newsreels we just improvised at the organ. So I really was used to composing for films before I started writing for cartoons. I just imagined myself playing for a cartoon in the theater, improvising, and it came easier.

MB: Did you have certain instruments that you liked to use more than others in your cartoon scores?

CS: The bassoon . . . the trombone, the slides on the trombone . . . the violin, with the glissandos, for comic effects. The viola is very good for mysterious effects.

MG: Did you ever record your music at Warner's before the exposure sheets were completed, so that the cartoon was fitted to the music?

CS: Yes, when there was a song, usually one that Mel Blanc sang. They'd indicate so many frames for each word on the exposure sheets.

BS: Did you write the music for the opening of the Warner cartoons, with the shield and the bullseye?

CS: No, I selected it, but that was a tune already owned by Warner Bros., "Merrily We Roll Along."

BS: How was the opening sound done, that "boinngg"?

CS: That was done with an electric guitar.

BS: Was the sound electronically altered?

CS: No, they just struck a chord and brought it down.

MB: Playing for a cartoon score would be hard for many musicians to get used to, wouldn't it?

CS: The musicians said they enjoyed the cartoons more than anything else. They looked forward to coming down to record the cartoons. It was screwy stuff, you know.

A cartoon score was usually made up of about ten sections. We'd run through a section once or twice—usually just once—and then record it. We had a wonderful orchestra at Warner's. It took about three hours to record a cartoon score.

MG: Did the directors show you the storyboards, and you then decided from that what music would be most suitable?

CS: That's right.

MB: Did the directors tell you what they wanted in the way of music? Did they want a certain kind of music for particular scenes?

CS: As a rule, no. Sometimes they'd just want something with a twelve-beat for one sequence, and then maybe an eight-beat for the next sequence, and so on. Sometimes they'd build a whole picture around a song like "What's Up, Doc," which I wrote, but many popular songs were treated likewise, using the song title as the cartoon title.

I'd say Chuck Jones and Friz Freleng were the easiest directors to work with, because they had something there. Tex Avery was also great, and Bob Clampett was really inspiring, he really had ideas. He was a fascinating guy. I hated to see Bob go.

MB: Were there any cartoon characters that it was especially enjoyable to write scores for, or did it make any difference?

CS: Each character had a different feeling, enjoyable, and, of course, very original, but there weren't any that were especially enjoyable to work with, unless it would be Bugs Bunny. He was the standout.

BS: Did you ever get tired of doing music for cartoons with "funny animals"?

CS: No, there were several directors at Warner's, and when you got through with one there was another one waiting for you. There was plenty of variety.

MG: Many times, you used the music to tell the story. In *Catch as Cats Can* (1947), Sylvester the cat swallowed a bar of soap and was hiccupping bubbles, and the music was "I'm Forever Blowing Bubbles." Did you make up those gags yourself, or did the directors help you with that?

CS: It happened both ways.

MB: You worked closely with the sound effects men, didn't you, to keep the music and sound effects coordinated?

CS: Yes; Treg Brown handled all the sound effects. Treg had thousands of sound effects on short reels, and he would make up a whole soundtrack out of these, as well as adding new ones for each cartoon. He had been there for three or four years when I came to Warner's. His room was next to mine.

MB: Did you ever actually write your music so that a sound effect came out as part of the music?

CS: Yes, and sometimes I'd just lay out altogether and let the sound effect stand alone.

MB: In some of Chuck Jones' Road Runner cartoons, there are long, involved gags for which there's no music; nothing is heard except the sound effects: Was this something Chuck wanted to do, or was this your idea?

CS: I don't remember, but I do remember that if the sound effect called for it, we'd stop the music altogether. And, of course, for a lot of the dialogue we would stop the music or we'd cut it down to just a few strings.

MG: Did you find a cartoon with lots of dialogue harder to compose for?

CS: Yes, because you don't dare drown out the voices. Sometimes on television, or in features, the music is way too loud, and you can't hear what they're saying. One trouble with cartoons today is that they do so much dialogue that the music doesn't mean much.

MB: Was it your idea to use Mendelssohn's "Fingal's Cave" for the Minah Bird's walk in Chuck Jones' Inki cartoons?

CS: Yes, and it went over so well that we had to use it every time.

MB: Did you ever suggest a cartoon idea to a director that would involve a certain kind of music? Did you, say, ever suggest to Chuck Jones that he might make a cartoon using a certain piece of classical music?

CS: It could be, but as a rule, he worked out the ideas first.

MB: Did you ever do any composing for live-action features?

CS: I did one reel of a feature for Jack Benny, *The Horn Blows at Midnight* [1945; score by Franz Waxman], and it was just as bad as the picture, which was a big flop. I didn't want to do it, but Leo Forbstein, the orchestra's general musical director—he'd hire all the musicians—and head of the music department, wanted me to. I'd played with him in Kansas City theaters, the Royal and Newman Theaters. So when I came out here, I liked it much better at Warner Bros. than at Disney's, because of that association. We'd known each other and worked together for years. He played violin and I played piano, and sometimes for the morning shows, that's all we'd have for an hour or so, and then I'd go up and play the organ.

MB: When you'd written your music, and had it ready to go, did anybody else have to look at it first and approve it before you recorded it?

CS: No, no one.

MB: Was there ever a time when you'd recorded your music that somebody said something should be different, and wanted to change it?

CS: Yes, once. Ray Heindorf, director of the Warner orchestra now, took Leo Forbstein's place when Leo passed on. He said a certain four bars sounded like the tune "Chicago." I thought I knew that tune, and I couldn't hear any similarity, but he had me change it. They didn't want anything that might cause a lawsuit over copyrighted music.

MG: Before you retired, did you start training other composers to take over your job? I know that some screen credits list you and another composer, Milt Franklyn.

CS: He was my arranger, and then he took over composing after I left. He died, I think in 1962. He was a very fine musician. . . .

12

Dimitri Tiomkin: *Please Don't Hate Me!* (1959)

Another prolific Hollywood composer with European origins, Dimitri Tiomkin (1894–1979) was born in the Ukraine and studied at the St. Petersburg Conservatory before emigrating to the United States in 1929 with his first wife, the choreographer Albertina Rasch. Tiomkin's budding career as a concert pianist was halted abruptly when he broke his arm in 1937, and this misfortune resulted in his decision to pursue a career as a film-music composer. He had already written sporadically for Hollywood productions, early assignments including film versions of Tolstoy's *Resurrection* (dir. Edwin Carewe, 1931) and Lewis Carroll's *Alice in Wonderland* (dir. Norman Z. McLeod, 1933), but it was his close association with Frank Capra that propelled him into the limelight with a succession of scores for the brilliant director, including *Lost Horizon* (1937), *You Can't Take It with You* (1938), *Mr. Smith Goes to Washington* (1939), *Meet John Doe* (1941), *It's a Wonderful Life* (1946), and a number of wartime documentaries.

As Tiomkin recounts in these extracts from his colorful autobiography (which derives its title from his characteristic phrase of deprecation when attempting to contradict his Hollywood employers), Capra was responsible for broadening the composer's musical horizons to extend from a conventional Eurocentric romantic style to an idiom more in tune with American subject matter. This experience served Tiomkin in good stead when he gained a particular reputation for the scoring of westerns, such as *Duel in the Sun* (dir. King

Source: Dimitri Tiomkin and Prosper Buranelli, *Please Don't Hate Me!* (New York: Doubleday and Company, 1959): 182–87, 192–99, 202–6, 220–22, 224–26, 230–36, 252–54.

Vidor et al., 1946) and *High Noon* (dir. Fred Zinnemann, 1952). For the latter, Tiomkin received Academy Awards for both his orchestral score and the hit song "Do Not Forsake Me, Oh My Darlin'." The song's spectacular success was partly responsible for changing the course of film-music history, since it had been plugged relentlessly in advance of the film's release and showed the enormous potential for cross-marketing between the film, broadcasting, and recording industries: thereafter, would-be hit songs became de rigueur in the movies. Tiomkin's Oscar for a later western score, *The High and the Mighty* (dir. William Wellman, 1954), elicited his legendary acceptance speech in which he thanked a number of great composers—a gesture widely misunderstood at the time, to the point where he felt its meaning had to be clarified at the end of his book.

Also included here are reminiscences of Tiomkin's work on features directed by Julien Duvivier (*The Great Waltz*, 1938), Henry Hathaway (*Spawn of the North*, 1938), and Alfred Hitchcock (*Shadow of a Doubt*, 1943).

Albertina and I gave many parties, some of them outrageous, the most anti-musical in Hollywood. We rented our house from Buddy Rogers who had married Mary Pickford. We got it furnished—and what furniture! Rogers was a remarkable musician, for the number of instruments he could play—saxophone, piano, horn, drums, clarinet, everything, it seemed, including the piccolo. The living room was full of them, and our guests could not resist the temptation to play them. One of them would take a trumpet and blow terrible sour notes; another would try the saxophone. Soon a dozen would be making appalling sounds in an ear-splitting imitation of a jam session.

The Capras always came to our parties, and Frank was an enthusiast at getting infamous notes out of an instrument he couldn't play. The bedlam included other gifted directors, [Ernst] Lubitsch and [Erich] von Stroheim. One of the noisiest of our antimusicians was Charlie Chaplin, as funny as a clarinet player as he was on the screen. I tried any instrument I couldn't play, while Albertina officiated at the drums, which she could play. She was, in fact, an excellent tympanist and could roll out a thunderous rhythm. Sometimes our late jam sessions were so sleep-destroying that the neighbors called the police. . . .

Then the time came when Capra decided to make *Lost Horizon* for Columbia Pictures. The James Hilton novel caught his imagination: Himalayan adventure at a Buddhist monastery in Tibet, Shangri-la, far away and mysterious. He had great ideas for the picture and wanted a large musical treatment to develop the feeling of the exotic, the occult, the remote. The locale was Central Asia, and Russian composers had always used Asian themes, for example, in [Rimsky-Korsakov's] *Scheherazade*, a supremely competent work, though now a musical chestnut. Capra and I talked about the film; the theme was as beguiling to me as it was to him. Sooner or later I was bound to get an assignment from him, and this was it. It was his way to go all out on a decision, and he gave me the job without reservation. I could write the score without interference, and he would hear it when it was done.

Lost Horizon offered me a superb chance to do something big. I wrote a score for an orchestra of eighty pieces, including instruments appropriate to the Himalayan scene—special horns, drums, and percussion. I thought I might be going a little too far in the matter of expense, and went to Frank one day as he sat in the projection room.

"For death of lama scene, Frank, is good using oriental xylophone, also special tympani for large effect. Is necessary, no?"

He looked shocked. "No, Dimi, the lama is a simple man. His greatness is in being simple. For his death the music should be simple, nothing more than the muttering rhythm of a drum."

"But, Frank, death of lama is not ending one man, but is death of idea. Is tragedy applying to whole human race. I must be honest. Music should rise high, high. Should give symbolism of immense loss. Please don't hate me."

"Dimi, it should be simple."

I saw he was reluctant to disagree; but once he had thought of it he was set on simplicity in the musical treatment of the scene; and he could be remarkably resolute. I went away depressed. I was convinced I was right, much as I respected his intelligence and taste.

Not until next day could I make up my mind. After all, he had given me a free hand, and was not one to take an agreement lightly. I decided to go ahead with my own conception of the scene, and wrote theme, chords, and orchestration to express a soaring grief for the death of the lama. Nor did I neglect the special xylophone and drums. I said nothing to Frank, and he didn't mention the subject again.

One day he asked me to come to his house in the evening for a party. It was his birthday. We were working late, putting the music on the sound track; I told him I would be at the studio most of the evening and would get to his party late.

The score called for orchestra and chorus, and I had engaged the Hall-Johnson Choir, one of the best in Hollywood. Everything went well until the dinner break. I went out, never thinking anything could go amiss. When I came back to the sound stage I found a jamboree going on. The orchestra and chorus, taking advantage of Capra's absence, had had a few drinks, and the uproar was hilarious.

I was gazing on the scene of confusion when my eyes strayed. Who was standing there but Harry Cohn, the studio despot! He was the last person we ever expected to see. They had had disagreements from time to time about the way a story should be filmed, and Capra, with his insistence on no interference, would not allow him on the set when he was making a picture. In this the toughest man in Hollywood had to defer to the ace director. But Harry Cohn knew that Capra was at home at his birthday party and had taken the opportunity to appear on the sound stage.

Harry Cohn said nothing and walked off. My knees were shaking. I could guess what was coming. Soon I was summoned by telephone to Cohn's office. I expected to be blamed for the unseemly outbreak on the sound stage. Cohn sat at a desk big enough to be a dance floor. With him sat the head of the music department, who was getting hell in a peculiar way. Cohn was shouting:

"Who does he think he is to have such a big orchestra and a chorus too? It costs a fortune. Where does he think he is, Carnegie Hall?"

The head of the music department listened silently to the tirade. It was unfair. He had nothing to do with it. But Cohn was indirectly ranting at me. He was a little awed by my reputation as a concert pianist.

My conscience hurt. Had I done wrong? I felt I was robbing Columbia Pictures, and remembered those exotic instruments I'd added for the death of the lama. Finally Cohn turned to me. Now I expected the storm to break. He asked:

"Who is that cello player?"

I was steeled for an outburst, and it took me a moment to recover. I knew what he meant. There were half a dozen cellists in the orchestra, and one of them was the most beautiful in the history of bowed instruments. She was Helen Gilbert, a lovely blonde with alluring blue eyes. During the bedlam on the sound stage, she'd sat at her music stand playing practice passages.

"Fine, Mr. Cohn, you appreciating Helen Gilbert. Seldom you see beautiful blonde in orchestra. Wonderful blue eyes with sweet smile, and she plays good cello."

He said nothing more. I don't think he'd even noticed the disorder on the stage or was concerned with the expense of the orchestra and chorus. For some reason, he'd had to raise hell before asking about the beautiful cellist.

In the orchestra Helen Gilbert sat in front of the contrabass player, Bakalenikov, a Russian and a friend of mine. He fell in love with her and they were married, and he helped to promote her screen career. She was engaged by M-G-M for a series of pictures and became a star. Then with her success as an actress, the marriage broke up. Not long ago Helen Gilbert died. I remember her as the most beautiful cellist in the world.

When the music for *Lost Horizon* was on the sound track, we ran the film for Capra. I sat near him in the projection room, nervous, tense. What would he say when it came to the death of the lama? In due time it did, and the orchestra rose to a lamentation in symphonic style laced with the rhythms of bizarre instruments. Glancing at Frank I thought I noticed moisture around his eyes.

He never mentioned the subject. The picture went on its lucky way, one of the hits of the time.

A few years later, while we were out on the desert, he spoke suddenly, as if out of nowhere:

"You were right, Dimi, about the music for the death of the lama."

At the Hollywood première of the picture, I met George Gershwin going into the theater. "They tell me, Dimi, you have something special here," he said. He spoke with his usual smiling courtesy, but I thought I detected an amused

A recording session for the music track of Frank Capra's *Lost Horizon* (1937), performed by the Columbia Studio Orchestra conducted by Max Steiner. Behind Steiner, at far right, is the score's composer, Dimitri Tiomkin; seated in front of them is the studio's music director, Morris Stoloff. Capra stands at far left. (Courtesy of Mrs. Olivia Tiomkin Douglas; © Volta Music Corporation)

skepticism—the Russian pianist who played Gershwin jazz at the Paris Opera now a composer for Hollywood films.

During the picture I sat just behind him, and soon he turned, nodded, and gave the Broadway-Hollywood sign of excellence—thumb and forefinger making a circle. That, I felt, was tops in criticism. . . .

Capra's contract difficulties with Columbia were settled on a basis of making two more pictures for them. He made two of his finest, *Mr. Smith Goes to Washington* and *You Can't Take It with You*. They needed all the musical Americana I could bring to them. *Mr. Smith* presented the idealist in national politics. Arriving in Washington, he stands gazing at the Lincoln Memorial. I based the music for this on a slave song of the Old South, to echo the black man's appeal to the Emancipator. Other pictures called for the style of Civil War songs or hillbilly ballads, which were not so hackneyed then as they are now.

I worked at other studios, too, and prepared the music for *The Great Waltz*. It was based on the life of Johann Strauss, with a score consisting of "The Blue Danube," "Thousand and One Nights," songs from *Die Fledermaus*, and others—eternal youth in three-quarter time. My job was to put the Strauss waltzes together, develop them, and thread them with connecting passages.

The producer wanted Lily Pons, the French coloratura soprano, as the star. The director and I were opposed. I had a high regard for Lily Pons as Marguerite in [Gounod's] *Faust* or Gilda in [Verdi's] *Rigoletto;* but her style was better suited to French or Italian opera, and Johann Strauss needed the true Viennese lilt.

"French elegance has Lily Pons," I argued. "Right style for *chic* and *soigné*, but Johann Strauss is needing schmaltz of Vienna. I must be honest. Paris is wonderful city, but for *Great Waltz* is Vienna needed."

He replied, "Lily Pons."

The director and I learned of a soprano in Germany, Milizia Korjus; from all accounts she seemed to be the right type, as I explained to the director:

"Milizia Korjus is fine coloratura. Has voice like Vienna, like Viennese dialect. Good-looking, good actress. Not engaging her is big mistake. Please don't hate me."

He said, "Lily Pons."

What to do? The director and I found a recording of Milizia Korjus singing a Strauss waltz; she was magnificent. The record was our weapon. We knew the producer was most amenable in the morning when he got up feeling well; so one morning we took the record to his house. There, when we were admitted, we found that he was in the bathroom. Good. In the living room was a record player. We put the disk on it, and in a moment the whole place was filled with the gaiety of the soprano voice.

The producer came running out in his dressing gown. He was jubilant. He thought it was Lily Pons. Then we told him, and he said, "Engage Milizia Korjus."

We followed orders, and that was how Milizia Korjus came to the United States and made her success in *The Great Waltz*.

At the same time I was working on Capra's *You Can't Take It with You*, doing the two jobs simultaneously. The story had turns of irony and I wanted the musical beginning to be in an impish, capricious vein. For this I resorted to the style of Richard Strauss, as in, say, *Till Eulenspiegel*, that symphonic poem of elfin roguery. It is common practice for a trained musician to write in the style of some great composer to achieve certain effects, just as a prose writer might use the idiom of the eighteenth century or of Ring Lardner for his own purposes. A composer may employ the modal colors of the Gregorian chant; and it's part of the great tradition to write in famous styles, as the modernist Prokofiev did in his *Classical Symphony*. This is not to be confused with stealing tunes from master works, or other outrages of plagiarism.

Recently in writing the score for the Cinerama *Search for Paradise* [1957], I put in a passage that somebody said sounded like Handel. It did. I wanted that feeling for a scene of large action. In the same picture I used the Venetian barcarolle in six-eighths time for scenes of boating on the canals of Kashmir, and for a Himalayan polo game the brio in triplets of the Neapolitan tarantella. The standard forms provide many resources for motion picture scores.

Richard Strauss has a highly individual style, easy to recognize. Most characteristic are flickering phrases that appear in the orchestra, with a touch of chromatics and dissonance that produce a twist of levity and a mocking effect. These were typical Strauss mannerisms I used for a comic impression in *You Can't Take It with You*.

When I rehearsed the orchestra, the veteran musicians recognized them immediately, nodded sagely, and said, "Strauss." The word got around and Capra picked it up. He was worried. "Strauss"—and at the same time I was working on *The Great Waltz*, with music by Johann Strauss. He thought I might be using the same music, and foresaw suits for plagiarism and other alarming possibilities.

He asked me about it. What did it mean, Strauss here and Strauss there? I felt like laughing, but merely gave him a simple assurance that he needn't worry. "Music, Frank, is different—one hundred per cent." He took my word for it.

Some years later I explained to him the difference between the two Strausses. He laughed and said, "You so-and-so, why didn't you tell me?" . . .

My research into American music extended into the music of the Indians. Henry Hathaway was making *Spawn of the North*, starring George Raft, for Paramount. It was a story of Alaskan Indian salmon fishermen. Hathaway was using a documentary technique in fiction films and required authenticity. When he offered me the music job, I gave him enthusiastic assurance:

"I am Russian musician. Once was Alaska Russian. I must be honest. Picture is for me, naturally."

However, he didn't want Cossack tunes, he wanted real Alaskan Indian music.

Los Angeles had a magnificent Indian museum where you could find out anything about the redskins, including their music. I consulted book after book and found studies of the culture of the Hopis, the Apaches, the Pueblos, the Indians around Palm Springs, and fascinating aboriginal music in notation, but none of it Alaskan. I asked advice of an Indian who did small-part acting at the studio. He knew nothing about Alaska, but told me to come to his house and I'd hear some real Indian music.

He got together a dozen California Indians, some of them Mexicans perhaps, and they brought with them their musical instruments—mostly percussion, such as drums and xylophones, and also a double flute with a single mouthpiece branching out in two pipes. On this the melody was played, if you could call it a melody; I could distinguish only a series of warbling notes of peculiar tonality. It was extremely interesting, and the aboriginal orchestra got a bizarre effect, but nothing that would last long in a motion picture score.

It was clear I wasn't going to get Alaskan music, and something else would have to do. It was equally clear I'd have to have something more than the sounds produced by my California Indians. I had an idea.

"Boys, we come to my house tomorrow. Have party. Have music." I said I'd pay them each a dollar or two, and they were happy.

Returning home I wrote a piece based more or less on the Indian music I'd found in the books. There was a vogue for music with an aboriginal flavor, using the five-tone scale, like Cadman's "Land of the Sky-Blue Water." I concocted something with a similar effect and a flowing lyric line.

When the Indians, dressed like desert rats, assembled with their strange instruments in our living room, Albertina gazed with a cold eye at this offense to the dignity of her household but summoned her patience. I gave them real Russian vodka, not the raw alcohol that desecrates the honorable name nowadays, and they were pleased. It created an uninhibited mood that helped the musical performance.

"Now, boys, we have music, yes. We play hot number."

First I played the piano piece I had written. The Indian cadences left them unmoved. Apparently they didn't recognize their own kind of music.

"Now, boys, we together play same tune. Everybody give big music."

What an uproar, as they banged away and the double flute squealed, while I played the piano! They tried to reproduce the melody I had written, but got it wrong in pitch and rhythm. But it was wrong in an interesting way. We tried again, and they got the hang of it better, making curious changes that improved the piece and gave it a wild, strange character.

This jam session lasted for several hours, and when it was over we had a new piece of music. They memorized it and I wrote it down for the piano. It was the reverse of the usual method of adapting primitive music to our manner; here, a conventional piece was adapted to the Indian manner. Alaska never produced anything half as exotic and interesting to the ear.

We engaged the Indians for the scoring of the picture. I put in several appropriate woodwinds, such as bass and alto flutes, to supplement the double flute, and the ensemble played against the background of a full orchestra. When we rehearsed, everybody agreed it sounded perfectly Alaskan.

The rehearsals were going on one day when visitors appeared in the sound studio. I recognized a tall, lean, blond fellow with a long face. It was Prokofiev. I hadn't seen him since the old days back in Russia twenty years before. He had changed little; he looked more mature and less eccentric.

I knew, of course, that after some years of exile in the West, he had returned to Bolshevik Russia. Several reasons were given, probably all true. He had a family there. He had been offered the life of ease and luxury the Soviets provided for important artists who accommodated themselves to the regime. He was so completely Russian he could not feel at home in a foreign land. The Stalin regime had not yet hardened toward artists, dictating the character of their work, as it was soon to do, when Prokofiev and other composers had to make abject confessions of error and promise to follow the Party line in music. He had been given permission to make concert appearances in the West and was playing recitals in the United States.

A meeting again after all those years might seem an occasion for an exchange of reminiscences of old St. Petersburg, the Conservatory, Glazunov, the *Homeless Dog*, even a recollection of the time when he, a gawky boy, had thumbed his nose at me, a miserable mite playing a Haydn sonata interminably. So many recollections, the two revolutions, the coming of the Bolsheviks.

Possibly Prokofiev didn't remember me after twenty years. Possibly he didn't choose to remember me. We spoke together in Russian, and I made no reference to our former acquaintance. I understood his position. Stalin's reign of terror, with the great purges, had begun. Russians had to be circumspect about contacts with anti-Communists, and I was a Russian-American. We talked impersonally about the Indian music he had come to hear.

The orchestra and my band of redskins went through it for him, and he was greatly impressed. Barbaric music always fascinated him. What could be more barbaric than his *Scythian Suite?* The Indian double flute with its curious tonalities beguiled him, and his general opinion was that the music was a revelation of the truly aboriginal. I didn't explain how it had been created in an Indian jam session, working on a conventional pentatonic melody. . . .

In Hollywood many of the studio orchestra conductors were routine second-class musicians who had picked up the trick of timing music to film footage and neither knew nor cared how to get the best out of an orchestral score. They considered movie music as a sort of neutral tonal background for the screen play, and were not concerned with its having any dramatic point. This was an attitude against which composers of the period had to struggle. It took time, endless wrangling, and the experience of the box office to establish the truth that it is the business of music to heighten moods and dramatic situations. In opera, music does this in a much more elaborate way, and motion pictures are a different medium; but the principles are a good deal the same.

I was constantly in revolt against the way my music was murdered, played as merely so many notes, with little care for nuance, phrasing, or orchestral balance. The studio conductor bothered only to time it correctly so that the march accompanied the soldiers and the romanza fell precisely on the love scene.

I always insisted on having some supervision over the performance of my music, and could be a nuisance.

"Please, phrasing is not right. Strings should give crescendo for melody, giving expression."

The conductor replies they can bring it up in the mix—as if you could shape a musical phrase by turning a knob.

Then there's a passage for flutes, and I point out that the counter melody for the solo viola is not heard. I get a mocking reply:

"Who pays any attention to the solo viola in Milwaukee?"

I speak my mind, which takes a good deal of speaking:

"Music should be partner of picture. Orchestra comes in on scene for expressing feelings of people in act. Melody, harmony, giving emphasis to dramatic meaning." And more to that effect.

It was a gospel I'd been speaking for years on behalf of the composer as a co-creator of a film. The arguments that ensued caused delays, and delays increased expense. Orchestra players loved me, because they got more overtime according to union regulations. Studio officials hated me. Heads of music departments were concerned with keeping down costs. I had a bad reputation, was considered long-hair and expensive. This made it harder for me to get jobs.

Albertina urged me not to give in. "Tell them to go to hell." She could give this defiant advice all the better because she was doing well at choreography in the studios and performances of ballet in the Hollywood Bowl.

Lost Horizon spoiled me completely. The conductor was Max Steiner, who was also a first-rate composer. Composers are usually jealous of each other, like rival tenors in an opera company; but Steiner had only one idea—to get the best out of the score. If I made a suggestion, he wanted to find out what was in my mind and do it that way. He was responsible for much of the musical success of the film.

That made it harder for me to go back to the routine studio conductors, and I began to have an idea.

"Albertinotchka, maybe is better for me conducting my music." . . .

So I made my debut as a conductor in Hollywood Bowl. I got through well enough, though hardly with the showmanship of a prima donna of the baton. I never did acquire a spectacular style or become an electrifying figure on the podium. I stand a little hunched over, with a musclebound beat.

I might have gone on then to conduct my music for one of the Capra pictures, but I didn't want to risk a fiasco on an important job. I made a start in minor studios, writing music for second-rate pictures at small fees, so as to have a chance to conduct for the experience. The orchestras were small and the scores were simple.

Some great maestro might tell you that motion picture conducting is easy. Let him try it. Suppose you are scoring the picture, which runs on a screen behind the orchestra. You watch the action on the film as you beat time, making sure that the music matches the scenes. In an opera the singers and the action follow the beat of the conductor; but film runs at a constant speed, and you have to follow that. The dialogue and action won't wait for you. You're on an inexorable treadmill; and yet you must make the music sound expressive and spontaneous. Too rigid a tempo will sound mechanical; but if you take liberties, the picture may run away from you.

I'm not a good conductor. Musicians say that sometimes my beat is none too clear. I don't enjoy the work as a gifted conductor does. I became a conductor in spite of myself, and the job's a chore. I get results by dint of sweat and toil. Albertina should be the orchestra conductor. . . .

I take as detached a view of myself as I can. I could never have been a Beethoven, Chopin, or Wagner. Anyway, the age of musical titans seems to be past. If I had devoted myself seriously to composition in the concert field

I think I might have been as good as Rachmaninoff. But the vogue in highbrow music today is the harsh, atonal school—enough to lacerate your ears, and I'm not in sympathy with it. I've gone over to the technology of motion pictures, music for the masses, music for the machine in an age of machines.

When I say I write music only for money, it isn't entirely true. Music for movies gives me many opportunities to compose in as fine a style as I am capable of. There's a chance for a fugal passage trimly written, here a rondo; and I can even speak learnedly of a passacaglia in a picture. The score I wrote for Hemingway's *The Old Man and the Sea* [1958] was in the style of a symphonic poem for concert.

After the successful pictures I'd worked on with Capra I could have gone to work at one of the big studios as a staff member. The salary would have been large, but I'd have been circumscribed in income and in what I could do. Instead I took assignments from the major companies on a contract basis.

Selznick was producing *Duel in the Sun*, a romantic, flamboyant picture. I worked on that. Music was a prime consideration. Some Hollywood moguls disliked music, paid little attention to it, considered it a necessary nuisance. Not Selznick, by all the notes in *Parsifal*. He had a way of directing operations by means of office memoranda, copious and precise. Soon I got one giving an outline for the score I was to write, a sort of musical prescription. The memo listed the ingredients to be compounded, the themes, the kind of music required for various scenes. Something like this:

> "Sentimental love,
> "Old memories,
> "Jealousy,
> "Flirtation,
> "Conflict,
> "Orgiastic."

These Mr. Selznick would want to hear before the film was scored. I wrote the music and rehearsed the orchestra, then played half a dozen themes for Selznick. The producer and his assistants sat in the last row of seats in a sound-recording studio. Things began well. "Sentimental love" got applause from Selznick, followed by his assistants. "Old memories" also fared well, and so did all the others down to "orgiastic," a swirl of soaring lyric intensity of which I was proud. When the orchestra finished, there was not a sound. The assistants waited for the boss to start clapping, but he never did. Instead he got up and walked out by himself.

This, it was well-known, meant that he would discuss the matter later in private. Out of courtesy Selznick did not reprove anyone when other people were around. Soon I was called into his office.

"Dimi, those other parts are splendid, but 'orgiastic' is not right."

"What wrong is?"

"It sounds sentimental, like 'sentimental love,' when it should be violent, uncontrolled, orgiastic."

"Okay, I write other music."

It was disconcerting. I had the orchestra ready to score the picture, but had to call everything off while I wrote another version of "orgiastic." This time I gave it a stronger rhythmic effect; but when I had the orchestra play it for him, he simply dismissed his assistants and called me to speak to him alone.

"No, Dimi, it still is not right. It hasn't the unbridled, throbbing urge."

So I had to write it again, this time giving it plenty of throb, with violent palpitations in the orchestra. If this wasn't it, I was going to shoot somebody.

It wasn't. When the orchestra had played through the feverish measures, I saw Selznick leave the auditorium alone.

I was ready for murder. When the summons came, I went to his office. If he said once more that "orgiastic" wasn't satisfactory, I might kill him.

"What is wrong now?" I restrained myself with difficulty.

"Dimi, that is not the way I make love."

With that, my Russian inflections thickened in a shout of rage:

"But is the way I make love."

He burst out laughing. That was the end of it. He agreed I should make musical love in my own way. When the story got around, everyone laughed; and "orgiastic" went into the picture the way I'd written it the third time. . . .

One of the singular geniuses of Hollywood was Alfred Hitchcock, who in the postwar period was rising to success with mystery thrillers, a dash of Sherlock Holmes with a flavoring of Dostoevsky. An Englishman who had started out to be a cartoonist, he had obscurely turned out an inexpensive horror picture which had surprised everybody by making a hit in the theatres. Now he was becoming the master producer of horror and suspense.

When I knew Hitchcock first he was ponderous and rotund. Then, when I saw him again, he was thin. Next he was fat again. It seemed to me that he could take off or put on seventy-five pounds with the greatest facility. As for gaining weight, you might say it was not because of eating. He told me: "Some people eat, and some dine. I dine." While working on a picture, he disdained to join the others for lunch in the studio cafeteria. Instead, he'd drive miles to Perino's for an epicurean repast. No cafeteria hash for Hitch.

I worked with him on a melodrama of suspense, *Shadow of a Doubt*, in which one musical task was to rewrite "The Merry Widow." Somehow or other—I don't remember—the graceful waltz played a sinister part in the picture, and at one place it appeared with horror harmonies and orchestration. I gave "The Merry Widow" the atonal treatment and worse.

Shadow of a Doubt had the usual preview, which was held at Long Beach, I think, and before going there Hitch and the studio executives had a fine dinner at Chasen's, where they all tried to follow the Hitchcock maxim of not eating but dining. Then to Long Beach in a fleet of automobiles, big ones. It was the practice of automobile dealers to sell oversize cars either to undertakers or to motion picture executives.

I've been to many a motion picture tryout, but that one was the most excruciating I ever suffered through. With a gripping thriller on the screen, most of the studio executives, having wined and dined in sumptuous Hitchcock style, went to sleep. One, sitting near me, snored in two notes. Even my ear-torturing version of "The Merry Widow Waltz" didn't wake him up. The audience? No, they didn't sleep through the nerve-tingling suspense. They laughed. They giggled through my sinister waltz harmonies and laughed loudly in moments of terror.

I was utterly depressed. I thought I had never witnessed such a fiasco. When it was over, I left in gloom and went back to Chasen's, and there at the bar I saw Hitch with his wife and writer, Van Druten. I expected to see them in the depths of woe after such a flop, but Hitch was having a brandy with a smiling air. Going to condole him, I said it was too bad.

"What?" he asked.

I refrained from saying that the studio executives had gone to sleep. That was perhaps to be expected. I concentrated on the main point.

"Is calamity, Hitch, audience laughing."

"Oh, that? It was quite all right."

"But, Hitch, when should be fear, terror, they going ha-ha."

"That was tension, Dimi. The laughs were a sign the picture had them on edge."

He explained that American audiences will break into nervous laughter when they are overwrought, a good sign for a suspense picture. At the time I hadn't had much experience with the Grand Guignol type of melodrama and could only reflect that in moments of shuddering apprehension a Russian audience would have been in tears.

Hitch was right about it. *Shadow of a Doubt* did big business in the theatres. . . .

Back in the mid-thirties the master of atonality took a post as professor of music at the University of California. A top producer heard that Schönberg was a great name in music and was persuaded that it would be a good idea to get him to write a score. Of course his harsh, bleak ultramodernisms would have driven audiences out of the theaters, but the producer didn't realize that. So he asked the composer if he would write a score.

No, he would not. But his wife told him that for one film he'd get more money than he'd ever made in his life, and he agreed to go to the studio to talk it over. It began with a mix-up. One of the studio magnates had invited his physician to make a tour of the studio, escorted by the chief of the studio police. When Schönberg arrived, he was mistaken for the doctor and taken all over the place, stages, sound-recording and cutting rooms, projection rooms. I don't know what happened to the doctor; but it was some time before Schönberg and his wife were taken to the producer's office.

The composer was a small, aging man with an austere face. He spoke English with a heavy German accent. When English was spoken, he'd turn to his wife and ask in a harsh voice, "*Was sagt ehr?*" She would explain what it meant.

The producer began by telling Schönberg how many famous people had worked at the studio, and gave their names.

Schönberg turned to his wife. "*Was sagt ehr?*" She explained about the celebrities. Schönberg shook his head. He'd never heard of them.

Then he asked his host what he did.

"I'm the producer."

"*Was sagt ehr?*" Frau Schönberg tried to explain, but he didn't understand.

"Do you operate the camera?" he asked.

"No."

"Do you direct the acting?"

"No."

"Do you write the story?"

"No."

How can you explain what a producer does? Schönberg never did find out.

The producer asked Schönberg what music he had written and was told *Verklärte Nacht*, the Wind Quintet, *Pierrot Lunaire*. The producer shook his head. He'd never heard of them.

"Well," said Schönberg, "if you want to know about me you'll find half a page in the Encyclopedia Britannica."

That sounded impressive, and the producer came to the point.

"What, Mr. Schönberg, will be your method of work?"

"I," said Schönberg, "will write the music, and then you will make motion pictures to correspond to it." . . .

Before they left the Hollywood Motion Picture Center, Stanley Kramer and Carl Forman produced what looked like the ugliest duckling of all. It was a Western, and when the film was put together the experts looked at it and said there never was such a stinkeroo. Such was the inauspicious beginning of *High Noon*.

I was not so pessimistic. The star was Gary Cooper, as a sheriff who waits for the noon train, knowing that there are outlaws aboard it who are coming to kill him. Gary Cooper was no young handsome hero. He was not beautified by make-up; you could see the bags under his eyes. He looked real. Director Fred Zinnemann had produced a curious quality of reality, and Carl Forman's dialogue was strong and effective, yet all this drew little approbation.

I thought it might be saved by a song. Perhaps a melody, a lyric, could make it take wing. It would be a title song, featured throughout the film, a device relatively new then. The rule book says that in movies you can't have singing while there's dialogue; but I convinced Stanley Kramer that it might be a good idea to have the song sung, whistled, and played by the orchestra all the way through.

Now all I needed was a song. I had worked before on dramas of the cattle country and gold camps. I had studied the songs of the Texas range and the Mexican border and the traditional British tunes of the frontier, modified by the pioneer minstrels of the plains and mountains.

A melody came to me. I played it on the piano at home and developed it until I thought I had it right. Albertina was in the kitchen preparing one of her specialties. She appeared in the doorway. I thought she had been drawn by my fine tune.

"Is good, Albertinotchka, is beautiful. Listen."

I played the melody with feeling.

"It's no good. That's what I came to tell you. It won't do."

She disappeared back into her kitchen and I was left discouraged. I trust Albertina's judgment in such matters.

I worked at the piano for a long time that day, expanding the melody, making it more complex. Finally I got it into a form that suited me and played it with full chords.

Albertina appeared in the doorway. "That's fine. That's it." She went back into the kitchen.

Now I needed a lyric. Sometimes the words of a song are written first, then the music; and sometimes it's the other way around. I had to have something romantic, with a heart-throb. The trouble was that the pattern of the melody was far more complicated than a popular lyric writer was likely to have thrown at him. The usual form is a melodic line of eight bars, then another eight bars in more or less similar rhythm. But this tune ran into changing phrases and varying patterns. It would be hard to fit the notes with rhymes, and they'd have to be of the sticky sentimentality dear to the popular ear.

I called in Ned Washington, a veteran of the Hollywood muse. Debonair, sophisticated, he cuts a dapper figure with his hair-line black mustache. He's hardly the type you'd pick to write a Western song; but he's adept at it, and excels in popular pathos. I told him what I needed and played the melody on the piano. He listened with a puzzled expression.

"What are you doing, Dimi, playing variations?"

I couldn't blame him. It sounded more like variations on a theme than a tune for Tin Pan Alley.

"Is melody, Ned. Is melody for you writing words. Please don't hate me."

He agreed the tune was appealing, but doubted that any kind of lyric for a popular song could be fitted to it. I pressed him; *High Noon* would have to be saved by a song. Finally he agreed to try.

I don't know what mental travail he went through, but in due time he came back with a lyric.

> Do not forsake me, oh my darlin'
> On this our wedding day
> Do not forsake me, oh my darlin'
> Wait, wait, alone.
>
> I do not know what fate awaits me
> I only know I must be brave
> And I must face a man who hates me
> Or lie a coward, a craven coward
> Or lie a coward in my grave!
>
> Oh to be torn 'twixt love and duty
> 'Sposin' I lose my fair-haired beauty
> Look at that big hand move along—near-in'
> High Noon.*

This may not be for an anthology of immortal English verse, but it's a masterpiece in its way. It fit the notes well. It was not only sentimental enough, but stated the central idea of the picture. "Do not forsake me, oh my darlin'" made an excellent beginning for a popular number, and the last line suited the formula ingeniously.

Next I needed a singer. I chose Tex Ritter, who sang cowboy ballads in a low, husky voice, with a group of cowboy guitar players. For concert or opera, you'd give the singer a copy of the song to read and learn; but that's not the Hollywood way. Many popular singers know little or no music, and think that even reading the notes might cramp their free and easy style. They depend

* Copyright 1952 Volta Music Corporation. Used by permission.

Dimitri Tiomkin (far right) conducting actor Chill Wills (far left) during a
recording session for George Stevens's Texan epic *Giant* in 1955–56. Stevens
(second from left) looks cheerfully on, and between him and Tiomkin stands
second-unit director Fred Guiol. (Courtesy of Mrs. Olivia Tiomkin Douglas; © Volta
Music Corporation)

more on personality and mannerisms than on vocal technique. The way to do
it was to have Tex Ritter come to my house and hear the song.

He arrived with his guitar players in full cowboy dress. I played and sang
the song; the vocal quality may not have been good, but the tune was clear, and
I rendered the lyrics with fervor.

> "Do not forsake me, oh my darlin'
> On this our wedding day."

The cowboys looked at each other. Never before had they heard a Panhandle
drawl with a Russian accent. Tex and his cowboys nearly fell off their chairs
laughing, and Ned Washington doubled up with mirth at hearing such a parody
of his song.

Nevertheless Tex Ritter learned the song in fine style, and sang it with a
simple, haunting quality. I wrote the score with all my ingenuity. "Do not forsake me" was there from beginning to end, sung, whistled, and played with

instrumental variations. While dialogue was going on in cattle-country lingo, a voice was softly singing, "Do not forsake me, oh my darlin'."

A final touch for the orchestration was provided by the pianist Ray Turner, who played in the orchestra. We were rehearsing a passage with strong rhythmic effects when he suggested a novel trick on a new-fangled electronic instrument with a piano keyboard. He struck it with his elbow, hitting several keys. It had a curious percussive effect, and we used it.

High Noon had a preview in a town near Los Angeles. It was a flop. The audience was given cards on which to mark its reaction, and the verdict was unfavorable. Film experts agreed that the picture, music and all, was a flat failure. Now it was time to sing "Do not forsake me" in a low sad voice.

The producers hesitated to release the picture. It might never reach the theaters. After all the work I'd done, what a percentage! It looked like the worst misadventure in the history of the Hollywood Motion Picture Center, that place of many misadventures.

I tried to salvage something. I asked the producers to give me the publication rights to the song. They were quite willing. After the calamity, what good was the song?

One of the prodigies of the music business in recent years has been the sale of phonograph records. People buy them by the millions to play at home, on the radio, on juke boxes. Now I would see if I could make anything on the song on phonograph records. A flop song from a film fiasco didn't look very promising, but there was no harm trying.

The record company that handled Tex Ritter wasn't interested, at least not at first; they came along with a Tex Ritter record later. I persuaded another company to issue the song with the popular singer Frankie Laine.

The record was an immediate success, one of the hits of the year. They couldn't turn out copies fast enough. The song was heard everywhere, in fact around the world. I read in a newspaper that President Eisenhower liked it, and sent him a stack of records in German, Japanese, Hebrew, every important language except Russian.

The picture was released four months after the record, and packed the theaters, a box-office gold mine. The success of the record promoted it. Why had *High Noon* got such an unfavorable reception at the preview? Picture business is full of such puzzles. . . .

The biggest name in Hollywood is Oscar. Nobody is more dearly loved, more ardently desired. The Academy Awards are an annual source of hope, jubilation, disappointment, envy. I think motion picture people would commit murder to win an Oscar if murder would help. Probably I would. Hitherto I'd never won the big prize, although music of mine, beginning with *Lost Horizon*, had been placed in nomination.

The way it works is this: There are a number of categories, from "best motion picture" to "best special effects." The list includes writing, acting, music, directing, and so on. In each category five candidates are selected and placed in nomination, and from each five a winner is picked. The nomination itself is a distinction; but I'd always missed the big prize. I explained my disappointment by saying that I worked mostly for small studios which did not have the prestige and publicity facilities to carry off Oscars. The alibi was a consolation.

This year the music from *High Noon* was on the list of nominations. Would it be another disappointment for me? I thought a bit of maneuvering would help.

M-G-M had a nomination on the list for music and threw a big party for disk jockeys, popular singers, and the press. Our small company could not afford expensive promotion. I knew the M-G-M title song would be featured at the party.

The master of ceremonies was Russ Morgan, the band leader. I happened to meet him, and did not lack courage.

"Would be great favor to me when you run performance if including my song. Now I know you will hate me."

He said he'd do it. He liked the song, and he also must have a magnificent sense of humor. At the party the M-G-M title song was rendered with feeling. Then followed "Do Not Forsake Me." The audience laughed. They knew there was a twister somewhere.

The night of the presentation of the awards, the Pantages Theater crawled with men in dinner clothes, women in the most resplendent gowns money could buy. Scattered here and there, waiting hopefully, were those who had been nominated. No one was more anxious than I, sitting with Albertina.

After the formalities, the master of ceremonies announced the award for the best motion picture of the year. Applause as a studio official goes to the stage and is presented with the shining effigy of a stern-looking fellow who presumably represents Motion Pictures. The same procedure followed for the best actor, the best actress, the best director, and so on. Each made a brief speech expressing a deep sense of humility, praising his co-workers, the company executives, and especially the little people at the studio.

Finally the category of music came up, and I heard the name Dimitri Tiomkin, like the sweetest of music. My feet seemed to fly as I went to the stage to be presented with the Academy Award for the best motion picture score of the year, the music in *High Noon*. I clasped the shining Oscar like the others and made the same speech, although not in the same kind of English.

"Is with great humility I'm accepting award. However, great credit must give to people at studio. I must be honest." I don't remember what I said, but it must have been something like that.

I left the stage clutching the Oscar. A hand grasped my arm.

"Don't go. Wait." It was Frank Capra. I hadn't seen him for some time. "Take it easy, Dimi, wait."

He kept me there until another award was called.

"Dimitri Tiomkin," the M.C. announced. Back to the stage I went and got a second Oscar, this one for the best motion picture song of the year, "Do Not Forsake Me." Holding the two trophies, I could only say:

"I feel now I have twins." . . .

Now I must tell you how I became "famous."

In 1955 I was granted an Academy Award for the music in *The High and the Mighty*. Since I had previously won two Oscars for *High Noon*, this was Oscar Number Three. But that was not the reason I suddenly attracted nationwide notice.

The presentations were memorable for the appearance of Grace Kelly, who was awarded an Oscar as the best actress of the year for her performance in *The Country Girl*. Since her debut in *High Noon* she had become one of the brightest of stars. A figure of blond loveliness, she came to the stage to receive the treasured token.

However, the laugh of the evening was won by me. The audience at the presentation, an enormous television audience, and the newspapers gave me credit for getting off the big joke of the occasion. I was hailed as a wit. Upon receiving my Oscar for the best motion picture score of the year, I expressed my thanks to Beethoven, Brahms, Wagner, Strauss, Rimsky-Korsakov, and other great composers.

A howl went up all over the country. A prize-winning Hollywood composer kidding Hollywood, poking fun at motion picture music. What could be funnier? The joke was applauded as a twice-welcome relief from the usual solemnity of Oscar awards. Even today people congratulate me: "I saw you on television when you got that Oscar and it was one of the best laughs I ever had."

What's wrong with a laugh? Nothing. I love a laugh. There's nothing I like better than to be entertaining, tell a good story, or make a droll remark. Perhaps I am at heart a jokester. Nothing could please me better than to contrive a bit of comedy that would bring down the house on such a magnificent occasion as the ceremony of the Academy Awards.

Unfortunately I didn't intend to be funny. It was a mistake. I was misunderstood. What I wanted to say was something entirely serious, even solemn.

Year after year I'd attended the presentation of the awards, and every time I had heard the winners, stars, producers, directors, musicians, technicians, praising the studio executives, fellow workers great and small—and especially the little people in the studios. I myself had talked the same trite line. I was tired of it. I thought: To whom should a musician give the greatest recognition but the masters who developed the art of music and created the traditions that we, their humble successors, follow? To whom should a writer or a painter give praise but to the giants of his art? What I wanted to express was a musician's homage to the heroes of the musical past.

A recording was made of the ceremony of the awards, and if you play it you can hear exactly what happened:

The master of ceremonies says: "And now for the best score for a comedy or a dramatic picture. The winner—*The High and the Mighty*—Dimitri Tiomkin."

Then follows the sound of applause as I went to the stage. Next, the playing of a selection from the score. The film tells the story of a drama aboard an airplane flying across the ocean, and the music seeks a symphonic expression of sublime strength rising to the heavens.

Now comes the speech recorded as I made it:

"Ladies and gentlemen: Because I am working in this town for twenty-five years, I like to make some kind of [pause for the right word] appreciation to very important factor which makes me successful and adds to quality of this town. I like to thank Johannes Brahms, Johann Strauss, Richard Strauss, Richard Wagner [laughter drowning out several other names], Beethoven, Rimsky-Korsakov [laughter drowning me out completely] . . ."

A voice rising above the din: "You'll never get on this show again."

I couldn't finish the speech. In the pandemonium I couldn't explain what I meant. I could only leave the stage with my Oscar.

That night people congratulated me for having an inspired sense of humor. I didn't know what to say, so I said nothing. At the rear of the hall I was accosted by several fellow composers who berated me angrily for having cast accusation and ridicule on our profession. Again I said nothing.

I've kept the secret until now. Why try to explain? Why not take the laugh for a good joke even if I didn't mean it as a joke? But now I must be honest. It was unconscious humor, and the laugh was on me. I must tell the truth. I gained more fame in those two mistaken minutes than in forty years of music. Please don't hate me.

13

A Radio Interview with
Franz Waxman (1950)

Franz Waxman (né Wachsmann, 1906–67) began his career as a jazz pianist in Germany, where before his emigration to the United States in 1934 he had been musical director for the famous Marlene Dietrich film *The Blue Angel* (dir. Josef von Sternberg, 1930). Waxman quickly came to prominence in Hollywood with his adventurous score to James Whale's *Bride of Frankenstein* (1935), an early landmark of the horror genre pioneered by Universal. Moving to MGM in 1935 and thence to Warner Bros. in 1942, Waxman went freelance in 1948. Among his best-known film scores were those to Alfred Hitchcock's *Rebecca* (1940), Billy Wilder's *Sunset Boulevard* (1950), George Stevens's *A Place in the Sun* (1951), and J. Lee Thompson's *Taras Bulba* (1962). With his music for these Wilder and Stevens films, he made AMPAS history by becoming the first composer to win Academy Awards in successive years.

Like Miklós Rózsa and Bernard Herrmann, Waxman was committed to pursuing a dual career as a composer of both concert and film music, and in 1948 he founded the Los Angeles International Music Festival to promote the work of modern composers. He resigned from AMPAS in 1954, as Herrmann was to do some years later, as a result of the failure of Newman's score to the biblical epic *The Robe* to be nominated for an award; both Herrmann and Waxman passionately felt that Hollywood did not take its music seriously enough, and were prepared to vote with their feet.

The radio script reproduced here preserves the content of a broadcast aired in April 1950 as part of an ambitious series of interviews with American film

Source: "'Music from the Films': A CBC Broadcast," *Hollywood Quarterly*, 5/2 (Winter 1950): 132–37.

Franz Waxman conducting in the 1940s. (Photofest)

composers recorded in Hollywood for the Canadian Broadcasting Corporation. The interviewer was Lawrence Morton, a pioneer in the field of film-music criticism (see pp. 327–40). Here Waxman discusses his interest in modern music, his activities as a conductor, and his views on the dramatic appropriateness of specific contrapuntal and thematic techniques in film scores. He also provides insights into his work on the films *Objective: Burma* (dir. Raoul Walsh, 1945), on which Morton had published a detailed article in 1946 (see p. 327); *God Is My Co-Pilot* (dir. Robert Florey, 1945); and *Possessed* (dir. Curtis Bernhardt, 1947). The broadcast concluded with a recording of Waxman's music from *The Paradine Case* (dir. Alfred Hitchcock, 1947).

ANNOUNCER: This is "Music from the Films"—a program prepared for all who are interested in film music and the composers who create it—arranged by Gerald Pratley and presented by Max Ferguson. . . . Good evening. Tonight, Lawrence Morton, film music critic and writer, discusses the composition of film music with Franz Waxman. This is the fourth of Mr. Morton's series of thirteen interviews with Hollywood composers.

Franz Waxman is one of the most prolific composers in Hollywood today. Not only has he scored over sixty motion pictures since his arrival in the cinema capital, but he has also achieved fame and recognition for his achievements in other forms of composition, and as a conductor. His suite from the score of Alfred Hitchcock's *Rebecca* has been presented by symphony orchestras throughout the country.

Waxman was born in Germany in 1906. He studied piano as a youth in Dresden and later went to Berlin to study composition, harmony, and counterpoint. His work in Germany received early recognition with the result that he was asked to score many important films for the well-known UFA Motion Picture Company. The year 1933 found him in Paris, where he immediately went to work scoring the Charles Boyer version of *Liliom*. When producer Erich Pommer, who had known Waxman's work both at UFA and in Paris, went to Hollywood in 1934, he took Waxman to Twentieth Century-Fox with him. Waxman remained at Twentieth for only a few months, leaving that studio for the more favorable assignment as head of music for Universal Pictures. In 1935 he signed a seven-year contract with Metro-Goldwyn-Mayer, where he wrote the scores for such well-remembered productions as *Captains Courageous, Fury, Dr. Jekyll and Mr. Hyde,* and *Three Comrades.* In 1942 he accepted a contract with Warner Brothers which he recently terminated in order to free-lance. While at Warners, he scored *Humoresque, Mr. Skeffington, Old Acquaintance,* and *Possessed,* among others. He has written the music for three of Alfred Hitchcock's films: *Rebecca, Suspicion,* and *The Paradine Case.* His score for the last-named film will be played later on the program.

His most recent music is that which he wrote for Paramount's *Sunset Boulevard,* made by William Wilder and Charles Brackett, a picture which brings back to the screen those two great artists of silent movies, Gloria Swanson and Erich von Stroheim.

With the coming of summer, Franz Waxman's name can often be found as conductor in the famous Hollywood Bowl. He is also the music director and conductor of the Los Angeles Music Festival, an annual series of symphonic concerts which takes place each May. Mr. Waxman mentions this now in the following interview which he recorded in Hollywood with Lawrence Morton. . . .

MORTON: Good evening, ladies and gentlemen. A few days ago, in preparation for this broadcast, I visited Mr. Waxman in his home high up in the Hollywood hills. It's a very handsome house, and it commands a magnificent view of the San Fernando Valley. The view is framed by a large bay window in

Mr. Waxman's study, and I could have been quite happy to contemplate the scene for a long time. But this was what might be called a professional visit, not a sight-seeing tour. And besides, being a musician, I was truly most interested in the musical paraphernalia of a composer's workroom—the books and scores and phonograph records which seemed almost to crowd the furniture out of the room.

It was apparent, Mr. Waxman, that your interests are by no means confined to film music.

WAXMAN: Indeed not, Mr. Morton. Composing for films is, of course, the main part of my work. This is how I make my living. But a composer has to keep up with the times just as much as a doctor or a businessman. And I try as much as possible to follow the activities of the important composers and writers of our time. And I'm also interested in the discoveries of the musicologists, particularly the new editions of old composers like Haydn and Vivaldi and Bach.

MORTON: I presume that this is important to your work as a conductor, too.

WAXMAN: Of course. I've been giving more and more time to conducting in the last few years. I've just finished my fourth season as musical director of the Los Angeles Music Festival, a series that takes place every spring. In past seasons I've conducted such important works as the Prokofiev Fifth Symphony, Honegger's *Joan of Arc at the Stake*, Strauss's *Metamorphoses*, and Stravinsky's *Story of a Soldier*. This year we presented the Mahler Ninth Symphony and Schubert's E-flat Mass. I'm leaving soon for Europe to conduct again in Paris—I gave a concert there a year ago. And then I'll conduct in Italy this summer.

MORTON: Is there much difference between conducting for concert and conducting for films?

WAXMAN: There isn't much difference from a musical point of view. But there are special problems in films: timing, balance for microphones, and so on.

MORTON: But many of these problems are solved already in the composition of a film score, aren't they?

WAXMAN: To a certain extent, yes. When I compose for the films, I try to imagine just what the sound will be in the theater—not only the sound itself, but its relation to the dialogue and the action on the screen.

That is why I often think of the tone color of music before I actually know what the notes are going to be. When I first see a picture in the projection room, certain scenes seem to call for a specific tone color—three trombones, for instance, or a flute or an English horn. In *Objective: Burma* I underlined General Stillwell's angry words ("I say we took a hell of a beating") with a solo trombone. And perhaps you remember the high string music in the main title of *God Is My Co-Pilot*, with which I tried to convey the religious feeling that was the underlying motif.

MORTON: But tone color still leaves the problem of the over-all character of the music.

WAXMAN: Sometimes this is quite obvious. Just reading a script might give all the necessary clues. In a film like *Objective: Burma*, you can tell immediately that the music will have to be military, epic; some orientalism might be required by the Burmese locale; there will have to be music for the cruel enemy, and for a lot of violent action.

You might say that, on the whole, the music is extrovert. But in a psychological drama like *Possessed*, a Joan Crawford picture that I scored a few years ago, the problem is more subtle. There are no battles, fires, chases, and so on. There are very few external events to be illustrated. There are mostly states of mind, conditions of feeling. You might say that in *Objective: Burma* the composer has only to *watch* the characters, while in *Possessed* the composer has to *get inside* the characters.

MORTON: That's an interesting differentiation, Mr. Waxman. Can you give an example of what you do when you write music for "inside a character"?

WAXMAN: In *Possessed* there was a direct cue given by the picture itself. Let me describe the situation in the film: Joan Crawford plays the part of a young woman emotionally unbalanced, a real psychiatric case. Her condition has, of course, a complicated history, but for our purposes here it is perhaps sufficient to say that it is based on an unreciprocated love for an engineer, played by Van Heflin.

A number of times during the picture, Van Heflin plays the piano—plays a passage from Schumann's *Carnaval*. Frequently, in the underscoring, I used this piece as an expression of Miss Crawford's attachment to Heflin. Now at the point in the film where she realizes that he really doesn't love her, which is the point at which her mind and emotions begin to crack up, Heflin plays the Schumann piece again. Heflin is apparently playing the piece correctly, what the audience hears this time is a distorted version, omitting all the sharps and flats, which suggests what Miss Crawford is hearing. That is, the distortion of the music corresponds to the distortion of normal emotions. What formerly had been a beautiful piano piece now sounds ugly to Miss Crawford because the man who is playing it does not return her love.

This illustrates what I mean by *getting inside* a character.

MORTON: Isn't it almost a cliché in film music that mental disturbance should be illustrated by dissonances and strange sounds?

WAXMAN: Yes, it's a common procedure. I don't know who started it, but there is plenty of precedent in concert music. Smetana, in his Quartet *From My Life*, used a high harmonic to illustrate the ringing in his ears that was one of the symptoms of his deafness. Religious mystics, like Joan of Arc and Bernadette, often claimed to hear voices and heavenly choirs. So there is some basis in reality for doing this sort of thing in music. I think composers have to take advantage of all these suggestive powers of music. It's one way of reaching audiences very directly.

MORTON: When you speak of audiences, Mr. Waxman—and before, when you mentioned trying to hear in advance what your music would sound like in the theater—you are really thinking of the function of music in films rather than purely musical qualities, aren't you?

WAXMAN: Yes, I don't believe that music as function and music as art are necessarily opposed to each other. But it is true that film music operates in a set of circumstances quite different from the circumstances in which other music is heard. Film music is heard only once—not many times, as concert music is. The audience comes to the theater unprepared—it is not like going to a concert to hear familiar music of Bach, Beethoven, Brahms. And besides, nobody goes to a movie theater to hear music.

MORTON: If film music is heard in a special set of circumstances, just what qualities ought it to have?

WAXMAN: It should have simplicity and directness. It must make its point immediately and strongly. The emotional impact must come all at once. It's not like concert music which is full of secrets that are learned from long acquaintance and many hearings.

MORTON: What are the musical equivalents of "simplicity" and "directness"?

WAXMAN: For me, music that is simple and direct is music that has strong melodic lines, simple accompaniments; and also a number of musical ideas expressed by solo instruments, even without accompaniments.

MORTON: When you have a simple style, strong melodies, and solo instruments, you still don't have a score. You have only the materials out of which a score is made.

WAXMAN: That is another problem—the problem of what to do with your materials. I regard a film score as essentially a set of variations. In concert music, variations are usually written around a single theme. But in film music, where there are many themes, the variations turn out to be variations on a group of themes. Another difference is that in film music the variations are not motivated by purely musical considerations, as they are in concert music. The motivation comes from the screen action.

MORTON: I've noticed in your own scores, Mr. Waxman, that you follow screen action very often by attaching musical themes to characters or ideas of the drama, and then varying the themes as the dramatic situations change. That is, you employ what is commonly known as the leitmotif technique.

WAXMAN: Yes, I find this very practical in writing film music. It is an aid in composition, and an aid to listening. Motifs are characteristically brief, with sharp profiles. They are easily recognizable. They permit repetition in varying forms and textures, and help musical continuity.

MORTON: On the other hand, Mr. Waxman, the use of leitmotifs often results in rather complicated counterpoint—as it does in Wagner, for instance. Do you think this contributes to simplicity and directness?

WAXMAN: There are many kinds of counterpoint, and each has varying degrees of complexity. I think this can be evaluated only by the final effect it makes. I have used the *fugato*, for instance, very frequently. Now I don't expect an audience to stop looking at the picture and say, "Ah, Waxman has written a *fugato*." But I think an audience will notice that somehow the music is growing in tension and excitement—because the reiteration of a single short motif, in a contrapuntal style, is a fairly obvious way of driving toward a climax. The technique of a *fugato* is strictly my own business. The dramatic effect is the audience's business. I don't think an audience will miss the dramatic intention if the composer has written a good *fugato*.

MORTON: That seems to me to be a fair division of responsibility, Mr. Waxman. Perhaps we might say that the ideal situation will be reached when good composers write good music for intelligent audiences.

WAXMAN: Don't forget one other factor, Mr. Morton—we composers feel that the situation, to be ideal, requires also good critics.

MORTON: That is another matter altogether, Mr. Waxman. And before you make this an opportunity for reversing our positions, with you asking the questions, I think I should quickly say goodnight to our CBC audience, and then thank you for having come to the studio tonight.

WAXMAN: Thank you, Mr. Morton. It's been a great pleasure.

ANNOUNCER: Franz Waxman's score from *The Paradine Case* has been arranged and recorded as a symphonic poem for piano and orchestra. It's described as a "recomposition" of the thematic material from the score presented in rhapsodic form for piano and orchestra. The main theme, which runs throughout the piece, is a rather haunting nocturne which pictures the sphinx-like beauty and strange attractiveness of the film's main character, Mrs. Paradine (played by Valli). This theme is heard in many variations and in different rhythmical patterns. Toward the end of the suite the introduction of the "Keane Theme" as a horn solo is heard. This plaintively portrays the emotion of Gay Keane (played by Ann Todd) when she realizes that her almost idyllic marriage is slowly being destroyed because her husband, Tony Keane (played by Gregory Peck), has become fascinated by the beauteous Mrs. Paradine. Near the end of this symphonic poem comes a short piano cadenza. This is joined by the woodwinds, which drive the cadenza to a final climax in a recapitulation of the theme. Franz Waxman's music from *The Paradine Case* then concludes with a short and brilliant coda.

(**RECORDS**: *The Paradine Case.*)

ANNOUNCER: Writing in *Film Music Notes* of January–February, 1950, Lawrence Morton said of Waxman's music: "In general, it has the grandiloquent expressiveness, the splendor and luxuriousness of texture that are characteristic of late German romantic music. If one had to ally him with any established 'school' of composition, it would perhaps be that of Richard Strauss. To this basic style he has added some of the elements of a more contemporary music—sharp dissonances, motor rhythms, angularity of phrase. He is fully aware of the new trends in music, for he is a thoroughly alert and trained musician; but they do not happen to correspond with his own feelings about the emotional content of music, nor with his convictions about structural principles. Nevertheless, he has such technique and facility that one feels he could easily absorb these later 'systems' if he wished to. Waxman's music may be summed up as being that of grand gesture and expansive emotion. His themes are strong, positive, clearly drawn, and calculated to communicate their ideas in their first statement. Considering these principles together with the variety and extent of Waxman's activities, they show him to be a musician of intense intellectual curiosity and boundless energy."

Good night.

14

Gail Kubik: "Music in Documentary Films" (1945)

Although Marc Blitzstein, Aaron Copland, and Virgil Thomson all composed music for fine social documentaries filmed by directors such as Robert Flaherty, Joris Ivens, Pare Lorentz, Ralph Steiner, and Willard Van Dyke in the 1930s and 1940s, and found that their inventive music was in this context accorded a prominence often lacking in feature films at the time, it was America's entry into the Second World War that arguably did most to draw public attention to the documentary genre. Wartime "morale" films made in the United States—many of which were shown in allied countries—were often of an execrable standard and blighted by blatant propagandism, but the initiative benefited from Frank Capra's sterling creative work on the "Why We Fight" series, to which many established Hollywood composers contributed (often uncredited) scores. Following Capra's example, director William Wyler made some of the finest wartime documentaries of all, working closely with composer Gail Kubik (1914–84), who specialized in the genre and had previously collaborated with directors George Gercke (*Men and Ships*, 1940), Sam Spewak (*The World at War*, 1942), and Jerry Chodorov (*Earthquakers*, 1943). After the war, Kubik pursued parallel careers as a film and concert composer, his output including such disparate projects as a score to the Oscar-winning cartoon *Gerald McBoing Boing* (dir. Robert Cannon, 1951) and a *Symphony Concertante* that won him a Pulitzer Prize in 1952.

In 1943–45, Kubik scored two of Wyler's most impressive documentaries. *The Memphis Belle* (1943) and *Thunderbolt* (made in 1944 but not released until

Source: *Music Publishers' Journal*, 3/5 (September–October 1945): 13, 54–56.

1947) were unsentimental and vivid portrayals of the U.S. Army Air Force's B17 bomber and P47 fighter crews on active service in Europe, endowed with soundtracks making resourceful use of both music and the visceral sounds of airborne combat. *The Memphis Belle* is mentioned in the article reproduced below, in which Corporal Kubik reveals his unusually fierce commitment to the documentary genre, not only calling for composers to write in their own personal styles for reasons of originality and self-expression, but boldly linking this aesthetic ideal with the overall democratic goals of wartime information films.

Documentary films are made with a point of view. The measure of their success is the extent to which they move an audience to act for or against something. To spur us to all-out effort in our war against the German and Italian Fascists and the Japanese, our government has made hundreds of documentary films—films which press home the fact that democracy is very much worth fighting for. They tell their story so convincingly that they make a real contribution to the war effort.

Just how, if at all, does music in these films help to sell democracy? Music in the documentary film aids democracy to the extent that it is creatively composed music. If the documentary film composer wants to represent a positive force in the fight against Fascism, the *only* thing he can do is to work with producers, directors, and writers who *will permit him to write creative music.*

It is impossible to overemphasize this last factor. There are many composers writing for films—documentary or otherwise—who are not permitted to write in their own creative style. Some music helps the democratic cause tremendously; some helps only indifferently; some actually hurts it. A score dominated by the aesthetic standards of the "front office" refutes the principle of democracy just as effectively as does the script that is mangled and emasculated to the point where its creativity disappears. Music *really* aids democracy to the extent that it reflects the feelings of a free and unrestricted personality. I cannot believe that the democratic, the American, concept of living is furthered by the writing of music dominated by any aesthetic values other than the composer's.

The music of the documentary film is, to my mind, more distinguished for its essential democracy than the music in other types of films because composers in the documentary field have more often been allowed the luxury of writing what *they* felt than have our colleagues in the more commercial films.

Not that the documentary record in music is anywhere near perfect. Many times I have witnessed the scoring of documentaries with music that might have been written by Strauss, Sibelius, or Ravel, with the old master, Tschaikowsky, represented by a main and end title! Of course, there are numerous instances of documentary film directors and producers who are quite certain that the music for their film just will not work unless it reminds them consciously or unconsciously, of the "Pathétique." Perhaps the film shows the problem in 1945 of getting iron ore from Duluth to Buffalo. In that case only the Pathétique's scherzo movement is recalled. After all, 5/4 is such an unusual time signature, and *so* modern!

No, the record of documentary films is not perfect, but the percentage of creative music in them still remains higher than that in the Hollywood product. Few composers on the west coast have been allowed the artistic freedom that characterizes the music which Virgil Thomson wrote for *The Plow That Broke the Plains* and *The River*; or that Douglas Moore wrote for *Power and the Land*; or Aaron Copland for *The City*; or Louis Gruenberg for *The Fight for Life*. Few producers of commercial films have given their musical directors as much freedom as I was permitted in the scoring of the many films produced by the OWI [Office of War Information] Motion Picture Bureau. But then I had only a few directors around who were sure that, since they liked [Sibelius's] *Finlandia*, for example, *Finlandia* was the only music to point up their little epic.

This record of the use of creative music in the documentary film is based upon the premise that creative music, like any other creative art, has the power to move people—a quality that is lacking in a stereotyped, synthetic style. This is true in music because the sounds that the listener hears are removed from the associative values inevitably called up by a synthetic style. It seems obvious that only when a composer is allowed to react to a film with complete sincerity and conviction will he create music that will reflect the particular drama and emotional values peculiar to that film. Why have one composer portray in sound the drama of *The Memphis Belle* and then ask another composer to do the music for *Farmer at War* in the same style? While the photographer, director, and writer are knocking themselves out trying to produce pictures which distinguish between the two subjects, the composer is blithely writing as though the farmer is a Flying Fortress; the Fortress is a farmer; God's in His heaven and all's right with the world—down to the last singing string and oboe solo.

There are other qualities and skills which a composer must have if he is to aid the screen's story—among them a talent for dramatic music. Abstract or purely musical forms are in most cases out of the question, though occasionally, in the documentary as in the Hollywood film, there is an opportunity to write a sequence which has only a time limitation. For a long scene which shows the unloading of coal from a lake freighter, it would be perfectly possible to write a scherzo which followed a strictly formal outline. The music would be required only to underscore the basic mood of power or elemental strength that was portrayed visually.

Most film-music problems, however, pose this question: Can the composer discover the architectural form which the film itself takes and, assuming that he has the instinctive dramatic talent which enables him to perceive this form, can he then translate his reactions to the film's structure into sounds which are musically satisfactory and convincing, yet which also supplement the dramatic impact of the film itself? In the example of the coal-loading scherzo, if one of the stevedores is killed, the composer should be able to construct his score so that the tragic, dirge-like mood of the accident is introduced into the scherzo just as convincingly and with the same feeling of inevitability as though the composer had normally arrived at the trio which would be found in the abstract scherzo form.

I am not a follower of the school that believes that music should never function in a literal, imitative fashion. "Mickey Mousing" can oftentimes supply just the touch that is needed. This is particularly true of films intended to provide a simple, extrovert kind of humor and amusement. The Disney films are perfect examples of this sort of thing. A training film on camouflage, done in animation, will require a less expressive score than a film like *The World at War*. The use of strictly imitative effects in a film score are effective in inverse ratio to the film's emotional and subjective intent. Serious, creative composers know what most directors and producers do not seem to know—that music is an art that exists in time, and that for it to work its wonderful enchantment, for it to penetrate into our emotional awareness, it must have time, time, time! To hit ten contrasted cues in sixty seconds will not, in a documentary or fictional film of serious intent, result in music that will move anyone to a greater understanding of that film's message. Most composers, and, I believe, a great number of movie-goers, resent most directors' inability to see this point of view. It is not necessary to do a musical take-off every time a plane leaves the ground. This "Mickey Mousing" is wonderful in a Mack Sennett comedy, but it is disconcerting and a bit irritating when it appears in a serious film. It is really tragic if music takes up precious time to make clear something our eyes have already adequately recorded, when it could be used to move us to understand the full dramatic implications of the scene.

Documentary films are being used today in the war effort on a scale not dreamed of even five years ago. The motion picture industry, through its "Victory Shorts"; the Office of War Information, through its numerous film reports; the Navy; through its Office of Strategic Services (*Battle of Midway*) and Bureau of Aeronautics (*Fighting Lady*); and the Army, through the Signal Corps (*Desert Victory*) and Special Services ("Why We Fight" series) and the Army Air Forces First Motion Picture Unit (*Memphis Belle*), are working feverishly to keep the world informed about work accomplished, work being done now, and work ahead. They are presenting our point of view to hundreds of millions of people. We are still engaged in a mighty struggle of ideas—a struggle ultimately as important as our military operations. The essence of our propaganda front— this publicizing of democracy—is a concept in which freedom is the corner-stone. At the core of all human activity, the artist stands as the finest symbol of man's dignity, individuality, and insistence on freedom. The documentary film composer, therefore, has an obligation to continue his work to maintain the dignity and freedom which is achieved only through genuinely creative effort. He has this obligation, not merely because of his personal gratification at being able to work creatively, but also because now, as never before, millions of people seeing our documentaries are at the same time listening to the scores to see if they can actually hear for themselves an evidence of man's dignity and freedom in his work. Here is the opportunity for the artist to show that he is qualified to stand as a symbol of democracy at work.

15

Adolph Deutsch on *Three Strangers* (1946)

Born in London, Adolph Deutsch (1897–1980) followed an early career path typical of several Hollywood composers in the Golden Age: emigration to the United States was followed by activities on Broadway as an orchestrator and music director, and with various dance bands, before he began work for the movies in earnest in the 1930s. From 1938 to 1946 he was contracted to Warner Bros., where among other features he scored Raoul Walsh's *High Sierra* and John Huston's *Maltese Falcon* (both 1941). In 1943 he was a founding member of the Film Composers' Committee, whose campaigning resulted two years later in the formation of the Screen Composers' Association as part of an on-going effort to ensure fair working conditions and royalty distribution for its members. Moving from Warner to MGM, Deutsch worked on a succession of famous musicals, receiving Academy Awards for his scoring and musical direction of *Annie Get Your Gun* (dir. George Sidney, 1950), *Seven Brides for Seven Brothers* (dir. Stanley Donen, 1954), and *Oklahoma!* (dir. Fred Zinnemann, 1955), and nominations for *Show Boat* (dir. George Sidney, 1951) and *The Band Wagon* (dir. Vincente Minnelli, 1953). Uncharacteristically for an arranger of musicals, Deutsch did not believe that their composers' interests were best served by overelaborate orchestrations and strove for clarity and directness in his scores, especially when tackling melodies by Jerome Kern in *Show Boat*. Deutsch retired from film composition in 1961, shortly after he worked with director Billy Wilder on *Some Like It Hot* (1959) and *The Apartment* (1960).

Source: "Three Strangers," *Hollywood Quarterly*, 1/2 (January 1946): 214–23.

In this article, published toward the end of his contract with Warner Bros., Deutsch provides a detailed account of his work on *Three Strangers* (dir. Jean Negulesco, 1946). At this time the studio's music department was still under the leadership of Leo Forbstein (1892–1948), who had helped Warner make the transition from Vitaphone sound-on-disc technology to celluloid soundtracks in the late 1920s and, as departmental head, had personally collected the Academy Award later earned by Korngold's score to *Anthony Adverse* (1936). Like many musical directors, Forbstein was widely considered to be more effective as an administrator than as a musician.

Reviewing *Three Strangers* for the *New York Times* on 23 February 1946 following its opening at the Strand, critic Bosley Crowther described it as

> full-bodied melodrama of a shrewd and sophisticated sort. Never so far away from reason that it is wholly incredible but obviously manufactured fiction, it makes a tolerably tantalizing show, reaching some points of fascination in a few of its critical scenes. . . . Of course, we seriously question whether it was so much the hand of Fate as it was the fine hands of the scenarists, John Huston and Howard Koch, that pulled the strings. Frankly, we suspect the latter. The plotting and writing have style. But whoever it was, they have turned out an efficiently intriguing show.

Three Strangers is a perfect example of my pet theory that there ought to be much more writer-composer collaboration in films, so I might as well start from the beginning and describe exactly what happened—and generally happens—in the scoring of a motion picture. The telephone rings; it is Miss Samson of the Warner Brothers music department. I am notified that the rough cut of *Three Strangers* will be run in Projection Room 6 at ten o'clock tomorrow morning. Arriving a few minutes early, I wait outside of Room 6 to enjoy the morning sun, remembering that for the next two and a half hours I shall be breathing air conditioned by yesterday's cigars and cigarettes. A small group of people arrive: I recognize Jean Negulesco, the director; Wolfgang Reinhardt, the supervising producer; and George Amy, the cutter. Greetings are exchanged, and I am introduced to Howard Koch, one of the two writers of the screen play. I am surprised to learn that his collaborator is Major John Huston, who, at the time, is away on official business for the U.S. Signal Corps. Mention of his name brings to my mind the stimulating experience I had in composing the musical score for *The Maltese Falcon*, which he adapted for the screen and also directed.

Promptly at ten, Leo Forbstein, the music department head, arrives and we file into the dimly lit projection room. It resembles a small theater and seats about fifty. Halfway forward is a long desk upon which are telephones, a volume regulator to control the sound, a buzzer signal, and an intercommunication phone that connects with the projectionist's booth. There is an air of expectancy as we await the two buzzes which is Eddie's "ready" signal. Eddie Higgins is our projectionist (operator, in studio language), and he is an expert at handling work prints so that they don't come apart at the splices or tear at the sprocket holes. As the small group settles itself in the divan-like chairs it occurs to me that this is the first time any of us will have seen the entire picture in continuity. It is the end toward which writer, director, producer, actors, and technicians have been working for several months.

I reflect upon their intimate knowledge of each scene and compare it with the few meager hints I had gleaned from reading the script, wondering if some day I would be invited to sit in at a story conference or the preparation of a shooting script. The phone at Mr. Forbstein's elbow rings. He is called away. Awaiting his return, we discuss the immediate musical problems of the picture. I am told that *Three Strangers* is a story that picks up the lives of three persons unknown to each other and follows each separately to a tragic denouement. One is a woman inclined toward Oriental mysticism and superstition; the second, a lawyer who is the trustee for several large estates; and the third, a down-at-heel but literate young man who plays classical piano pieces, quotes fragments of poetry, and contemplates life through an alcoholic haze. From George Amy, the cutter, I learn that in the process of editing the film he transposed several sequences to clarify the story line which wove in and out of the lives of the three people, and that more recutting may be necessary.

"The music," Jean Negulesco says, "will be a big help in identifying the main characters"—"What do you think," interjects Mr. Reinhardt, "of having three distinct themes?" "Excellent," I agree, recalling how well the leitmotif device served the operatic composers—a quaint old Wagnerian custom. At this point Mr. Forbstein returns, signals the operator with two buzzes, and we're off.

As the lights dim we focus our eyes on the screen, where the first atmospheric shot of Piccadilly Circus fades in. My mind automatically registers: music must reflect cosmopolitan London, around 1938; that's easy, I was born there. The camera wanders through the crowd and picks out Geraldine Fitzgerald (the most prepossessing of the three strangers). I concentrate on her characterization, seeking clues for an appropriate theme. Even though she has spoken no words, I am influenced by her appearance, her bearing, and her facial expressions. All these must be reflected in the music. The second stranger looms out of the crowd; he is Sydney Greenstreet, "the Fat Man." The camera lingers on him as his eyes follow Miss Fitzgerald appraisingly. I ask myself, "What kind of music does one write for a susceptible barrister?" The question remains unanswered as the film progresses unfalteringly to the first meeting of the three strangers. The third stranger is an old projection-room friend of mine, he of the soft-boiled eyes, Peter Lorre.

It is not long before the narrative, in the hands of such capable performers, absorbs my interest to the total exclusion of musical considerations. This is a healthy sign and I don't resist it. Music has no place in this scene, I register subconsciously. Hold on! Here's that Chinese image, Kwan Yin, the "Goddess of Mercy"—here a symbol of mysticism and superstition. Big Ben starts tolling. The wind whips the curtains. A candle goes out. "Make a light!—The matches!" Miss Fitzgerald cries. Aha! I think . . . looks like a music cue. George Amy volunteers some information. "The chimes ought to last longer." Nobody answers. It is a point for later discussion.

The first episode, the meeting of the three strangers, comes to an end and we watch the unwinding and interweaving of the three separate story threads. This is a uniquely daring essay in screen craftsmanship. It is no easy task to tell part of a story, part of a second story, part of a third story; pick up the first story again, the second and the third where they left off, and finally merge the three in a gripping climax. To be sure, there were some sections where the meanings became obscured, but they were not too opaque to be cleared up by recutting and by the proper handling of music and sound effects. One has to imagine the finished print with these elements added.

The final reel is before us and the three strangers, propelled by an evil fate, are brought together. I see Miss Fitzgerald seated near a radio, listening transfixed and oblivious to the ranting of Sydney Greenstreet and the piano playing of Peter Lorre. This being the work print, the sound of the piano is indicated for only a measure or two; the complete piece will be added in the re-recording process. The same applies to the radio announcer who is presumed to be describing the Grand National Steeplechase. Inexorably the emotional stress of the scene increases; I have a momentary flash of the musical problems to be solved, but the threat of impending violence again commands my attention to the exclusion of technical problems. The film fades out on a bizarre note; the lights flash on, and we look at each other. To the question marks which I see in the eyes of the Messrs. Reinhardt and Negulesco I give an honest nod of approval. The looks give way to conversation. We voice our opinions in generally favorable terms, meanwhile standing and stretching. Once these preliminaries are out of the way, we settle down to a review of the picture in relation to musical treatment. The odds are very one-sided. Nine reels of picture (roughly ninety minutes of screen play) are not quickly assimilated. The writer, the director, and the producer have lived with the picture from its beginnings, whereas I am basing my opinions on the superficial impressions of a single screening. My only advantages are a fresh perspective and my past experience in scoring dramatic films.

Thus begins a belated and makeshift collaboration. The music I am about to write is expected to become an integral part of the screen play, heighten the emotional appeal, be so deftly a part of the drama that it has its effect upon an audience without their being conscious of it. "Unobtrusive" is the gold standard for a dramatic score. In the weeks of preparation of the script and with the knowledge that music was going to play an important part in their film the writers did not discuss this basic component with the composer. The problem for me is now one of adapting music to the tempi of acting, the spaces between spoken lines, fade-ins and fade-outs, gestures, reactions, and a dozen other conditions arbitrarily crystallized on the film. My job has become one of conforming rather than of collaborating.

We begin with Mr. Reinhardt's suggestion of identifying each stranger with a distinctive theme. I add to the idea by naming specific instruments to characterize them further. Negulesco would like a violin for Miss Fitzgerald. I do not quarrel with the idea; a violin can express the kind of femininity portrayed by Miss Fitzgerald. In her more violent moods I can harden the string quality with a muted trumpet. We are debating the proper place at which to introduce these individual themes (a decision that should have been made before the picture started shooting). "If you would precede the main title with individual close-ups of the three principals and give each one footage enough, I could introduce their themes effectively before the story begins." There is some hesitancy over my suggestion, because it will involve a radical change in the format of the title. The idea appeals to all present, however, and we decide to use it if the "front office" authorizes the change.

The discussion moves on to the sequence with the chimes in it; it is an involved one. Preceding the chimes there is a period of dramatic silence, the lights are switched out, Miss Fitzgerald lights some candles and the group intently watches the image of Kwan Yin. The script, I recall, directs that the first chime be heard as the picture cuts to a "BIG HEAD CLOSE-UP OF KWAN YIN," and the last chime, just before Mr. Greenstreet strikes a match. The picture wasn't shot to the accurate length of twelve chimes, and we are obliged to consider ways of stretching the chimes so that they begin and end in the right places. This, we decide, will be a job of manipulating the spacing of the music, and of the chimes, and some discreet cutting of the film. Messrs. Reinhardt and Negulesco are content to leave this in our hands.

Our next point is the very important one of finding a suitable device to punctuate the beginnings and endings of the three stories that interweave throughout the play. The audience must see and, if possible, hear where one story is interrupted and another is begun. The visual problem can be solved by using any one of a variety of optical distortions; it is the oil dissolve that is chosen. To the audience it will appear as a series of ripples across the screen that blur the images as they melt from one to the other. In matching this oil dissolve I must devise an unusual sound as if the music were being blurred by the same ripple. My inner ear suggests a small combination of instruments, some electric, that will produce an oily sound contrasting sharply with the legitimate instrumentation preceding it. Two vibraphones, two harps, marimba, and cymbal, recorded with a fluctuating volume control, will do the trick. The audience will see and hear the ripples, I assure my collaborators.

The final scene now receives some attention. Here again the screen action dictates the handling of the accompanying sounds. We know that a radio announcer is describing the Grand National and that at a certain point in the sequence the screen characters react to his shout of "They're off." We see Lorre start and stop playing the piano, and we will record a suitable length of piano music to match his actions. The scene presents a rare problem in dynamic levels of sound. Our theater audience must hear the spoken lines of the cast, so these will have to be re-recorded at the top range of audibility. At a slightly lower level the piano must be heard; still lower, the radio announcer, and behind his voice the murmurs and exclamations of the crowd at the race. "The idea," Reinhardt says, "is to play Greenstreet's lines against a confusion of sound that seems intent on frustrating his desire to be heard. He is competing with the radio and the piano for the attention of the other two persons in the room." It is the kind of drama that is ideally suited to the film medium, where one has complete control over the elements of sound. "I'll work with George and Alex (a sound engineer) on this. It won't be easy, but I think we'll give you the effect." Having seen examples of sound wizardry in other pictures of ours, Reinhardt, Negulesco, and Koch are content to leave the scene to us.

The ending of the picture presents no further problems and so our little group in Projection Room 6 begins to melt away. After a screening of this sort there is always some reluctance to break up a meeting before double checking with each other to be sure that we all understand what was agreed upon during the running. Howard Koch, the writer, moves off. He is glad to have met me. "So am I," I answer (fervently), considering myself fortunate to have had even one casual meeting with him. Mr. Reinhardt and Mr. Negulesco say their goodbyes fully confident that the music department will do a good job. Mr. Forbstein assures them that they will be happy with the music and suggests that, in view of a tentative preview date, we had better get right on the first three reels.

"Getting right on the first three reels" means that we will run each one through several times, analyzing them carefully for music cues. Upon deciding which sequences are to be underscored, we look for the exact spot, within the fraction of a second, to begin and end the music. Each musical entrance must coincide with some significant event on the screen. Sometimes it comes in on a change of facial expression, the sharp reaction of a character, a threatening gesture, a walk, a change of scene, a sudden cut from long shot to close-up or vice versa, a meaningful remark, an off-screen noise, a letter, or a weapon, violent physical action, or some other dramatic reason.

During this crucial stage of what really amounts to dramatic construction, my inventiveness is circumscribed and dominated by the preestablished pace of direction and camera movement crystallized on the film now before me. Collaboration with the writer and director is no longer possible. The cutter will cooperate as far as he possibly can, but he, too, works within these limitations. For example, if a musical phrase cannot be uttered without undue distortion of tempo, either fast or slow, it might be possible for the cutter to cheat a foot of film to accommodate the music. The word "cheat" is used literally here because the cutter, in making changes after the reels have been approved by the producer, runs the risk of being called to task for making unauthorized changes. It is a significant commentary on standardized film production that so much composer-cutter collaboration is carried on furtively, like the Underground.

When the reels have been analyzed, the actual task of composing music begins. To supplement the mental images formed in my mind I will have typewritten cue sheets. Every spoken word, action, camera movement, and cut is written down and measured; the timings are given both in footage and in fractions of seconds. The mysterious process by which composers create music has never been fathomed. Add to this mystery the self-control, the discipline of subordinating one's inspiration to a cue sheet, and further complicate the procedure with a delivery deadline, and you gain some idea of the conditions under which I shall write approximately one hour's worth of music (the equivalent, in length, to one act of *Tristan*) in four weeks.

The composer is not worth his salt who assumes that his obligations as a collaborator end after the music is written. A new and vital phase of mutual effort begins, on the sound-recording stage. My next collaborator is the recording engineer, David Forrest, whose handling of the sensitive microphones and volume controls on the music-recording stage is termed "mixing." The responsibility of getting the best possible music recording is placed squarely upon the mixer's shoulders by his department head. Left to his own judgment, Dave, who reads an orchestral score in addition to his volume indicators, will capture a picture of my music on the sound track that meets the required standards of the studio. He will not, however, plumb the inner dramatic meanings of the score unless I make them clear to him first. By exploiting the acoustic flexibilities of film recording I can invest my music with qualities that will complement the mystic atmosphere of *Three Strangers*. Parts of the score must be recorded with clarity, others with a diffused quality; some must sound intimate, others distant; here and there I take "stage liberty" and ask for excessive reverberation in one section of the orchestra, combined with natural presence in the others.

The microphone is a camera that records sound, and, like the cameraman, the mixer will direct the placement of the microphones to obtain the quality of recording I have asked for. Many times during the playing of a piece of music the microphone becomes a mobile unit, swinging in to pick up at close range, then returning to a normal placement. If necessary, Dave will employ several microphones at varying distances from the source of sound. There is nothing static about a recording stage. Instruments are at times moved and regrouped for special results; in fact, the very walls of the room are mounted on hinged sections that can be adjusted to alter acoustic characteristics. Equipped with all these devices, the mixer is an important factor in contemporary film technique and certainly a collaborator to be accepted by every writer as well as composer if screen plays are to possess a multidimensional aural quality rather than a flat single plane of sound.

Three Strangers presented many opportunities for the manipulation of recording qualities. Right in the introduction, for instance, where the close-ups of the principals were used, we decided to match the photographic proximity with a corresponding close pickup of the solo instruments. The image on the screen was big and the tone of the instrument was big. Following the title came the London atmosphere, Piccadilly Circus at night, traffic and crowd noise. The music I had written attempted to sound British and at the same time to give the feeling of a lot of things going on simultaneously. Dave and I agreed that we should attempt to get as much clarity of recording as possible, to bring out the counterrhythms and contrapuntal lines in the orchestra. Later on in the picture we had a scene on the bank of the Thames, a night shot, damp and foggy. The orchestration reflected this mood, which we further enhanced by using a very reverberant pickup. The result was a diffused shimmer of sound like the distant murmur of a metropolis, a perfect accompaniment for the occasion. For the image of Kwan Yin I wanted a detached quality as if the Oriental strain, played by seven instruments, were coming from a great distance. This was accomplished by performing the music softly and picking it up at twice the normal distance.

In one of the final sequences there was a frightening shot of Sydney Greenstreet walking into the camera, his huge hulk filling the screen. The full orchestra was used, but to heighten further the feeling of the demoniac characterization we "miked" the bass section of the orchestra to get a massive sound that became louder as the actor came closer. The result was a gripping combination of sight and sound.

The deliberate distortion of musical balance and perspective is thus an important adjunct to film technique. The uses of this device should be fully exploited, not only by the composer working in collaboration with the mixer, but also by the screen writer in collaboration with the composer. A shooting script may very well incorporate notations on aural perspective to supplement the camera angle and all the descriptive material considered necessary to achieve a well-integrated and artistic result.

Once all the music for *Three Strangers* is recorded on film, the negative goes to the laboratory to be developed. Usually this is an overnight job. The positive prints of the music tracks are sent to the Dupe Building to be cut into their respective reels.

Let me take you to the Dupe Room where Jerry Alexander is dubbing the first reel of *Three Strangers*. Jerry and his assistant sit at a sound-control panel facing the screen. Each knob on the panel controls a different sound track, and the number of knobs required depends upon the complexity of the sound pattern in the reel. The speech of the principals, the shuffling of feet on the pavement, traffic sounds, crowd sounds, the tap-tap of a steel-ferruled cane, the chimes of Big Ben, a wind effect, and the musical score comprise the setup of the sound pattern for the first reel. Detailed cue sheets serve as a guide to indicate the exact footage at which the sounds and music will occur.

Jerry signals his projectionist, the room is darkened, and we watch the illuminated footage meter at the right of the screen, which is synchronized with the projection machine. The meter serves as a warning guide for incoming and outgoing sounds, also as a quick check if any imperfection of quality or bad synchronization of sound with the picture is apparent. "This is only a rough rehearsal, so don't expect too much," Jerry always says when the composer is present, usually to forestall a request for more music—louder, louder. The rehearsal is rough; some effects are too loud, some too soft; music entrances are faded in too slowly and the whole reel seems a confused jumble. "Rewind," Jerry signals, "and we'll run it again." The second rehearsal is smoother and the pattern of sound begins to make more sense. While the reel is being rewound for a third rehearsal I talk over the musical dynamics with Jerry. "Hold it down a little so that the tapping of Greenstreet's cane comes over." "Fade in sooner when they sign their names." "Blend it with the wind effect and increase the volume as the candle goes out." "Hold the Kwan Yin theme down." The next rehearsal gets under way and my suggestions are tried; they all work out except the cane tapping; that is out of balance. Jerry is now becoming familiar with the sound content of the reel, and each successive rehearsal shows a marked improvement. A few more adjustments and we are ready for a final take. Overhead a red light indicates that this run is a take; there will be no conversation in the room to distract the two dubbers from their sensitive task. The picture fades in, the title music starts, and we know that downstairs the light valve is recording on a strip of film one-tenth of an inch wide a pattern of modulations that will reproduce the speech, music, and noises in exactly the same relative proportions as those in which Jerry is mixing them. The reel is over, the lights brighten. "How do you like it?" "O.K. for me," I reply, and the first thousand feet of *Three Strangers* is ready to print. "Lunch," announces Jerry. It has taken three hours to rehearse and record ten minutes of sound.

Returning from lunch, I notice the NO ADMITTANCE sign on the door of the Dupe Building and ask Jerry whether that includes writers and directors. "It sure does; departmental rule," he replies. "Hum," is my guarded comment, as I ponder the wisdom of keeping these talents ignorant of this important phase of film making.

The dubbing of the next seven reels moves along smoothly. We have occasion to add an echo to the sounds in two places: one is a scene under Battersea Bridge; the other, a corridor in a jail. We work out an interesting transition from a train effect underscored with music to a cracked phonograph record repeating a phrase monotonously. We exaggerate an orchestral crescendo and punctuate it with the impact of a weapon hitting the floor—pure cinematic liberty to shock an audience.

The final reel containing the critical scene of the Grand National coming over the radio, the tense dialogue in the room, and Lorre's piano playing, commands our attention for the better part of a day. We are occupied, for the most part, with finding the proper dynamic levels, playing them higher or lower as the camera follows the action from one side of the room to the other, and never once losing the intelligibility of the on-screen dialogue. It is fascinating to watch the hands of Jerry and his assistant as they play the multiple controls during this scene. Satisfied with our last rehearsal, we decide to try our luck. We have notified Leo Forbstein and George Amy that reel 9 is ready for a take and they are in the room as the reel starts. Our audience is augmented by some sound cutters and technicians, since word has reached them that reel 9 of *Three Strangers* is up; they watch with critical attention. The take is made, but proves unsatisfactory. We ask for reactions and get them. Some discussion follows. It is decided to cheat the piano out sooner and play up the dramatic scoring in one spot. This time the take is good and our dubbing job is done.

The completed sound track now goes to the laboratory to be developed, printed, and combined with the picture in a master negative. A positive print will be made as quickly as possible because our sneak preview deadline is two days away. The exact time and place of the sneak is a studio secret, known only to a few department heads. On the evening of the event, a favored few of us will receive two hours' advance notice, naming an outlying theater and an approximate starting time. "Eight-thirty tonight at the Cascade Theater." At eight-thirty we submit our work to the public. By ten o'clock we shall have its verdict, not in writing but through an intangible series of telepathic signals—"audience reaction."

Outside the Cascade Theater the same group which four weeks ago met in Room 6 greet each other. Awaiting the arrival of Jack Warner and his associates, we make conversation, carefully avoiding the topic uppermost in our minds. My eye wanders over the line of cash customers—our jury. I am counting the infants in arms and the popcorn bags, wondering if their cacophony will obliterate the subtle nuances of our play.

The arrival of the Jack Warner party is our signal to file into the theater. As the last newsreel clip thunders from the screen, we settle ourselves in the section reserved for us. Recorded several decibels higher than feature pictures, all newsreels leave the ears tingling. A normal recording following the news sounds puny, and if the proscenium curtains are closed the effect is that of an underwater performance.

"Ladies and gentlemen, we present a Warner Brothers feature preview," the voice from behind the closed curtains announces, with an air of confidence not shared by us. A murmur of anticipation fills the house and as the close-up of Geraldine Fitzgerald fades in the murmur surges into exclamations of approval. Another surge as the patrons recognize Sydney Greenstreet and his co-artist Peter Lorre. The musical themes of identification are lost in the shuffle, but I am not too concerned, knowing that the element of surprise will not be present in a regularly advertised performance. As the title fades out and the picture begins, we concentrate on the screen as though we had never seen *Three Strangers* before. This is not entirely because an audience is present; much of the unfamiliarity stems from the fact that the screen play has acquired a new aural dimension since it was run in Room 6.

The background of music and sound against which the actors perform and speak their lines is at this time doubly conspicuous to the writer, the director, and the producer. Accustomed as they are to the simple picture-and-word form of the work print, these added sounds must seem obtrusive. More than once during the preview I glance in Howard Koch's direction as a piece of musical underscoring begins while his lines are being spoken. As we did not collaborate on the script, I am sure he is having many surprises. It is a disquieting thought.

As the picture nears its end the cumulative result of the nine reels run in continuity before an audience manifests itself in a number of ways. We see our work in true perspective and all the details merged into a whole. Our senses of self-appraisal and criticism are sharpened; the glow of accomplishment is tempered by the sobering knowledge that some places might have been better. As for the score, I am acutely aware of some irritating musical mutilations and incoherences that could have been avoided if I had been able to work with Howard Koch, John Huston, and Jean Negulesco *before* the picture was shot. It is incongruous that two such vital ingredients as the music and sound effects should receive so little consideration in the plotting of the script. The musical score of this film was heard during two-thirds of the running time, more than 60 per cent of its total footage—by no means an inconsequential contribution. Is music the leavening in the loaf of bread, or merely the gaudy icing hastily poured over a cake to conceal some doubtful ingredients? Surely, it's the leavening.

The curtain closes, the audience applauds, but long before this we are aware of its favorable verdict.

Our group files out of the theater and assembles in the manager's office for the usual confab and review of notes made during the running. This time, the notes are few and the changes are slight. Jack Warner nods his approval to the circle of inquiring faces and, as if to confirm his feelings, offers Reinhardt a cigar. The tension eases, there are some pleasantries, and we gather our hats and coats. Reinhardt smiles from behind his Havana perfecto.

In the lobby Howard Koch approaches me. Is he thinking that I have smothered some of his best lines? My momentary suspense is relieved by his smile. "The music helped a lot," he remarks quietly. Jean Negulesco joins us as we walk to the parking lot. "Beautiful score, Adolph"—his enthusiasm is sincere. "Thanks, Jean! Maybe on our next picture we won't have to work like *Three Strangers*."

16

Miklós Rózsa: *"Quo Vadis"* (1951)

Along with Erich Wolfgang Korngold, who enjoyed a formidable reputation as
a front-rank opera composer in Europe long before he worked for Warner Bros.
in the 1930s, Miklós Rózsa (1907–95) came to the West Coast in 1940 as an
already successful classical composer of impeccable pedigree. At the age of
nineteen he had left his native Hungary to study musicology and composition
at the Leipzig Conservatory, and his early concert works received regular performances in Continental Europe during the late 1920s and early 1930s. His time
in Paris led to an encounter with Swiss composer Arthur Honegger, who, fresh
from scoring *Les Misérables* (dir. Raymond Bernard, 1934), encouraged him to
seek employment as a film composer. This Rózsa duly did: in 1937 he joined
the British film company London Films, whose guiding spirit Alexander Korda
(a fellow Hungarian expatriate) took him to Hollywood three years later when
he was writing the music for *The Thief of Baghdad*—a movie that quickly earned
the composer the first of a remarkable series of no fewer than seventeen
Academy Award nominations.

Although Rózsa was to maintain his output of concert music in later life,
writing (among many other classical works) a violin concerto for Jascha Heifetz
in 1953, he is best remembered for his innovative film scores. His dual composing careers are referred to in the title of his fascinating autobiography
Double Life (Tunbridge Wells: Midas Books; New York: Hippocrene Books,
1982), its title borrowed from a film (dir. George Cukor, 1947) for which
his score won one of his three Academy Awards. Rózsa's book, which is long

Source: Film/TV Music 11/4 (November–December 1951); reprinted in James L. Limbacher, ed., *Film Music: From Violins to Video* (Metuchen, N.J.: Scarecrow Press, 1974): 147–53.

overdue a reprint, is not only a vivid account of his Hollywood days, but also an important source of information on musical life in Europe and America in the twentieth century.

Rózsa remained loyal to his European cultural roots and always felt something of an outsider on the West Coast. He had an unwaveringly low opinion of hack film composers, inane producers, and untrained music directors, and the views he expressed both of them and of their working environment were sometimes caustic. It is difficult, for example, to imagine many other multi-Oscar-winning composers describing the usually treasured awards as "those stupid little statuettes." In several places in his memoirs Rózsa refers to an anonymous "Musical Director" who constantly attempted to interfere with his compositional style, which was in some quarters felt to be too dissonant and modernistic for its humble purpose; this figure was Louis Lipstone, head of the music department at Paramount Pictures when Rózsa was scoring a succession of films for director Billy Wilder, including *Five Graves to Cairo* (1943) and *Double Indemnity* (1944)—the latter a fine film noir, a genre for which Rózsa evolved a new and influentially gritty musical style well suited to the uncomfortable angst-ridden atmosphere prevalent in the bleak Hollywood films emerging as the Second World War came to a close. His noir modernism, sometimes colored by the distinctive electronic timbre of the theremin, proved equally appropriate for psychological and social dramas such as Wilder's *Lost Weekend* (1945), Alfred Hitchcock's *Spellbound* (1945), and Fritz Lang's *Secret Beyond the Door* (1948).

During Rózsa's highly productive period as a staff composer at MGM (1948–62), he worked for directors Vincente Minnelli (*Madame Bovary*, 1949) and John Huston (*The Asphalt Jungle*, 1950), before pioneering a new sense of musical authenticity in the scoring of such lavish "historico-biblical" epics as *Quo Vadis* (dir. Mervyn LeRoy, 1951), *Ben-Hur* (dir. William Wyler, 1959), *King of Kings* (dir. Nicholas Ray, 1961), and *El Cid* (dir. Anthony Mann, 1961)—projects that gave Rózsa the chance to work for prolonged spells in his beloved Europe as Hollywood increasingly shot its "sword and sandal" spectacles abroad in a rather misguided attempt to keep otherwise wildly escalating costs down. In the article below, written in 1951 shortly after he completed his innovative music to *Quo Vadis*, Rózsa recounts his first attempts to spearhead a new kind of historical realism in scoring motion pictures with a period setting.

A motion picture with historical background always presents interesting problems to the composer. There have been innumerable other historical pictures produced before *Quo Vadis*, and they were all alike in their negligent attitude toward the stylistic accuracy of their music. It is interesting to note what pains-taking research is usually made to ascertain the year of publication of, let us say, "Yes, We Have No Bananas," if it is used in a picture about the twenties, but no one seems to care much if the early Christians in the 1st century A. D. sing "Onward Christian Soldiers" by Sir Arthur Sullivan, composed a mere 1800 years later! When a period picture is made, the historical background of the script is naturally based on historical facts and the dialogue tries to avoid any anachronistic term or reference. The art director, interior decorator, costume designer, hair-stylist and makeup man start their work only after thorough research, and the greatest care is taken that every building, every piece of furni-ture, every costume and every hairdo is absolutely authentic according to the period of the picture. During the actual photographing a historical advisor, usu-ally a scholar of reputation, supervises this procedure so that nothing can slip in and spoil the absolute authenticity.

Why is it then when we come to music an exceptionally lofty attitude is felt and no one seems to care much about the genuineness of this most important factor of picture making? The countless dramatizations of antiquity in operas and oratorios naturally have not attempted to recreate the music of the period, as opera is stylized art and, therefore, the music is also a stylized adaptation of a certain historical or nationalistic style. No one expects to hear 16th-century Min-nesanger music in *Die Meistersinger*, antique Greek music in *Electra*, or ancient Hebrew music in *Salome*. The orientalism in *Aida, Samson and Delilah* or *Queen of Sheba* is only used as color and they are full-blooded, romantic operas mirror-ing the style of the period of their creation with no attempt whatsoever to represent the true style of the period of their action. But the motion picture is different. It is realistic and factual. It not only tries to capture the spirit of bygone eras but also tries to make believe that it projects before the eyes of the spectator the real thing. There are no painted backdrops, fake props, cardboard shields and wooden swords as in an opera, but everything is realistic to the fullest limit and if the public doesn't believe that the Christians were actually eaten by the lions, the photoplay would have completely failed in its objective.

When *Quo Vadis* was assigned to me I decided to be stylistically, absolutely correct. First, thorough research had to be made. Though my old studies of the music of antiquity came in handy now, I am most indebted to the librarian of Metro-Goldwyn-Mayer studios, Mr. George Schneider, who with unfailing enthusiasm and unceasing effort produced every reference to the period that could be found in the libraries throughout the four corners of the world.

Our first duty was to prepare the blueprints for the antique instruments which had to be made. We reconstructed these from Roman statues (in the

Vatican and Naples museums), antique vases and bas-reliefs on columns and tombstones, giving exact measurements for all details. The actual instruments were then produced by Italian instrument makers, so a great array of lyras and cytharas (the chief instruments of the Romans), double pipes (aulos), curved horns (buccina), straight trumpets (salpynx or tuba), tambourines, drums, sistrums, clappers and other percussion instruments were made with amazing likeness to the real ones.

Then the music which was to be performed on-scene had to be prepared. To select music for a historical picture of the middle ages, for instance, would have been an easy task, as there is a wealth of material available. But this is not the case with Roman music from the year A.D. 64. In spite of the fact that a great amount of Roman literature, painting, architecture and sculpture has been preserved, there is absolutely no actual record of any music of the classical times of Roman history. There are a lot of references to music in literary works of the time, so we know what an important part music played in the life of the Romans. Seneca complains that orchestras and choruses grew to gigantic proportions and often there were more singers and players in the theater than spectators. There were numerous schools of music, and daughters of the rich bourgoisie had to learn to play the lyre just as they have to learn the piano today. The slaves of the aristocrats entertained constantly and Seneca complains that "at table no one can talk for the music!" (An early forerunner of the menace of our radios.) All this proves that music was widely practiced and belonged to everyday life.

In *Quo Vadis* there were three distinguishable styles in which music had to be created. Firstly, the music of the Romans, such as the songs of Nero and the slave girl Eunice, sacrificial hymn of the Vestal, marches and fanfares. Secondly, the hymns of the Christians; and thirdly, the music performed by slaves, which I call the Roman Empire music. As nothing remains of Roman music, this had to be recreated by deduction. We know that the culture of the Romans was entirely borrowed from the Greeks. Greek civilization and religion dominated Roman life and Nero himself preferred to speak Greek rather than Latin. As Greek musicians and instruments were imported and Greek musical theory adopted, the music of the Romans cannot be separated from its Greek models and ideas. It was, therefore, not incorrect to reconstruct this music from Greek examples. About the music of the Greeks we know considerably more. We know their thorough and involved musical systems, we can read their musical notations and we also have about twelve relics of actual music, preserved mostly on tombstones and old papyri. These were of the greatest value in this attempt at reconstruction. The Skolion of Sikilos, which is perhaps the oldest known musical relic with a definite melody in our modern sense, became the basic idea from which I developed Nero's first song, "The Burning of Troy." It is in Phrygian mode and dates from the 1st or 2nd century.

The second song of Nero, "The Burning of Rome," uses a Gregorian anthem, "Omnes sitientos venite ad aquas," as a point of departure. This is a reverse method of reconstruction, but if we accept the theory that much Roman music became Christian (as we shall see later), we can select from the early Christian music where the origin cannot be proven, and presume that the original source was Roman. For Eunice's song I used the first Ode of Pindar, music for which was allegedly found in a Sicilian monastery in 1650. Its authenticity is doubtful, but it is constructed entirely on Greek principles and it is a hauntingly beautiful melody. Fragments from an anonymous composer from the 2nd century, which probably were written for a cythara school, were interesting enough to serve as a point of departure for an instrumental piece, used as a bacchanale at Nero's banquet. The 5/8 time is characteristic of Greek music.

The main problem that arose with all these original melodies was how to harmonize them. Whether the Greeks or Romans knew harmonies, or was their music entirely monodic, is still a hotly debated question. Polyphony in our modern sense was, of course, unknown except that of parallel octaves, which hardly can be called polyphony. Only six intervals, the 4th, the 5th, the octaves, and their higher octaves, were known and allowed as consonances.

As the music for *Quo Vadis* was intended for dramatic use and as entertainment for the lay public, one had to avoid the pitfall of producing only musicological oddities instead of music with a universal, emotional appeal. For the modern ear, instrumental music in unison has very little emotional or aesthetic appeal; therefore I had to find a way for an archaic sounding harmonization which gives warmth, color, and emotional values to these melodies. A parallelism with open fifths and fourths came in most handy and also a modal harmonization suggested by the different (Lydian, Phrygian, Dorian, Mixolydian, etc.) modes of the melodies in question. In the second category for which authentic music had to be supplied, were the hymns of the early Christians. These also had to be reconstructed by deduction. Saint Ambrose's collection of liturgical music for the Catholic Church appeared about four hundred years after our period and I wanted to go back to the very source from which the Ambrosian plain chant and later the Gregorian hymnology blossomed. As the early Christians were partly Jews and partly Greeks their liturgical music naturally originates from these two sources. These two influences have been proven and are prevalent in the Gregorian hymns which are the fundamental of the Roman Catholic Church music.

The first time we meet organized Christianity in the picture, we see Saint Paul baptizing new believers and we hear them singing a hymn. A Babylonian

Jewish liturgical melody (which found its way into the Gregorian hymnody, becoming a Kyrie) served as basis for this hymn. I used it in the manner of a cantus responsorius, where the priest intones a phrase and the congregation answers it. To achieve the authentic timbre and feeling of its rendition, we engaged a Jewish cantor to sing the part of the priest.

As the second major influence on the early Christian music was Greek, I selected a melody from a Greek hymn which had the beauty and fervor needed for the Christians to sing in the arena. The Hymn to Nemesis which was discovered by Vincenzo Galilei in the 17th century but dates from the 2nd century, seemed to me perfect for this purpose. The third hymn, which is sung by the Christians burning on the crosses in the arena, had to have a plaintive character which I found in the Ambrosian Aeterna Conditor.

It goes without saying that all these hymns are performed in the picture in unison (or octaves) unharmonized, as they were sung two thousand years ago. The English words were written by Hugh Gray, who also served as historical advisor on the picture and displayed great feeling for the style and character of the time of antiquity.

The third category of the music was the music of the slaves, mostly Babylonians, Syrians, Egyptians, Persians and other conquered nations of oriental origin. There were fragments of the oldest melodies found in Sicily (a Roman province), with Arabian influence, and others found in Cairo, which I could utilize.

The orchestration of the music performed on-scene was another problem. None of the old instruments were available and, therefore, the archaic sound had to be created with our modern instruments. I used a small Scottish harp, the clarsach, and this delicate instrument gave a remarkably true likeness to the sound of the lyre and antique harp. For military music, cornets, mixed with trumpets and trombones, gave the roughness of the early brass instruments. Bass flute and English horn replaced the sound of the aulos. Our modern percussion instruments come close to the antique ones and therefore it was safe to use tambourines, jingles, drums of different shapes and sizes, and cymbals. Bowed stringed instruments, however, could not be used. These came into usage nearly a thousand years after our period so they would have been completely anachronistic. For music that was supposed to be performed by a large group of players I took the liberty of using the string group of the orchestra playing pizzicato to reinforce the main body of the orchestra. Harps and guitars were also added to achieve the percussive quality. Melodic lines, however, were only given to the woodwind and brass instruments to perform.

"Another part of the forest" is the dramatic accompanying music which, for yet undetected reasons, Hollywood semantics calls "the score." The main function of this music is to heighten the drama, create the atmosphere and underline the emotional content of certain scenes. A stylistically, strictly correct music corresponding to our period could not have supplied these aims to the modern spectator and listener. Although I have constructed my themes on classical principles and was able to use a few fragments from historical relics, these had to be harmonized to make them emotionally appealing. A romantic, chromatic harmonization would have been out of place and a simple modal harmonization seemed to me the closest to the character of this music. The modern major and minor triads were unknown factors to the Romans, but our modern ears are so used to these sounds that it would have been impossible to ignore them completely.

The main themes of the score of *Quo Vadis* are the following: The opening prelude is a choral setting of the words "Quo Vadis Domine?" and its translation, "Lord, Whither Goest Thou?" The melodic line of this theme was modeled on the Gregorian, "Libera me Domie," and Kyrie. Behind this urging question of Christianity we hear the interrupting fanfares of Roman buccinas. A recurring of faith first appears in the garden where Lygia draws a fish, the symbol of the early Christians. The love theme is first heard in Plautius' gardens in the scene between Lygia and Marcus and is a musical reflection of Lydia's gentle character and deep faith. The Triumph introduces Marcus Vinicius' contrasting theme of pagan heroism and self-confidence. An interesting chromatic motif from the second Delphic hymn was utilized as a motif of menace and tension in the scene where Lygia is taken as hostage. A motif from "The Hymn to the Sun" appears majestically in the brass when Rome is in flames. A motif of four chords introduces the Miracle scene, when the Lord talks to St. Peter and then the voices of angels intone the "Quo Vadis" theme. A theme of doom accompanies the suicide scene of Nero.

The dramatic music of *Quo Vadis* is much less polyphonic than my previous film scores, for the only reason that extended polyphony would have clashed anachronistically with monodic music performed on-scene throughout the picture. At the end of the picture the voices of humanity take up the "Quo Vadis" theme and after the answer of Christ they join in a jubilant reprise of the hymn, "By the Light of the Dawn." For those who want to study the music of *Quo Vadis* more thoroughly, there is a record album from the sound tracks and a piano score, with the most important themes together with pictures and historical notes.

17

André Previn: *No Minor Chords* (1991)

André Previn (b. 1929) began work at Metro-Goldwyn-Mayer as a precocious teenage pianist, arranger, and would-be composer. Miklós Rózsa became something of a mentor to the prodigy, declaring in *Double Life* (New York: Hippocrene Books, 1982): "I am proud to claim the credit for making him use a proper full orchestral score at recording sessions rather than the 'piano-conductor' parts in vogue. . . . [A]t the studios it was a real and rare pleasure to come into contact with someone who both was musical and loved music" (157). Rózsa's pride here looks knowingly ahead to the classical conducting career for which Previn is best known today, though the successful conductor has also remained active as a pianist and composer. In the 1960s he had become much in demand on the international orchestral circuit, and abandoned the film industry in order to hold major conductorships with the symphony orchestras of Houston, London, Pittsburgh, Los Angeles, and Oslo.

During Previn's time as principal conductor of the London Symphony Orchestra (1969–79), his friendship with film composer John Williams resulted in the LSO's engagement to record Williams's seminal scores to George Lucas's first *Star Wars* trilogy (see p. 233), but otherwise Previn left his movie roots firmly in the past. This was much to the bafflement of Hollywood musicians who well knew how much money he might have earned had he continued to pursue a career as a film composer. During his London years Previn delighted in recounting how two former Hollywood associates came to

Source: No Minor Chords: My Days in Hollywood (New York/London: Doubleday, 1991/1992): 16–21, 33–36, 38–40, 62–64, 102–5, 121–24, 138–42, 150–52, 155–59.

hear him conduct Beethoven's Ninth Symphony at the Royal Festival Hall, and as they sat in the audience, one was overheard to remark to the other (without the trace of a smile): "Gee, isn't it tragic how André has screwed up his career?"

These excerpts from Previn's often hilarious memoirs begin with his initial experiences of jobbing work at the MGM studios as a bright-eyed sixteen-year-old, where his first encounter was with musical director Georgie Stoll, and his later work for composer Herbert Stothart and studio moguls Sam Goldwyn, Dore Schary, and Irving Thalberg. (It was the latter's legendarily inept edict instructing MGM composers to refrain from using minor chords that gave Previn's book its title.) Previn describes the tense atmosphere prevailing at the studio during the anticommunist witch hunts that began in the late 1940s and came to have a seriously detrimental effect on the industry's creative talent during the 1950s. Among the film-scoring assignments discussed in his book are the superior western *Bad Day at Black Rock* (dir. John Sturges, 1955), *Designing Woman* (dir. Vincente Minnelli, 1957), and the four musicals for which he won Academy Awards: *Gigi* (dir. Minnelli, 1958), *Porgy and Bess* (dir. Otto Preminger, 1959), *Irma La Douce* (dir. Billy Wilder, 1963), and *My Fair Lady* (dir. George Cukor, 1964). In contrast to Rózsa, Previn cheerfully admits to having been temporarily brainwashed by the "Twilight Zone" of the AMPAS award ceremonies and offers an amusing musician's-eye account of how they were organized at the time.

Looking at the Irving Thalberg Building, and admiring its thirties facade, I turned to my right and found myself looking into the drive-in gates of the studio itself. These gates were closely watched and guarded. No one drove or walked in without being checked and identified by the uniformed gateman, a gentleman named—no, I'm not making this up—Kenneth Hollywood. Whether the name came before the job, or the job before the name, remained a mystery throughout my dozen years in the place, but surely no Restoration play ever boasted a more directly named personage.

When I arrived, he checked his list of the day and found that I had indeed an appointment with one of the studio's composers, Georgie Stoll, and I was waved through with the instruction that I should report to the music library first, to fill out a few papers.

All the music department bungalows were clumped together, on a street to the left of the main thoroughfare. These little houses were truly dilapidated, with banging screen doors and peeling paint, but to my sixteen-year-old eye they all resembled Le Petit Trianon. I found the music library. It consisted of many huge, high-ceilinged rooms, all filled with every note ever written for the studio. Songs, scores, arrangements, utility music, Academy Award efforts, and football marches, all in the manuscripts of the composers. I subsequently spent countless hours idly going through these drawers and coming up with really fascinating musical relics, all irreplaceable. A couple of decades later, a new studio chief, James Aubrey, ordered all the music in the MGM library burned, in order to make some extra space. Tons of score paper were incinerated, all covered with penciled notes—hours, weeks, months, years of effort thrown away. In the rooms immediately beyond these vaults were the copyists' offices. In 1946 there must have been at least twenty copyists under contract, each of them working all day long, just to keep up with the ceaseless flow of new music being handed in. Presiding over this was Arthur Berg, one of the three chief librarians.

'You hand in all your work to me,' he said. 'I'll get it copied, make out your union bill, and then you can get paid.'

He was a man then in his sixties, with the kind of immaculate white hair that usually goes with Florida car salesmen. He had the sort of reddish baby complexion that looks as if he had never found it necessary to shave. I was in awe of him that first day, figuring that the keeper of such archives would be a walking Grove's Dictionary of Music. I was wrong about that. He liked to compose, from time to time, not movie music, but little, anachronistic piano pieces, usually called 'Album Leaves' or 'Dance of the Elves', suitable for display on the music rack of upright pianos. While I was filling in the employment forms Arthur handed me, I sneaked a look at the roster of the music department, nailed to the wall. The contract composers were Miklós Rózsa, Herbert Stothart, Bronislaw Kaper, Lennie Hayton, Georgie Stoll, Scott Bradley, David Snell, Adolph Deutsch, and David Raksin. I knew all about them. I could recite all their credits. I was not anywhere near being able to join their company, but I was very pleased to be in the same place. My reverie was interrupted by the entrance of another librarian, Jules Megeff. Jules was relaxed and always seemed slightly amused. He introduced himself to me and asked what I was supposed to be doing at the studio. I told him.

'Well, well,' he said, smiling. 'So you're another little helper for Georgie! You'll have an interesting time. Let me tell you how to get to his office; it's not easy.'

I thanked him and paid attention to his set of directions. He followed me to the door. 'Have you ever worked for anyone before?' he asked. 'What I mean is, you're kind of young, have you orchestrated for anyone before?'

I felt it was time to assert myself, and I told him of my days at the Paris Conservatory, and of my musical studies since. Jules's face betrayed nothing of his thoughts; he would have been a perfect John Le Carré hero.

'Paris Conservatory, eh?' he mused. 'Well, good luck, kid. And listen'—and his voice became just a trifle conspiratorial—'don't be taken aback by Georgie. He's a little—unusual.'

Georgie Stoll was quite an apparition, with hair like the woolliest of the Three Stooges, and clothes he could have found only by diligently combing the thrift shops of the Bowery. He drove an ancient Duesenberg and lived in a house that would have inspired Bram Stoker. He was also sweet-natured and kind and never hurt anyone. I must confess that I never actually saw him write anything, and I don't know whether a genuine Georgie Stoll Urtext manuscript exists anywhere, but he always had a keen nose for the talented newcomer, and dozens of Hollywood's best arrangers went through his particular school. There are many people who play the piano with just one finger, but Georgie was the only one I ever met who played with just his thumbs. It was very weird, but you got used to it. He would stand at the piano—he was too restless to sit—and sing and bang his thumbs and shriek and explain, and somehow some kind of mysterious message got through and you would go home and write something that was undeniably based on his singing and banging and shrieking, and it would work quite well in the film.

As far as his ability to read music was concerned, well, he was an ex-fiddler, so treble clef held no fears for him, but the rest was the Dead Sea Scrolls to him, most particularly the transpositions that are necessary to any orchestral music. To the uninitiated, a page of orchestral score must look as hopeless as a page of calculus looks to me. When it came to the recording of the music, Georgie would always conduct from a sort of simplified piano part, while the orchestrator who had actually put all those dots on paper would sit, unobtrusively, near the podium and field any questions that might arise from within the ranks of the orchestra itself.

One day this caused a problem. The music we were recording had been written partly by me, and to a greater extent by a remarkable French arranger called Leo Arnaud. Leo had listened to a rehearsal of the sequence he had written, and there had been no mistakes or problems. Leo thought it was a safe time to go to the bathroom, so he disappeared, taking his scores with him.

Almost immediately one of the trumpet players had a question.

'Georgie,' he called out, 'what's my second note in bar 37?'

Georgie looked around for Leo. No Leo. He knew I was of no use, since I hadn't written the piece in question. He panicked and stalled for time.

'Would you run that sequence again, please, I want to check something,' he shouted at the projectionist. I sensed impending disaster and went off at a trot to find Leo. I found him down the street, in the Gents, sitting in contented privacy. I explained the situation hurriedly.

'*Mon dieu!*' said Leo, coming out of the door at a dead run. We burst back onto the recording stage in time to hear the aggrieved voice of the trumpet player.

'Jesus, Georgie, what do you mean I'm wasting everybody's time, I just want to know what's my second note in bar 37?'

At this point Leo was flailing through his manuscript pages with one hand, and trying to hold up his unbuttoned pants with the other.

'F sharp,' he suddenly yelled. 'Ralph, you should have an F sharp!'

Ralph shot Leo a grateful look, but he knew the rules of the game as well as we did.

'Thank you, Georgie,' he said, and the recording resumed. . . .

I soon found out, coached by my friends the arrangers and orchestrators, that the only musical job totally controlled by union fees and not covered by weekly stipends was actual orchestrating. The musicians' union decreed that a page of orchestration was to consist of four bars, that payment was to be made by the page, and that, therefore, each four bars was worth whatever the traffic might bear over and above the minimum, which was of course what I worked for. The brilliant musician Leo Arnaud, whom I mentioned earlier, was also deciphering Georgie Stoll's thumb melodies; he was French, had studied in Paris, and knew everything worth knowing about the orchestra. He became my benefactor, unofficial teacher, advisor in how to write for the harp, and my Baedeker to the Rules of the Game.

'Listen, *mon vieux,*' he confided one day. 'When you are orchestrating for a true musical illiterate, then it is perfectly okay to take advantage of that situation here. We don't get any credit, so the idea is to make as much money as possible. When I am asked by one of our innocents to ghost-write some chase music, for Western posses or gangland car rides, the music has to be very fast, eh? Well, write the meter in 3/8. This means that'—and he sang a demonstration—'bubbidy bubbidy bubbidy bubbidy, two seconds of music, is already a page, whereas a more normal 4/4 or 12/8 bar would only take up a quarter of a page with the same notes. Mind you,' he continued, 'this must only be done with those employers of ours who can hardly read music. With the good ones, it would be dishonest.'

These were interesting lessons in variable morality for a teenager.

More important, I was getting a thorough schooling in the practical aspects of music making. Nothing teaches as much as experience, and I was surrounded by talented people who were willing to be helpful. I learned how to orchestrate quickly. I have, in recent years, received some compliments on being a good and supple accompanist to my soloists. The reason for that, in my opinion, goes back to my studio work of the late forties and fifties. I had to conduct for a lot of unorthodox, or to put it more bluntly, unmusical singers, and once a conductor has learned to cope with the vagaries of musical naiveté, none of the occasional way-wardnesses of genuine musicians is a problem.

Best of all, and most important of all, I was privileged—later on—to stand up in front of an orchestra of superlative players countless times, probably several times a week for ten years, rehearse them in brand new music, make the necessary changes, and record it, all as quickly as possible without sacrificing the performance. I learned how much an orchestra can be put through, what makes them tired or angry or irritable, and what pleases them. All orchestral players, whether at MGM or in the Berlin Philharmonic, like to get on with it: don't waste a lot of time, don't talk too much, and have a conductor firmly in charge without being arrogant or self-aggrandizing. Only a few months ago I watched a young conductor in front of the Vienna Philharmonic for the first time. He was frightened of them, which is totally understandable. At one point in the rehearsal the principal violinist asked about a bowing at a certain place. Should they start the phrase upbow or downbow? The young conductor wanted to ingratiate himself with this august body of players. 'Well,' he said winningly, 'what would you like?'

And from the back of the viola section came the answer. 'What would we like? Well, a decision would be nice!'

All this I learned in, of all places, Culver City and Burbank. It would have been nice to be a *répétiteur* in an opera house in Wiesbaden and learn all those things while in the service of immortal music instead of in the service of Kathryn Grayson, but learn it I did, and at an early age. When I composed, I heard my music played by the orchestra within days of completion of the score. No master at a conservatory, no matter how revered, can teach as much by verbal criticism as can a cold and analytical hearing of one's own music being played. I would mentally tick the results as they came at me: that was pretty good, you can use that device again, that was awful, too thick, that mixture makes the woodwinds disappear, those trills are not effective, that's a good balance, and so on and on. I paid very close attention and tried to be reasonably ruthless with myself. . . .

When I think, from my present vantage point, to some of the demands made on musicians at MGM, I cringe in retrospect. For example, early on I worked for a composer named Herbert Stothart. He had been an operetta composer in the twenties and had achieved a firm foothold at MGM, with his name on most of that studio's heavy dramas. Hardly a tear was shed on screen for better than twenty years without Herbert Stothart's accompanying music. His method was to devise pretty themes and melodies which were then turned over to one of the musical drones for metamorphosis into something orchestrally usable. I was assigned to concoct the title music to an 'important' epic, and Stothart had been explicit in his instructions to me. He handed me his tune, which was very nice indeed, and said 'Big! Big! Impressive! Use a huge orchestra! Add a chorus if you want to. Or an organ. Or extra brass. Big!!'

By this time stoic acceptance had become second nature to me. I went to my office and wrote sort of an anthology of effective bad taste; the ending of [Respighi's] 'Pines of Rome' was modest by comparison. On the day of the recording, Mr Stothart was on the podium, his gestures reeking with authority, his head leonine. At a respectful distance behind him were the producer and director, in attitudes of awe and admiration, pilgrim students at the feet of Beethoven. I was sitting, as invisible as possible, on the bottom step of the conductor's rostrum, following my score. As the music headed for yet another fortissimo wallow of excess, Stothart leaned down toward me without missing a beat.

'Young man,' he stage-whispered, 'did I write this?'

But I loved the studio, I loved the way it smelled, I was crazy about Indians in the lunchroom, and Romans making phone calls, and the highly charged and technically dazzling music making on the recording stage. Most of all I loved being a part of it, a part of a peculiar fraternity, belittled and superior at the same time, envied for all the wrong reasons and commiserated with for the stuff we all took in our stride. . . .

Nearly a decade later I was working on *Porgy and Bess* for Sam Goldwyn.

McCarthyism's hold on the public's paranoia had lost some of its grip, but Hollywood was still submissive to such arbiters of patriotism, defenders of morals and deciders of careers such as Ward Bond, Ginger Rogers's mother, and Adolphe Menjou. The climate was still truly creepy, and just about the only safe discussion in the studio commissary was about the salads on the menu, and even then you had to be careful about Russian dressing. One day, the daily gossip column of the *Hollywood Reporter* carried an item that stated that it was a disgrace that André Previn allowed so many Pinkos to play in his film studio orchestra. That same day I was summoned to Sam Goldwyn's office. Goldwyn was sad, but he wanted to remind me that at MGM those musicians who had been accused of being fellow travelers had been dismissed so summarily that they had been prevented from coming onto the lot in order to clear their instrument lockers of their possessions.

I took a deep breath and assured Mr Goldwyn that I was quite certain that the musicians in the *Porgy and Bess* orchestra were neither Communists nor

Fascists, they were just musicians. I told him that they were much too busy playing music to pass out pamphlets, that the criterion of their having been hired had been the fact that they were the best people available, and that I would give him my word that the playing of the orchestra would not subvert the audience into attempts to overthrow the government. Goldwyn thought about it. Then he said, okay, he believed me. However, he went on, if any one single member of the orchestra ever turned out to have questionable politics, I would be fired the same day.

A few weeks later, a letter came, requesting that I come to the offices of a gentleman who was running a small, private magazine dedicated to the 'exposure' of Hollywood Reds. Armed with total ignorance, I showed up at the man's desk at the appointed time. He gave me hardly a glance but shuffled through a stack of papers in front of him, his face positively radiant with booze. Finally, he leaned back, envisioning himself as the Burbank Inquisitor, and said, 'I have certain information that you gave benefit concerts for the Abraham Lincoln Brigade during the Spanish Civil War. What do you have to say to that?'

I was almost sorry that my answer was so simple. I reminded him that although I had sometimes been on the receiving end of the flattery that I had been precociously talented, I could not take credit for concerts in 1936, since (1) I was six years old when the war began, and (2) was living in Berlin.

It was so obviously the unadorned truth that even my inquisitor recognized it as such. He thought about it. Then he stood up and grasped my hand across the desk. His hand was very warm, and so wet that I thought a large animal had licked my palm. He smiled and chuckled. 'No harm in trying, eh?' he asked. He was, for a while, a feared personage in Hollywood; then he went to prison for blackmail. . . .

Jazz and the army were only an interlude. Soon I was back at MGM, where the studio had a new boss. Mayer's successor was a tall, affable, likable man named Dore Schary. He had put in some years as a screenwriter and had produced some successful films at RKO before becoming Mayer's second in command. It wasn't long before new names were painted on the office doors and Dore became the Master of All He Surveyed. From time to time he would personally produce a film at MGM (as opposed to impersonally supervising the rest of the product), and I was tapped to compose the music for two of these efforts. The first one was actually a hell of a good movie, *Bad Day at Black Rock*, with a superb performance by Spencer Tracy. It dealt quite realistically with prejudice during the Second World War years, and Schary had a specific wish for the music.

'I want it to sound military,' he said. 'Lots of French horns,' and to emphasize his wish, his arms pumped out the unmistakable gestures of a slide trombone.

'You mean,' I began carefully, 'that you want a lot of brass instruments?'

'No no no'—a little impatiently—'French horns, lots of them,' and again the charade of a very busy trombonist.

'Fine, okay,' I agreed, and proceeded to write a vaguely dissonant and sinister score that seemed to make the producer very happy.

My other assignment started out disastrously, and it was entirely due to my stupidity. Schary had produced a film called *Designing Woman*, with Lauren Bacall and Gregory Peck. The picture was finished and edited and I was invited to see it, along with quite a few others. Now, the run-of-the-mill producers had these screenings in one of the studio projection rooms, but Dore had the clout to run them in his own living room. He was a hospitable man and invited about ten of us to dinner prior to the running of the film. His house was furnished in Early Unamerican, with every room crammed and stuffed with spinning wheels, weather vanes, quilts, salt boxes and whirligigs, and primitive portraits, most of them made in Taiwan. The dinner was enormous and the wine was heavy. After a sickeningly rich dessert, I made my torpid way into the living room. I sat in a very soft chair. The lights were dimmed at the flick of a switch, the prize Grant Wood slid soundlessly upward, disclosing a screen, the film started, and I went into a deep, dreamless, happy, babylike sleep. I woke for the first time when the lights went back on, and realized that I had not seen a single frame of the movie. I had not been given a script to read and I didn't know whether *Designing Woman* was a biography of some designer, or of Mata Hari, or of the only female member of the Bauhaus. Mr Schary smiled at me.

'Well, André, do you have unusual ideas of what you'd like to compose for this?' I went into a sort of manic overdrive. I couldn't very well admit that I hadn't seen a single frame of his brainchild because I had had the best sleep in months, and so I improvised rashly.

'Dore,' I said with conviction, 'I'd like to write the whole score for just strings and harp, and possibly piano.'

Dore was stumped, but game. 'Just strings, eh kid?' he said. 'I would never have thought of that, but listen, what the hell, by all means try it.'

The next morning I was at the studio bright and early and looked up Benny Lewis, the film editor of *Designing Woman*. I wasted no time. 'Benny, can you run me the film again, right away, please?'

'I can't get a projection room this morning, André, and aren't you a bit anxious?' he asked. I confessed the whole predicament and he laughed until the tears ran down his face. 'Come into the cutting room,' he offered, then ran the whole film for me on a Moviola, which is a great clattering machine used by film editors and has a viewing screen of approximately four inches. Two hours later I realized that 'just strings and a harp' had been total nonsense, but now I was stuck with it, and actually the challenge was advantageous. I wrote a light and pleasant comedy score, it all fitted quite reasonably, and everyone was happy. I had been lucky, but it was a near thing. . . .

Vincente Minnelli was certainly one of the very best directors of musical films ever. His visual sense was immaculate and his taste impeccable. He was a pleasure to work with and should have given lessons in how to make a film look beautiful and move gracefully. However, Vincente was also given to being nervous and a bit irritable when things did not go smoothly.

An interesting manifestation of this foible came to light on the set of *Kismet*, a turkey if there ever was one, which was being shot in Hollywood in 1955. Vincente was shooting the 'Stranger in paradise' number, during which the young Caliph, serenading his lady love, wanders down a path in the palace gardens. The paths were multicolored gravel, the bushes were laden with exotic blooms, and peacocks strolled through the shot. Now Vincente had an idea. Vic Damone, who played the caliph—could you possibly think of anyone else to play him?—had a very effective high note in the middle of the song, on the words ' . . . like a dream, I hang suspended.' On the second syllable of the word 'suspended', I had thoughtfully provided a shimmering chord in the orchestra, and at this point Vincente wished one of the peacocks to unfurl its gorgeous tail right on cue, a sudden and gigantic fan of colors. The peacock trainer—oh yes, we had a peacock trainer—was called over and given the problem.

His solution was pretty simple: He would lie down behind a prop bush, safely out of camera range, holding a stick with a point on the end of it, much like the implement park cleaners use to spear debris off the grass. On the cue word 'suspended', he would jab the stick smartly into the bird's behind, the bird would be surprised and shocked, and *voilà*! a gorgeous fan would be produced. And by God, it worked. Evidently peacocks unfurl all that glory either when courting or when angry, and it certainly could be said this particular peacock was furious at the indignity.

However, no one had counted on Vincente's famous perfectionism. Two takes, three takes, four takes, still it wasn't good enough. And then the bird got wise. Why stand still and have someone jam a sharp stick up your rear? Maybe this peacock wasn't Stephen Hawking, but he did figure that one out. And so he would simply move out of reach, scampering away just at the moment when it was necessary for him to provide a stationary target. Half a dozen futile attempts later, Vincente's nerves got the better of him.

'Make him stand still,' he yelled at the trainer. 'Do something!!'

'Can't do it, Mr Minnelli,' the man apologized. 'He's got wise to the trick now.'

Vincente was deep in thought. He wasn't about to be beaten by a peacock, not even a smart one. 'Prop man,' he shouted, and the man came running. 'George, see that peacock?' Vincente demanded and George nodded. 'Nail him down,' said Vincente. 'I don't want him to move, nail him down.'

It was an interesting moment. George pondered for quite a while. 'I can't do that, Mr Minnelli,' he finally offered. 'I can't and I won't.' Vincente was really jumpy now, a whole set-load of people were waiting, including a small army of 'Arabian Nights' extras.

'I tell you, nail him down!' he repeated doggedly. 'Or at least do *something*, think of something, and quickly!'

George was an inventive prop man, he liked his work, and he was a good fellow. He invented a sort of bracket, a kind of staple, and duly fastened the bird to the gravel path without actually nailing him. He eyed his invention judiciously and said, 'That oughta work,' and Vincente screamed for the shot to be lined up again. The playback record was turned on, the orchestra played, Vic Damone hit his high note, the trainer speared the peacock's bum, the peacock flared his tail with abandon, and Vincente was very happy. Next time *Kismet* is on the late show, you might wait for this scene. Luckily, it's early on in the picture, and you can watch the peacock during the musical lead-up to the high note; I can't be sure, of course, but I could swear that bird knows what's coming. . . .

During the period of my life with which this book is concerned, I was quite involved with the [Academy] Awards, having been nominated more than a dozen times and having actually won an Oscar on four occasions, for *Gigi*, *Irma la Douce*, *Porgy and Bess*, and *My Fair Lady*. No matter how critical I appear right now, it must be admitted that while I was in the thick of things I was just as brainwashed as the rest of the town and spent a ludicrous amount of time speculating about the little statuettes. Who would win for best black-and-white art direction, and supporting actress, and short subject? Were Reuters and Tass and the BBC standing by to flash the news to travelers on the Burma Road? It is virtually impossible to exaggerate the film industry's self-importance at this time of year; no Pulitzer, no mere Nobel, no knighthood, no ascendancy to the peerage could compete. Even during the less frantic seasons, the insularity of Los Angeles is amazing; beyond the borders of Burbank to the south and Culver City to the north, *nothing* is seen to be of importance. It makes life a good deal more sanguine, but it is of course the Twilight Zone.

During my fourteen years in the film industry, I attended five of the awards ceremonies in the audience, and another three as the conductor of the pit orchestra. It might be interesting to disclose how it is possible for the forty-piece orchestra to play the appropriate theme music every time a winner is announced, so that the overwhelmed recipient can stumble up on stage, accompanied by his or her very own melody. There are five nominations in every category, and therefore five apropos pieces of music. To prevent orchestral chaos following each disclosure of a winner, the five themes, labeled by the title of the film and with the name of the individual nominee, are reduced to an eight-bar loop, repeatable as many times as necessary, and copied onto a single page of music manuscript paper. Each member of the orchestra has his instrument's correct page in front of him. The envelope is opened, the name is read, and there is the inevitable scream of jubilation from the audience. This scream is all-pervasive for a few seconds, thus giving the orchestral players time to fix their gaze on the correct theme on the page, the conductor to give a downbeat, and the strains of the winning film's music to be played. It's all done very smoothly and quickly, thus giving rise to the theory that the winners are actually known in advance, because how else could the right tune be played? No, in fact, the secrecy of the winner's identity is scrupulously guarded, and the envelopes are probably kept on a nuclear submarine which surfaces backstage only in time for the show.

I know from practical experience, having won and lost several times, that there is no way to stay perfectly cool and above it all when the list of nominees is read. Maybe it would be easier at home, listening to the TV set, but when you are right there, reserve and common sense are put into a hammerlock by adrenaline, and for that one minute *You wanna win, you wanna win!!* Of course it's nonsense, of course it's like Prize Day at school, but as Mike Nichols observed with typical candor, 'If you're in any contest at all where you can win or lose, try to win.' It's true.

The rules and bylaws of the Academy, perhaps cognizant of the fact that the general audience cares only about the actors, decree that a great many of the other categories are lumped together as 'Technical Awards'. The music awards are filed under 'Technical', a misconception that has enraged a great many composers. For some churlish reason Aaron Copland, Erich Korngold, Miklós Rózsa, Bernard Herrmann, David Raksin and others don't consider themselves technicians rather than artists. Another quibble I might mention is the rule that every single member of the Academy, regardless of his individual branch, is allowed to vote on every category in the final ballot. I know I am not equipped to vote on the niceties and details governing the prize in set decoration or film editing, and conversely, I am not prepared to put too much credence in Sylvester Stallone's opinion on composition.

The show itself, at least in the theater, is usually a merciful blur. The nominees are in a haze except for those minutes concerned with their own category, and the nonconcerned spectators find out very quickly that it is a lot better to watch at home. Ennui is more easily dealt with, the overpowering urge to grab a short nap is not embarrassing in private, and getting dressed in evening

clothes at five in the afternoon is either decadent or foolish. The most mysterious part of the show seems to be the opening song-and-dance number. With
all the talent of the motion picture industry available and willing to contribute,
why is it this number seems to be staged by the same people responsible for the
Elks' Club Picnic in Fargo? What keeps the nominees in their seats, smiling
stiffly, is the suspense of sweating out their eventual victory or loss. Once that
moment has passed and rational standards return, it's a tough evening. When
you win, collect the Oscar, and come offstage, you are requested to go to the
press room for a session with the photographers. The first time it happened to
me, I demurred and indicated that I should really return out front fairly quickly.
Ella Fitzgerald was backstage and came over to me, beaming with friendship.
'Don't be silly, honey,' she said. 'After all, how many times does this happen?
Enjoy it, relax, have your picture taken!' 'Okay, Ella,' I said, 'but I think your
song is due next and I'm supposed to conduct for you.' She had her arm around
my shoulder and gave me a little squeeze. 'Honey,' she said again, 'get the hell
back in that pit!!'

The Oscars meant a lot to me at the time I won them. I was pleased and
proud of them. Now that I view my film work from a distance, and across a
wide gulf of the intervening years, they have taken on a different perspective—
they have become three-dimensional objects of nostalgia. It is always a problem
to know where to keep them. Too blatantly displayed is awful. A well-known
actress had a niche built into the wall of her sitting room, and a pin spotlight
concealed in the ceiling. When the light was on, it bathed her Oscar in a mysterious golden reflection, and one expected a healing spring to gurgle forth
miraculously under the figurine. On the other hand, using Oscar as a door stop
is bending over backward too far. I keep mine in the corner of a bookcase,
where I like to think they are visible but not pushy. . . .

Periodically the big studios, driven by guilt and fear, went on an economy
drive. This usually resulted in the firing of a few secretaries and a futile attempt to
inflict some stringent rules on the workday patterns of the employees. At Warner
Brothers, Jack Warner issued the ukase that all writers had to check in at nine in
the morning. Approximately a month later he sent for Julius Epstein, a marvelous
screenwriter whose credits included *Casablanca*. 'I just read your new script, Julie,'
he said, 'and I've never read such unmitigated crap before in my life!'

Julie was bewildered. 'But Mr Warner, how is that possible? The script simply can't be bad. After all, I was here every morning at nine sharp!'

At Metro, in the music department, a similar rule was instigated by the department's bookkeeper and accountant, a Mr I. M. Halperin, a pale man with rimless
glasses and a rimless sense of humor. All composers, the rule stated, had to be on
the lot between ten and six every day, and should there be a deviation from these

hours, he had to be notified. The rule was posted, and we waited in vain for Zorro to come and make his mark on the memo. However, as it happened, I had to work straight through the night soon after, and when I finally tottered out of my office, with eyes red as a rabbit's, I noticed that it was four in the morning. I went back to my desk and rang Mr I. M. Halperin at home. It took quite a few rings before he answered. 'Hello,' I said cheerfully, 'I'm so sorry to bother you, but this is André. I've just finished work, it's not six in the evening, it's four in the morning, so I thought I had better let you know that I'm going home now.' The rule was rescinded two days later, and for a very little while I was a folk hero.

All these attempts by executives to marshal the muse into line pale into insignificance in comparison to an edict once issued by Irving Thalberg.

He was the most renowned of all the MGM producers but his reign at the studio was in the early thirties, so I missed out working for him. He was the model for Scott Fitzgerald's *Last Tycoon*, and is generally held to have been an awesome figure of intellect, taste, and drive, and the old-timers in Hollywood still speak of him as a sort of combination Ziegfeld and Teilhard de Chardin. It is entirely possible that he was a beacon of enlightenment, but when it came to music his fund of information was minuscule. One day, the story goes, he was in his projection room running a new MGM film when something on the sound track bothered him. 'What is that?' he asked irritably into the darkness. 'What is that in the music? It's awful, I hate it!'

The edge in his voice required an answer, even if that answer was untainted by knowledge. One of his minions leapt forward. 'That's a minor chord, Mr Thalberg,' he offered. The next day, an inter-office memo arrived in the music department with instructions to post it conspicuously. It read as follows: 'From the above date onward, no music in an MGM film is to contain a "minor chord".' Signed, 'IRVING THALBERG'. When I left the studio for the last time, twenty-five years after this missive's arrival, it was still on the wall in the music department, under glass and heavily bolted. I must now confess that I actually tried to get the thing off the wall with a heavy-duty screwdriver, but nothing would budge the rusted screws. Maybe there would have been a curse attached to it, and I would have been doomed to spend eternity in a projection room, running and rerunning Norma Shearer in *Marie Antoinette*. . . .

The orchestrators were my first, and probably my closest, friends. At MGM alone there were Conrad Salinger, Bob Franklyn, Al Woodbury, Sandy Courage, Leo Arnaud, and Ted Duncan—not a household name among them but every one of them schooled to a real perfection of his craft. Often they were saddled with the problem of making the scrawls or verbal wishes of *soi-disant* composers into something glamorous and wonderful, and so it was necessary for them to have the maximum of expertise and the minimum of conceit. It is source of great pride to me that I was a member of this incognito band for a while.

I have a vivid memory of Al Woodbury filling page after page of the giant yellow score pads while avidly listening to the ball game on the radio, and never missing a note or mistaking a clef or a transposition. One night I had been working terribly late, two in the morning, and as I made my stumbling way out of the studio and toward the parking lot, I noticed Bob Franklyn's cubbyhole office still lit. I stuck my head in and there was Bob, meticulously orchestrating someone's music in his elegant French-schooled manner, yawning luxuriously and peering up at me over his rimless glasses. We chatted for a few minutes, competing as to who had the worse assignment, when a gust of wind from the open window blew the page Bob was working on from his desk onto the floor. Now, it must be explained at this point that a page of score for full orchestra consists of about thirty-two staves, four bars per stave, and that this particular page was almost completely filled in Bob's fine hand. For the normal, talented composer, it would represent several hours of hard work. Bob looked at the page on the floor a full six feet away, and thought about physical effort versus mental application. He sighed and picked up a brand new page from the ream of paper by his side.

'The hell with it,' he said and started over, the pencil gliding effortlessly over the woodwind parts.

All of us were expected to be total chameleons. 'I want this to sound like . . .' Fill in the name of your preference: Ravel, Tchaikovsky, Strauss, Count Basie, a Broadway pit; that was an instruction we all heard, many times during working hours, and we were expected to nod submissively, go away, and produce the musical goods. I was never in the pantheon of Hollywood orchestrators, but I learned a lot and was able to put it to use for the rest of my life. Don't let anyone mistake these gentlemen's unquestioning music habits as hack work; any examination of their scores would prove the most enviable, sophisticated knowledge of what makes an orchestra sound.

Naturally, some of the composers were more capable of doing their own orchestrating. My point of view has always been that, given the hair-raising shortness of time allotted to the completion of a score, if help is needed, then that is fair dues. On the other hand, if orchestrating help is sought by a composer because he doesn't know how, then that is meretricious.

When Aaron Copland wrote music to *The Red Pony*, his detailed sketches were scored by a staff orchestrator at the studio. A colleague of Copland's, shocked by the disclosure of this weakness, asked Aaron how he could allow such a thing. Aaron produced a page of his handwritten sketch. 'Look at this,' he said, 'and answer me the following: If I dictate a letter and it is typed for me, who actually wrote the letter, me or my secretary?'

It's a valid point, but only if the composer's sketch, or short score, is as complete as Copland's obviously was. I orchestrated for Hugo Friedhofer once. Hugo, in his early days, had scored the music for Korngold and Steiner, and there was nothing about the orchestra he didn't know. His sketch could have been handed right to a copyist, and I felt as if I were stealing as I translated his dots onto individual lines on the big pages. There was nothing left for me to do except the wearying mechanics of it all. Hugo was a sensational musician, capable of being moved to tears by music, and just as capable of some of the most ribald and awful jokes extant.

He also kept his individuality. He once composed the music to a Western; in the projection room, the producer was baffled. 'Hugo,' he demanded, 'your music for the villains is, if anything, more heroic than for the hero! Why did you do that?' Hugo was sanguine. 'I liked them,' he explained.

It isn't just actors who get typed in a specific mold. Composers suffer the same fate. I had done some successful musicals; therefore, I was the one to get for a musical. Then I did four of Billy Wilder's comedies in a row and I became the comedy expert. After I did 'Elmer Gantry,' every script that was tough and uncompromising came my way. Producers love pigeonholing everybody; it makes assigning and casting so much easier.

Miklós Rózsa is one of the film world's most famous and prestigious composers. When I knew him at Metro, he was knee-deep in his religious phase. *Quo Vadis?*, *King of Kings*, *Barabbas* [not in fact scored by Rózsa], *Ben Hur*—he did 'em all. As soon as there were actors in sight wearing white robes and sandals, poor Miklós was called. These were tough films to compose, if for no other reason than the fact that they were absolutely crammed with music, wall-to-wall pious *tuttis*, and it must have been wildly boring for someone of Miklós's standing.

Once I saw him come out of a projection room really in despair.

'I just don't know what else to write for that scene in which that fella carries the cross up that hill,' he complained. This might not have been Bach's problem, but for lesser mortals, it was a genuine challenge. In order to keep himself interested, Miklós did an amazing (and probably unnecessary) amount of research for each of his projects, and so he was a real expert in biblical instruments, plainsong, Gregorian chant, and the like. He was, in other words, a scholar, and an anachronism in Culver City. During *Ben Hur*, he was beside himself with impotent rage when the director, William Wyler, suggested that 'Silent Night, Holy Night' be played during the Nativity scene.

Poor Miklós: he was always the most European of gentlemen, and his dark suits in the blazing sunshine typified how out of place he was.

18

Henry Mancini: *Did They Mention the Music?* (1989)

Arguably no composer did more to refresh the potentially moribund art of film scoring in the 1950s and 1960s than Henry Mancini (1924–94), whose combination of classical compositional training and wide experience of jazz and dance music allowed him to bring together the best of both worlds: he forged a flexible and immediately recognizable style of jazz-tinged scoring that was deftly poised in the middle ground between structural sophistication and commercial appeal, and this at precisely the time when the ailing fortunes of the Hollywood film industry desperately required a financial boost from tie-in record sales of the kind that Mancini was comfortably able to achieve. Unlike compilation pop scores based on preexisting and self-contained hit songs, Mancini's film scores—which at times seemed carefully designed to maximize the potential for their individual cues to be readily assembled as a pleasingly contrasted LP soundtrack album—could switch easily between conventional structured underscoring that supported the narrative and foregrounded original songs and memorable instrumental themes, a strategy soon adopted by other film composers with a background in popular music (for example, John Barry and Ennio Morricone).

In Mancini's autobiography, authored in conjunction with distinguished jazz writer Gene Lees, the composer recounts his early years at Universal (1952–58) before he came to attention as the Oscar-nominated musical director for *The Glenn Miller Story* (dir. Anthony Mann, 1953), in which James Stewart starred as the bandleader under whom Mancini had himself played as a member

Source: Henry Mancini with Gene Lees, *Did They Mention the Music?* (Chicago: Contemporary Books, 1989): 69–73, 75–84, 86–90, 97–102, 104–10, 140–42, 178–85.

of the 28th Air Force Band during his military service. In 1958 Mancini provided a notable source-music-dominated score for Orson Welles's *Touch of Evil* and achieved a popular success with his poundingly bluesy and enormously influential big-band theme tune for the TV detective series *Peter Gunn*. Mancini here relates details of his work for Howard Hawks on *Hatari!* (1962), for which he composed "Baby Elephant Walk," and his long-term collaborator Blake Edwards, for whom he wrote the famous saxophone theme for the animated title sequences in the *Pink Panther* comedy franchise (1963–93) and the song "Moon River" in *Breakfast at Tiffany's* (1961). His music for the latter became one of the most successful film scores of all time, spawning four hit records and netting two Academy Awards and five Grammy Awards.

The days of the music department at Universal were almost over; indeed the days of Universal itself, as an old-line movie studio, were about finished. Unlike those at Warner Bros., who were deeply involved in television, the executives at Universal lacked foresight. Theaters around the country were closing as more and more television sets went into American homes. By order of the Supreme Court, the studios were no longer allowed to own theaters and had been stripped of guaranteed distribution for their pictures. Staff musicians earned an average of $300 or $400 a week, a lot of money at that time, which made the big studio orchestras difficult to justify and sustain. One by one they were dismissed. Finally, Universal was up for sale, and MCA bought it in 1957 and in time turned it into the biggest television factory in the world. MCA acquired it for a ridiculously low figure, something like $11 million, for its entire catalog of films, its physical plant, and all that backlot real estate.

The whole studio system, and with it the star system, was coming to an end. The new films were being made by independents. The ax fell, as we knew it would. When the Universal orchestra's contract expired, it was not renewed. Along with Herman Stein, David Tamkin, Frank Skinner, Nick Nuzzi, and the copyists, I was given my notice. Our friendly little family of musicians was broken up.

At the time, I was working on a picture with Jimmy Cagney, *Never Steal Anything Small* [1958], the last film I did there. I was making $350 a week and, with three children to care for and mortgage payments, we counted on it. When I told Ginny I'd lost my job, she was concerned. In later years she has said that the experience taught her never to fear the future. "One door closes, another opens," she says.

I had worked with Blake Edwards on three pictures. One was *This Happy Feeling* [1958], with Debbie Reynolds. Another was *Mister Cory* [1957], with Tony Curtis; it was about a professional gambler and had rumblings of what was to become the TV series "Mr. Lucky." Blake had written the screenplay. I didn't write the score for that picture, but as often happened when they needed music in a pop vein, I had been brought in for some source cues. The third picture I worked on with him was *The Perfect Furlough* [1958], with Tony Curtis and Janet Leigh. . . .

Blake had set up a production company, Spartan Productions, in partnership with Don Sharpe. Don was a golden boy in those days, a master. If he wanted to do something, he got at least to make a pilot. In those days, you didn't have to audition if you had a sponsor. And he already had a sponsor for "Peter Gunn," Procter & Gamble. He had a commitment from them, their ad agency, and NBC for thirteen weeks; as it turned out, we did thirty-three episodes that first year. . . .

Blake and I immediately established a comfortable working relationship, yet we rarely had meetings, even then. In our thirty years together I can remember few actual meetings, and usually they had to do with concepts of songs, planned in advance, as for *Victor/Victoria* [1982] and *Darling Lili* [1970]. In the pictures I scored for Blake, I would always let him hear the theme, and from then until the recording dates he always left the music entirely to me.

The idea of using jazz in the "Gunn" score was never even discussed. It was implicit in the story. Peter Gunn hangs out in a jazz roadhouse called Mother's—the name was Blake's way of tweaking the noses of the censors—where there is a five-piece jazz group. In the pilot, five or six minutes took place in Mother's. That's a long time, so it was obvious that jazz had to be used.

It was the time of so-called cool West Coast jazz, with Shelly Manne, the Candoli brothers, and Shorty Rogers, among others. And that was the sound that came to me, the walking bass and drums. The "Peter Gunn" title theme actually derives more from rock and roll than from jazz. I used guitar and piano in unison, playing what is known in music as an *ostinato*, which means obstinate. It was sustained throughout the piece, giving it a sinister effect, with some frightened saxophone sounds and some shouting brass.

The piece has one chord throughout and a super-simple top line. It has been played through the years by school marching bands as well as rock bands throughout the world. The synth group The Art of Noise had a major hit with it in 1987. Never has so much been made of so little.

The music budget for each segment of "Peter Gunn" was $2,000. That was for me, copying, and musicians. Musically in situations like that you fall back on your string section. I didn't have any money to buy a string section, so I was happy that a small jazz group could be used. The original orchestra was four woodwinds, four trombones, one trumpet, and five rhythm. At the same time, so small a band made me find different ways of producing tension and suspense.

That's when I started using bass flutes. The instrument was virtually unused at the time, and still isn't used much. The reason is simple: it has little power and doesn't project. You can use it only with microphones; it's impractical for a symphony orchestra. The first time I recall hearing a bass flute in film was in Alex North's score for *Death of a Salesman* [1951]. I knew what the sound was, and as a flute player I'd seen a few of the instruments. A man in Los Angeles named Ogilvie made bass flutes. Harry Klee, one of my fine flute players, owned one. Some of the other players acquired them, and I used three at first in the "Peter Gunn" music and four when another one became available. It was probably the first time a section of bass flutes had ever been used. I used them for a dark effect, sometimes writing a fall—a descending figure—at the end of a note, which gave a kind of paranoid effect. That sound, along with the walking bass, became one of the trademarks of the "Peter Gunn" music. Another was the use of free improvisation under dramatic scenes.

Several of the musicians I used had been with me with Tex Beneke, including Rolly Bundock, bass; Jack Sperling, drums; Jimmy Priddy, trombone; and Pete Candoli, trumpet. My favorite trombonist, Dick Nash, joined the band. We used to record once a week, on Wednesday nights. Later, when Rolly and Jack went to work on staff on "The Tonight Show," I replaced them with Shelly Manne on drums and Red Mitchell on bass. John Williams played piano the first year. When he left to pursue a brilliant career as a film composer and conductor, he was replaced by Jimmy Rowles.

It was unusual enough for movie-score albums to be released. Certainly no one thought of putting the music of a dramatic television show out on record. And "Peter Gunn" hadn't even gone on the air yet. When the pilot was completed, Blake took it to NBC. One of the people who heard it there was Alan Livingston, who had a background in the record business. He called Si Rady at RCA Records and told him he thought the company should consider releasing the score on record. By now we were in production, and we had a lot more music. Si Rady pointed out to me that Shorty Rogers, who was under contract to RCA, had a guaranteed sale of eighty thousand albums, which was big for jazz. If Shorty would record the music, Si said, we might have that kind of sale. I was pleased by the idea, and Si said he'd set up a meeting with Shorty.

Blake was friendly with Ray Anthony, who had just had a hit with the "Dragnet" theme. In keeping with record-company mentality, it seemed logical to the people at Capitol that Ray should do the next detective-show theme that came along, and the "Gunn" theme was taken to him. He liked it. I asked Ray if he wanted me to do an arrangement on it for him, which I did. He had a big hit on that one too.

I had lunch with Shorty, a small, compact man with dark hair and a trim vandyked beard. He is a genuinely sweet man, very pure—pure of body, of heart, and of mind. He had seen the pilot. And immediately he said to me, "Hank, I have no reason to record this. It has no connection with me. *You* wrote it, *you* arranged it, and *you* should record it. This music is *yours.*"

I said, "But, Shorty, I'm not a recording artist. I'm just a film writer, nobody know who I am. You have a name." But he was adamant, and at the end of lunch he repeated, "It's your baby, and you should do it."

So Shorty Rogers became another of the people who represented a turning point in my life. I don't know what would have happened to my career if Shorty had decided that day to make the record.

RCA finally chose to record the "Gunn" music under my name, though not with what I would describe as burning enthusiasm. The best I can say for their attitude toward the project is that is was perfunctory. They did two things, the first of which no record man in his right mind would ever do. They signed me for one album only, with no options. The second tip-off to their attitude was the number of pressings. Furthermore, they didn't put out a single until long after Ray Anthony had the hit on the main theme.

"Peter Gunn" went on the air in September 1958. RCA had pressed only eight thousand copies of the album and had printed only eight thousand covers. When you had a hot record, the pressing plant could gear up to turn them out immediately. The problem was the covers—they took longer. And suddenly all hell broke loose. Within a week they had sold those eight thousand albums. RCA used to have stock covers, with abstract designs on the front, that could go on any record. And so the second pressing of *The Music from "Peter Gunn"* came out in those stock covers. They were running around like madmen at RCA, trying to keep up with the demand.

The album promptly became number 1 on the *Billboard* chart and held that position for ten weeks. And even when it dropped back a bit, it stayed on the charts for a total of 117 weeks, more than two years. In all, it sold more than a million copies, which was unprecedented for a jazz album. Since it was released under my name instead of Shorty Rogers's, suddenly out of nowhere, I was a successful recording artist. Almost overnight *"Peter Gunn"* put me in the public eye. . . .

About the time I was doing the score for *High Time* [1960], Blake said, "The next one is at Paramount. We're going ahead on *Breakfast at Tiffany's.* I'd like you to come over and do it." Blake was to direct it; Dick Shepherd and Marty Jurow were the producers, and the screenplay, based on the Truman Capote novella, was by George Axelrod. They had considered a number of actresses for the role of Holly Golightly and finally chose Audrey Hepburn. It was the first time I'd met her.

I went over to Paramount for a meeting with Blake and the producers. Dick and Marty felt that because the story had a New York location they should hire a Broadway composer to write the song that the script called for—a scene where Holly Golightly goes out on the fire escape with her guitar and sings. I would do the score, with someone else doing the song. This was not unusual—we'd used a Cahn–Van Heusen song in *High Time*—but this time I felt differently about it, and I was not happy when I left that meeting.

My agent at MCA, Henry Alper, said, "You have a hell of a picture here with a great director and a great star—don't rock the boat. Let someone else do the song; you do the score."

But the albums "*Peter Gunn*" and "*Mr. Lucky*" were nothing if not a series of songs without words, and I knew I could write a tune. So I said to Blake, "Give me a shot. Let me at least try something from that scene." Blake took it up with Dick and Marty, who relented and agreed to let me try it.

No decision had been made on who would sing the song. Audrey was not known as a singer. There was a question of whether she could handle it. Then, by chance, I was watching television one night when the movie *Funny Face* [1956] came on, with Fred Astaire and Audrey. It contains a scene in which Audrey sings "How Long Has This Been Going On?" I thought, You can't buy that kind of thing, that kind of simplicity. I went to the piano and played the song. It had a range of an octave and one, so I knew she could sing that. I now felt strongly that she should be the one to sing the new song in our picture—the song I hadn't written yet.

That song was one of the toughest I have ever had to write. It took me a month to think it through. What kind of song would this girl sing? What kind of melody was required? Should it be a jazz-flavored ballad? Would it be a blues? One night at home, I was relaxing after dinner. I went out to my studio off the garage, sat down at the piano (still rented), and all of a sudden I played the first three notes of a tune. It sounded attractive. I built the melody in a range of an octave and one. It was simple and completely diatonic: in the key of C, you can play it entirely on the white keys. It came quickly. It had taken me one month and half an hour to write that melody.

I took it in and played it for Blake, who loved it. He asked, "Who would you like to do the lyrics?"

I went for the best. I knew Johnny Mercer, who was in the habit of writing lyrics for melodies he just happened to hear and like. He would hear some music on his car radio and call the station to ask what it was; that was another of his habits. He heard "Joanna," from the second "*Peter Gunn*" album, and wrote a lyric for it. Nothing came of it, but that was the start of my professional relationship with Johnny. We wanted to write together.

So I called him.

This was the low point of Johnny's artistic life. Illiterate songs were high on the charts, and doo-wop groups were thriving. Johnny came to see me. He talked about the condition of the music business. We were almost ten years into the rock era, and he didn't have much hope for his kind of lyric or my kind of music. After I played him the melody, he asked, "Hank, who's going to record a waltz? We'll do it for the movie, but after that it hasn't any future commercially." I gave him a tape of the melody and he went home.

Had Johnny been a military man he would have been another Patton. He used to attack a song three ways. He could hear a melody and see different angles from which to approach it and then write three different lyrics, each one valid, each one fully worked out, and each one different from the others.

Once Blake and the producers decided they loved the melody, they left it to John and me to decide what the lyric should be—another example of the trust Blake put in me. John called me one morning and said he had three lyrics to show me.

That evening I was conducting the orchestra for a benefit dinner at the Beverly Wilshire Hotel. The rehearsal call was for four o'clock. I told John, "Meet me in the ballroom of the Beverly Wilshire around noon."

I waited in the ballroom, which was deserted and dark but for a couple of bare-bulb work lights. John came in with an envelope full of papers. I sat down at the piano and started to play. The first lyric he sang was a personal one about the girl, with the opening notes covered by the words "I'm Holly." John said, "I don't know about that one."

Then he showed me another, quite different, and finally a third one. He said, "I'm calling this one 'Blue River.' But it may change, because I went through the ASCAP archives and found that several of my friends have already written songs called 'Blue River.'" There was nothing to prevent John's using it: legally, you cannot copyright a title. But John was reluctant to use "Blue River." His kind of honesty has not caught on with many of the young songwriters today.

John said, "I have an optional title. 'Moon River.'"

I said, "You know, John, there used to be a radio show coming out of Cincinnati that had that title."

"It wasn't a song, was it?"

"No, it was just a late-night show where a guy would talk in a deep voice about various things."

"Okay," he said.

Sitting there on the bandstand in that deserted ballroom, I started to play the melody again, and he sang the third lyric. Every once in a while you hear something so right that it gives you chills, and when he sang that "huckleberry friend" line, I got them. I don't know whether he knew what effect those words had or if it was just something that came to him, but it was thrilling. It made you think of Mark Twain and Huckleberry Finn's trip down the Mississippi. It had such echoes of America. It was one of those remarkable lines that gives you a rush. It was the clincher.

A day or two later we played it for Blake, then for Dick Shepherd and Marty Jurow. Everybody loved the song. And everybody was convinced that Audrey should do it. I taught it to her, and we prerecorded.

There have been more than one thousand recordings of "Moon River." Of all of them—and I am not overlooking the recordings by many of my singer friends—Audrey's performance was the definitive version.

But I made a mistake with it.

The quality of sound recording in movie and television scoring was poor. The control board at Universal, where we did "*Gunn,*" was ancient. Although they had good mikes, the technique of placement was primitive—one mike for the whole rhythm section, for example. Sound was never given priority, and the equipment was falling further and further behind. The recording studios around town were always ahead of the movie studios in equipment and technique.

Breakfast at Tiffany's (dir. Blake Edwards, 1961): Holly Golightly (Audrey Hepburn) sings Henry Mancini and Johnny Mercer's famous song "Moon River."

While film and television scores were still being recorded in mono, stereo, which for years had been in the experimental stage, was coming into the general marketplace. And one of the reasons I had re-recorded "*Gunn*" was the demand for stereo. *The Music from "Peter Gunn"* was one of the first of the stereo albums, which may have contributed to its success. After that I continued re-recording my scores in stereo for album release.

That started me on a method of operation. I re-recorded *Mr. Lucky* and then the *Breakfast at Tiffany's* music. When it seemed appropriate, I rewrote some of the cues so that they would be complete tracks in the albums rather than tailing off into silence.

One of my bigger goofs was having a chorus, not Audrey, sing that song in the album version of the score.

A problem arose from the re-recording of those scores. The albums were made up of the most melodic material from the films. A lot of the dramatic music—which is what I really loved to do and really thought I had a feeling for—was left out. *Days of Wine and Roses* [1962] and *Charade* [1963] had a lot of dramatic music that was never released on record. For the albums, I used the source music that was the common denominator for my record-buying audience. And there was pressure from the record company: they didn't want to know about dramatic music. It may have hurt my reputation as a writer of serious film music. To this day, I would love to have an album of some of those scores as they were heard in the film. The albums gave me a reputation, even among producers, as a writer of light comedy and light suspense, and at that time it was not easy for them to think of me for the more dramatic assignments. I did that to myself.

We recorded the song and scored the picture. Everyone was very high on it. Audrey, Mel Ferrer—who was then Audrey's husband—Blake, Ginny, Marty Rackin, who was head of Paramount, Dick Shepherd, Marty Jurow, and I went up to a preview near Stanford. The limousines took us back to our hotel in San Francisco, where Marty Rackin had a suite. The preview had gone very well. We continued to be excited about the song, no one more so than Blake, and we were elated about the picture as a whole, although we realized it was running long and would have to be cut. As is usual in those situations, everybody has different ideas about what should and should not go. It is a subjective process, with everyone trying to protect his or her own interests and involvement in the picture. We were all sitting around, nobody saying anything. Marty Rackin had his arm on the mantelpiece of the fireplace. He was very New York and personable, a tall, trim, and lovely man in his forties, with fine features.

The first thing Marty said was, "Well, the fucking song has to go."

I looked over at Blake. I saw his face. The blood was rising to the top of his head, like that thermometer when I put a match under it. He looked like he was going to burst. Audrey moved in her chair as if she were going to get up and say something. They made a slight move toward Marty, as if they were thinking about lynching him.

The song stayed in the picture.

But I still wish I'd had Audrey sing it on the album. . . .

No matter how blasé anyone pretends to be about the Academy Awards, there is a rush when you are nominated. My first nomination had come in 1954, when Joe Gershenson and I were nominated for Best Score for a Musical Picture for *The Glenn Miller Story*. I received three nominations in 1961: one for the *Breakfast at Tiffany's* score, a joint nomination with Johnny Mercer for "Moon River," and another for the title song of the film *Bachelor in Paradise*, which had a lyric by Mack David. Ginny and I decided to do it right. On Academy Awards night we hired a limousine and picked up Johnny and his wife, Ginger. They had a lovely home in Bel Air, not really very large in view of Johnny's incredible catalog of songs and his ASCAP rating, but beautifully decorated and charming. It seemed to be snuggled in a hollow of trees next to the golf course, and at the back of the property Johnny had a studio where he wrote. I guess the lyric to "Moon River" was written here. Johnny had been a champion typist when he was a young man, and he wrote his lyrics on a typewriter.

We were already feeling a little high on excitement as we drove that March evening to Santa Monica, where the award ceremonies were held in those days. We drove down Pico Boulevard and turned right at the ocean to arrive at the Santa Monica Civic Auditorium. The limousine was moving slowly because of the traffic, and ours and all the other vehicles were surrounded by teenage girls, screaming when the movie stars arrived. They crowded around the cars and peered in the windows in search of celebrities. Movie composers did not fall into that category, and in the age of rock, Johnny—who had had a solid career as a singer—was not recognized either. I remember one little girl with a squeaky voice who stuck her head in our open window and inquired, "Are you anybody?"

We went in and found our places. Surprisingly, the only seating for all these people in tuxedos and evening gowns was hard folding chairs, set out on the floor of the auditorium. The longer you waited to see if your name would be called, the harder those chairs seemed to get.

As pleased as I was about the nomination for the song, being nominated for the score was much more gratifying, because I didn't—and still don't—think of myself as a songwriter. Most of the songs in my career have been written as instrumental themes for scores and had lyrics added later. I write themes that can be used in different ways, and developed in the course of the scores.

The people in your own branch vote for the nominations, whereas the full membership votes for the actual awards. Thus, to be nominated for a score means your fellow composers have made the selection. I had grown up as an arranger, and to be nominated by my colleagues among such peers as Miklos Rozsa and Dimitri Tiomkin made me feel as if I had suddenly arrived exactly at the end of the rainbow. But I didn't think I could win.

For one thing, my score was up against tough competition: Rozsa's for *El Cid*, Tiomkin's for *The Guns of Navarone*, Morris Stoloff and Harry Sukman's for *Fanny*, and Elmer Bernstein's for *Summer and Smoke*. For another thing, while it was a very successful film, *Breakfast at Tiffany's* was not a true box-office hit. It had such style in the acting and directing; it was as hip as you could get for that time. Nor was it a big picture in scope, just a gentle, softly humorous, introspective picture about a girl named Holly. It was not the kind of score you'd think would win an Academy Award. Even though it served all the purposes required of it, it did not seem to be in the dramatic sense parallel to many of the great Alex North and Al Newman scores. In all honesty, without the enormous success of "Moon River," I don't believe the score would have been nominated. All this was running through my mind as we sat there on those hard, getting harder, chairs.

Nominees are always given aisle seats, so they won't have to climb over a row of knees if they should win, so Johnny was seated on the aisle just in front of me. Johnny and I felt pretty good about "Moon River"'s chances. In a way, though, I was at a disadvantage. It isn't a good thing to have two nominations in one category, because you are competing against yourself, and if you are getting any kind of sympathy ballot, you're splitting it. Still, "Moon River" had had much more exposure than "Bachelor in Paradise" and already seemed to be on its way to being a standard.

As was the custom, all the nominated songs were sung during the course of the ceremony. Ann-Margret sang "Bachelor in Paradise." Virtually unknown, she was then working with a little group down in Newport Beach, and her appearance on television that night was the real launching of her career. And of course Andy Williams, who had the big hit record of it—so much so that for all practical purposes it has become his theme song—sang "Moon River."

They announced the nominations for the best score for a dramatic or comedy picture. Then I heard my name. I felt as if I'd been hit with a cattle prod. I jumped up, gave Ginny a kiss, and ran up to the stage where my old Air Force buddy, Tony Martin, and his wife, Cyd Charisse, handed me an Oscar. It was a long way from Seymour Johnson Field.

The next category was best song. I was still in shock from winning for best score when I heard my name again. Johnny grinned that impish smile of his, and we went up and picked up two Oscars presented by Debbie Reynolds. . . .

In 1962 I got a call from Paramount. I was hot over there because *Breakfast at Tiffany's* was their picture. I was asked to come in to look at a picture that already had music by another composer that they didn't think worked for the picture. He was actually a recording artist, not experienced at film, although he was talented.

I went to Paramount and took a look at it. It hadn't yet been edited down to its final cut, but it looked good, and there were a lot of very interesting things in it. The film was *Hatari!* The star was John Wayne, and the director was the great Howard Hawks. Hawks, one of the industry's legends, directed such films as *The Road to Glory, Dawn Patrol, Scarface, Sergeant York, His Girl Friday, Ball of Fire, To Have and Have Not, Red River*, and many more. I jumped at the chance to work on a picture with him.

Further, it offered an opportunity to score a big-scope film of a kind I hadn't done up to that point. I saw it as a way to open up and broaden my image, one associated with romantic strings and flutes and jazz.

I had a meeting with Hawks in his office. I found him to be a true gentleman. He was a tall man with gray hair cut short. He was a ramrod, straight as an arrow. We discussed the picture, and I told him my ideas about the score. I went to work. Shortly after I started into the score, Howard called and told me he had a lot of musical instruments he had brought back from Africa. He asked if I wanted to take a look at them. Of course I did!

I went over to see him. He dragged out a big box and opened it, an absolute treasure chest of authentic African musical instruments, including the thumb piano, shell gourds, and giant pea pods. These instruments are just what you'd think they are, huge pea pods, about two feet long, which African musicians dry in the sun. When you shake them, the seeds inside set up a rustling rhythm, like maracas but with a very distinct sound. I was entranced and immediately decided to use them in the score. Howard also had some tapes of chants of the Masai, and so, with those instruments and the tapes from which to adapt authentic material, I was in pretty good shape to score the animal scenes, of which there were many. In fact, the picture opens with an animal scene. The music starts out very softly, gaining momentum as the scene unfolds until finally the rhino charges one of the jeeps and gores one of the characters.

Howard shot a lot of material without knowing exactly where or even if he was going to use it. And he shot one such scene with Elsa Martinelli, a sort of cameo or vignette.

In the story there were three baby elephants who had taken to the girl played by Elsa Martinelli because she was the only one who had been able to figure out how to feed the little creatures. Howard had written this detail into the story because this had happened in real life, during the shooting. Those little elephants were crazy about Elsa. They followed her everywhere.

Elephants like to wallow in cool mud, and they love the water. Elsa took the elephants to a watering hole to bathe them. They filled their trunks and squirted each other and Elsa. It simply happened, and Howard shot it. He had now edited this material into a scene that, while absolutely charming, was not really necessary to the story. Howard said, "I don't know what to do with this. I'm thinking of cutting it out. But before I do, take a look at it and let me know if you have any ideas."

So I looked at the scene several times and still thought it was wonderful. As the little elephants went down to the water, there was a shot of them from behind. Their little backsides were definitely in rhythm with something. I kept thinking about it; it reminded me of something. I thought, Yeah, they're walking eight to the bar, and that brought something to mind, an old Will Bradley boogie-woogie number called "Down the Road a Piece," a hit record in the old days, with Ray McKinley on drums and Freddie Slack on piano. Those little elephants were definitely walking boogie-woogie, eight to the bar. I wrote "Baby Elephant Walk" as a result.

I went in to see Howard. You didn't have demo tapes to give to producers in those days. I played it for him on the piano. He loved it.

I was always looking for unusual instruments and somehow had become aware of an electric calliope made by a man named Mr. Baccigalupi in Long Beach. You didn't get all the spit and whoosh you do with a regular steam calliope. It had a perfect sound, light, airy, and perfect for what I had to put there on the screen, and there was only one like it in the world. On top of that I thought that, because the elephants were little creatures, I would use an E-flat clarinet over the calliope. It created something with a really different sound to it, especially in the middle of Africa. This is another example of how the incongruous in scoring sometimes works best—what we call playing against the scene. . . .

Blake returned home to edit [*The Pink Panther*]. He dropped the little piece of information on me that we were going to have a cartoon opening to the picture. He had hired David DePatie and Friz Freleng to do the animation.

By now I was quite familiar with the script and saw the David Niven character, the phantom jewel thief, as an interesting character to score. It was a beautifully written role. He was suave and sophisticated, with a lot of class. The character reminded me of a song called "Jimmy Valentine." There were a number of scenes in which David would be slinking around on tippy-toes. I started to write a theme for him—one of the few times I wrote a theme before seeing the actual picture. That music was designed as the phantom-thief music, not to be the Pink Panther theme.

I had no idea what DePatie and Freleng were going to come up with, what the little Pink Panther character would look like, until they showed me a cell, one frame, that they had done. Cartoonists are very set in their ways, and among their other quirks, they love to have a piece of music they can animate to.

The scoring date was still far in the future. But they wanted to see what I had. I said, "Well, boys, I don't think I have enough scoring to show you, I don't have a piece big enough for you to animate to. And I don't know how long the titles are going to be. It's ass backward."

I told them that I would give them a tempo they could animate to, so that any time there were striking motions, someone getting hit, I could score to it. I said, "Let me come in after you're finished, and I'll do the music."

They weren't thrilled about this, because from their point of view it was working backward.

They finished the sequence and I looked at it. All the accents in the music were timed to actions on the screen. The brass accents and of course the theme worked in perfectly with the little "dead ant" figure, as it came to be known, in the beginning of the piece. I had a specific saxophone player in mind—Plas Johnson. I nearly always precast my players and write for them and around them, and Plas had the sound and the style I wanted. He is the saxophonist on the original *Pink Panther* film.

I realized that the theme I had written for David Niven's character, the jewel thief, was perfect for the opening credits and the cartoon of the little Pink Panther character. I used it for both.

The picture was released in 1965 [*recte* 1964]. It was an immediate and big success. It had a style, as *Breakfast at Tiffany's* did. It was a very "in" picture. Even the people who wouldn't normally go to a romantic comedy went to see it because of Niven and the Clouseau character, which was a personal triumph for Peter [Sellers].

A few years later I conducted the music for the Academy Awards show. David Niven was on the program. The conductor of the Awards show is responsible for choosing the music for the presenters or the guest stars. Usually the choices are obvious, and I picked the Pink Panther music for David. After we had run the theme down, the production manager told me, "David would like to talk with you. He's in his dressing room."

David said, "Hank, as much as I love *The Pink Panther*, the movie and all the work that I've done with Blake, I don't feel that this theme is 'my song.'"

I said, "David, you're absolutely right. How about 'Around the World in 80 Days'?"

David smiled, and that's what we did. . . .

"What do you do? Do you see a rough cut of the film? Do you read the script first? Exactly what do you do?"

I have been asked these questions hundreds of times over the past years, as has every film composer.

It all starts, of course, with someone somewhere saying, "Let's get Mancini for the score."

Sometimes I get the call directly, but most of the time the producer or director calls my agent, Al Bart, to check on my availability. This call can come at any phase of the production of the picture. Sometimes it is in an early stage of the writing of the script, sometimes after the entire film has been shot. If the script is available, I'll read it, and if there is a cut of the picture, I'll see it. If I decide to accept the assignment, Al Bart will start his negotiations. The "negotiations" go through the same legalese that everything else does in Hollywood. Most of the time, I sign my contract for the film long after it has been released.

Sometimes there is a humorous side to this ritual. Recently, the ABC-TV network bought "Peter Gunn" to be presented as a two-hour Movie of the Week. Al proceeded to make my deal with the production company. When the subject of ownership of the copyright of the "Peter Gunn" theme came up, Al told them that I was the sole owner of that copyright, and therefore they would not share in it. The attorney, who was on the sunny side of thirty, inquired with a straight face, "Would Mr. Mancini write a new 'Peter Gunn' theme?"

Now the process starts. Before a single note is written, a meeting of all those involved takes place. The number of people in the room gives an indication of how many people will have something to say later on. Specifics of the music are not really discussed at this time. The main purpose is to reach a sort of agreement on the overall approach to the score—what themes, if any, are needed, and how they should be applied.

What comes next is, for me, the most difficult hurdle: the composition of the thematic material. This can be agonizing, not to mention time-consuming. In the heat of developing themes, sometimes one is guilty of petty theft—a little pinch here and there of other people's thoughts, plus outright stealing from yourself, which is worse. I prevent this by the use of my second set of ears, Ginny's. Every theme or song that I write must first pass her scrutiny. More than a few times she has saved me from embarrassment down the line.

My old boss, Joe Gershenson, once gave me a sage bit of advice, "Take partners," meaning: let the other people in on what you intend to do. Following Joe's advice, I take the next step: letting the front office hear what I have written, with a simple tape of the material played on the piano, as in the old days, or a more elaborate demonstration using synthesizers. I have a basic four-track recording setup in my studio at home, which includes synthesizers, drum machine, and an echo unit. A good demo can only enhance the music to the ears of nonmusicians.

Once everyone agrees to go with what I've written, we wait until the final edit of the film, then proceed to the next step, which is called spotting. This is the process of deciding where the music will be placed and the exact beginning and ending of each piece of music. (The "pieces" are called cues in film parlance.) It is here that we discuss the fine points and nuances. By now a few more people have joined the team. The film editor is usually there and, sometimes, the sound effects editor. Some scenes may be carried by sound effects alone, and at this point such matters are decided. Now another person enters the story, who is invaluable to the composer—the music editor. His job is to provide all the technical information I will need to get the music onto the sound track of the film. He will provide timing sheets that show, down to one-tenth of a second, exactly where I am at each point in a cue. To aid me later, when I am conducting and recording the music, he will prepare each sequence with both visual and sound references that I will need to keep the music in perfect synchronization with the film. I work mostly with two music editors: John Hammell, an alumnus of Paramount Studios, whose experience and credits go back to the days of Cecil B. De Mille; and Steve Hope, who came up through television and is up-to-the-minute with the synthesizers and other toys and gadgets that have become necessary in the electronic age.

When the spotting session is completed, the work begins. The film editor gives me a VHS cassette of the picture, and the music editor starts to feed me the timing sheets. It helps me to look at the film straight through several times before starting to write. Film composing is a problem-solving process, and each time I see the picture I find that more problems are resolved.

Usually I try to score the film in sequence, starting at the beginning and going right through to the end. If I am having difficulty with a certain sequence, I will put it aside and turn to another, knowing, however, that I will fret over the uncompleted sequence until it is finished.

For purposes of identification, each cue is given a numerical identity such as 1-M-1, which indicates that it is the first music cue in the first reel of film, and so forth. It is also given an actual title for purposes of copyright. Ever since film composing began, composers have been vying to see who could make the worst pun on the title of a cue. The entries are legion. However, one sticks in my mind, although I'm sure the author intended no pun. A prominent Viennese composer who spoke English perfectly, except for a slight accent, was scoring a western. He was quite a proper fellow, not taken to much joviality. On the first day of scoring the very first cue, he mounted the podium, tapped his baton, and announced, "Gentleman, . . . Hoof Hearted."

A film, from spotting to recording, takes me about four weeks. When writing music for dramatic purposes, you start to take on in your mind the pace of what is happening in the film. One's own emotional reaction is dictated by what's up there on the screen. Pace and tempo are critical. Four different conductors performing Beethoven's Fifth Symphony will come up with four different timings for the first movement, sometimes minutes off from each other. Unless grossly exaggerated, each of them will be artistically valid. A film composer has no such leeway, as he is boxed in by precise timings that must be adhered to. That perfect tempo to your music, the one that is neither too slow nor too fast, is sometimes elusive. To me, tempo is of prime importance. It could be a deciding factor in whether a scene works or not. It gives me great pleasure to hear one of my friends' scores and be touched by it. I know what he's gone through.

The orchestration of my sketches comes next. Some of my colleagues prefer to do their own orchestration, but in most cases the time crunch does not permit me to do this. Jack Hayes has been my orchestrator since the early days of *Breakfast at Tiffany's*. Jack wrote with a partner, Leo Shuken, for many years, until Leo died. Jack is a consummate musician. More than a few times in the past, he has been called on to ghostwrite film scores for people who have been assigned to them but can't write a note. These "composers" are known among musicians as "hummers," for obvious reasons.

Upon completing his orchestration, Jack turns the music over to the copyist. My copyist is my old friend from the Tex Beneke days, Jimmy Priddy. When it comes time to record, Jack sits in the control booth, monitoring the music. Because the engineer is hearing it for the first time, Jack is a big help to him.

Even as I wallow in the muse while writing, another part of me has to remain aware of the logistics of recording the score. The best studio musicians are, of course, constantly in demand, and the top players are often booked two or three months in advance. Therefore I must decide very early in the process what the exact instrumentation is going to be.

Now another person comes into the picture: my orchestral contractor. For many years my contractor was Marion Klein, wife of the master trumpeter Mannie Klein, but Marion retired recently and now their son, Gus, has taken over. I give Gus the instrumentation, most times accompanied by a list of specific musicians I want. Gus then puts out the call and hires the musicians for me.

At this point the decision must be made as to where to record and who will be the music mixer. In contrast to earlier days when studio soundstages were aging and inadequate, they have been refurbished and are now state-of-the-art. Over the years I have mainly used three engineers: John Richards, whom I first met at CTS in London and who is now at Evergreen Studios in Los Angeles;

Dan Wallin, who at present is at MGM; and Bobby Fernandez, who has been with The Burbank Studios for several years. Discussions between the composer and engineer are necessary to achieve the intended sound of the orchestra.

Now that the music has been composed and copied, the orchestra assembles in the studio in a small forest of music stands and microphones. There is the usual banter and joking among the musicians. I stand on a podium, facing the orchestra, my back to the double-paned glass window to the control booth, through which the engineer and any interested observers—the producer, the director, sometimes even some of the cast—can watch us. This is my favorite time. Now I will find out how close the sounds in my head are to the sounds I am about to hear. I give the first downbeat and run the musicians through whatever cue is to be recorded first, checking for mistakes—either my own or those of the orchestrator or copyist. It is difficult indeed for three men to write all those thousands of notes by hand without an occasional error creeping in. If I hear a wrong note from one of the instruments, I tell the player about it and he corrects it.

These first run-throughs are made without viewing the picture. Now it is time to hear the music in conjunction with seeing the scene it was written for. I ask for it to be projected on the screen, without dialogue or sound effects. The screen is behind the orchestra, so that I can see both—orchestra and picture. We play the music as the scene goes by. This is the moment I have looked forward to most. I can tell now whether or not I have accomplished my job. If the music works, it's pure heaven. If it doesn't, I fix it, and then we start going for a final take, one that is both musically satisfying and perfectly synchronized to the film.

Musicians are hired for three-hour sessions. Thirty minutes of those three hours are taken up by rest periods, in accordance with union regulations. I have found that, under normal financial pressures and taking into account the difficulty of the music, I can record up to ten minutes of music in that time. Television scoring demands up to fifteen minutes of music in the same time. Incidentally, the only real differences I find between feature film composing and television composing is that television pays less and you have less time to complete the job. The average film contains thirty to forty-five minutes of music. The epics, of course, can have wall-to-wall music.

In the old days, the music was recorded in mono, but nowadays it is recorded on thirty-two or more tracks. After the final recording session, it is ready for the mix-down process. I spend many hours with my engineer, going through each musical sequence in the film, condensing and balancing all the tracks into the final mix, which is on three tracks. This is to make the music more manageable for the next phase, which is called re-recording or dubbing.

At this point real life takes over. The euphoria of the scoring stage play-back, with its large speakers, is history. The music will now become part of the overall sound of the film. Of the three sound elements in a picture—dialogue, music, and sound effects—dialogue is the prime concern. A great deal of care is expended to ensure that every word is clearly audible. The music and sound effects must take their proper place, subordinate to the dialogue.

The dubbing room is actually a small theater containing a full-size screen on one wall and a large mixing panel facing it. Usually there is a three-man crew at the panel, one of whom handles the music tracks. All the sound tracks—dialogue, music, sound effects—are fed into the mixing panel from machines in an adjoining room. The film is mixed one reel (one thousand feet) at a time. In earlier years, you had to complete an entire reel to achieve a "take." If a cue was missed at, say, 750 feet, you had to start over again from the beginning. Today, by means of a system called "rock and roll," you need only replay the miscue and insert the correction. The system, among other advantages, permits you to run the film forward or backward at high speed. Electronics has entered the field. This whole procedure can be accomplished by means of videotape. Indeed most television shows are either shot on tape, or shot on film and transferred to tape for editing and dubbing.

Many a composer's heart is broken in the dubbing room. Sometimes music is severely subdued, or cut out entirely. Sometimes it is used under scenes it was not intended for. Cries of "How can they do this to my music?" have been heard. "They" can and "they" do.

The film is now ready for the first screening. Changes may be made—scenes tightened or even omitted, for example—but essentially the process is now completed.

I feel that the old adage, "A good score is one that you're not aware of," is only half true. To be sure, this is so of scenes with important dialogue. But if the viewer is unaware of the music during a three-minute main title—as the part of the film giving the opening credits is called—the composer isn't saying much. The importance of music at this point in a picture is attested to by the "Moon River" title sequence in *Breakfast at Tiffany's*, by Bill Conti's music for the opening of *Rocky* [1976], and by John Williams's music for *Star Wars* [1977], among many examples I could cite.

With the new technology that keeps entering the media, film composers are constantly being placed in new learning situations. Acknowledging this and realizing that one must keep up, I maintain, nonetheless, that the real creative power is in the mind and heart of the composer.

19

Bernard Herrmann: A Lecture on Film Music (1973)

Bernard Herrmann (1911–75) is widely considered to be one of the most important film composers of all, and his fame does not rest merely on the fact that he had the good fortune to work with a succession of front-rank directors responsible for making some of the most critically acclaimed films in the history of the medium; the first of these was Orson Welles's legendary debut feature, *Citizen Kane* (1941), and Herrmann discussed his structurally sophisticated music for this movie in a contemporaneous newspaper article ("Score for a Film: Composer Tells of Problems Solved in Music for *Citizen Kane*," *New York Times*, 25 May 1941). Always something of an outsider to the Hollywood milieu—he hailed from New York and was to remain a respected composer of concert music and opera—Herrmann refused to pander to either the widespread clichés of film-music composition or the sometimes inane demands of musically illiterate producers and directors, in the process earning a formidable reputation for (often decidedly tetchy) outspokenness. His innovative compositional style took an entirely different route from the nationalistic neoclassicism of Aaron Copland, drawing heavily on the stubbornly repetitive and dissonant ostinato techniques of modernist composers such as Béla Bartók and Igor Stravinsky, while at the same time transforming a darkly romantic expressionist vein into a distinctively brooding and unsettling idiom that musicologist Royal S. Brown memorably branded as "music of the irrational."

Source: "Bernard Herrmann, Film Composer," in Evan William Cameron, ed., *Sound and the Cinema: The Coming of Sound to American Film* (Pleasantville, N.Y.: Redgrave Publishing Company, 1980): 117–35.

Herrmann's score for *Citizen Kane* is particularly notable for its use of autonomous musical forms that parallel aspects of the drama, some of which were outlined by the composer in his *New York Times* article. While this strategy was utterly familiar to the twentieth-century opera composer, it was to remain rare in mainstream film music, and was possible in this instance only because Welles was unusually sensitive and respectful toward the structural integrity of the musical cues Herrmann had provided. In some instances, Welles edited his visual images to suit the proportions of precomposed sections of music—another rare phenomenon in Hollywood film production, both then and now. As Herrmann noted, his use of leitmotifs in this score was not typical of his usual approach to film scoring, and in writing shorter cues he drew on the experience he had gained composing economical and inventive music for Welles's experimental radio dramas at CBS in the 1930s.

A little over two years before his death, Herrmann gave the address reprinted below to a symposium titled "The Coming of Sound to the American Film, 1925–1940," held in October 1973 at the International Museum of Photography in George Eastman House, Rochester, New York. Although none of the film scores he chose to discuss as case studies was in fact released during the period with which the conference was primarily concerned, his speech was a wide-ranging and characteristically trenchant discussion of his experiences as a film composer, including comment on the origins of film music in opera and melodrama (omitted from the selection below), the development of music for silent films, the various functions of music in the sound film, and working with directors of the stature of Orson Welles, Alfred Hitchcock, and François Truffaut on (respectively) their seminal films *Citizen Kane* (1941), *Psycho* (1960), and *Fahrenheit 451* (1966).

By this stage in his career, Herrmann had become disillusioned with Hollywood filmmaking, his attitude toward the commercial bias of the film industry having grown implacably embittered following the undignified rejection by Hitchcock of his music to the Cold War thriller *Torn Curtain* (1966), for which both director and producers had insisted on a pop-based score that Herrmann refused to provide. (In his lecture, Herrmann hints that Hitchcock's growing egotism had been a further factor in the breach between them.) Herrmann resigned from AMPAS in 1967, furious that they persisted in regarding film music as merely a "technical" credit, and moved to the United Kingdom in 1971. In addition to his work for Truffaut, which also included *The Bride Wore Black* (1967), his career ended with a handful of scores for young independent American directors Brian De Palma (*Sisters*, 1973; *Obsession*, 1975) and Martin Scorsese (*Taxi Driver*, 1975), both of whom aimed to tap specific emotional characteristics of the classic Hollywood scores Herrmann had composed years before and gave him the respect and, indeed, veneration he had in other quarters found sorely lacking.

The use of music in films is a completely unstudied territory. In the old days there used to be atlases of the world with unexplored regions marked in white and labeled 'unknown'. Well, that's still what cinema music is like. Some of the most sensitive directors are complete ignoramuses concerning the use of music in their own films, while sometimes an inferior director will have a great instinct for it. Whatever music can do in a film is something mystical. The camera can only do so much; the actors can only do so much; the director can only do so much. But the music can tell you what people are thinking and feeling, and that is the real function of music. The whole recognition scene of *Vertigo* [1958], for example, is eight minutes of cinema without dialogue or sound effects—just music and picture. I remember Hitchcock said to me, 'Well, music will do better than words there'.

Remember also, whenever speaking of music in the cinema, that the ear deludes the eye as to what it is seeing. It changes time values. What you think is long may be only four seconds, and what you thought was very short may be quite long. There's no rule, but music has this mysterious quality. It also has a quality of giving shape to a mundane stretch of film. Let me explain that to you.

You can cut a scene ABA, or CBA, or BCA—any way you like. But if you put music from one point in a film to another, there is no alternative to that music as it is in itself. Music is a kind of binding veneer that holds a film together, and hence is particularly valuable in the use of montage. It's really the only thing that seals a montage into one coherent effect. That's why it was used in the newsreel in its most primitive form. (Have you ever watched a newsreel without music? Try it!) This sort of binding is one of the mysterious things that music can do.

The other thing that the sound film permitted music to do for the first time is to give a musical close-up (analogous to the way the camera can give a visual close-up). Let me explain this to you. A lone clarinet playing one note in a concert hall means nothing; but given the way you can manipulate its sound on a sound track, it can be made to take over the whole auditorium. This is another valuable way of using music.

There are some directors who say 'We can make a film without music—we don't need it'. A wonderful example of this attitude was [Tony] Richardson's

Mademoiselle [1966], a film with Jeanne Moreau. Jeanne Moreau, I believe portrays a school teacher who's a pyromaniac. As great an actress as she is, however, she couldn't do anything to give the audience a sense of her inner turmoil. Mr. Richardson (who was so sure that he'd gotten it all on film) had no score prepared, and so the picture went no place. When you saw Moreau's face in the film while her emotions supposedly burnt within her, you heard just silence and some crickets. But with the proper score that would have been a most moving and exciting film!

There's no reason why you can't have a film with sound effects and no music. *The Grapes of Wrath* [1940], *A Tree Grows in Brooklyn* [1945], and *Diabolique* [1954], for example, had no music.[1] Every once in a while there's an exception—a good film without music. But generally the odds are against it. I've been associated with so many films whose music pulled them through. Not only me, but many colleagues of mine have saved films in a similar way by making them acceptable for an hour or two.

Music really is something that comes out of the screen and engulfs the whole audience in a common experience. It isn't something away from the screen. I've spent a long life in films, trying to convince people of this. They don't see it. It's partly because making a film is a cooperative effort of many talents and gifts working together. But, you see, at the present time there's this hysterical cult of the director. No director can make a film by himself. No one man can do it. The nature of the cinema requires cooperative pulsation. And I, having had the privilege and pleasure of working for many great directors, can tell you: the ones who have the greatest humility in this way achieve the greatest films!

I have the final say about my music; otherwise I refuse to do the music for the film. The reason for insisting upon this is that all directors—other than Orson Welles, a man of great musical culture—are just babes in the woods. If you were to follow the taste of most directors, the music would be awful. They really have no taste at all. I'm overstating a bit, of course. They are exceptions. I once did a film, *The Devil and Daniel Webster* [1941], with a wonderful director, William Dieterle. He was a man of great musical culture. Hitchcock is very sensitive: he leaves me alone! (Fortunately, because if Hitchcock were left by himself, he would play "In a Monastery Garden" behind all his pictures!) It depends on the composer, and I'm not making a rule about it. But for myself, personally, I'd rather not do a film than have to take what a director says. I'd rather skip it, for I find it's impossible to work that way. Many years ago [Stanley] Kubrick asked me to write the music for *Lolita* [1962]. When I agreed to do it, he

---

1. In fact, limited music for the first two of these films was provided by Alfred Newman, and George Van Parys contributed music to the third.—Ed.

said 'But there's one thing I've forgotten to tell you: you've got to use a melody of my brother-in-law'. So I told him to forget it.

It shows vulgarity, also, when a director uses music previously composed. I think that *2001: A Space Odyssey* [1968] is the height of vulgarity in our time. To have outer space accompanied by "The Blue Danube Waltz" and the piece not even recorded anew! They just used gramophone records. The best you can come up with for the whole epic of outer space is to play "The Blue Danube Waltz"! They even had a Howard Johnson's in the film! (*Death in Venice* [1971] is a different kind of thing altogether.)

There are directors and directors and directors. Some are so egotistical that you can't say anything to them, while others are sensitive to anybody's opinion and want to hear it. For example, you must never tell Hitchcock about a book you think would make a wonderful film. If you do, it's dead. What you should suggest, rather, is that *he sent you* the book and that you think it's great. Then it's got a chance!

Hitchcock generally was very sensitive about the use of music. He sometimes said to me 'I'm shooting this scene tomorrow. Can you come down to the set?' I'd come to the set and watch, and he'd say 'Are you planning to have music here?' I'd say 'Well, I think we should have it'. 'Oh good', he would say, 'then I'll make the scene longer; because if you were not going to have music, then I would have to contract it'. Some directors are considerate about things like that. Hitchcock, at least, likes people to work with him through the shooting of the film. So do Welles and Truffaut. But there are many directors whom I never even met until the picture was completely shot. They're not even interested enough to care.

Of course there are disappointments in this business, but most are unintentional. Things just don't fuse together sometimes. People go off in different ways. Generally what happens is that somebody's ego (usually the director's) is so great that everybody else becomes superfluous to him. His attitude becomes 'I can do it without you'. This attitude has been the reason for some of Hitchcock's greatest films, and, unfortunately, one of the reasons why Hitchcock and I don't get along any more.

Today the cinema has become a medium for young people's ego expression. I wish they'd just make films and forget about their egos. I recently went to talk to a director who was making a film, and I suggested that one of the things we should do was to go to one of the great cathedrals of England and record the diapason stop on the organ. He said 'No, I don't want no Catholic instrument in my film!'

There are no fixed rules in this business. There is nothing, for example, in the nature of a film that says we should use what they call an 'orchestra' on the sound track. An orchestra was a device developed over several hundred years—an agreed representation of certain instruments to play a certain repertoire. If you wish first to play the music of Haydn at Esterhazy, and then to play it in Paris, you have to use the same kind of instruments. But music for film is created for one performance—for that one film—and there is no law that says it has to be related to concert music. As a matter of fact, such an opportunity to shift the complete spectrum of sound within one piece has never before been given to us in the history of music. You can't do this in an opera house. I know! If you write an opera and you request something a little unusual, they say 'Well, we can't do Wagner if we do yours'. Or 'For Puccini we use this, why can't you use that?'. But not with film! Each film can create its own variety of musical color.

The screen itself dictates musical forms: the way a picture is cut, or the way it's shaped. I myself am very flexible to the demands of the screen itself. I don't think, for example, that one can do a film score that has the musical vitality of, say, a work by Richard Strauss, and get away with it. I mean that in all seriousness! If you could do a score for a picture, and *really* play Strauss's "Don Juan", no one would watch the picture! The music would completely sweep you away and the film would not be seen. Sound and music, after all, are only part of the illusion which is cinema, not all of it. Filmed opera, therefore, won't work because film is primarily visual, while opera is not primarily a visual art. Film aims at melodram, not opera—at an integration of all the arts, not one in isolation.

You may have noticed that the tempi of the gramophone recordings of my film scores frequently differ from the tempi of the soundtracks themselves. Why? The tempo of the music on the film is dictated by the film itself; on a film everything is dictated by the screen. But the tempo of the music on a record is dictated by musical reasons which have nothing to do with cinematic reasons. After all, there is no 'right' tempo for a piece of music. Even with great classic music there is a difference of opinion concerning tempi. (I hate to think what Toscanini would think of Karajan's tempi!)

Now I must discuss a terrible thing, namely, most of the people who write music for films! I would say (and I'd go to the gallows for saying it) that roughly 98 out of every 100 persons making film music would have no more interest in making films if it weren't for the money. Only about 2% are interested in the cinema, and the cinema is a very demanding art form. The rest have figured out how to cheat. Most film music is created by assembly line: one fellow sketches it, another fellow completes it, another one orchestrates it, and yet another adapts it. Consequently the music is dissipated; it has no direction. Then some man of the lowest denomination says 'It'll be a hit!' I don't see what merit this approach has for the creation of a film, but that's the way it is.

There is enormous pressure to write film music which can be exploited afterwards. Out of every 100 film scores we make, the producers would want a gramophone record of 99 of them. *Dr. Zhivago* [1965] is a good example. Notice: nobody ever talks about the *film*. David Lean said recently in London that without its wonderful music his film would have been nothing. If that's what he feels about his film, too bad! But do you see what a terrible and really revolting circle it is? What does that piece of harmless legitimate music have to do with a big saga of the ending of the aristocracy in Russia? Nothing! But to the studio it's great!

I have a friend who was denied a film music contract from a studio and asked for the reason. 'Oh', they said, 'we're using so-and-so. His music sold over a million records.' My friend replied 'But I've sold three-quarters of a million records!'. 'Yes', they said, 'but it wasn't a million was it!'. This is what I've hated all my life. The cinema is a great vehicle for contemporary expression, and a contemporary *art* form. Yet I was recently in the Museum of Modern Art (the museum *called* 'the Museum of Modern Art'!), and the people working there are not interested in music for the cinema at all—not at all. One museum after another is devoted to the contemporary cinema, yet uninterested in film music. And they're proud of it, too, because they don't understand. Even the people who should understand cannot comprehend what's happening to them. I've spent my entire career combating ignorance.

I shall say no more about this. I want to speak about cinema, not the way people abuse cinema and make it rubbish. Let me, therefore, discuss some of my scores, beginning with *Citizen Kane*.

Citizen Kane

Citizen Kane originally had no main title. When it was initially shown, there was no 'RKO' or 'CITIZEN KANE' title, just a black screen. The first thing you saw was the pan up to the sign 'No Trespassing'. I remember at the premier that people shouted all over the place 'lights, sound, sound, sound, projection, sound', because they could not accept a film that started in complete silence. Since the studio couldn't put sound in, they unfortunately added a trade mark and a title instead.

Imagine the opening of *Kane* if it were silent, without music. That is the way it was turned over to me. Does the sequence seem long to you, imagined without music? This was the first sequence I scored. If I remember correctly, I didn't have the idea of a 'Rosebud' theme, nor of a 'Destiny' or 'Fate' theme. Both themes sort of automatically presented themselves to me. You don't write music with the top of your mind; you write it from a part you don't know anything about. Anyway, I was very lucky in the first hour of composition: I hit on two sequences of sound that could bear the weight of this film. (I was just in luck; if I had not had that luck, it might have been a disaster for me.) The picture opens with a motive I call 'the Motive of Destiny', of Kane's destiny. Later in the film the permutations of this theme become a can-can, jazz, all kinds of things. Then, when Kane sees the flickering snow, we hear for the first time the motive of 'Rosebud' around which the whole picture pivots. This second theme tells everybody what Rosebud is, even though they soon forget about it. But the music has told them, right away.

This opening sequence also uses an unconventional orchestra of eight flutes (four being alto), four bass flutes, very deep contrabass clarinets, clarinets, tubas, trombones, deep lower percussion, and a vibraphone.

Imagine now the sound track to the opening sequence alone, without the visuals. Decide for yourself whether or not you think the music by itself is too long. I think the music's too long. I, of course, had no choice about its length. The director gives you the visuals because this is his vision. Sometimes one can go to a director and complain, feeling that things are disproportionate and should be changed—but certainly not in a film like this!

Imagine now the full opening sequence, visuals and sound together. Do you still feel that the sequence is too long? I think not—and that's one of the great mysteries of the power of music in cinema! Without the music the picture is incomplete, and the time scale is skewed.

Why didn't I use percussive or rhythmic effects rather than music here? *Citizen Kane* is a romantic picture. It's about a man obsessed by a little gadget called 'Rosebud'. Percussive sound effects would have been inappropriate in the opening, and wouldn't have worked later on either, for similar reasons. As a matter of fact, later on in the film Kane picks up Susan in the street, and says 'I was on my way to the warehouse to look at some things my mother left me'. The reason he responds to the girl is that she faintly resembles his mother—and the orchestra gives out the 'Rosebud' theme! Nobody's ever caught it, nobody's ever written about it. They don't have to because it's there! Sometimes with a subject this romantic you must do romantic things.

On the other hand, there is a great [Japanese] picture, *A Woman in the Dunes* [1964], which was all done with electronics, with the most marvelous use of electronics. Every picture is unique. I'm not implying that there's only one way to score a picture, because there are many ways providing imagination is used. But I doubt whether one could have substituted percussive effects for music in a picture like *Kane*, a kaleidoscopic picture. A certain greyness would settle over it.

The opera sequence in *Citizen Kane* presented a very great problem. Perhaps you have read Miss Pauline Kael's book about the making of the film. I would like to say publicly that she never wrote me or approached me to ask about the music, even though she has included pages of spurious wisdom about it, including the purported 'fact' that we evidently were so poverty stricken that we couldn't afford to use Massenet's "Thais"!

Why did we have to write an opera for this sequence? Kane's girlfriend, Susan, is partially modeled on a friend of William Randolph Hearst; but she is also partially modeled on Ganna Walska, the lady friend and later wife of Harold McCormick whose former wife, Edith Rockefeller, was instrumental in getting Samuel Insull to build the Chicago Opera House. Our problem was to create something that would give the audience the feeling of the quicksand into which this simple little girl, having a charming but small voice, is suddenly thrown. And we had to do it in cinema terms, not musical ones. It had to be done quickly. We had to have the sound of an enormous orchestra pounding at her while everyone is fussing over her, and then—'Now get going, go!'—they throw her into the quicksand.

There is no opera is existence that opens that way. We had to create one. But this doesn't stop Miss Kael from saying that we could not afford "Thais", with its lovely little strings, which we could have afforded any time. The point is that it wouldn't have served the emotional purpose. I didn't particularly care to write an opera sequence like this, but *Kane* demanded it. Not Welles, but *Kane*. It was the only way, from a cinematic point of view, that we could convey the terror that this girl was in.

How could we achieve this effect musically? If Susan couldn't sing at all, then we know she wouldn't have found herself in this position. But she had something of a little voice. So I wrote this piece in a very high tessitura, so that a girl with a modest little voice would be completely hopeless in it. (Later on, singers like Eileen Farrell would sing it to great effect.) We got a very charming singer to dub Susan's voice, explaining to her the purpose of the effect. Notice: the reason Susan is struggling so hard is *not* that she cannot sing but rather that the demands of the part are purposely greater than she can ever meet.

One should note this opera sequence carefully, because this is a case where the music had to be created for the film, and it's my contention that no other approach could have solved the problem. Had we played the last scene of "Salome", we'd have gotten the same effect, but it wouldn't have shown Susan *starting* the opera. (The beginning of "Salome" anyone can sing.) The problem was: can Susan survive the *beginning*? That was the problem the film posed.

Look and listen to Susan in her music lesson. In this case the music was written before the scene was filmed; the scene was photographed to a playback.

If you think about it, you'll understand why a conventional opera wouldn't have worked. It wouldn't have worked because there doesn't exist that terror-in-the-quicksand feeling at the beginning of any conventional opera.

It's discouraging to see an eminent critic dispose of the problem by saying that we couldn't afford to use "Thais". People think that Pauline Kael is the gospel. That's how falsehoods are perpetrated. If this is how good she is about the music, I hate to think how good she is about anything else. I happen to disagree with the premise of her whole book on *Kane*, because she tries to pretend that Welles is nothing, and that a mediocre writer by the name of [Herman] Mankiewicz was a hidden Voltaire. I'm not implying that Mankiewicz made no contribution: the titles say so on the screen, and Orson says that Mankiewicz did make a valuable contribution. But without Orson all of Mankiewicz's other pictures were nothing, before and after. With Orson, however, something happened to this wonderful man. (He was a wonderful man in a way, except that his life was very disappointing to him. But he could not have created *Kane*.)

There are so many people interested in trying to pretend that Orson didn't do anything. This is in great vogue today: to pretend that all the great masters of the past and of today really didn't do anything. It was the bootblack who did it for them!

This gets me into the realm of authors and authorship. There's nothing that says a film should be like the novel from which it's adapted, or that a visualization of a piece of music has to resemble the music, and I think people who think that are wrong. If you don't like movies and think that the picture they are making is distorting your novel, then don't let them make a film of your novel. But if you like their money, just take it and shut up! I'll tell you a great story about Stravinsky. Selznick asked Stravinsky to do the score for a film, and Stravinsky agreed. Selznick asked his price. Stravinsky answered '$100,000'. Selznick retorted, 'We don't spend that kind of money for music!'. 'Ah', Stravinsky replied, 'it's not for the music. That's cheap. It's for my name!'

The next part of *Kane* I'd like to consider is the little marriage breakfast scene in Kane's first marriage. Imagine the visuals alone, without the music. This is what I was given. The popular music of this period corresponding to the image would have been a romantic waltz. So each change in mood and each cut was designed to be a variation on a basic waltz theme. The structure of the sequence is therefore simple: a series of waltz variations in absolutely classic form, giving unity to the scene and making it whole.

The ending of *Kane* gave me a wonderful opportunity to arrive at a complete musical statement, since the ending contains no dialogue with the exception of perhaps one or two lines. I wished at the end of the film to summon forth and draw all the dramatic threads together. This last musical sequence is played by a conventional symphony orchestra. I used a full orchestra for the simple reason that, from the time the music of the final sequence begins to the end of the film, the music has effectively left the film and become an apotheosis of the entire work.

I was fortunate indeed to start my cinema career with a film like *Citizen Kane*. It's been a downhill run ever since! I receive all kinds of requests from producers, most of whom say 'I want you to write a score like you did for *Kane*'. I reply 'Do you have a picture like *Kane*?' They don't realize that you can't write another *Kane*, or *Psycho*, because there's only one *Kane*, or *Psycho*. People always tell me how difficult Welles is to work with. I would say about my own career that the only people I've met worth working for were difficult people, because they're interested in achieving something. Just spare me the charmers! Welles in every other way of life may be difficult, but when it comes to making artistic decisions he's a rock of Gibraltar. . . .

Psycho

I wish, lastly, to discuss some parts of *Psycho* by Hitchcock. In film studios and among filmmakers, there is a convention that the main titles have to have cymbal crashes and be accompanied by a pop song—no matter what! The real function of a main title, of course, should be to set the pulse of what is going to follow. I wrote the main title music for *Psycho* before Saul Bass even did the animation. They animated to the music. The point, however, is that after the main title nothing much happens in this picture, apparently, for 20 minutes or so. Appearances, of course, are deceiving, for in fact the drama starts immediately with the titles! The *climax* of *Psycho* is given to you by the music right at the moment the film begins. I am firmly convinced, and so is Hitchcock, that after the main titles you know that something terrible must happen. The main title sequence tells you so, and that is its function: to set the drama. You don't need cymbal crashes or records that never sell! (The only orchestra used, incidentally, is a string orchestra, the same kind of orchestra with which one plays Mozart. I mention this because people have all kinds of ideas about the instrumentation used, including a wonderful new study of *Psycho* which says I wrote wonderfully for woodwinds!)

When I was first shown this film, Hitchcock was depressed about it. He felt it didn't come off. He wanted to cut it down to an hour television show and get rid of it. I had an idea of what one could do with this film, so I said 'Why don't you go away for your Christmas holidays, and when you come back we'll record the score and see what you think'. (Hitchcock always goes away for 5 or

Bernard Herrmann (left) with Alfred Hitchcock during their collaboration on *Vertigo* in 1958. (Photofest; photograph by G. E. Richardson, © Paramount Pictures)

6 weeks for Christmas.) 'Well', he said, 'do what you like, but only one thing I ask of you: please write nothing for the murder in the shower. That must be without music.'

When Hitchcock returned we played the score for him in the mixing and dubbing studio (not at a recording session). We dubbed the composite without any musical effects behind the murder scene, and let him watch it. Then I said 'I really do have something composed for it, and now that you've seen it your way, let me try mine'. We played him my version with the music. He said 'Of course, that's the one we'll use'. I said 'But you requested that we not add any music'. 'Improper suggestion, improper suggestion', he replied.

Many people have inquired how I achieved the sound effects behind the murder scene. Violins did it! People laugh when they learn it's just violins, and that's interesting to me. It shows that people are so jaded that if you give them cold water they wonder what kind of champagne it is. It's just the strings doing something every violinist does all day long when he tunes up. The effect is as common as rocks. (The soundtrack on *The Birds* [1963] is another story. It was all done electronically. At that time the only place which possessed the equipment to do the sound was in West Berlin, so we went there. I worked with a chap named Remi Gassman at the West Berlin Radio Workshop. The whole score is electronic.)

I wish also to explain something interesting about the murder scene itself in *Psycho*. The final shot, which appears to be a pan and zoom shot into the drain hole of the bathtub, was the most expensive and difficult aspect of the entire film. Every frame was printed separately and enlarged gradually, millimeter by millimeter. People think it's an ordinary zoom shot, yet every frame was enlarged, one by one, by Eastman. To get that effect took the longest time and cost more money than any other aspect of the production of the film.

There's a rumor that *Psycho* was shot in color, but released in black and white. This is only a rumor, for *Psycho* was not made in color; it was made as cheaply as possible. The whole picture was shot by a television crew in a little under three weeks, and was purposely shot in black and white. That's one of the reasons why I use a string orchestra; I wanted to get a black and white musical color. It never was shot in color. Don't believe everything you read!

Conclusion

The cinema is a great contemporary art form. I believe that when we're all gone, people in the 21st century will be interested neither in our literature nor in our music but only and completely in our cinema. That will be our legacy to them. (Just think if we could see a film made in 1870!) The people, therefore, who view the cinema as a hack way of making money are betraying one of the greatest means of expressing themselves completely and fully—a means directly related to that ancient Greek ideal of melodram because it consists of spoken drama with music. I admit that there have been other attempts to change the function of cinema, but essentially it retains this ideal, and the ideal will persist.

I don't think that it's possible to advise up-and-coming young composers on special areas of training which will enable them to become expert film composers. Creators of film music must have it in their bones, and their imaginations must be triggered by working in films. Many people have their egos stimulated by working in films, but they haven't got much imagination. Ego stimulation is no rarity, but to have a fertile imagination is quite another story. Mozart once said that whenever he saw a piece of music paper and thought of the word 'aria', he got excited! By an empty piece of music paper and an idea! That's how one has to feel about cinema. Nobody ever starts out to make a bad piece of film. Everybody starts wanting to make something good, but there's a long road to be traveled to make it good, and it requires a certain flexibility. I myself don't feel that film music is of much interest divorced from the film. Many people disagree with me, but to me it seems like playing the accompaniment to a song without the melody.

I don't know how you begin to understand the function of film music. You can study counterpoint all you like, and then write a piece of music, for you've been studying the rules of composition. But rules and sensitivity can be miles apart. Hundreds of films have died for lack of a sensitive musical score, though written by men who knew the rules. Jean Cocteau once made a fine remark concerning sensitivity in film music. He said that a film score should create the sensation that one does not know whether the music is propelling the film, or the film is propelling the music. This use of cinematic music is so mysterious that I can actually say, after surviving 60-odd films, that I don't know much about it myself. I know *instinctively* about it, but I don't know intellectually. I have to leave that to my superiors.

20

A Conversation with Jerry Goldsmith (1977)

In this interview conducted by his friend and fellow film composer Elmer Bernstein, Jerry (Jerrald) Goldsmith (1929–2004) begins by recalling his early career
as a composer of music for CBS radio and television before he was talent-spot-
ted by Alfred Newman and invited to score the contemporary western *Lonely
Are the Brave* (dir. David Miller, 1962). The assignment proved to be the first in
a long series of resourceful movie scores composed by Goldsmith, who quickly
became a leading light of a dualistic modernist approach that on the one hand
updated traditional orchestral techniques with a high degree of dissonance and
textural fragmentation, and on the other experimented with the more radical
electronic timbres increasingly in vogue during the 1960s and 1970s. By 1977,
when this conversation took place, Goldsmith's credits included several
acclaimed films by director Franklin Schaffner (*The Planet of the Apes*, 1968;
Patton, 1969; *Papillon*, 1973), his scores for which demonstrated unusual versa-
tility in their willingness to adapt to the contrasting requirements of markedly
different dramatic topics. Goldsmith had also given a fresh lease of life to two
well-worn genres: the detective thriller, which he imbued with a neo-noir atmosphere in *Chinatown* (dir. Roman Polanski, 1974), and the horror film, his
much-imitated score for *The Omen* (dir. Richard Donner, 1976) earning him
his sole Academy Award. Goldsmith habitually worked in close collaboration
with veteran orchestrator Arthur Morton (1908–2000), who had been active in
Hollywood as an arranger and composer of stock music since the mid-1930s.

Source: Film Music Notebook, 3/2 (1977): 18–31; reprinted in *Elmer Bernstein's Film Music Notebook: A Complete Collection of the Quarterly Journal, 1974–1978* (Sherman Oaks, Calif.: Film Music Society, 2004): 392–405,
396–97, 400–404.

In the later 1970s Goldsmith became closely associated with the burgeoning of sci-fi epics, scoring *Capricorn One* (1978), *Alien*, and *Star Trek:
The Motion Picture* (both 1979), and thereafter was also much in demand for
action films well suited to his propulsively dissonant idiom; his contributions to this genre included the first three *Rambo* movies (1982–88). He
remained active as a film composer until shortly before his death, his last
major assignment being *Star Trek: Nemesis* in 2002, and frequently conducted film music in the concert hall and championed neglected or rejected
scores by other composers (for example, Alex North's music jettisoned from
Stanley Kubrick's *2001: A Space Odyssey* [1968], which Goldsmith recorded
in 1993). Like other film composers with a solid classical training, Goldsmith strongly believed in the value of good film music away from its original context.

EB: Do you have a particular notion of what the function of music in a
given film is? How do you approach it? What do you look for when you start to
spot a film?

JG: Well, basically, I am looking for the humanistic values. I want to find a
character that I can get inside of, my focal point at least, I don't believe in the
leitmotif style of composing something for this, something for that. I want a
central character which will motivate the score thematically and I want everything out of the score to develop from there. I'm looking for some meaning or
emotional values that are not on the screen. We're not set decorators.

EB: In other words, what you're saying is you are looking for music as an
emotional element to the film.

JG: Absolutely. It may seem like a sophomore answer but that's what it is.

EB: No, that's a very straight answer.

JG: You really have to bring something emotionally to the picture that's not
there. Otherwise the music is redundant.

EB: How do you approach communication with command people (usually
the director)?

JG: Generally, I've worked with literate people, for example, Franklin
Schaffner is very, very knowledgeable musically although he never studied
music. But Franklin has incredible sense. He also can read music. He goes in
the booth with the scores actually. Even so, I can still not communicate with
him verbally in *musical* terms. I am really, basically dealing in terms of *dramatics*. That is the method of communication. The kind of director I am afraid

to work with talks about sounds! Sounds! I hate that! Don't talk in terms of sounds. What does that mean? I think in music that makes sounds.

EB: Well, you are concerned with content, and unfortunately many people see music as wallpaper, as you say, set decorations.

JG: For example, in *Chinatown*, [producer] Bob Evans had fallen in love with *I Can't Get Started* by Bunny Berigan and he thought the whole picture and the music should really have that flavor. Well, now that's tangible, we can pinpoint it. I explained, "I don't feel that that would be right for the film because the picture is the 1930's all over again, I grew up in Los Angeles and that's amazingly enough the way it looked. I can remember this whole ambience as a kid. It's too much of a re-emphasis of 30's with that kind of music. Let me go in another direction." He understood and said, "You're right!" So here was one means of communication because we had the plans already set up. When you don't have this, you know you are dealing in terms of dramatics. What elements to explore dramatically. As you know, we're the first people to see the picture.

EB: Yes, of course.

JG: The studio heads haven't seen it, nobody has seen it except the editor and the director. We come in and they're very insecure and uncertain because they have been living with this for so long. So here, two fresh eyes, two fresh ears and people they hope and feel have some taste and knowledge. I don't feel that first meeting should be a sounding board of what I think of their film. From their feedback, I gain a great insight into where their insecurities lie, if they are there and immediately start to psych out what are the dramatic possibilities, where am I going to go dramatically and that's really the first line of communication. As time goes on, I get more and more specific in terms of dramatics, but I think the basic line of communication is dramatics.

EB: Of course. Composers come to a film as strangers. We're often a stranger to the director. When he comes to the first scoring session, music is sort of an elegant, emotional stranger entering his life and that becomes a very crucial period. Have you found for instance, on going on to the stage to do the recording that you find the director nervous or apprehensive about what's going on on the scoring stage or have you psyched him out by that time so that he is not uncomfortable?

JG: Well, it's sort of hard to answer that question. First of all, I'm so nervous that I can't be worried about the other guy. It's my problem, not his that I'm most concerned about. After so many years, I still have many insecurities about how my music is going to sound. There are times when I am not quite sure how things will sound. At times I know exactly. There is a strange thing that will happen. Most of the time I have found that when you are at the stage with a big orchestra (this goes back to the days of radio), there is some kind of magic that happens. You put all these musicians in a room and they can play a unison C and all of a sudden everyone is very turned on, there is a lot of electricity. So, unless it is really a total miss, you get a tremendous feedback from the director or producer—they are all excited about everything but from then it's all *up* hill.

EB: What happens for instance, where there is a disagreement on a particular sequence?

JG: On a score page?

EB: Yes.

JG: Lots of times I invite this,—I say, "Please, for God's sake if there is something that bothers you, ask me *now* or tell me *now* while I can still do something about it! I can rewrite it tonight, but *don't* do it when we get to the dubbing stage!"

EB: As I understand the expression, you feel perfectly willing to rewrite something if you consider a valid reason has been given.

JG: Absolutely, when it comes to making a change I think 95% of the time it is quite valid and I'll tell you, 80% of the changes are of my own volition. I will make them before someone else suggests it. I think the most particular person is Schaffner because he will go right down to the particular instrument, because he knows his picture so well, and he is so meticulous. He will say, "Look, I am worried about the range, maybe you should put it an octave lower? I am worried about blocking the dialogue." This is a marvelous calibration. Let us say the director has been working with sound effects, and he says, "Look, we have a terrific effect here—we can't possibly get both it and the music in. I think maybe the music should start here." I would rather it be worked out on the scoring stage instead of having someone go with a pair of scissors to the dubbing stage!

EB: Has your experience been that you are involved after the picture is shot, or do you get an opportunity to talk to the people while it is in production?

JG: It varies, Elmer. Sometimes they can't make up their minds, sometimes they call you the night before the director has been hired. It seems lately I have been more and more involved before the production has started and at least have had some meetings with the director ahead of time, based on the script. But I don't find this terribly helpful because as far as I'm concerned, I could not sit down and write a theme from the script. I never have been able to. We are dealing in a visual media and I have to see the film. . . .

EB: What was the most difficult thing you had to do?

JG: The first was *The Sand Pebbles* [1966]. I could not get a theme for love nor money, and I battled and battled for weeks on that thing and then I said, "I can't wait any longer" and I scratched out a really cornball tune. I had elected to do the first cue first, and I don't know what happened, but what I had originally written I started to write as the theme and it took a whole different shape—a whole different direction and it became a very pretty tune and I guess it was one of my most successful in terms of being commercial—you know, the theme from *The Sand Pebbles*—it's a standard now. One of the big hits in Musak!! All of a sudden that magic thing happened. The other was *Papillon*. As well and as close as I have worked with Schaffner for twenty years, I fought his ideas (going back to our other discussion earlier about organization). For this picture he was able to say, "Look, I feel there should be a thread of Montmartre in the music," but I fought with him—in my mind it seemed too "on the nose" but he was right, and I kept fighting this. I was so miserable. I spit more blood on his picture than anyone else and as Arthur Morton said to me, he said to Frank Schaffner: "I don't know what you do to Goldsmith—you sure freak him out!" Then all of a sudden I really came to a big emotional moment and the theme went together. The little snippets I had been playing with for weeks became the theme for Montmartre and again that became a very successful tune, especially in Europe.

EB: What do you do when you find you are not making headway? Let's say in those two weeks. Do you go to your studio every day and keep hacking away at it or do you go for walks? How do you deal with that?

JG: I just keep hacking away at it and get more and more miserable. My wife can't stand me another minute during that period of time! You know, it's just discipline or lack or it. Stravinsky would get up and start working at 8 o'clock and finish at 1 o'clock and take his nap. It was discipline—*every* day whether he wrote or he didn't, Thomas Mann was the same way. He would sit at his typewriter for a prescribed number of hours with a fingernail file and clean his fingernails and sit there and work. I wish we all had the same kind of discipline. So many marvelous composers cannot adapt themselves to the regime and the pressures we have in writing for motion pictures. We have an orchestra of 70 musicians five weeks from now and we have to be there with the music! My recurring nightmare is that I'm walking on the stage and the score isn't finished!

EB: You're a member of a large club! Talking on the subject of concepts, take-off position for creation of scores, one of your works which particularly impressed me, because of the concept, was *Patton*. After all, here is this basically unpleasant character in a war situation. You hit upon a solution which in my opinion elevated the entire film to a level which it could not have achieved without what you did for it. I am curious—how did you arrive at what you did?

JG: Well, that was probably the most intellectual exercise that I ever put forth on a film. My relationship with Schaffner, besides working for him is that for many years we have been close friends personally and I absolutely worship the man creatively and humanistically and when I'm on the picture, the phone rings every morning at 7:30 a.m. with some silly joke, or "How are you doing?" and we will talk for five minutes or an hour and he will drop some little remark which has some creative purpose. On that picture I felt very little demand for music—I didn't see a hell of a lot of music for the picture! As a matter of fact, there wasn't very much music in the picture. Only 30 minutes and the picture ran almost 3 hours. I felt the picture was an anti-war picture. That was my feeling. It wasn't made that way but that was the point of view I took. The audiences took two points of view. If one looks back in history, there isn't a war that doesn't have some religious implications somewhere, including Viet Nam. The man was a religious man and first my idea was to use a doxology and I told Frank about this and he thought about it and said it might be a good idea. I used that, and said I would write a march as a counterpoint to that and so the actual march I wrote was a counterpoint to the doxology. So now I get a call from him one day already anticipating what he was going to say and he said, "You can't do it. You are really reaching a little far and insulting the Protestants." I said, "You are absolutely right!" So I wrote a reverse counterpoint, but I was still going to make a chorale of religious character which I did. The march was to represent the militaristic character of the man, the chorale the religious part of the man and the trumpet fanfare was to represent his belief in reincarnation!

EB: That's the one thing I was most interested in because obviously that was the most striking feature of the score. The fanfare—the whole use of the brass. Was that trumpet electrified?

JG: Yes, there were two trumpets put through echoplex.

EB: I don't know what it meant to you but it seemed to conjure up warriors of old. It had a very ancient feeling to it.

JG: Well, that's what it was supposed to do, and by doing it electronically it added another element. I mean doing it live still never gets the same effect as electronically. It was one of those things—how do you get the idea—it just came to me, that's all!

EB: What were you looking for when it came to you?

JG: Just to somehow subtly be able to remind the audience that this facet of his character was alive. This was a three-fold character I was telling. My feeling is that all of these elements musically had to stand by themselves or in various combinations of their parts so that you had the summation of the character when you have all three elements going, or you were seeing one particular facet of the man when he was reliving the battle of Carthaginia. When he was preparing for battle, it was more of a religious rite. I mean it was a ritual. There I took the chorale and expanded it. As I said, it was really the most intellectual score I had ever written. Patton attracted my emotions and my mind. But the picture lent itself more to the intellect. It was a portrait of a man. *MacArthur* [1977] is the same thing.

EB: That must have been very difficult—tackling another like character!

JG: The fortunate thing was that they weren't alike. Neither man did I admire as a human being!

EB: They were alike in the sense that they were "bigger than life" characters in their own eyes.

JG: You are absolutely right, but MacArthur was a much more complex person, but a much more overt person than Patton. There were not that many facets to him. There was a more regal quality about the man that I really tried to get musically. You can write the most brilliant pieces construction wise, you can be so involved but some little gimmick will catch someone's fancy!

EB: The first time I did a motion picture was in 1950, and Morris Stoloff was the head of the Music Department at Columbia, and he told me one thing which I think is eminently true about our art, and that is, we are basically working for an audience that will see the film only once, and the impression that we have to make is an impression that must be immediate. I think those gimmicks of which you speak are so successful because those are the things that are easily latched on to.

JG: That's right. What I really try to do is to take one simple motif of the material for the picture, and a broad theme, and construct it so they always can work in concert with each other or separately. A repetitive value of an identifiable motif does have an accumulative effect upon the audience if they hear it enough times.

EB: Do you work from cue sheets or do you use a moviola?

JG: I use both. I haven't used a moviola the last couple of years, but I like it for two reasons. I needn't tell you, but there probably isn't a more lonely profession than a composer. If you are a writer you can have music on. If you are an actor, you are with others. The composer has a really lonely existence. If I'm doing a scene, I will pick a particular close-up of a character and leave the moviola lamp on it and I feel like I have company with me. Not saying anything approving or disapproving, but I'm not there alone. And also I really have found that I have been missing a lot by not being involved in the scenes.

EB: Tell me about how you work with orchestrators. That's something that is apparently of great interest to our readers. We have had some requests for whole articles on the function of orchestrators. There is probably some misunderstanding about what orchestrators do.

JG: I think there is a terrible misunderstanding about that because there is an arranger, and then there is an orchestrator. You know in the heyday of Fox and Metro when they did all those musicals there was the *arranger* who would come in and write the arrangement and then there was the *orchestrator* who would come in and orchestrate the arrangement. I have done about 70 films with Arthur Morton. I find besides being my closest friend, he is a colleague and collaborator to a great extent and a very strong shoulder to lean on. I write a nine line sketch, two lines for brass, two lines for strings, one for the percussion and I pretty well indicate what I want. All the musical elements are there, every note, counterpoint, harmony—that's all there. I don't know how a composer can write for the orchestra without sketching for the orchestra. I know there are some that do, but I can't work that way. I can see the orchestra right here so I write down what I hear and indicate what instruments are going to play what.

EB: In other words, you are totally satisfied with the final result exactly as you intended it to be.

JG: Hopefully, yes; then I will sit with Arthur. Some sequences don't need to really be discussed. He knows me so well by now he knows my shorthand—he can read my bad writing—he knows what I am talking about! Others we will spend a great deal of time discussing. Because of the limitation of time, we don't have that second chance to think. When you are really pressured, you can't give it the kind of thought you would like. I can sit for hours deciding how should I write this for the brass, but Arthur would say, "Don't waste your time." We'll discuss it, how we are going to lay it out, and we'll spend a great deal of time at the piano and work it out and many times I'll rewrite things while he is there. The whole fabric I conceive ahead of time. For instance in *The Omen*, Arthur was absolutely invaluable. I would have to say at least 65% of the choral writing was arranged by Arthur. I had written it, but he really opened it up in such a fashion that it sounded much better than the way I had written it. You know I hadn't written that much for chorus in the last 25 years and I must say I got a bit rusty at it and he made a tremendous contribution in that area alone. It's things like that where the orchestrator is a tremendous help.

EB: You are one of the few composers that I know that has successfully integrated the use of the electronic instruments which I consider to be an intelligent way of doing scoring. Is that a result of any philosophy concerning electronic music or do you consider the electronics a gadget or tool?

JG: I read an article somebody wrote about me and they were very angry with me because I used electronic music in *Logan's Run* [1976]. Somewhere I must have put down the use of electronics. Perhaps I might have said this four or five years ago although I can't remember. Doing *The Satan Bug* in 1963 and

Paul Beaver was just getting going, he had this little Solovox he had souped up, and it was fascinating using it then. My feeling about electronic music then was that it's not a means to an end, but it's a modern gadget, a new section of the orchestra, and I guess in the last three years I started to re-educate myself in the use of electronics. If a composer is going to write electronically, I feel he has to have it in his head the same way as if he is writing for an orchestra. When you are writing for an orchestra, if you can see it electronically, then you have some concept of what you are going to accomplish electronically. The only way I can do it is by investing heavily in the electronic equipment and learning the process that does this. It's very logical if you understand how the electronic elements interact with each other then you can more or less predict what is going to happen. Of course there are accidents, but there are accidents that happen with an orchestra too. I must do it at home. I pre-record it at home and take it to the studio to combine it with the orchestra. . . .

21

John Williams and *Star Wars* (1997)

This interview marked the twentieth anniversary of the first film in George
Lucas's original *Star Wars* trilogy, which was released in 1977 (netting several
Academy Awards, including one for its score) and quickly became a box-office
and merchandizing phenomenon; its impact on the Hollywood film industry's
financial and artistic aspirations is still very much in evidence today. Along with
Steven Spielberg, Lucas revitalized commercial film production by returning to
old-fashioned adventure stories told on an epic scale with lavish special effects.
Composer John Williams (b. 1932) worked closely with both directors, strength-
ening their incident-laden narratives with finely crafted music that was firmly
rooted in the tonal and structural procedures of orchestral scores from the earlier Golden Age. For Spielberg, Williams had already composed his famously
threatening music for *Jaws* (1975), one of the first blockbusters of the so-called
New Hollywood school, and his later successes with this director included *Close
Encounters of the Third Kind* (1977); *E.T. the Extra Terrestrial* (1982); the Indiana
Jones trilogy spawned by *Raiders of the Lost Ark* (1981); *Schindler's List* (1993);
Jurassic Park (1993) and its first sequel; *Amistad* (1997); *Saving Private Ryan*
(1998); and many more.

Lucas and Williams revisited the *Star Wars* format in a second trilogy of
films released in 1999–2005, for which the music (as in the first trilogy) was
recorded in the United Kingdom by the London Symphony Orchestra. By this
time Williams had long been reputedly the most highly paid film composer in
the world, and well known in the concert hall through his work with the Boston

Source: Craig L. Byrd, "The Star Wars Interview: John Williams," *Film Score Monthly*, 2/1 (1997): 18–21.

John Williams recording his score to *Star Wars: Episode I—The Phantom Menace* (dir. George Lucas) at London's Abbey Road studios in 1999. Courtesy of Lucasfilm Ltd. *Star Wars: Episode I—The Phantom Menace*™ & © 1999 Lucasfilm Ltd. All rights reserved. Used under authorization. Unauthorized duplication is a violation of applicable law.

Pops Orchestra. In addition to his high-profile work for Lucas and Spielberg, he had been involved with two other hugely successful movie franchises, working for director Chris Columbus on *Home Alone* (1990) and *Harry Potter and the Philosopher's Stone* (2001) and on several of their sequels. Although the frequent claim that with his 1970s blockbuster scores Williams single-handedly rescued the old-fashioned orchestral film score from incipient oblivion (its survival having been constantly threatened by pop and electronic music) has been somewhat overstated, his development of a rich and often memorably tuneful orchestral idiom with considerable commercial potential has been enormously influential in the industry.

CRAIG L. BYRD [CB]: How did the *Star Wars* project first come to your attention? How did you become involved?

JOHN WILLIAMS [JW]: My involvement with *Star Wars* began actually with Steven Spielberg, who was, in the '70s when these films were made, and still is, a very close friend of George Lucas's. I had done two or three scores for Steven Spielberg before I met George Lucas, *Jaws* being the principal one among them. I think it was that George Lucas, when he was making *Star Wars*, asked his friend Steven Spielberg who should write the music, where will he find a composer? The best knowledge I have is that Steven recommended me to George Lucas as a composer for the film, and I met him under those circumstances, and that's how it all began.

CB: How did you feel when you were first contacted about his project? Was it about one film at the time, or all three?

JW: The first contact had to do only with *Star Wars*. I didn't realize that there would be a sequel and then a sequel after that at that time. I imagine George Lucas planned it that way and perhaps even mentioned it to me at the time, but I don't remember. I was thinking of it as a singular opportunity and a singular assignment.

CB: What was your reaction when you read the script?

JW: I didn't read the script. I don't like to read scripts. When I'm talking about this I always make the analogy that if one reads a book, a novel, and then you see someone else's realization of it, there's always a slight sense of disappointment because we've cast it in our minds, and created the scenery and all the ambiance in our mind's imagination. There's always a slight moment of disappointment when we've read a script and then we see the film realized. Having said that I don't even remember if George Lucas offered me a script to read.

I remember seeing the film and reacting to its atmospheres and energies and rhythms. That for me is always the best way to pick up a film—from the visual image itself and without any preconceptions that might have been put there by the script.

CB: When you first saw an assemblage of footage, what were you looking at and how did that inspire your work?

JW: I think the film was finished when I first saw it, with the exception of some special effects shots that would have been missing. I remember some leader in there where it would say "spaceships collide here," "place explosion here," this kind of thing. But they were measured out in terms of length so that I could time the music to what I hadn't in fact specifically seen.

The first chore I really had was to spot the music of the film with George Lucas, which is to say sitting with him deciding where we would play the music and what its particular function would be for each scene.

CB: The film set any number of standards. How do you explain the *Star Wars* phenomenon as it occurred back in 1977?

JW: Well, along with others involved with the film, I was surprised at what a great success it was. I think we all expected a successful film. In my mind I was thinking of it as a kind of Saturday afternoon movie for kids really, a kind of popcorn, Buck Rogers show. A good, you know, sound and light show for young people, thinking that it would be successful, but never imagining that it would be this world-wide international success, and never imagining and even expecting that the sequels would (a) be along and (b) be as successful as they all were.

I can only speculate about it along with others. I remember Joseph Campbell, the great mythologist and teacher and author, who was a friend of George Lucas's and who went to Skywalker Ranch and talked to George Lucas about the films. He began to write about the mythology, or pseudo-mythology if you like, that formed the basis of these films. I learned more from Joseph Campbell about the film, after the fact, than I did while I was working on it or watching it as a viewer.

Having said all that, I think the partial answer to your question is the success of this film must be due to some cross-cultural connection with the mythic aspects of the film that Campbell described to us later. The fact that the Darth Vader figure may be present in every culture, with a different name perhaps, but with a similar myth attached to it. The films surprised everyone I think—George Lucas included—in that they reached across cultural bounds and beyond language into some kind of mythic, shared remembered past—from the deep past of our collective unconscious, if you like. That may be an explanation as to why it has such a broad appeal and such a strong one.

CB: You would also have to assume that the hero's journey then would be a part of that.

JW: That's right. All of these aspects of journey and heroic life and aspiration and disappointment, all of the great human subjects that this seems to touch and tap in on, must be one of the reasons for its great success. I suppose for me as a composer for the film, these forces that I'm struggling to put my finger on must have been at work subconsciously. The music for the film is very non-futuristic. The films themselves showed us characters we hadn't seen before and planets unimagined and so on, but the music was—this is actually George Lucas's conception and a very good one—emotionally familiar. It was not music that might describe *terra incognita* but the opposite of that, music that would put us in touch with very familiar and remembered emotions, which for me as a musician translated into the use of a 19th century operatic idiom, if you like, Wagner and this sort of thing. These sorts of influences would put us in touch with remembered theatrical experiences as well—all western experiences to be sure. We were talking about cross-cultural mythology a moment ago; the music at least I think is firmly rooted in western cultural sensibilities.

CB: It's interesting that you brought up opera and Wagner. On a certain level it seems like the three scores are almost your "Ring Cycle." How did it become so interwoven when you originally were only scoring one film?

JW: I think if the score has an architectural unity, it's the result of a happy accident. I approached each film as a separate entity. The first one completely out of the blue, but the second one of course connected to the first one; we referred back to characters and extended them and referred back to themes and extended and developed those. I suppose it was a natural but unconscious metamorphosis of musical themes that created something that may seem to have more architectural and conscious interrelatedness than I actually intended to put there. If it's there, to the degree that it is there, it's a kind of happy accident if you like.

That maybe sounds deprecating—I don't mean it quite that way—but the functional aspect and the craft aspect of doing the job of these three films has to be credited with producing a lot of this unity in the musical content the listeners perceive.

CB: The album itself was in the top 20 on *Billboard*'s charts. That was relatively unheard of for a non-pop score. How did you respond to that?

JW: I don't think we ever had in the history of the record industry or a film business something that was so non-pop, with a small "p," reach an audience that size. I have to credit the film for a lot of this. If I had written the music without the film probably nobody ever would have heard of the music; it was the combination of things and the elusive, weird, unpredictable aspect of timing that none of us can quite get our hands around. If we could predict this kind of phenomenon or produce it consciously out of a group effort we would do it every year and we'd all be caliphs surrounded [*laughs*] with fountains of riches.

But it doesn't work that way, it's a much more elusive thing than that. Any composer who begins to write a piece would think, "this will be a successful piece." But you can't and we don't pull them out of the air that way. It also reminds us that as artists we don't work in a vacuum. We write our material, compose it or film it or whatever, but we're not alone in the vacuum, the audience is also out there and it's going to hit them. With all the aspects of happenstance and fad, and the issue of skirt length for example, which is to say style and fad, and what is à la mode? When all of these things come together and create a phenomenon like this, we then, as we're doing now, look back on it and say, "Why did it happen?" It's as fascinating and inexplicable to me as to any viewer.

CB: It's also got to be intensely gratifying.

JW: It's enormously gratifying and it makes me feel very lucky. I'm not a particularly religious person, but there's something sort of eerie, about the way our hands are occasionally guided in some of the things that we do. It can happen in any aspect, any phase of human endeavor where we come to the right solutions almost in spite of ourselves. And you look back and you say that that almost seems to have a kind of—you want to use the word divine guidance—behind it. It can make you believe in miracles in any collaborative art form: the theatre, film, any of this, when all these aspects come together to form a humming engine that works and the audience is there for it and they're ready for it and willing to embrace it. That is a kind of miracle also.

CB: It also changed the shape of film music. A lot of filmmakers had really abandoned the idea of big full orchestral scores.

JW: Well, I don't know if it's fair to say the *Star Wars* films brought back symphonic scores per se. We've been using symphony orchestras since even before sound. Anyone interested in film knows that music seems to be an indispensable ingredient for filmmakers. I'm not exactly sure why. We could talk about that for days, but mood, motivation, rhythm, tempo, atmosphere, all these things, characterization and so on—just the practical aspect of sounds between dialogue that need filling up. Symphony orchestras were enormously handy for this because they're elegant and the symphony orchestra itself is one of the greatest inventions of our artistic culture. Fabulous sounds it can produce and a great range of emotional capabilities.

I think if the use of symphony orchestras went out of fad in the '50s and '60s for some reason it was just that: it was out of fad. Someone would have brought it back. It's too useful and too successful not to have it back. I think after the success of *Star Wars* the orchestras enjoyed a very successful period because of that—wonderful, all to the good. I don't think we can claim that it was a renaissance really, more than just a change of fad if you'd like.

CB: Or a little goose if nothing else.

JW: Right. A little helping push.

CB: All three scores were recorded with the London Symphony Orchestra. Was there a particular reason why that orchestra was chosen?

JW: We decided to record the music for the films in London. I say we, I think George Lucas decided that. He shot some of the film in Africa and England and did some of his post-production work there. It was part of the plan that we would record there and that was fine with me. I had done *Fiddler on the Roof* [1971] and some other large-scale productions in England and I knew the orchestras very well and liked them; I was very comfortable recording there.

We were going to use a freelance orchestra, as I had done with *Fiddler* and other films. I remember having a conversation with the late Lionel Newman, who was then the music director of the 20th Century Fox studios, and we were talking about the practical plans of when to record and where and so on, booking facility stages and the rest of it. He suggested to me, "Why don't we just use the London Symphony Orchestra for this recording? We won't have to be troubled with hiring freelance players, we'll just make one contractual arrangement with the London Symphony."

It also happened at that time that our friend from Hollywood, André Previn, was then the music director of the London Symphony. I rang him up and said, "How would it be if we borrowed your orchestra for this recording?" André was very positive and very excited—he had no idea what *Star Wars* was going to be about or what the music would be like, but just the idea that the orchestra would have that exposure seemed to be a good plan for him. So, it was a combination of a lot of nice things. I had worked in England for years and knew the orchestras well; I knew the London Symphony well. They had played a symphony of mine under Previn's direction a few years before, and played other music of mine in concerts and so on. It was a coming together of a lot of familiar forces in a nice way and I had a good time.

CB: At the risk of sounding like someone from *Entertainment Tonight*, it sounds like the Force was with everyone involved.

JW: [*laughs*] The Force did seem to be with us, yes.

CB: How do you see the scores changing from one film to another, through the three films?

JW: The scores do seem unified to me, now that I look back on the four, five or six years involved in making the films, with the distance of time making it seem to be one short period now in my mind. The scores all seem to be one slightly longer score than the usual film score. If that contradicts what I said earlier about writing one at a time, I hear that contradiction, but given the distance of time now I can see that it's one effort really. The scores are all one thing and a theme that appeared in film two that wasn't in film one was probably a very close intervalic, which is to say note-by-note-by-note, relative to a theme that we'd had.

I mean we would have the Princess Leia theme as the romantic theme in the first film, but then we'd have Yoda's music, which was unexpectedly romantic, if you like, in the second film, but not such a distant relative, musically speaking, intervalically/melodically speaking, to Princess Leia's music. So you can marry one theme right after the other. They're different, but they also marry up very well and you can interplay them in a contrapuntal way, and it will be part of a texture that is familial.

CB: I'd like to touch on some of the characters' themes. A lot of people remember the Darth Vader theme. What was the idea behind Darth Vader and how do you see his theme?

JW: Darth Vader's theme seemed to me to need to have, like all of the themes if possible, strong melodic identification, so that when you heard it or part of the theme you would associate it with the character. The melodic elements needed to have a strong imprint.

In the case of Darth Vader, brass suggests itself because of his military bearing and his authority and his ominous look. That would translate into a strong melody that's military, that grabs you right away, that is, probably simplistically, in a minor mode because he's threatening. You combine these thoughts into this kind of a military, ceremonial march, and we've got something that perhaps will answer the requirement here.

CB: And then also the hero, Luke Skywalker. What about his theme?

JW: Flourishes and upward reaching; idealistic and heroic, in a very different way than Darth Vader of course, and a very different tonality—a very uplifted kind of heraldic quality. Larger than he is. His idealism is more the subject than the character itself, I would say.

CB: And Han Solo?

JW: I would make similar comments there about Solo's music. Although they overlap a lot; I mean it's one thing really in my mind, a lot of it. And of course the Luke Skywalker music has several themes within it also. You'd be testing my memory to ask me how I used them all and where [laughs].

CB: At the *Star Wars* Special Edition screening in December, when the main theme came on, the audience responded. What were you looking for in the main theme?

JW: The opening of the film was visually so stunning, with that lettering that comes out and the spaceships and so on, that it was clear that that music had to kind of smack you right in the eye and do something very strong. It's in my mind a very simple, very direct tune that jumps an octave in a very dramatic way, and has a triplet placed in it that has a kind of grab.

I tried to construct something that again would have this idealistic, uplifting but military flare to it. And set it in brass instruments, which I love anyway, which I used to play as a student, as a youngster. And try to get it so it's set in the most brilliant register of the trumpets, horns and trombones so that we'd have a blazingly brilliant fanfare at the opening of the piece. And contrast that with the second theme that was lyrical and romantic and adventurous also. And give it all a kind of ceremonial . . . it's not a march but very nearly that. So you almost kind of want to [laughs] patch your feet to it or stand up and salute when you hear it—I mean there's a little bit of that ceremonial aspect. More than a little I think.

The response of the audience that you ask about is something that I certainly can't explain. I wish I could explain that. But maybe the combination of the audio and the visual hitting people in the way that it does must speak to some collective memory—we talked about that before—that we don't quite

understand. Some memory of Buck Rogers or King Arthur or something earlier in the cultural salts of our brains, memories of lives lived in the past, I don't
know. But it has that kind of resonance—it resonates within us in some past
hero's life that we've all lived.

Now we're into a kind of Hindu idea, but I think somehow that's what happens musically. That's what in performance one tries to get with orchestras, and
we talk about that at orchestral rehearsals: that it isn't only the notes, it's this
reaching back into the past. As creatures we don't know if we have a future, but
we certainly share a great past. We remember it, in language and in pre-language,
and that's where music lives—it's to this area in our souls that it can speak.

CB: Can you tell me what it was like working with George Lucas on these
three movies?

JW: Working with George Lucas was always very pleasant. For a great innovator and a great creative artist and a great administrator, he's a very simple,
very accessible man. Now people will hear that and they'll say he's a very private
man, he's very inaccessible. I suppose that is also true. But when you're working
with him as a colleague sitting in the room, he's very informal, very approach-
able, very reachable, and communicates very well.

In discussing the spotting of the music for the film he's very particular in
a way. He would say, "The music could get bigger here, or would be softer
there"—you would think these ideas would be obvious, and sometimes they
are, but sometimes it's very helpful to articulate the obvious. Especially in this
interpersonal way that he's able to do it, he has made it a very comfortable
thing for me. When he first heard the music he liked it very well, it was encour-
aging—I felt positive reinforcement always with George. A lot of people will
say, "Don't go in that direction"; it's always "Don't do this, don't do that." With
George, my experience with him was, "That's right, keep going." With that
kind of collaboration, we get better results I think. He has the secret of this
naturally.

He was even then, when he hadn't done a lot of films, a very experienced
filmmaker and a very serious and assiduous student of filmmaking. He brought
a lot of knowledge to it and a lot of knowledge about how music could be used.

I found him pleasant, a good communicator, a good leader and an expert
filmmaker. And it's quite a combination of good, positive things I think.

CB: Are there any scenes that stand out for you?

JW: Well I have stand-outs in my mind because of the music that we play
in concerts more recently: the asteroid field I remember from, I think it was the
second film. It had a musical piece that was like a ballet of flying spaceships
and asteroids colliding. That was a very effective and successful scene in my
mind both musically and visually.

I remember the finale of the first film, which had that stately procession, where I made a sort of processional out of the middle theme of the main title music—for the beginning, I took the second theme of that and made a kind of imperial procession. And that was a very rewarding musical scene also. So many things, but I would say those two just right off the top of my head.

CB: A lot of people have said that their favorite scene is the cantina scene in the first film. And they often speak of the music.

JW: The cantina music is an anomaly, it sticks out entirely as an unrelated rib to the score. There's a nice little story if you haven't heard this, I'll tell you briefly: When I looked at that scene there wasn't any music in it and these little creatures were jumping up and down playing instruments and I didn't have any idea what the sound should be. It could have been anything: electronic music, futuristic music, tribal music, whatever you like.

And I said to George, "What do you think we should do?" And George said, "I don't know" and sort of scratched his head. He said, "Well I have an idea. What if these little creatures on this planet way out someplace, came upon a rock and they lifted up the rock and underneath was sheet music from Benny Goodman's great swing band of the 1930s on planet Earth? And they looked at this music and they kind of deciphered it, but they didn't know quite how it should go, but they tried. And, uh, why don't you try doing that? What would these space creatures, what would their imitation of Benny Goodman sound like?"

So, I kind of giggled and I went to the piano and began writing the silliest little series of old-time swing band licks, kind of a little off and a little wrong and not quite matching. We recorded that and everyone seemed to love it. We didn't have electronic instruments exactly in that period very much. They're all little Trinidad steel drums and out-of-tune kazoos and little reed instruments, you know. It was all done acoustically—it wasn't an electronic preparation as it probably would have been done today.

I think that may be also part of its success, because being acoustic it meant people had to blow the notes and make all the sounds, a little out of tune and a little behind there, a little ahead there: it had all the foibles of a not-very-good human performance.

CB: In the Special Editions there's some added footage. Did that require any rescoring?

JW: George has changed the lengths in some of these films for the reissue because of his improved animatics and so on. It required some change in the music, mostly additions and subtractions of a small sort. This was all attended to by Ken Wannberg who was originally a music editor and still is today.

The only thing I had to re-record was a short finale for *Return of the Jedi* [1983], the very end of the film where George created a new scene of Ewoks celebrating. He had some ideas for new music and gave me a film without any sound but with a tempo, with Ewoks dancing and reacting and reveling in their success. You and I are now talking in January 1997; just a few weeks ago, the end of '96, I went over to London and recorded that music for the new finale. And as a matter of fact this very day that we're talking, George is dubbing that new music into the final reel of the reissue.

CB: These films are classics. Why tinker with them now?

JW: Well, this is a very interesting question. If the *Star Wars Trilogy* is a kind of classic, why would we want to tamper with it? I'm not particularly in favor of coloring all the old early films in black and white and might come down on the side of saying, leave things alone. That's one side of the argument.

The other side of it is true for music also. For example, every time Brahms went to hear one of his symphonies played, he would go in the audience and listen to the symphony, and the next day he would go to the Bibliotheque in Vienna, get the original score out and make changes—he never could leave it alone. Some sage said that a work of art is never finished, it's only abandoned. That's really true of all of us; it's like one of our children. You never finish trying to groom it; the child could be 60 years old, and you're still saying, "Well you look better if you dress this way."

So I think George is well within the predictable and understandable and probably correct area of an artist's prerogative to continue to try to want to improve what he's done. He complained that he didn't have the animatics 20 years ago and he wants to do it now. So I think on the one hand don't tamper with it, and on the other an artist can, should and, I think, must be excused for wanting to continue to improve his or her work. That's the two answers.

The third answer could be for those traditionalists who want the original the way it is—it's there. They don't have to go; they can listen to the Brahms without his latest edition. So they can see the original version and they can also see the new, updated George Lucas wish-list for his work.

I think it's a wonderful question and the answer has to admit all of these possibilities for us to be fair.

CB: The original negative for *Star Wars* was in horrible condition.

JW: I didn't know that.

CB: Because of the stock that they were using at the time. What is your take on the whole idea of film preservation and how that affects both the films themselves and the scores?

JW: I can't speak with an expertise about film preservation, but I can talk emotionally and not as a serious art historian. I would make this observation: In the last 20 years or so, I've been very heartened—I guess we all have—by the consciousness that has emerged about preservation.

We're suddenly realizing as the 20th century comes to a close, one of the greatest cultural legacies, especially American but around the world also, is our filmmaking, and that we need to be very serious about preservation and about the archival aspects of all of these things that we do. It isn't only film, it's also music. The horror stories are myriad about the great MGM library that had *Doctor Zhivago* original music and *Singin' in the Rain* original music and musicals from the '30s and '40s—all these scores and orchestra parts that people want to perform now were all destroyed in the fire after some real estate company took over the physical lab of the studio.

The American Film Institute and other interested people, their preservation sentiments are wonderful in film and I think they should extend to original scripts that people have their marginalia on, and the original scores and sketches and orchestra parts of all this material. Imagine our grandchildren fifty, a hundred years from now, the interest that they would find in being able to take the orchestra parts to *Wizard of Oz* and sit down and play the whole score.

That is something devoutly to be wished. I don't confuse popular arts with high art. That's another discussion not suitable for this kind of time. But, however you evaluate the popular art of American filmmaking, as a high, middle, low, wherever you place it in your mind, doesn't alter the fact that this preservation task is desperately needed. I'm just delighted that we're seeing in the recent period of years people being very conscious of it, especially young people.

CB: I understand that George Lucas is in pre-production for the first three films. Can we look forward to another John Williams/George Lucas collaboration?

JW: Oh, I very much hope I can do the new trilogy, or as much of it as I'm granted the energy and time to do—I would welcome the opportunity and hope I will be able to do it. There's no reason why I shouldn't be able to. And I would look forward to it and I hope that that happens.

CB: Has there been a conversation about it?

JW: Well George is—yes, we talk about it all the time. It's more in the area of George threatening to say, you know, I'm going to get these three things done so get ready. So the conversation is kind of on that level, and he knows I'm ready and willing and hopefully able and certainly keen to do it.

CB: It sounds like the ultimate hurry up and wait. Thank you very much.

JW: Thank you.

22

Thomas Newman on His Film Music (1999)

Thomas Newman (b. 1955), son of the legendary Alfred Newman, is one of the most distinctive composers working in Hollywood today. His music offers a rare example of an original and flexible idiom that differs fundamentally from either traditional symphonic writing, clear-cut pop styles, or the athematicism of the avant-garde: in managing to achieve a balance between memorable melodic hooks and sonic experimentation, his writing is instantly appealing, commercially successful, and (not surprisingly) widely imitated. A key factor in its success is his idiosyncratic use of minimalist techniques based on the often obsessive repetition of short, catchy ideas, a manner of writing also to be heard in contemporary film scores by Philip Glass and Michael Nyman. Whereas these last two composers have been criticized for the dramatic stagnation that can arise from an unrelenting application of sometimes rather bland minimalist devices, Newman's music has a freshness and spontaneity all its own and at times makes attractive allusions to pop, jazz, and folk music.

As he reveals in the interview below, he is sensitive to the various ways in which listeners might respond to his music in filmic contexts and, like other modern film composers, is gratefully dependent on the creative talents of the performers with whom he regularly works—several of whom play decidedly unorthodox instruments. Initial ideas are explored and honed in a collaborative workshop environment that involves a degree of improvisation. Both the imaginative electronic manipulation of sampled acoustic timbres and a careful

Source: Michael Schelle, *The Score: Interviews with Film Composers* (Beverly Hills: Silman-James Press, 1999): 269–92.

combination of electronics with live acoustic sound are key elements in the final sonic mix.

Films mentioned by Newman in his interview cover a wide range of genres and include *Reckless* (dir. James Foley, 1984), *Desperately Seeking Susan* (dir. Susan Seidelman, 1985), *The Man with One Red Shoe* (dir. Stan Dragoti, 1985), *The Lost Boys* (dir. Joel Schumacher, 1987), *The Rapture* (dir. Michael Tolkin, 1991), *The Player* (dir. Robert Altman, 1992), *Little Women* (dir. Gillian Armstrong, 1994), *The Shawshank Redemption* (dir. Frank Darabont, 1994), and *Unstrung Heroes* (dir. Diane Keaton, 1995). Among his more recent credits are *American Beauty* (1999) and *Road to Perdition* (2002), both directed by Sam Mendes; the CGI animated features *Finding Nemo* (2003) and *WALL•E* (2008), both directed by Andrew Stanton; and the quirky theme tune to the darkly comic TV series *Six Feet Under* (2001–5).

I'm intrigued by a statement of yours that I came across in Fred Karlin's book *Listening to Movies*: "Even if you don't particularly like the music, you can recognize its effectiveness in the movie." Your scores rarely blast the audience with a big tune. Take *Shawshank Redemption*, for example: Your score uses evolving musical material that almost yearns to be a big tune, but which you seem to consciously hold back for the good of the film.

I guess that comes from experience. You can't force the square peg in the round whatever. As much as you may want the form, as much as you may yearn to be heard, the forward motion of the whole film experience will never allow it to be anything more than it is. By that comment, I mean that you must see the situation for what it is. Don't try to fight it; don't try to slip in under the door, through the keyhole.

Music is secondary. It's there to help, it's not there to be listened to, unfortunately. You can argue that it *is* heard and listened to, but usually that's accidental or that's because it's appropriate for a particular dramatic moment in the movie, as opposed to, "Well, gee, I really wanna be heard." Find the moments when you can speak out and the moments when it's inappropriate to speak out. I don't want to say, "Well, I'm a composer and I want to be heard" as much as, "Here's what I can do in this environment." Some environments are more avant-garde, more progressive, than others. Some are very conservative, and you kind of have to do what you have to do.

As you're trying to stick to one of these particular environments and the film is moving your musical imagination, do you find yourself saying, "Hey,

this is great. I wouldn't have come up with this on my own had not I had this particular scene, this particular character"?

Sure. It's the whole issue of referencing anything against anything. You're often surprised by the direction it takes you. If you're not totally concept-oriented, it's very interesting to see where it leads you and then to try to follow it. I think that's probably one of the great attractions of film music.

Let's talk about some of the unusual sounds and timbres for which you've become well-known.

You know all the people.

Well, I've met Rick Cox and Chas Smith. Is it a collaborative process with these guys and the other musicians you regularly use? Do you look to them for ideas, or do you bring ideas to them and say, "How can we elaborate on this?"

I try to give them vague direction. I try to capitalize on their talents as players and sound conceptualists. I try to corner them and, at the same time, try to keep them wild, because the minute you start dealing with odd sounds and try to be specific, it just doesn't work. When you sample sounds or try to find sounds, it's best to dumb down in terms of questioning the appropriateness of a particular sound or how is it going to work. Normally, you just find sounds that are either useful or less useful.

I've gotten such a shorthand with people like Rick that often we'll improvise—we'll just mess around with colors. Both he and I will take material and sample it. We'll sometimes sample a similar phrase and, by virtue of the manner of sampling, the sounds will be different. If you take any small phrase and alter it just a bit, it becomes something almost entirely different. I tend to like where sounds lead me, so I tend to give musicians like Rick some information and then let them feed information back to me. I guess I'm kind of the great bandleader or something.

So, sometimes, the sounds become for you, a stepping stone into the completed score in a way that perhaps a theme or melody would have functioned for your father?

I guess so. The danger of working with abstract sound is that it can be anything for any amount of time. So, sometimes, I wonder how deep down into this well I dare dive, discovering my own instrumentation, my own orchestrations, along the way. It *is* a discovery process. And that's good *and* bad. It can be very time-consuming; you can do five hours of work for ten minutes of result. Yet it's fun because a lot of the sounds that are explored are exceptionally interesting, but probably too complex for movies.

Often a complete film score needs to be delivered in four or five weeks. Can you build a little extra time into such a composing schedule to allow you to explore sounds?

If it's appropriate. It's less appropriate for some movies, period movies, which you realize aren't going to be sonically experimental, so you just step away from it. But, when it is appropriate, you've got to roll up your sleeves and do it faster, and maybe the ways in which you're trying to cull these sounds come in a more abbreviated manner. You rise to the experience and do what you can.

What's your process for scores that fuse electronics with acoustic instruments? Does one of those elements tend to come before the other?

Usually the electronics come first because, to me, they're the more interesting sounds—they're the things that give a more unique, dramatic flavor. The minute you start putting an orchestra on top, you're kind of doing that movie thing, which, in a way, is a requirement because, to a degree, people want to sit around as they did way back in the old days, watching their movie while listening to a full symphonic complement as it's going down.

I think that music for movies is so abstract that the orchestra has become a ludicrous ritual in a way, although it's very effective, and huge orchestral sounds are great in movies. Probably their best asset is how large and full-bodied they can be. With electronics, the ear often has no reference to decide if a sound is too loud or too soft because you don't know the source of the sound. Electronics are usually taken at face value. If you hear a loud trumpet, the ear has a reference for what a loud trumpet sounds like. With electronics, that doesn't happen.

Do you often find the director saying, "More orchestra"?

Yeah. It's how they see things. It's a way of bringing class to an environment, and I say that pejoratively because, obviously, good music is good music however it's created, however it's motivated. Sometimes I ask myself, "Why am I adding strings to this? Why am I taking it in that direction?" Often it's because that's where the ritual of dramatic film music takes it. To a degree, I fight the ritual. At the same time, I understand it and embrace it. That's the yin and the yang of this—you want to fight it, but there's no fighting it. It is what it is. To a degree, it's an obligation. And once you've fulfilled that obligation, then you think that it isn't really necessary.

Postproduction in movies is just not a hugely experimental time—people don't want to spend more money, and they're scared that you're going to ruin a movie if it's good and not save it if it's bad. So you face just huge philosophical and political requirements. What I've tried to do is recognize the requirements and not be stunned by them, not feel stifled by what I'm supposed to be doing.

In many of your scores, you seem completely comfortable working within the traditional expectations.

I never would have been able to survive out here otherwise. In Hollywood, you are what people *think* you are. If you're just this guy with electronics, this guy who just primarily does electronics, you're "the electronics guy."

The famous Newman film-music family—Alfred, Emil, Lionel, etc. As you get older, do you look back on that with great pride and emotion, whereas, when you were growing up, it was just dad's job?

Yeah. When I was quite young, it was just the thing he did. The family would go down and watch him record, which was very dramatic because he would almost never use a click track—there would always be free time, with double punches and the streamer and things. The stage would darken, and there was just something very *wow* about it all, kind of like when the lights go down in the theater. It was interesting and fun, but I had no interest in it whatsoever. It was just something over there that he did.

He died when I was fourteen, and I started getting interested in writing a year or two later. It all came very late to me. And then it became very daunting that he was who he was.

Emil and Lionel?

Uncle Emo was a good man. He was music director at Fox, and was basically retired by the time I started to write. He taught me to conduct a bit, and he was very interested in my music and encouraged me when I was in high school.

And then, along the way, it all became rather daunting for me in terms of what it was that I was supposed to be. You look at the job of film music, and what are you supposed to be? There's a lot of "Supposed to be" written into the bylaws of film music in terms of "Well, this is an action scene; it's *supposed to be* done in this way." I never thought I'd do it very well. It was tough enough to write music, much less write it in a week and be greeted by people who were not interested in your effort, only in your result.

I struggled when I first started. I struggled a lot with "What could I do?" and "How could I be different yet be myself?" I think that's what drove me toward electronics—the idea that I could lock myself up in a room and discover what I liked about music and what I didn't like. All the book knowledge I'd had up to that point, and I'd been well-trained, was not applicable for some reason. Everything I knew in terms of aesthetics or what orchestral music was was over there, and I was over here. The early part of my career was spent trying to understand the over-here part of it, and then, bring the over-there into the over-here.

It took me quite a while to put together a sense of who I was and how I was to deal with musicians. I'd had some experience just talking to players, and I was always told, "You get on the podium and you kind of talk Italian—whatever

Italian you know." I remember the first time I got on a podium to conduct, it was just *wow!* Then you realize that it's not that big a deal. A musician friend of mine once said, "You get out on the podium and you look at all those players, and you think they're looking at you as if to say, 'Now what do you want us to do?' But no, they're asking themselves, 'When's the next break? When's lunch?'" Once you start to realize that, some of the mysticism goes away, which is a good thing. I don't want it to be mystical. When my dad was doing it, it was always mystical to me, like jazz is always magical. But when you finally learn enough about it, you realize that people turn tricks and that they do their thing.

A couple of your early scores—*Reckless* and *Desperately Seeking Susan*— were mostly electronic, if not entirely.

There were actually a couple of solo players, but never an ensemble of any kind.

In those scores, did you record the electronic parts first and then put the solo players on top?

Yeah. I remember my first *Reckless* session: I came home and said, "I don't have a clue about how to do this." I'd had some drum programs and I had tried to use a live drummer. I thought, "Well, a live drummer has got to be better that a drum machine." But I was wrong. Not that the machine was better but that, the minute you try to change course, your sense of where sound goes and how the ear perceives it suddenly changes. So the process was certainly a "from scratch" thing—mostly trial and error, with a lot of things going wrong. And then you finally realize, "Well, this sounds good now. Why? Why did this work out okay?" Then you work backward from there, and you learn another trick or two. It's all trickery, and it all adds up.

In *Desperately Seeking Susan*, there are little hints of Newmanisms-to-come—sounds that show up later in *The Player, Unstrung Heroes,* and other scores.

It's true. That was kind of the start of understanding a little more. A lot of that's Rick Cox, whom I've worked with since my very first job. It's funny how some things don't change.

The Man With One Red Shoe has a great opening sequence where your tiny musical events dart through the initial orchestral tuning-up section.

The main character was the concertmaster of an orchestra, and the idea of tune-ups have always interested me. Tune-ups are interesting because the players are noodling around, doing their own thing. But what they're doing is musical—usually haphazard or unconscious, but instinctively musical. I thought, "What if I take this big orchestral tune-up over a period of twenty seconds or so and, *boom,* immediately go to someplace different?" That was the beginning of *Aha!* If you put a tune-up next to something electronic, what does that do to the ear? How does that jag the ear?

The Lost Boys seems a more traditional score in terms of orchestration and requisite mickey-mousing. For example, at the close-up of a vampire baring his teeth, there's a big, scary diminished chord. But even within that kind of classic Steiner horror-shock technique, the scenes maintain personal, modernistic edges to them.

Thanks. Those were the days when I was trying to reconcile my scores with rock tunes. I thought about how one could deal with that. And then there was the whole idea of this deep, dark, Gothic organ music. To a certain degree, you could argue it was a circumspect choice. But, again, the directions that we go in often are not solo ideas—this was a Joel Schumacher opus. How much of that had to do with him and how much of that had to do with me? To tell you the truth, I thought that I was a little lost in *The Lost Boys*.

The Rapture was one of the first Thomas Newman scores that really nailed me. It had a very strong presence of that experimental orchestral sound. Is *The Rapture* maybe the film that helped you break through, break out of teen comedies and allow the more sophisticated Thomas Newman to breathe?

I think it was. Before that, I did *Men Don't Leave*, which was not a comedy. But before that, *Desperately Seeking Susan* was probably my best credit. It was a comedy, but it was a very stylish comedy. It was certainly a movie I was proud of.

I remember wanting to do *The Rapture* because it was a fairly small-budget movie. I thought it would be fun to get together with players I knew and just mess around in an experimental environment. I worked with Rick Cox on it, and Chas [Smith] may have worked on it. George Budd did great scratch phonograph work on it. *The Rapture* was an opportunity to do some bizarre, wild things that I always felt I was capable of doing.

But you start where you start, and people don't allow you to do much. I used to have this theory that as long as I could write something that didn't offend me, I was going to be okay. If it was something that would interest my ears on some level, it would be all right. When I finally got around to *The Rapture*, I was starting to think that I was just getting better at it, too. It's funny how, after you do it for a while, you feel like you improve at it. Or you kind of get the exercise.

There are many avant-garde/contemporary elements in that score—experimental timbres, tone clusters, extreme dissonance, synthetic scales and harmonies.

Right. But in a totally dramatic context. When you're doing comedies, you can use weird sounds, but it's a lot like you do in hip-hop, not that my music is anything like hip-hop. But, if you think about a popular music using strange sounds, a lot of it is rap and some alternative music. You can get away with some of that in comedy, especially if it's contemporary comedy, because that's kind of the current popular language. To be able to finally use strange sounds in a more serious, dramatic context was new and fun.

Did you have anything to do with the Meredith Monk material in _The Rapture?_

I had nothing to do with it. I usually won't have anything to do with music that's not my own, unless I'm asked. Normally, directors hire music supervisors to do that.

Often, directors will come in with their own conceptions. I remember Michael Tolkin, the director of _The Rapture_, wanted to use some horn tune and a fragment of a Brahms symphony for the last horn calling in the apocalypse scene. I thought it was just not a good idea. But, nevertheless, it was an idea I needed to entertain because this was _his_ concept—he had written the script, he had directed it and, as much as I didn't get it, I had to deal with it. You have to deal with such ideas from directors and writers somewhat delicately because there's something to be said for their having that concept or having written a scene while some kind of music was going on in their head. In the case of the Meredith Monk, I think that was Tolkin's idea. And not a bad one.

In _The Rapture_, you used a xaphoon, along with many other curious instruments. What the hell is a xaphoon?

Oh, the Maui xaphoon! That's a Rick Cox instrument. It sounds fluty when he plays it, although I bought one in Hawaii and it sounds more like a saxophone. They actually call it "the Hawaiian saxophone." But the way Rick plays it, it sounds like a deep flute.

Okay, that's an authentic instrument, but what about "door," which is listed on the CD liner notes? What's the "door"?

Ha! The door was literally this. [Newman goes to his studio door and slowly closes it. It squeaks and creaks.] I was doing some sampling while my buddy Bill Bernstein was in the bathroom. When he came into the studio, he closed _the_ door, and it ended up on this one sample! You can argue that it was precious of us to name it "door," but it was just there and I kind of wanted to remember it.

Other things: there are resonators and bowed plates and things—those were Chas [Smith] instruments.

Processed hurdy-gurdy and prepared guitar? We know Cage's prepared piano, is this similar?

Yeah. That's a Rick Cox thing. Rick did that before I knew him. That was one of his calling cards: putting all kinds of small metal objects toward the fingerboard part of his guitar and sometimes bowing the strings with beveled glass and sponges. Processed hurdy-gurdy: If Rick and I mess around on hurdy-gurdy, we do odd things to it. I think the reason I wanted to call it by its acoustic name is because it was the acoustic side of the instrument that interested me. I like the idea of processing acoustic sounds. That interests me a lot.

You take all these different sound sources and pull them together into individual, unique-sounding bits.

That's right! Then no one can touch you in terms of color, and color is what I find most interesting. The sky's the limit—from bowing to blowing to knocking. I've played things on tables. Anything's possible. But I don't mean to imply that I'm this great experimentalist. I just find abstract color really interesting.

I remember playing the sound of some cicadas for someone who said, "Ah, cicadas. That's bug sound," as opposed to saying, "Wow, here's this *sound*. Now what happens if you listen to the sound of a xaphoon next to it?" Often, I get criticized for being "ethnic." But if I play an instrument that sounds like a koto, but it's just an instrument that kinda plucks, that's all it is to me—it's an abstract sound. But, unfortunately, people often hear it as "ethnic," which, I guess, would make an interesting study in itself: Why are people drawn to such conclusions?—bells, oh, sure, it's Christmas time, right?

There's a scene in *The Player* where you have a lot of music-box sounds—multiple music boxes playing at the same time.

Do you remember the name of the piece? Was it "Six Inches of Dirty Water"? It wasn't music boxes so much as it was kids' toys that you roll like little spools.

Do people ever say, "Thomas Newman is great if you want these modern, experimental sounds, but what about traditional orchestral scores?"

[*Laughter*] Yeah. See, again, we go back to the notion of obligation and expectation. Most people expect the traditional orchestral score. I think you could argue that it's valid. Right? If you go see *Star Wars*, you're kinda knocked off your seat by just the sound of all that brass coming at you. That's a great thing, and it's a fun thing. In a way, it embraces the whole tradition of what movies are and what movie scores are.

But *Star Wars* definitely looks back to Korngold, Steiner, and the Golden Age. What do *The Rapture* or *The Player* or *Unstrung Heroes* look to?

No looking back! That's what's fun about it.

But with *Little Women*, you do look back.

Well, you have no choice. In the case of *Little Women*, the film didn't have a big budget and they needed to record out of the country. I had to go to London, so I wasn't going to have my regular team. And it was a period piece, so it was

Thomas Newman composed the score for Robert Altman's satirical thriller
The Player (1992), set in a fictional Hollywood ridden with blackmail, sleaze,
and cameo appearances by real-life stars. Here troubled script-assessor Griffin
Mill (Tim Robbins, left) listens to a pitch from aspiring writers Andy Civella
(Dean Stockwell, center) and Tom Oakley (Richard E. Grant, right). Featured
prominently on the wall is a poster for *Laura* (dir. Otto Preminger), for which
David Raksin wrote an innovative monothematic score in 1944 (see p. 70).

actually less appropriate for whackings and pluckings. You could argue that a
less-traditional score could've been really interesting, but if you think about it,
if you were to score a movie like *Little Women* strangely, it would probably end
up being self-conscious. You'd probably say, "Oh, yeah, that composer's trying
to do something different just for the sake of being different." I guess that's
why, finally, we can never rise above our material. If we do, we're probably pretentious, we're probably not serving whatever it is that we're scoring. And that
really rankles a lot of us, because we always want to make smarter choices than
we're allowed to make.

**As you worked on *Little Women*, did you miss the experimental process or
did you find yourself simply enjoying this "new" environment of little set dance
pieces?**

I really did like scoring it. The reason I like being experimental is because
I find that's where I live—I think I'm most sophisticated in that environment.
When I'm scoring for traditional orchestra, I find it hard not to remember all
of the amazing composers who have preceded me and who have done it so ex-
quisitely. I feel like I'm immediately more like them. And by being more like
them, I bring myself up for comparison against them, and I don't enjoy that as
much, because it makes me feel I'm less than myself. Yet, at the same time, my
God, what power there is in a symphonic environment!

God, there have been amazing things written before any electronics or any sound processing existed! But I want to be a product of my own time. You always hear people say, "Well, if Beethoven and Mozart were alive today . . ." I hate all that. Beethoven's not alive today, and the world has gotten to where it is *because* Beethoven lived when he lived. Sometimes I think film music is an opportunity for people to justify their own basic conservative musical natures.

Do composers now, by the nature of the business, seem less creative, more derivative?

The other day, I was thinking about George Antheil. I was looking at his *Ballet mécanique* and its set design, wondering where all the thinking has gone. It seems like people used to think more about things. Now, it costs twenty million because you have to get David Hockney or Robert Wilson. Budgets are too expensive, People used to get a hundred bucks and a free meal, but, at least, it seemed like there was aesthetic foresight. Now, with movies, if it's a wheatfield scene, it's got to be the rough-hewn, rustic solo-trumpet melody. And, to a degree, we all get caught up in that. What bothers me is that it's always some kind of homage that's unique only in that it references the movie. It's certainly unoriginal in its concept and in its sense of harmony and in its own sense of how music happens. . . .

Shawshank Redemption is a terrific score. You wrote powerful, moving emotionally charged string lines, yet no big hummable tune. You wrote a quasi-tune that is constantly emerging, searching—perhaps a reflection of the characters themselves. What about the very opening of the picture, with The Ink Spots singing "If I Didn't Care"? I assume that you had that to work with.

After I had struggled with building my score around that tune, I played the whole opening for the director. He said, "You know, I've not quite decided on that or another Ink Spots tune." I said, "If you change it, I'm just going to kill you."

You begin *your* music in the same tonal area as the end of the Ink Spots' tune. The Ink Spots' tonal center of A gradually yields to your material arriving in A, then E and E^b on top. Outside of Wagner's *Das Rheingold*, I don't know of a longer opening pedal point.

Yeah! Did it get boring?

No, no, no. Quite the opposite, but there's always a little . . .

It's just a goddamn drone!

Everybody writes drones these days, but this drone had an extremely dramatic purpose, in the way *Das Rheingold* has its never-ending E^b opening.

Wow. That's interesting. I like the way that you're referencing me to *Rheingold*. Why not?

The gunshot shatters everything, and then there's silence for a long time—a silence pedal. What about the scenes where you are dealing with the

mini-duets of solo violin and guitar? Did these motivic fragments come to you while improvising at the piano or some other instrument or come to you mentally, while driving out to a get a cheeseburger?

Usually not when I'm driving. A lot of times, when I'm driving, if I have the radio on, I'll listen to it and ask myself what would happen if *that* piece of music were in this movie. It's like doing homework in any place you can do it. But, normally, I come here, take out certain instruments, and try to create as much of a playground environment as I can. I studied violin as a kid, so in the case of that *Shawshank* violin piece, I took out a violin and started experimenting with open strings. I got my ideas for that music on the violin, and then I went to the piano to actually plunk them out, thinking that, basically, it was going to be a fairly rough, folksy kind of melody.

In terms of the other stuff, I just tend to go back and forth. In terms of the main piano theme in *Shawshank*, I knew I wanted it to have kind of a quintal/quartal, open, non-consonant feeling to it. I guess the tritone was the big dissonance, the one bit of dissonance between the fourth and the fifth.

When I write, I mostly just let my mind go. I try not to over-think. I try to save the over-thinking for when I have accrued a lot of ideas, and then it's like taking spices off the shelves: There's an idea! What if I try that? Then I look at it against the movie, and it works or it doesn't work. I'm not much into playing at and looking like and trying to be the stern composer. I just try to have ideas and see if they work, all the while trying to have as much fun as I can, and being as inspired as I can be. . . .

III

Critics and Commentators

Alongside the often revealing personal testimonies of composers working in the highly pressurized environment of Hollywood studios, a body of critical literature on film music gradually arose from the late 1930s onward. Some was generated by the composers themselves; for example, Aaron Copland (whose listing of functional categories of film music was especially influential), Hanns Eisler, and Bernard Herrmann all successfully distanced themselves from their own creative work in order to publish their markedly contrasting viewpoints on the general aesthetic goals of—and practical demands on—film composers in the 1940s, as well as the differences and similarities between film music and concert music. This last consideration was to remain a burning critical issue, as the texts reproduced in this section demonstrate, and it was fueled by a steady growth in the number of concert suites and gramophone recordings directly tied in to film scores. However, as concert music increasingly espoused an international modernism inspired by the groundbreaking styles of Arnold Schoenberg and Igor Stravinsky (both of whom came to live in Hollywood), so the endemic conservatism of studio executives and music directors was thrown into ever sharper relief.

George Antheil was the first practitioner to write regular journalism on the subject of film music, beginning in 1936, and in his autobiography he offered a witty and vivid account of the Hollywood milieu in which he found himself during the late 1930s and early 1940s. As with other Hollywood composers who had parallel careers writing "serious" music (such as Miklós Rózsa and Franz Waxman), Antheil keenly felt the tension between the practical and commercial demands of composing for the movies and the higher artistic aspirations of the concert hall. After Antheil ceased publishing film-music criticism in 1939, the baton was taken up on the West Coast by Bruno David Ussher and especially Lawrence Morton, who was the first commentator to recognize the true functional value of film-specific compositional idioms and techniques that were (and indeed still are) routinely dismissed as mindless clichés by elitist critics; he also saw the value of artistic collaboration and was a notable advocate of the orchestrator's art, something most European (and some American) composers viewed with deep suspicion. Morton was incensed by what he viewed as the ignorant and prejudiced views of certain European musicians concerning film music, writing at a distance and with no real knowledge of the demands of the studio system, though it should be noted that several U.S. commentators in the 1940s (including Herrmann) wrote warmly of the fine scores composed by the likes of William Walton in the United Kingdom, Arthur Honegger in France, and Sergei Prokofiev in the Soviet Union. At the end of the decade, the British academic F. W. Sternfeld repaid the compliment by publishing the first substantial critical and analytical essays on film music to appear in a prestigious musicological journal—his subjects were films scores by Hugo Friedhofer and Copland—though even he did not escape modest censure from Morton. Sternfeld's articles were to remain almost unique examples in their field until the modern growth of film-music scholarship spearheaded from the 1980s onward by (among others) Claudia Gorbman, Kathryn Kalinak, Caryl Flinn, and Royal S. Brown.

All the writings in the present section predate the late-twentieth-century boom in academic film-music studies and are intended to capture the flavor of sporadic commentaries written contemporaneously with the films and other events they describe. The texts come from a wide range of journals (including national newspapers and periodicals devoted either to music or to movies—though rarely to both) that did sterling work to promote the field of film-music criticism in its earlier years, including *Films in Review*, *Hollywood Quarterly* (later *Film Quarterly*), *Modern Music*, *Music & Letters*, *Musical Digest*, the *New York Times*, and *Sight and Sound*. That these writings singularly ignore the use of popular music as an alternative means of scoring movies is a vivid testament to the widespread suspicion of such practices on the part of commentators predominantly schooled in classical music and preoccupied with a specious need for structural orthodoxy in film scores.

The present selection concludes with two texts that discuss the state of film music in the 1970s and 1980s, one written by a composer and the other by a director: Elmer Bernstein's summary of his legal campaign to improve the studio composers' harsh lot at a time when freelance livelihoods were seriously threatened by bullish and insensitive employers in the film industry, and Sidney Lumet's wide-ranging and nonspecialist appreciation of the contributions to his films made by a clutch of talented and versatile composers and musicians.

23

George Antheil: "I Am Not a Businessman" (1945)

In these extracts from his lively autobiography, the American composer George Antheil (1900–1959) briefly discusses the film scores he composed during the late 1930s, and provides an eyewitness account of Hollywood music departments in the Golden Age from the viewpoint of a "serious" composer who constantly felt himself to be an outsider in the industry. His remarks touch on what he saw as a fundamental tension between the writing of commercial and art music, and the inveterate resistance on the part of both music directors and studio executives toward even moderate stylistic innovation.

Antheil was an established composer long before he moved to Hollywood in 1936 with his wife, Boski Markus. He had acquired an international reputation as an *enfant terrible* during his formative years in Europe, where he had composed a succession of stunning avant-garde works, including *Ballet mécanique* (1923–25; performed in Paris in 1926 and at Carnegie Hall in the following year). This extraordinary piece, scored for multiple keyboards and percussion, had at one stage been intended to accompany Fernand Léger's experimental silent film with the same title, but the application failed owing to difficulties with unreliable synchronization equipment. In 1933 Antheil moved back to America, where, in addition to composing both film music and concert works (the latter including six symphonies), he supplemented his income with journalistic writings on an unusually wide range of subjects.

Source: Bad Boy of Music (Garden City, N.Y.: Doubleday, Doran & Company, 1945; reprinted, with a new introduction by Charles Amirkhanian, New York: Da Capo Press, 1981): 292–94, 297–303, 306–10, 312–16.

George Antheil composing at home in Los Angeles. (Photographer and date unknown; © Estate of George Antheil)

Among them was a series of regular columns on film music for the journal *Modern Music* ("On the Hollywood Front," 1936–39). His happiest film-scoring experiences were for the writer-directors Ben Hecht and Charlie MacArthur, for whom he wrote music for *Once in a Blue Moon* and *The Scoundrel* (both 1935), *Angels over Broadway* (1940), and *Spectre of the Rose* (1946). He also scored Cecil B. DeMille's *The Plainsman* (1936) and *The Buccaneer* (1938), and later worked for directors Nicholas Ray (*In a Lonely Place*, 1950), Edward Dmytryk (*The Juggler* and *The Sniper*, both 1952), and Stanley Kramer (*The Pride and the Passion*, 1957).

The extracts from Antheil's Hollywood reminiscences below include an amusing encounter with the painter Salvador Dali and a musical escapade involving the Marx Brothers. They were but a few of Antheil's many and varied West Coast acquaintances, who also included actress Hedy Lamarr. Lamarr, having read one of Antheil's scientific articles, sought him out specifically to ask his advice—in deadly earnest—on the options open to her for the enlargement of her famous bosom. Despite Antheil's initial embarrassment, the two became firm friends, and in 1942 they jointly patented a proposed technology for the radio-controlled guidance of missiles; the idea had apparently been conceived during their initial conversation on the subject of her breast augmentation.

I contacted Boris Morros, music director of Paramount Studios, and after a number of conferences he assigned me to De Mille's new picture, *The Plainsman*. This picture was just being "shot" in the autumn of 1936, and I immediately comprehended that it was very important for me to be able to play my sketches for De Mille. Accordingly I brought a piano into our hotel room, and this was the way the extraordinary soundproofness of the Hollywood-Franklin was discovered. (I have a theory about it which is not generally accepted: my theory is that the spirits of departed pixies who have lived in the hotel line the spaces between its walls, and that this stuff is 100 per cent soundproof.) . . .

I considered making "a fortune" through the writing of motion-picture scores. Many composers had come to Hollywood and done so. A former friend of mine, for instance, now owned a vast villa, a swimming pool, a movie-starlet wife and two lovely children; once he had been a very promising but hungry composer in New York. Today he was no longer promising, but his family ate and could look forward into the future with some measure of assurance.

But I became wary of the idea for several reasons. The first and most important was that I soon discovered that I could not write movie music all day and then write my own music (my Third Symphony) at night. Symphonic writing is just too organic a process. For instance, when I am working upon a knotty symphonic problem, I can often "put it to bed" at night and wake up in the morning with the entire problem solved. But when, during the day, I also write movie music (which cannot possibly be up to the same standard, no matter what anybody tells you about the excellence of present-day movie music), the two various kinds of music are very apt to become entangled in my subconscious brain at night, with the result that I more often than not have the damnedest time sorting them out again in the daytime. My symphonic writing incorporates corny movie-music solutions, while my movie music suddenly develops highbrow tendencies which please my director and producer not at all. (Unless it happens to be Ben Hecht.)

The most obvious solution to all this, of course, would seem to be to write one movie score for a goodly sum of money, then quit for four or five months to finish an orchestral work, then write another movie background, then quit for another four or five months, ad infinitum. This solution is good in theory only because, in the movie business, you must keep working to get future jobs.

The movie studios, unable to grasp the idea that you may just be holding back in order to write some unlucrative music of your own, simply figure that you must be skidding if you are not constantly employed on some scoring job or another. In other words, once you start you must continue, otherwise you're a has-been—and Hollywood is the place par excellence for cruelty to has-beens. . . .

But I'm ahead of my story again. This was still late 1936; I was still going every day over to Paramount (while composing my symphony on the side); and a fellow by the name of Salvador Dali was beginning to create a great deal of flurry in the press columns of Hollywood.

The first moment a fellow like me looks at a fellow like Dali, he thinks, "I wonder if this guy is really on the level? A great painter, all right. The greatest surrealist painter, all right. But what about that surrealist acting of his? Is he publicity-stunting?"

So when, for the first time, I met Salvador Dali at his own request, I said to him, "Look here, Dali, you and I are two of a kind. The only thing is, I'm a little older, and at this exact moment of my destiny I'm endeavoring to make a good impression over at Paramount. C. B. de Mille thinks I'm crazy and is watching me like a hawk."

"Ah! C. B. de Mille! He is the greatest surrealist in all the world!" Dali said ecstatically.

"Too true," I murmured, "but will you behave yourself if I take you over to see him? He is also my boss."

"But I only wish to kiss his hands," Dali said reprovingly.

"In that case," I said, "we don't go over. Do you know what sort of a situation I'm in over there? Boris Morros, the music director, has engaged me to write the music of C. B.'s latest masterpiece, *The Plainsman*. This was O.K. with De Mille, as he doesn't know my name from Adam, or that of any other musician. However, some of the yes men around him did, and they told him that Boris Morros is out to get him by assigning to his new two-million-dollar picture a raving maniac by the name of Antheil who once wrote a mechanical ballet for nineteen linotype machines and performed it at Carnegie Hall. This, at the moment, does not set well with De Mille, and he is brooding about it. If he detects the least sign of insanity about me, out I go. If I bring you in now, you may be that least trace of insanity."

Dali reflected. My logic was unassailable. "O.K., pal," he said at last. "No surrealism."

So I took Dali over to Paramount, where he kissed C. B. de Mille's hands anyhow. Most fortunately De Mille saw nothing whatsoever amiss in this.

Dali immediately started cooing:

"Ah, Cecil B. de Mille! I have met you at last, *you*, the *greatest surrealist on earth!*" De Mille looked first charmed, then puzzled. He turned around, but none of his henchmen were present to interpret. "What is a surrealist?" he asked.

I explained. "It's a new European art movement, Mr. de Mille, a kind of realism but more real than realism—'superrealism,' so to speak."

"Oh," said De Mille, getting it, "a kind of supercolossal realism?"

"To put it lightly," I said, "yes."

"Very interesting," said De Mille. "I should like to know more about it."

"Ah," interrupted Dali, "but you *do* know all about it, C. B. de Mille. *You* are the veritable *king of the surrealists.*"

De Mille accepted this title in silence. He was now the king of the surrealists, and Dali said so in the next morning's papers. Incredulous newspaper reporters interviewed De Mille and asked him if this was so. De Mille said it was. The item was read by everybody in Paramount.

Boris Morros, who is a nice right guy but who possesses to the extreme degree the typical Hollywood weakness of judging all and sundry according to the inches of space they are daily able to wangle out of the press, said to me, "George, you told me yesterday that your friend, Salvador Dali, would like to get a job at Paramount."

"That is correct," I said, "but he didn't say what kind of a job he wanted. He's a surrealist, you know. That might mean that he really has in mind the studio manager's job, or a producer's—which, incidentally, might not be a bad idea. Almost all the producers I know are surrealists at heart."

"Nonsense, nonsense!" Boris smiled his moon smile at me and brushed the idea of Dali's really being crazy aside. "Of course, what Dali wants is to design sets, dream sequences, and that sort of thing. He'd be marvelous at it, too, from what I've seen of his pictures printed in the newspapers. Now I've got an idea, but first tell me, have you ever seen that picture, *Le Chien Andalou?* It's a silent moving picture which Dali made around 1929, and everybody says it's terrific. But nobody seems to have actually *seen* it. If I were sure it was terrific, supercolossal, I'd invite all the producers and executives of Paramount over to see it at Projection Room One, including C. B. de Mille——"

"I've seen it," I interrupted, "and it *is* terrific. It's wonderful! It's beautiful!"

Now this was no pose with me. One summer night, six or seven years back, Jean Cocteau had phoned my Montparnasse hotel and excitedly told me to come right over to the Right Bank, as he had discovered something of incredible interest and beauty. Knowing Jean to have the best nose in Paris, I quickly entered the local subway and met him in front of his hotel inside of twenty-five minutes. He immediately took me to a nearby moving-picture theater, where, after the regular show, they were to run for him a private showing of a brand-new surrealist film, *Le Chien Andalou* (The Andalusian Dog). It was made by two Spanish surrealists, Salvador Dali and Luis Bunuel. . . .

Le Chien Andalou started unrolling, and the first thing Cocteau and I comprehended was a man shaving with a very sharp razor. Suddenly he turns to a wide-eyed girl sitting right alongside, and he cuts her left eyeball right open, while she placidly sits there and lets him do it. The horrid interior of the eyeball slithers down her face. This is only the beginning.

It gets worse or—depending upon whether you are surrealistic-minded—more beautiful as it goes along. The young man with the razor pursues the girl, who, as she runs from room to room in a building with apparently endless rooms in it, has her clothes alternately dissolve and materialize as she runs along. One moment she is nude. The next moment she is clothed. And so on, clothes, nudity, clothes, nudity, clothes. She runs through one room to the next, closing doors all the while. Sometimes the fellow gets his hands caught in the closing doors, and one sees a close-up of a clenched fist apparently decaying, with ants running all over it. None of this stops him, however; he keeps on going. The going gets harder towards the end. The girl comes to the last room and is huddling, nude, in the furthest corner of the room while the fellow strains towards her with two big cables attached to his shoulders. He strains and strains, hardly making more than an inch headway at a time. We pan along the cables, backwards, to see what's holding him up. Two pianos, grand pianos, are holding him up. They are filled with dead donkeys and crocodiles, their heads sticking out over the piano desk and the blood from their mouths dripping upon the white keys. There are two other cables attached to the two pianos, and these drag a number of priests who, as they slide along the floor on their backs, hold open prayer books as their lips move. . . .

When, seven years later, we ran the picture at Projection Room One, Paramount Studios, Hollywood, the first thing that happened was that one of the biggest producers on the lot got violently ill. He had to leave very suddenly. The rest were nailed to their seats as if hypnotized by a King Cobra.

Boris turned to me and hissed, "I thought you said this was the most beautiful picture you ever saw!"

Cecil B. de Mille, king of the surrealists (American branch) was a pale green when the lights went up. He got up and left without a word.

So did the others, when they recovered.

Dali ran out to a phone immediately. He called his wife, Gala.

"Gala," he said breathlessly, "it was the *greatest* success imaginable. *They were speechless!*"

The next day there were repercussions. De Mille sent word to the music department that he'd like to hear whatever Antheil had finished of the score of *The Plainsman*. We had a date in one of the music rooms for four o'clock. I was to be there promptly, and Boris sent word to De Mille that he might be a trifle late but would be sure to come.

He was going to let me face the music alone, coming in only for finalities, such as they might be!

When De Mille came into the music room he was in no mood to dicker. Knowing the end was plainly in sight, I resolved to play him the most dissonant sections of my score (on the piano) and go down with colors flying. I got out my Indian War Dance Torture Scene, the sequence where the Indians hang Gary Cooper to a sort of roasting stake and light a fire under him. Singing such melodies as there were, I accompanied them with a furious bedlam of discords on the piano. When I had finished the scene I turned around, ready to go.

"Go on, play the rest of the sequences," De Mille said. An astonished but not totally displeased look had come over De Mille's face. I played the rest of the sequences, most of them very simple and melodic, and I could see that De Mille was becoming more pleased with each one. Finally, after a half hour of this, Boris Morros suddenly burst into the room.

"I've got it, I've got it!" he whispered hoarsely.

"Got what?" asked De Mille, who slightly resented interruption at this point.

"Why, the theme for the Indian War Dance Torture Scene, of course!" And, without allowing De Mille to answer, Boris produced a copy of Rimsky-Korsakov's "Song of India" and began to whistle it. De Mille had quite a time to convince Boris that Indians from India and Indians in America were not at all ethnographically or ethnologically the same.

"And besides," C. B. de Mille insisted, "Antheil's music for *The Plainsman* Indian War Dance Torture Scene is fine, just what I wanted."

I never saw a man look so doubting or thunderstruck as Boris at this instant. He left the room mumbling, and somehow I felt that all in all I had sown the seeds of future trouble in the Paramount music department. This hunch turned out to be one hundred per cent correct, but not immediately.

In any case, when, finally, I brought Dali into the office of Paramount's chief executive, I did not feel any too safely entrenched. But in the meantime Dali's publicity in the daily Los Angeles press had been so terrific, pages of it, that the producers who had previously turned green at his *Chien Andalou* thought they had been mistaken. The word got up to the front office: Dali was seeking a job as a set designer, and the front office decided to snap him up with a generous contract. I was appointed to bring him in tow.

"Mr. Dali," said the All Highest, "we, Paramount Incorporated, are prepared to make you a set designer on this lot!"

Dali looked distressed. "Alas, Mr. President, I'm afraid there's been a ghastly mistake."

"A mistake? There can't be any mistake. You wanted to get yourself a position at Paramount, didn't you?"

"Yes, Mr. President, that is true. But *not* as an artist, a set designer. It is the job of scenario writer for which I am applying."

At which moment the interview was terminated. Fortunately, C. B. de Mille was "sold" on me for my composing merits alone; otherwise I should have flown out of Paramount Studios that day. . . .

In the meantime I had finished, with considerable success, two major pictures for De Mille. I was now even launched on my third, an epic to be called *Union Pacific* [1939].

Up until now, let me emphasize that I had had no trouble with the Paramount music department. But too, up until now, Boris Morros had been in charge. Now he left Paramount in order to become a producer at another studio and I was suddenly to learn how difficult it is to make a few extra dollars via movie scoring.

When I brought my first sketches for *Union Pacific* to Projection Room Number One of Paramount Studios, I noticed something very strange. Previously I could have played any amount of sketches for De Mille without ever encountering a single other movie composer in that projection room; now, however, every movie composer or arranger working at Paramount at the time was mysteriously present! Now C. B. de Mille is a man, if he will forgive my saying so, who likes to keep in touch with the public's pulse; to cut to the chase, he likes to make his pictures by popular vote.

He is much influenced by everything everybody tells him—especially *en masse.*

Everyone knew this and, therefore, when I saw the whole music department, which had previously never been too cordially inclined towards a musical radical like myself, I became exceedingly apprehensive—and, as it proved, not without due cause. I knew they were there to turn in a record vote and that vote would be against me.

I played one of my sketches for *Union Pacific.*

"Fine! Fine!" said De Mille, beaming, for he had grown to like my music, especially after the very successful scores of *The Plainsman* and *The Buccaneer.* Then he bethought himself.

He looked around to see how the rest of the music department liked it.

Their faces were a study.

I looked at De Mille. I could see him thinking.

"Good God, if even his own music department doesn't like it . . ."

"What do you think of it?" he asked them point-blank.

The jury hemmed and hawed. You could see they really didn't like to say, really. . . .

De Mille turned around to me and said, not unkindly, "Well George, perhaps you weren't feeling too well last night. Go home and try again." I was still ace high with him.

The next day I found the projection room filled again. The same jury. They didn't like my sketches again, not really. . . . "They're not bad, you know, but *really*, Mr. de Mille. . . ."

So I went home that night and rewrote everything again. I worked myself silly. Ditto the next night, and the next.

Inside of one week I was ready to say "uncle."

I did not score *Union Pacific*.

After this I decided that perhaps the Hollywood music departments considered me too aloof, snob, standoffish. Whereupon we rented ourselves a larger house, invited various movie composers, movie arrangers, and music directors to our fireside. Things now went better at the studios, but it all demanded precious time off from my own personal composition; it also greatly upped our expenses. One could never serve anything but the best liquor to these gents, and one had, of course, to keep two maids, to say nothing of [my son] Peter's nurse.

Constant dinners, night after night, ran into formidable sums—even though the movie-music business continued to provide me with interesting amounts of lucre.

Before long we saw that we could not continue in the movie business without losing practically everything, including first of all our self-respect.

One day we simply quit. We moved out of our large house into a very, very small one in a less fashionable section of Hollywood. I told the music departments to go pound sand. I planned to devote myself entirely to writing words and a new commercial proposition I called "SEE-Note." This was in early 1939, approximately April.

In early 1938 I had published in *Esquire* two articles on *popular* piano playing, called "Chopin in Two Lessons." It taught one how to play piano music immediately, but not by ear. It taught you to read music by eye, through a new music notation which I was afterwards to call "SEE-Note." (Although why I happened to call it exactly this I cannot remember.)

But before we left our big, palatial house, and I the movie business entirely, Ben and Charlie suddenly came to Hollywood, both on separate commissions.

Jointly they called me up and, in great glee, kept yelling over the phone that Ben was going to establish a chamber-music society called "The Ben Hecht Symphonietta," and they wanted me to be their pianist. (In his book, *A Smattering of Ignorance*, Oscar Levant has already explained that Ben plays the violin fairly well, likes to play it on every possible occasion.)

Ben would play first violin, and Charlie "clarinet in B flat major." Others were going to join the "symphonietta" too. Charlie Lederer for one, and Harpo Marx. Rehearsals would be held each Thursday night after dinner in Ben's recently rented Hollywood hilltop palace.

I accepted. The nucleus of the orchestra established, Ben now gave an interview to the movie trade papers in which he violently attacked "the general crass and low level of Hollywood musical taste," placing the budding "Ben Hecht Symphonietta" on record as intending to remedy it.

When he appendixed the symphonietta's personnel, Hollywood guffawed and knew it was being ribbed.

The "orchestra" commenced rehearsals. During our very first rehearsal we were together in a little quiet upstairs room of Ben's enormous rented house when, all uninvited, Groucho Marx suddenly opened the door and yelled:

"Quiet, please!"

We looked at one another, thunderstruck. Harpo managed to say, "Groucho's jealous." Ben said, "I wonder what the hell Groucho's up to—I've been hearing our front door open and close all evening."

The mystery remained a mystery until the door, with Groucho behind it, opened again.

"Quiet! You lousy amateurs!"

We took no notice. Previously we had discussed whether or not we should take Groucho into our group and had decided against it because the only instrument he played was the mandolin—which was considered vulgar and undignified for our "chamber music." We sat there in painful, austere silence until Groucho disappeared. We heard him thumping his indignant way down the stairs.

Then, after a minute, there was a sound which raised the rafters. . . .

It was the *Tannhäuser* Overture played by a full real symphony orchestra. Thunderstruck again, we all crawled down the stairway to look. There was Groucho, directing with great batlike gestures, the Los Angeles Symphony Orchestra. At least one hundred men had been squeezed into the living room.

Groucho had hired them because (as he later explained) he had been hurt at our not taking him into our symphonietta.

We took him in. . . .

When Ernst Krenek, the composer, came to town, Ben and I decided that Sam Goldwyn would have to hire him to write the score of a picture which Sam was then planning, one with a Czech background. As Krenek was Czech, had just arrived from Europe (where he had been persecuted by the Nazis), because he was an old and very good friend of mine, and finally because he was out of a job, Ben and I immediately went to Sam and started screaming at him that the greatest composer in the world was in town.

"Is that so?" said Goldwyn, without falling off his chair. "What's his name?"

"Krenek, Ernst Krenek!"

"Never heard of him! What has he written?"

"What's he written, what's he written!" screamed Ben. "Listen to that!"

"Well, what *has* he written? I never heard tell of the guy before."

"You tell him, Georgie," said Ben. I took over.

"He wrote one of the world's most successful operas, 'Jonny Spielt Auf.' It made over a million in Germany before Hitler came in."

"Never heard of it."

"Well," I said, reaching, "he wrote 'Threepenny Opera.'" (Actually, Kurt Weill wrote it, and I knew it, but all of Krenek's operas, symphonies, and other pieces seemed so feeble now.)

"Never heard of it."

"And 'Rosenkavalier,'" interrupted Ben. "He wrote 'Rosenkavalier.' It grossed over two million dollars last year on the Continent."

Goldwyn brightened up a bit. He thought he might have heard of "Rosenkavalier."

"And 'Faust' too; Krenek wrote that."

"No kiddin'!" said Goldwyn speculatively. I could see Krenek was going to get the job.

"And 'La Traviata' too," said Ben, to clinch it.

"So he wrote 'La Traviata' did he!" Goldwyn's smiling face suddenly turned black. "Just bring that guy around here so's I can get my hands on him. Why, his publishers almost ruined me with a suit just because we used a few bars of that lousy opera. We had to retake half of the picture for a few lousy bars."

As we quickly withdrew from his wrath, both Ben and I sadly realized that we oversold our product. . . .

But unless you attempt to do so with a really talented man like Ben Hecht or one of his large caliber, the trouble with trying to earn a fortune by writing movie music is that it's such an awful darned nuisance. Earning money is always a nuisance, but earning it through several not-to-be-mentioned-here Hollywood music directors is really the most irritating way one can imagine, particularly when (am I, perhaps, a bit too boastful?) one is a *known* composer with one's name in almost every musical encyclopedia, and the music directors are without their names in same. It just becomes a question of whether their inferiority complex or your superiority complex holds out the longest. Even so they, holding the whip hand, usually manage to outguess you.

But the over-all question of to be or not to be in the movie music departments is not only a question of music directors but of one's studio colleagues in music; mostly they are "composers" who are afraid that maybe you will come in and upset the whole technique of scoring pictures as once you've been reputed to have upset the technique of writing serious music, and where would they be then? (I mean in case you're Stravinsky, Copland, Toch, Schönberg, or somebody like that; they have these same troubles.)

The ensconced movie composers are mostly not alert enough, quick enough to learn a really new scoring wrinkle; in short, to move a new composer of reputation into a Hollywood music studio is murder, a matter of survival of the fittest, both for them and for you. And they know the ropes.

In 1936–37 two or three "modern" composers entered Hollywood studios, including myself. Our scores were very successful, giving all the directors and producers a new idea. The directors started demanding to know why all the scores of Hollywood were not at least as fresh, if not as expert. Oscar Levant tells the amusing story of how, during the latter end of this exact period, most of the old stuffy routine composers of Hollywood suddenly ran out to Arnold Schönberg in order to take "a few lessons in discords," this presumably to "modernize" their work, to make it as "up to date" as ours. (Horrors, what terminology!) As this, naturally, didn't work, the only other method of protection they could adopt was to gang up against newcomers.

There were more of them than there were of us, so it is redundant to observe that, mostly, they won.

This is not to say that I don't like Hollywood, or the motion-picture business. I very much do. I think that it is one of the few so-called "art colonies" of the world *which actually works*. It is a lot of fun to live here and be connected with the movies. Fresh air blows through them. But not around the music departments.

Around the movie lots there is a saying that the music departments are the last kicked-around dog of the motion pictures. For one thing they have the lowest budgets—important here. They also get the footage last and have less time to do their stunt with it than any other department, not even excepting the cutting. Nobody gives a damn about them.

It is really too bad. After all, Hollywood music is very nearly a public communication, like radio. If you are a movie fan (and who isn't?) you may sit in a movie theater three times a week listening to the symphonic background scores which Hollywood composers concoct. What happens? Your musical tastes become molded by these scores, heard without knowing it. You *see* love, and you *hear* it. *Simultaneously.* It makes sense. Music suddenly becomes a language for you, without your knowing it. You cannot see and hear such stuff week in and year out without forming some kind of taste for it. You do not have to listen to a radio program of stupid banal music. But you cannot see your movies without being compelled to listen.

In this special regard I sometimes wonder greatly at music critics. They take infinite pains with the molding of public taste, at least insofar as the concert hall and the symphonic radio program is concerned, but they absolutely ignore the most important thing of all, the background movie score. It is here that the great larger public taste is being slowly but surely formed. As I said before, the radio is something you can turn off. But you cannot turn this stuff off unless you refuse to go to the movies.

I am very worried about this state of affairs in American music, and I was very worried about it when I went to Hollywood, only then I thought I could do something about it. Now, at least, I know I can't; and so do my colleagues. With the exception of Waxman, Hollander, and possibly Rozsa, and my old squawking friend, Benny [Bernard] Herrmann, not a single composer of new vitality has appeared in Hollywood in years, and Benny entered Hollywood via radio and the great prestige of Orson Welles, so he doesn't quite count.

Hollywood music is a closed proposition for the likes of us.

24

Igor Stravinsky on Film Music (1946)

Although neither of them composed a single film score, Arnold Schoenberg (1874–1951) and Igor Stravinsky (1882–1971) both lived in Los Angeles during the Hollywood Golden Age—Schoenberg arrived there in 1934 and Stravinsky in 1940, though as dogged opponents they chose never to meet one another—and their shadows hovered over many aspiring film composers interested in modern concert music at the time. David Raksin, Leonard Rosenman, and other film composers studied with Schoenberg, who numbered film-music critic Bruno David Ussher and legendary music director Hugo Riesenfeld among his Hollywood acquaintances, and Schoenberg's twelve-note serial techniques occasionally made an esoteric appearance in film scores by composers as diverse as Raksin, Rózsa, Rosenman, Jerry Fielding, and David Shire—and even in the work of Tom and Jerry composer Scott Bradley (see p. 102). Stravinsky's stylistic influence on film music was more palpable, both filtered through the neoclassical leanings of Aaron Copland's scores and later in the more aggressive modernism of dynamic ostinato-driven scores by Jerry Goldsmith and others. Given the conservatism that was endemic in Hollywood at the time, however, the influence of these two leading modernist composers on film scoring did not obviously emerge until the 1950s and 1960s, many decades after they had introduced their innovative compositional methods to the concert hall.

Various attempts, some misguided and others serious, were made to lure Schoenberg and Stravinsky into the Hollywood film studios during their residency in Los Angeles. In the silent era, Schoenberg had been seriously interested

Source: Ingolf Dahl, "Igor Stravinsky on Film Music," *Musical Digest*, 28 (September 1946): 4–5, 35–36.

in the possibilities that cinema had to offer for the filming of opera in a nonrealistic manner, but now his megalomania and egotism soon put paid to any thought that he might work effectively as part of a team of artisans. Dimitri Tiomkin recalled a typical encounter between Schoenberg and Hollywood's studio moguls (see pp. 130–31), and in her book *The Kindness of Strangers* (New York: Holt, Rinehart and Winston, 1969, 206–8), actress and screenwriter Salka Viertel recounted an enterprising attempt by MGM producer Irving Thalberg to persuade Schoenberg to write the music for *The Good Earth* (dir. Sidney Franklin et al., 1937) after Thalberg had enjoyed listening to the Viennese composer's late-romantic tone poem *Verklärte Nacht* (*Transfigured Night*). Thalberg was seemingly unaware that Schoenberg had abandoned his early tonal style and had instead been composing grittily atonal music for some decades, and unwisely began the conversation:

> "Last Sunday when I heard the lovely music you have written . . ."
> Schoenberg interrupted sharply: "I don't write 'lovely' music."
>
> Thalberg looked baffled, then smiled and explained what he meant by "lovely music." It had to have Chinese themes, and, as the people in the film were peasants, there was not much dialogue but a lot of action. . . . I translated what Thalberg said into German, but Schoenberg interrupted me. He understood everything, and in a surprisingly literary though faulty English, he conveyed what he thought in general of music in films: that it was simply terrible. The whole handling of sound was incredibly bad, meaningless, numbing all expression; the leveling monotony of the dialogue was unbearable. He had read *The Good Earth* and would not undertake the assignment unless he was given complete control over the sound, including the spoken words.

Asked by an incredulous Thalberg to explain what he meant, Schoenberg declared that he would need to coach the actors in his own brand of *Sprechstimme* (speech song) after the manner of his avant-garde composition *Pierrot Lunaire* before he would even allow the film's director to work with them. Undaunted, Thalberg gave Schoenberg a copy of the script to peruse overnight. The next morning, Viertel received a telephone call from Schoenberg's wife:

> For his complete control of the film, including the dialogue, Schoenberg was asking fifty thousand [dollars—i.e., twice the fee that had been offered to him], otherwise it was not worth his time and effort. When I related this to Thalberg he shrugged and said that meanwhile the Chinese technical advisor had brought some folk songs which had inspired the head of the sound department to write some very lovely music.

Schoenberg's difficult behavior toward film executives was also true to some extent of Stravinsky, and a degree of sympathy must in all fairness be extended toward producers who were genuinely perplexed as to why these composers made such unreasonable demands when (in the producers' minds, at least) more reliable and certainly far cheaper scores could readily and quickly be obtained from others, and without the hassle of having to deal with temperamental geniuses.

In the somewhat eccentric text below, which appeared in a provocative 1946 article published in two parts in *Musical Digest*—an enterprising journal whose publication was made possible by the generosity of the chemical magnate, arts patron, and philanthropist Henry H. Reichhold (1901–89)—Stravinsky expounds on what he saw as the essential feebleness of film music. Stravinsky's views also appeared in France at this time in an article entitled "La musique de film?—du papier peint!" (*Ecran français*, 125 [1947]: 3), in which he curtly dismisses film music as aural wallpaper. The present article was the result of a conversation between Stravinsky and the composer Ingolf Dahl (whose account of early cartoon music is reprinted on pp. 93–99) that took place on 3 May 1946. At this stage in his rich and varied career, which in addition to composition included session work in film studios as a keyboard player and a spell as Gracie Fields's accompanist, Dahl was teaching music at the University of Southern California and was in regular contact with Stravinsky. In 1942, he had assisted Stravinsky by preparing a two-piano reduction of his *Danses concertantes*, and his later program notes on other Stravinsky works were written at the composer's personal request and warmly praised by Copland for their insights. Dahl also translated (with Arthur Knodel) Stravinsky's published lecture series, *Poetics of Music* (Cambridge, Mass.: Harvard University Press, 1947), and remained Stravinsky's confidante until he was supplanted in this role by Robert Craft in the 1950s—an abrupt shift in loyalty that occasioned much sadness on Dahl's part.

A spirited riposte to Stravinsky's prejudiced views on film music was published in *Musical Digest*, at the journal's request, by David Raksin: see the next chapter.

As Igor Stravinsky is eminently a "contemporary" composer and decidedly a "modernist," it is sometimes difficult to remember that this Russian innovator in tone, born in 1882, was already 15 years old when Brahms died. It is almost as hard to realize today that *The Firebird, Petrouchka* and *Rite of Spring* ballets were composed prior to the outbreak of World War I, while *Histoire du Soldat* was created before that war ended. Even the much later *Symphony of Psalms*,

Ingolf Dahl (left) with his protégé, the young composer Paul Glass, at
Twentieth Century-Fox in April 1957 during the recording of Glass's
modernist score to *The Abductors* (dir. Andrew McLaglen), for which
Dahl was the conductor. Among Dahl's writings on film music were his
pioneering article on cartoon scores and an interview on the subject with a
characteristically provocative Stravinsky. (Courtesy of Dr. Anthony Linick)

which had been composed for the fiftieth anniversary of the Boston Symphony,
dates as far back as 1930. Such biographical details are worth mention, not only
for the record but as collateral tribute to the vitality and verve of the composer
and his creations. As for the man himself, his opinions on the relation of music
to moving pictures set forth in this article acquire additional weight and momentum, of course, because Stravinsky's *Sacre du Printemps (Rite of Spring)*
reaches the celluloid in Walt Disney's *Fantasia*.

Some of the Russian's views may startle some readers; hardly one reader
will be shocked into anything less profitable than a fresh examination of his
own opinions.

Igor Stravinsky on Film Music

What is the function of music in moving pictures? What, you ask, are the particular problems involved in music for the screen? I can answer both questions

briefly. And I must answer them bluntly. There are no musical problems in the film. And there is only one real function of film music—namely, to feed the composer! In all frankness I find it impossible to talk to film people about music because we have no common meeting ground; their primitive and childish concept of music is not my concept. They have the mistaken notion that music, in "helping" and "explaining" the cinematic shadow-play, could be regarded under artistic considerations. It cannot be.

Do not misunderstand me. I realize that music is an indispensable adjunct to the sound film. It has got to bridge holes; it has got to fill the emptiness of the screen and supply the loudspeakers with more or less pleasant sounds. The film could not get along without it, just as I myself could not get along without having the empty spaces of my living-room walls covered with wall paper. But you would not ask me, would you, to regard my wall paper as I would regard painting, or apply aesthetic standards to it?

Misconceptions arise at the very outset of such a discussion when it is asserted that music will help the drama by underlining and describing the characters and the action. Well, that is precisely the same fallacy which has so disastrously affected the true opera through the "Musikdrama." Music explains nothing; music underlines nothing. When it attempts to explain, to narrate, or to underline something, the effect is both embarrassing and harmful.

What, for example, is "sad" music? There is no sad music, there are only conventions to which part of the western world has unthinkingly become accustomed through repeated associations. These conventions tell us that *Allegro* stands for rushing action, *Adagio* for tragedy, suspension harmonies for sentimental feeling, etc. I do not like to base premises on wrong deductions, and these conventions are far removed from the essential core of music.

And—to ask a question myself—why take film music seriously? The film people admit themselves that at its most satisfactory it should not be heard as such. Here I agree. I believe that it should not hinder or hurt the action and that it should fill its wallpaper function by having the same relationship to the drama that restaurant music has to the conversation at the individual restaurant table. Or that somebody's piano playing in my living-room has to the book I am reading.

The orchestral sounds in films, then, would be like a perfume which is indefinable there. But let it be clearly understood that such perfume "explains" nothing; and, moreover, I can not accept it as music. Mozart once said: "Music is there to delight us, that is its calling." In other words, music is too high an art to be a servant to other arts; it is too high to be absorbed only by the subconscious mind of the spectator, if it still wants to be considered as music.

Furthermore, the fact that some good composers have composed for the screen does not alter these basic considerations. Decent composers will offer the films decent pages of background score; they will supply more "listenable" sounds than other composers; but even they are subject to the basic rules of the film which, of course, are primarily commercial. The film makers know that they need music, but they prefer music which is not very new. When, for commercial reasons, they employ a composer of repute they want him to write this kind of "not very new" music—which, of course, results in nothing but musical disaster.

I have been asked whether my own music, written for the ballet and the stage, would not be comparable in its dramatic connotation to music in the films. It cannot be compared at all. The days of *Petrouchka* are long past, and whatever few elements of realistic description can be found in its pages fail to be representative of my thinking now. My music expresses nothing of realistic character, and neither does the dance. The ballet consists of movements which have their own aesthetic and logic, and if one of those movements should happen to be a visualization of the words "I Love You," then this reference to the external world would play the same role in the dance (and in my music) that a guitar in a Picasso still-life would play: something of the world is caught as pretext or clothing for the inherent abstraction. Dancers have nothing to narrate and neither has my music. Even in older ballets like *Giselle*, descriptiveness has been removed—by virtue of its naiveté, its unpretentious traditionalism and its simplicity—to a level of objectivity and pure art-play.

My music for the stage, then, never tries to "explain" the action, but rather it lives side by side with the visual movement, happily married to it, as one individual to another. In *Scènes de Ballet* the dramatic action was given by an evolution of plastic problems, and both dance and music had to be constructed on the architectural feeling for contrast and similarity.

The danger in the visualization of music on the screen—and a very real danger it is—is that the film has always tried to "describe" the music. That is absurd. When Balanchine did a choreography to my *Danses Concertantes* (originally written as a piece of concert music) he approached the problem architecturally and not descriptively. And his success was extraordinary for one great reason: he went to the roots of the musical form, of the *jeu musical*, and recreated it in forms of movements. Only if the films should ever adopt an attitude of this kind is it possible that a satisfying and interesting art form would result.

The dramatic impact of my *Histoire du Soldat* has been cited by various critics. There, too, the result was achieved, not by trying to write music which, in the background, tried to explain the dramatic action, or to carry the action forward descriptively, the procedure followed in the cinema. Rather was it the simultaneity of stage, narration, and music which was the object, resulting in the dramatic power of the whole. Put music and drama together as individual entities, put them together and let them alone without compelling one to try to "explain" and to react to the other. To borrow a term from chemistry: my ideal is the chemical *reaction*, where a new entity, a third body, results from uniting two different but equally important elements, music and drama; it is not the chemical *mixture* where, as in the films, to the preordained whole just the ingredient of music is added, resulting in nothing either new or creative. The entire working methods of dramatic film exemplify this.

All these reflections are not to be taken as a point-blank refusal on my part ever to work for the film. I do not work for money, but I need it, as everybody does. Chesterton tells about Charles Dickens' visit to America. The people who had invited him to lecture here were astonished, it seems, about his interest in fees and contracts. "Money is not a shocking thing to an artist," Dickens insisted. Likewise there will be nothing shocking to me in offering my professional capacities to a film studio for remuneration.

If I am asked whether the dissemination of good concert music in the cinema will help to create a more understanding mass audience, I can only answer that here again we must beware of dangerous misconceptions. My first premise is that good music must be heard by and for itself, and not with the crutch of any visual medium. If you start to explain the "meaning" of music you are on the wrong path. Such absurd "meanings" will invariably be established by the image, if only through automatic association. That is an extreme disservice to music. Listeners will never be able to hear music by and for itself, but only for what it represents under the given circumstances and given instructions. Music can be useful, I repeat, only when it is taken for itself. It has to play its own role if it is to be understood at all. And for music to be useful to the individual we must above all teach the self-sufficiency of music, and you will agree that the cinema is a poor place for that! Even under the best conditions it is impossible for the human brain to follow the ear and the eye at the same time.

And even listening is itself not enough, granted that it be understood in its best sense; the training of the ear. To listen only is too passive and it creates a taste and judgment which are too general, too indiscriminate. Only in limited degree can music be helped through increased listening; much more important is the making of music. The playing of an instrument, actual production of some kind or another, will make music accessible and helpful to the individual, not the passive consumption in the darkness of a neighborhood theatre.

And it is the individual that matters, never the mass. The "mass," in relationship to art, is a quantitative term which has never once entered into my consideration. When Disney used *Sacre du Printemps* for *Fantasia* he told me: "Think of the number of people who will thus be able to hear your music!"

Well, the number of people who will consume music is doubtless of interest to somebody like [impresario] Mr. [Sol] Hurok, but it is of no interest to me. The broad mass adds nothing to the art, it cannot raise the level, and the artist who aims consciously at "mass-appeal" can do so only by lowering his own level. The soul of each individual who listens to my music is important to me, and not the mass feeling of a group. Music cannot be helped through an increase in *quantity* of listeners, be this increase effected by the films or any other medium, but only through an increase in the *quality* of listening, the quality of the individual soul.

In my autobiography I described the dangers of mechanical music distribution; and I still believe, as I then did, that "for the majority of listeners there is every reason to fear that, far from developing a love and understanding of music, the modern methods of dissemination will . . . produce indifference, inability to understand, to appreciate, or to undergo any worthy reaction. In addition, there is the musical deception arising from the substitution for the actual playing of a reproduction, whether on record or film or by wireless transmission. It is the same difference as that between the synthetic and the authentic. The danger lied [*sic*] in the fact that there is always a far greater consumption of the synthetic which, it must always be remembered, is far from being identical with its mode. The continuous habit of listening to changed and sometimes distorted timbres dulls and degrades the ear, so that it gradually loses all capacity for enjoying natural musical sounds."

In summary, then, my ideas on music and the moving pictures are brief and definite:

The current cinematic concept of music is foreign to me; I express myself in a different way. What common language can one have with the films? They have recourse to music for reasons of sentiment. They use it like remembrances, like odors, like perfumes which evoke remembrances. As for myself, I need music for hygienic purposes, for the health of my soul. Without music in its best sense there is chaos. For my part, music is a force which gives reason to things, a force which creates organization, which attunes things. Music probably attended the creation of the universe. LOGOS.

25

David Raksin: "Hollywood Strikes Back" (1948)

This article was a direct response to Stravinsky's provocative views on film music, which had been published in *Musical Digest* in 1946 in an article written by Ingolf Dahl: see the previous chapter.

For more on David Raksin, and his personal account of his early work with Charlie Chaplin, see pp. 69–81.

I live in a land where deference towards one's elders is scarcely the rule; young people grow up to think in terms of a man's essential worth rather than his seniority. "Essential worth" is, of course, a fancy generalization. It is a variable, a term that permits too many subjective responses. Nevertheless, the essential worth of a man like Igor Stravinsky is hardly disputable—when he is writing music. In the role of critic, however, his greatness is questionable. His recent pronouncements make this abundantly clear.

In writing of a man who was composing *Le Sacre du Printemps* the year I was born, I must first make clear my great admiration for his genius and for the music he has created. It is not with this that I would quarrel, but with his opinions on artistic matters that appear to be quite beyond his understanding.

In his interview with Ingolf Dahl, which appeared in the *Musical Digest* of September 1946, Mr. Stravinsky contends that "there is only one real function

Source: "Hollywood Strikes Back: Film Composer Attacks Stravinsky's 'Cult of Inexpressiveness,'" *Musical Digest*, 30 (January 1948).

of film music—namely to feed the composer." Aside from the fact that I have found this function a consistently useful one, there are other less personal reasons for holding it in respect.

One wishes, as he reads the oftentimes sad history of music, that it might have operated on behalf of Mozart and Schubert. The world has so often neglected its great men that one looks with pleasure at the composer who eats regularly as a result of the indulgence of a wealthy patron or of an organization (sometimes called commission), or by composing or orchestrating for the ballet. In a world where man does not live by double-fugues alone, perhaps the composer who works in films is most fortunate of all. At least he works as a composer and does not wear himself out teaching dolts, concertizing or kow-towing to concert-managers, dilettantes and other musical parasites.

While he may sometimes work with people whose intelligence is somewhat below that of Leonardo da Vinci, this is in no way different from the "Classic" position of the composer, who has always had to cope with employers or patrons who were fundamentally unmusical, from the Archbishop of Salzburg to Louis B. Mayer. The whole struggle of the new generation of American composers has been just this: that they should be able to live from their work as composers. If film music makes this possible, so much the better.

Mr. Stravinsky is absolutely horrified at the esthetics of film music. "I find it impossible to talk to film people about music," he says, "because we have no common meeting ground; their primitive and childish concept of music is not my concept." So long as he assumes the position of godhead in esthetic matters, there are, of course, no grounds for argument. What is primitive and childish is often open to question. Mr. Stravinsky appears to be using against film music the same arguments that were directed against his own ballet, Le Sacre du Printemps, when it first appeared. And if complexity and maturity be the opposites of the qualities that Mr. Stravinsky so despises, he will have great difficulty in convincing all critics that these are the typical qualities of his own music.

A popular, non-technical magazine is hardly the place to be quoting musical examples; otherwise it would be easy to set Mr. Stravinsky's words against his music. For now, it must be sufficient to wonder aloud how the second movement of his Symphony in Three Movements and parts of Scènes de Ballet fit in with his dicta. It has always been interesting to see how often an artist's stated principles are contradicted by his art.

It is an inevitable corollary of Mr. Stravinsky's esthetics that film music, as he sees it, cannot "be regarded under artistic considerations." He said no; I say yes. Impasse. But it is an impasse arising out of a dogmatic assumption with which he could trap the unwary. Evidently Mr. Stravinsky's definition of art is a restrictive one, and if he can maintain it, he has indeed succeeded where philosophers have been frustrated for centuries. He, of all people, should beware of such restrictive definitions. A genuine orthodoxy, sanctioned by theories and accomplishments of generations of great artists before his own time, might conceivably exclude most of his own art. Mr. Stravinsky's definitions must perforce be broad ones, lest he find himself a pariah among those to whom he would appear as a god. Neither Mr. Stravinsky nor I will decide these matters. They will be decided through the same process of selection that constantly refines and revitalizes our musical heritage. Such selective processes have a way of disregarding respectability, theories and venerable age, and of deferring only to essential worth.

The doctrine of essential worth, if I may presume so to dignify the idea, is not one that requires definition. It is quite satisfied with illustration. If one cannot say what it is, one can at least say what it does. It has freed artists from oppressive esthetic standards of both the past and present. It has repeatedly sent the status quo crashing into ruins. It has broken the charmed circle and destroyed the exclusiveness of the daisy chain. It has assured universality and immortality to any piece of music that is good, whether it be a symphony, a popular song or a sequence in a film score. More than that, it has made room in the contemporary musical scene for Mr. Stravinsky.

It is true, of course, that a sequence of film music may not measure up as a musical entity—that is, it may not satisfy the logic of "pure" music. But it may, nevertheless, remain a good piece of film music; and as such, it may be as worthy of artistic consideration as other music for, say, the opera, or the ballet or the dramatic stage. If one were to quibble with Mr. Stravinsky's music as he quibbles with Hollywood's, it would be fair to ask just what "pure" logic is satisfied by the final bars of *Petrouchka*. By themselves they are hard to justify, but in the context of the ballet they are inevitable. So with film music: many a sequence derives its meaning from the context of the film and the rest of the music. The "wall-paper" theory of film music which Mr. Stravinsky so glibly expounds may help him to maintain the defensive position of a neo-classicist who does not wish his preconceived attitudes to be affected in any way by facts. But it cannot be other than ridiculous to the film-goer, to whom the function of film music is an actuality which he does not need to be convinced of, since he experiences it.

"Put music and drama together as individual entities," says Mr. Stravinsky, "put them together and let them alone, without compelling one to try to 'explain' and to react to the other." Then, contradicting himself, he explains that his ideal is "the chemical reaction where a new entity . . . results." Aside from the fact that Mr. Stravinsky thus rules out almost all of the operas the world has learned to love in favor of his own esoteric preferences, it seems sheer presumption to say arbitrarily that this reaction never occurs in film music. Anyone who has ever seen the silent footage of a film in its rough cut and then the final scored version can testify to the transformation. The expressiveness of film music has frequently been derided; too often it overstates the case. But to deny its eloquence requires an extreme degree of insensitivity.

Here one runs into another of Mr. Stravinsky's dogmas, the statement that "music explains nothing, music underlines nothing." This may be for Mr. Stravinsky a satisfactory defense of his own aversion to expressiveness. But it hardly conforms to the facts. Mr. Stravinsky's music may indeed be more expressive than he himself suspects. For even when he sets out to say nothing he succeeds in saying much about himself. And this is why he has come to be recognized as one of the great masters of our day. What we revere in his music is precisely what he has explained and underlined about himself, not what he has hidden from us.

Pursuing his idea, Mr. Stravinsky goes on to ask, "What is 'sad' music?" I confess that I find this question narrow, contemptuous, disillusioned, insensitive, precious—and deaf. Does the man who grew up in the land of Tchaikovsky and Moussorgsky really ask what is sad music? Ask the artist who painted *Guernica* what is horror, the author of the Twenty-ninth Psalm what is exaltation. Mr. Stravinsky seems hardly the one to pause for an answer to such questions, for his esoteric point of view excludes the simple, direct and accessible aspects of art.

I do not hold to the extreme opposite of insisting that every note of music must have some "significance"—social or otherwise—in order to justify it. This approach to art is as intolerable as it is dull. But somehow it seems closer to the realities of life than a philosophy of detachment and scorn.

No one can quarrel with Mr. Stravinsky's prerogatives as an artist, or with his analyses of his own music. They are interesting but not final. Just as Mr. Stravinsky has searched deeply for the intrinsic quality of the music of Pergolesi in *Pulcinella,* so do we who listen to Stravinsky's music search for the meaning that it has for us. These meanings, I suspect, are far greater than Mr. Stravinsky prefers to acknowledge. Consider, for a moment, the Introduction to the second part of *Le Sacre,* or Jocasta's aria, *Oracula, Oracula,* from *Oedipus Rex.* Examples fall over themselves to be heard, but if I may hark back to an earlier paragraph of this article, let us forget the author of the Twenty-ninth Psalm, and ask the composer of the last movement of the *Symphony of Psalms,* with its Hallelujahs, what is exaltation?

That Mr. Stravinsky is not unaware of the significance of his music is demonstrated by his acceptance of Ingolf Dahl's program notes for the *Symphony in*

C Major, which included the following sentence: "One day it will be universally recognized that the white house in the Hollywood hills, in which the Symphony was written and which was regarded by some as an ivory tower, was just as close to the core of the world at war as the place where Picasso painted *Guernica.*" Many of us were greatly surprised when Mr. Stravinsky approved this passage; some questioned its validity, which now seems to this writer more apparent than it was at first. The important thing is that Mr. Stravinsky, by his approval, admits to this significance.

The difference between the meanings that a composer intends and the meanings that an audience infers constitutes the very richness of art. Speaking of his *Scènes de Ballet,* Mr. Stravinsky says, "the dramatic action was given by an evolution of plastic problems." This is undoubtedly true—although one notes that he uses the word "dramatic" in describing the action. But it is not the whole truth. For not all of the problems of today's composers are plastic problems. Many of them are dynamic problems presented by events of the composer's inner and outer life. Expressive music does not have to dig very hard into the history of musical art to find examples in abundance. One can find them even in Mr. Stravinsky's music—in the opening of the *Symphony in Three Movements,* for instance, in the outer movements of the *Symphony of Psalms,* in the *Pas de Deux* of *Scènes de Ballet,* with its sentimental trumpet solo. These may have been plastic problems to Mr. Stravinsky; but the finished product, as we hear it, is packed with feeling and emotion.

On the basis of his music, Mr. Stravinsky, who has fathered the latest cult of inexpressiveness (an earlier one was sired by Nero), seems himself not quite able to fulfill the membership qualifications. This may come as a great blow to him, but the gulf between his own music and that of the films is neither so wide nor so impassable as he would like to imagine. A man who writes such pretty thirds and sixths, whose music from the ballet, *Firebird,* is soon to be the subject of a tap dance in a film, and whose new ballad, *Summer Moon,* may soon be a contender for Hit Parade honors, is hardly in the best possible position to espouse austerity.

I must now point out again that I admire and respect Mr. Stravinsky as a great composer. But as a critic of music in films he leaves much to be desired. Any Hollywood composer can tell him what is really wrong with film music. Mr. Stravinsky himself has pointed out none of the real defects. He has succeeded only in expressing an esoteric and snobbish attitude.

"Music," says Mr. Stravinsky, "probably attended the creation of the universe." Certainly. It was background music.

26

Theodor Adorno and Hanns Eisler: *Composing for the Films* (1947)

The German composer Hanns Eisler (1898–1962) studied with Schoenberg in Vienna in 1919–23 and, like his teacher, at first wrote in a modernist idiom in which unstable chromaticism was rationalized by the discipline of strict serial techniques. Closely involved with the Communist Party from 1926, Eisler began to write political essays and diatonic militant songs that were espoused by the left wing in several European countries. He started his lifelong collaboration with dramatist Bertolt Brecht in the early 1930s, but his composing career in Germany was cut short when his music was proscribed by the Nazis. Also banned was a docudrama for which Eisler had provided the music: *Kuhle Wampe* (dir. Slatan Dudow, 1932), a film based on a screenplay by Brecht about communist youth activities. Something of a specialist in the genre, Eisler wrote music for a series of documentaries made by Joris Ivens (*Komsomols*, 1932; *New Earth*, 1934; *400 Million*, 1938), and Alain Resnais's Holocaust memorial *Nuit et brouillard* (*Night and Fog*, 1956).

Having taught sporadically in the United States in 1935–37, Eisler in 1940 accepted from the Rockefeller Foundation a three-year research grant to investigate the nature of film music, during which he composed a Schoenbergian score to an early experimental film by Ivens (*Rain*, 1929), screened in Los Angeles in 1947. By this time Eisler had written music for several Hollywood features by top directors, including Fritz Lang (*Hangmen Also Die!*, 1943, with a screenplay by Brecht), Douglas Sirk (*A Scandal in Paris*, 1946), and Edward

Source: *Composing for the Films* (New York: Oxford University Press, 1947), newly published with an Introduction by Graham McCann (London: Athlone Press, 1994): 3–19.

Dmytryk (*So Well Remembered*, 1947). The score for *Hangmen Also Die!* was nominated for an Academy Award but lost out to Alfred Newman's music for *The Song of Bernadette*. Along with Brecht, Eisler subsequently fell foul of the 1947 anticommunist witch hunt in which the House Un-American Activities Committee ruthlessly investigated what it described as "the Communists' Infiltration of the Motion Picture Industry," and he wisely left the United States the following year. He was not allowed to return.

From the Rockefeller project emerged the provocative book *Composing for the Films*, which Eisler coauthored with Theodor Adorno (1903–69). Adorno, the leading light in the new discipline of music-related sociology and philosophy, was sharply critical of bourgeois musical values and the culture industry associated with them; he idealized intellectual musical modernism as a solution to the degeneracy of clichéd film music and was thus to some extent similar in outlook to Eisler. (It may be noted, however, that Eisler's own Hollywood film music was far less adventurous than might have been expected given the trenchant views expressed—with the luxury of theoretical abstraction—in the extracts below.) Another exile from Nazi Germany, Adorno lived in the United States between 1938 and 1949, moving from New York to Los Angeles in 1941; in addition to his work with Eisler on *Composing for the Films*, he undertook collaborative research on radio broadcasting and popular music.

Composing for the Films (which was first published in 1947 with only Eisler's name on the title page) comprised the following chapters, the extracts below being taken from the first: 1. Prejudices and Bad Habits; 2. Function and Dramaturgy; 3. The New Musical Resources; 4. Sociological Aspects; 5. Elements of Aesthetics; 6. The Composer and the Movie-Making Process; and 7. Suggestions and Conclusions. The volume ended with an appendix comprising a report on the Rockefeller project and an account of the "fourteen ways to describe rain" arising from Eisler's work on Ivens's film during his research. The book's content was in places controversial and struck some working in the film industry as both elitist and prejudicial. Reviewing the volume for *Hollywood Quarterly* (3/2 [Winter 1947–48]: 208–11), Lawrence Morton wrote:

> Mr. Eisler fulminates against these evils [the leitmotif, illustrative
> music, and clichés] as though he has discovered them. Yet they have
> been named and discussed many times before. . . . He has merely
> thrown himself (and rather late at that) into a struggle of long
> standing. He has done a more nearly complete job than the others;
> and he has employed the most telling weapons—irritation, idealism,

intelligence, musicianship, and a formidable power of irony and invective.

It must be said, however, that his analysis of the present state of film music is sometimes biased, oversimplified, and impolite. While all the evils he names do exist, they certainly are not universal; and there are variations of degree and kind. His indictment is so sweeping as to consign to hell fire a number of legitimate practices and an amount of good film music which, in a less Jehovah-like judgment, would be regarded as extenuating. . . .

It appears that many of Mr. Eisler's objections to today's film music are based less upon its actual failures than upon his desire to promote the twelve-tone aesthetic. This is the weakness of his position as a critic. But it is also the strength of his position as a composer. Out of his musical faith arises his second main thesis, that modern music (particularly twelve-tone) is what the films need in order to realize their fullest potentialities. His argument for it is excellent. . . .

. . . Mr. Eisler has a rare and original talent. If Hollywood is to be deprived of his services, which it can ill afford, it is fortunate in having at least a verbal exposition of his ideas. His book provides much food for thought during the impending famine.

Morton's closing remarks were a clear reference to the egregious and ongoing official purge of communist sympathizers from the film industry.

The character of motion-picture music has been determined by everyday practice. It has been an adaptation in part to the immediate needs of the film industry, in part to whatever musical clichés and ideas about music happened to be current. As a result, a number of empirical standards—rules of thumb—were evolved that corresponded to what motion-picture people called common sense. These rules have now been made obsolete by the technical development of the cinema as well as of autonomous music, yet they have persisted as tenaciously as if they had their roots in ancient wisdom rather than in bad habits. They originated in the intellectual milieu of Tin Pan Alley; and because of practical considerations and problems of personnel, they have so entrenched themselves that they, more than anything else, have hindered the progress of motion-picture music. They only seem to make sense as a consequence of standardization within the industry itself, which calls for standard practices everywhere.

Furthermore, these rules of thumb represent a kind of pseudo-tradition harking back to the days of spontaneity and craftsmanship, of medicine shows and covered wagons. And it is precisely this discrepancy between obsolete practices and scientific production methods that characterizes the whole system. The two aspects are inseparable in principle, and both are subject to criticism. Public realization of the antiquated character of these rules should suffice to break their hold.

Typical examples of these habits, selected at random, will be discussed here in order to show concretely the level on which the problem of motion-picture music is dealt with today.

The Leitmotif

Cinema music is still patched together by means of leitmotifs. The ease with which they are recalled provides definite clues for the listener, and they also are a practical help to the composer in his task of composition under pressure. He can quote where he otherwise would have to invent.

The idea of the leitmotif has been popular since the days of Wagner.[1] His popularity was largely connected with his use of leitmotifs. They function as trademarks, so to speak, by which persons, emotions, and symbols can instantly be identified. They have always been the most elementary means of elucidation, the thread by which the musically inexperienced find their way about. They were drummed into the listener's ear by persistent repetition, often with scarcely any variation, very much as a new song is plugged or as a motion-picture actress is popularized by her hair-do. It was natural to assume that this device, because it is so easy to grasp, would be particularly suitable to motion pictures, which are based on the premise that they must be easily understood. However, the truth of this assumption is only illusory.

The reasons for this are first of all technical. The fundamental character of the leitmotif—its salience and brevity—was related to the gigantic dimensions of the Wagnerian and post-Wagnerian music dramas. Just because the leitmotif

---

1. A prominent Hollywood composer, in an interview quoted in the newspapers, declared that there is no fundamental difference between his methods of composing and Wagner's. He, too, uses the leitmotif.

as such is musically rudimentary, it requires a large musical canvas if it is to take on a structural meaning beyond that of a signpost. The atomization of the musical element is paralleled by the heroic dimensions of the composition as a whole. This relation is entirely absent in the motion picture, which requires continual interruption of one element by another rather than continuity. The constantly changing scenes are characteristic of the structure of the motion picture. Musically, also, shorter forms prevail, and the leitmotif is unsuitable here because of this brevity of forms which must be complete in themselves. Cinema music is so easily understood that it has no need of leitmotifs to serve as signposts, and its limited dimension does not permit of adequate expansion of the leitmotif.

Similar considerations apply with regard to the aesthetic problem. The Wagnerian leitmotif is inseparably connected with the symbolic nature of the music drama. The leitmotif is not supposed merely to characterize persons, emotions, or things, although this is the prevalent conception. Wagner conceived its purpose as the endowment of the dramatic events with metaphysical significance. When in the *Ring* the tubas blare the Valhalla motif, it is not merely to indicate the dwelling place of Wotan. Wagner meant also to connote the sphere of sublimity, the cosmic will, and the primal principle. The leitmotif was invented essentially for this kind of symbolism. There is no place for it in the motion picture, which seeks to depict reality. Here the function of the leitmotif has been reduced to the level of a musical lackey, who announces his master with an important air even though the eminent personage is clearly recognizable to everyone. The effective technique of the past thus becomes a mere duplication, ineffective and uneconomical. At the same time, since it cannot be developed to its full musical significance in the motion picture, its use leads to extreme poverty of composition.

Melody and Euphony

The demand for melody and euphony is not only assumed to be obvious, but also a matter of public taste, as represented in the consumer. We do not deny that producers and consumers generally agree in regard to this demand. But the concepts of melody and euphony are not so self-evident as is generally believed. Both are to a large extent conventionalized historical categories.

The concept of melody first gained ascendancy in the nineteenth century in connection with the new *Kunstlied*, especially Schubert's. Melody was conceived as the opposite of the 'theme' of the Viennese classicism of Haydn,

Mozart, and Beethoven.[2] It denotes a tonal sequence, constituting not so much the point of departure of a composition as a self-contained entity that is easy to listen to, singable, and expressive. This notion led to the sort of melodiousness for which the German language has no specific term, but which the English word 'tune' expresses quite accurately. It consists first of all in the uninterrupted flow of a melody in the upper voice, in such a way that the melodic continuity seems natural, because it is almost possible to guess in advance exactly what will follow. The listener zealously insists on his right to this anticipation, and feels cheated if it is denied him. This fetishism in regard to melody, which at certain moments during the latter part of the Romantic period crowded out all the other elements of music, shackled the concept of melody itself.

Today, the conventional concept of melody is based on criteria of the crudest sort. Easy intelligibility is guaranteed by harmonic and rhythmic symmetry, and by the paraphrasing of accepted harmonic procedures; tunefulness is assured by the preponderance of small diatonic intervals. These postulates have taken on the semblance of logic, owing to the rigid institutionalization of prevailing customs, in which these criteria automatically obtain. In Mozart's and Beethoven's day, when the stylistic ideal of filigree composition held sway, the postulate of the predominance of an anticipatable melody in the upper voice would scarcely have been comprehended. 'Natural' melody is a figment of the imagination, an extremely relative phenomenon illegitimately absolutized, neither an obligatory nor an *a priori* constituent of the material, but one procedure among many, singled out for exclusive use.

The conventional demand for melody and euphony is constantly in conflict with the objective requirements of the motion picture. The prerequisite of

---

2. As a matter of fact, the modern concept of melody made itself felt as early as within Viennese classicism. Nowhere does the historical character of this apparently natural concept become more manifest than in the famous Mozart critique by Hans Georg Naegeli, the Swiss contemporary of the Viennese classicists, which is now made accessible in a reprint edited by Willi Reich. Musical history generally recognizes as one of the greatest merits of Mozart that he introduced the element of cantability into the sonata form, particularly the complex of the second theme. This innovation, largely responsible for the musical changes that led to the crystallization of the later *Lied* melody, was by no means greeted enthusiastically in all quarters. To Naegeli, who was certainly narrow-minded and dogmatic but had rather articulate philosophical ideas about musical style, Mozart's synthesis of instrumental writing and cantability appeared about as shocking as advanced modern composition would to a popular-music addict of today. He blames Mozart, who is now regarded by the musical public as the utmost representative of stylistic purity, for lack of taste and style. The following passage is characteristic: 'His [Mozart's] genius was great, but its defect, the overuse of contrast, was equally great. This was all the more objectionable in his case because he continuously contrasted the non-instrumental with the instrumental, cantability with the free play of tones. This was inartistic, as it is in all arts. As soon as continuous contrast becomes the main effect, the beautiful proportion of parts is necessarily neglected. This stylistic fault can be discovered in many of Mozart's works' (Hans Georg Naegeli, *Von Bach zu Beethoven*, Benno Schwabe & Co., Basel, 1946, pp. 48–49).

melody is that the composer be independent, in the sense that his selection and invention relate to situations that supply specific lyric-poetic inspiration. This is out of the question where the motion picture is concerned. All music in the motion picture is under the sign of utility, rather than lyric expressiveness. Aside from the fact that lyric-poetic inspiration cannot be expected of the composer for the cinema, this kind of inspiration would contradict the embellishing and subordinate function that industrial practice still enforces on the composer.

Moreover, the problem of melody as 'poetic' is made insoluble by the conventionality of the popular notion of melody. Visual action in the motion picture has of course a prosaic irregularity and asymmetry. It claims to be photographed life; and as such every motion picture is a documentary. As a result, there is a gap between what is happening on the screen and the symmetrically articulated conventional melody. A photographed kiss cannot actually be synchronized with an eight-bar phrase. The disparity between symmetry and asymmetry becomes particularly striking when music is used to accompany natural phenomena, such as drifting clouds, sunrise, wind, and rain. These natural phenomena could inspire nineteenth-century poets; however, as photographed, they are essentially irregular and non-rhythmic, thus excluding that element of poetic rhythm with which the motion-picture industry associates them. Verlaine could write a poem about rain in the city, but one cannot hum a tune that accompanies rain reproduced on the screen.

More than anything else the demand for melody at any cost and on every occasion has throttled the development of motion-picture music. The alternative is certainly not to resort to the unmelodic, but to liberate melody from conventional fetters.

Unobtrusiveness

One of the most widespread prejudices in the motion-picture industry is the premise that the spectator should not be conscious of the music. The philosophy behind this belief is a vague notion that music should have a subordinate role in relation to the picture. As a rule, the motion picture represents action with dialogue. Financial considerations and technical interest are concentrated on the actor; anything that might overshadow him is considered disturbing. The musical indications in the scripts are usually sporadic and indefinite. Music thus far has not been treated in accordance with its specific potentialities. It is tolerated as an outsider who is somehow regarded as being indispensable, partly because of a genuine need and partly on account of the fetishistic idea that the existing technical resources must be exploited to the fullest extent.[3]

Despite the often reiterated opinion of the wizards of the movie industry, in which many composers concur, the thesis that music should be unobtrusive is questionable. There are, doubtless, situations in motion pictures in which the dialogue must be emphasized and in which detailed musical foreground configurations would be disturbing. It may also be granted that these situations sometimes require acoustic supplementation. But precisely when this requirement is taken seriously, the insertion of allegedly unobtrusive music becomes dubious. In such instances, an accompaniment of extramusical sound would more nearly approximate the realism of the motion picture. If, instead, music is used, music that is supposed to be real music but is not supposed to be noticed, the effect is that described in a German nursery rhyme:

> *Ich weiss ein schönes Spiel,*
> *Ich mal' mir einen Bart,*
> *Und halt mir einen Fächer vor,*
> *Dass niemand ihn gewahrt.*

> [I know a pretty game:
> I deck me with a beard
> And hide behind a fan
> So I won't look too weird.] (Translated by N. G.)

In practice, the requirement of unobtrusiveness is generally met not by an approximation of nonmusical sounds, but by the use of banal music. Accordingly, the music is supposed to be inconspicuous in the same sense as are selections from *La Bohème* played in a restaurant.

Apart from this, unobtrusive music, assumed to be the typical solution of the problem, is only one and certainly the least important of many possible solutions. The insertion of music should be planned along with the writing of the script, and the question whether the spectator should be aware of the music

---

3. In the realm of motion pictures the term 'technique' has a double meaning that can easily lead to confusion. On the one hand, technique is the equivalent of an industrial process for producing goods: e.g. the discovery that picture and sound can be recorded on the same strip is comparable to the invention of the air brake. The other meaning of 'technique' is aesthetic. It designates the methods by which an artistic intention can be adequately realized. While the technical treatment of music in sound pictures was essentially determined by the industrial factor, there was a need for music from the very beginning, because of certain aesthetic requirements. Thus far no clearcut relation between the factors has been established, neither in theory nor in practice.

is a matter to be decided in each case according to the dramatic requirements of the script. Interruption of the action by a developed musical episode could be an important artistic device. For example, in an anti-Nazi picture, at the point when the action is dispersed into individual psychological details, an exceptionally serious piece of music occupies the whole perception. Its movement helps the listener to remember the essential incidents and focuses his attention on the situation as a whole. It is true that in this case the music is the very opposite of what it is conventionally supposed to be. It no longer expresses the conflicts of individual characters, nor does it persuade the spectator to identify himself with the hero; but rather it leads him back from the sphere of privacy to the major social issue. In pictures of an inferior type of entertainment—musicals and revues from which every trace of dramatic psychology is eliminated—one finds, more often than elsewhere, rudiments of this device of musical interruption, and the independent use of music in songs, dances, and finales.

Visual Justification

The problem relates less to rules than to tendencies, which are not as important as they were a few years ago, yet must still be taken into account. The fear that the use of music at a point when it would be completely impossible in a real situation will appear naive or childish, or impose upon the listener an effort of imagination that might distract him from the main issue, leads to attempts to justify this use in a more or less rationalistic way. Thus situations are often contrived in which it is allegedly natural for the main character to stop and sing, or music accompanying a love scene is made plausible by having the hero turn on a radio or a phonograph.

The following is a typical instance. The hero is waiting for his beloved. Not a word is spoken. The director feels the need of filling in the silence. He knows the danger of nonaction, of absence of suspense, and therefore prescribes music. At the same time, however, he lays so much stress in the objective portrayal of psychological continuity that an unmotivated irruption of music strikes him as risky. Thus he resorts to the most artless trick in order to avoid artlessness, and makes the hero turn to the radio. The threadbareness of this artifice is illustrated by those scenes in which the hero accompanies himself 'realistically' on the piano for about eight bars, whereupon he is relieved by a large orchestra and chorus, albeit with no change of scene. In so far as this device, which obtained in the early days of sound pictures, is still applied, it hinders the use of music as a genuine element of contrast. Music becomes a plot accessory, a sort of acoustical stage property.

Illustration

There is a favorite Hollywood gibe: 'Birdie sings, music sings.' Music must follow visual incidents and illustrate them either by directly imitating them or by using clichés that are associated with the mood and content of the picture. The preferred material for imitation is 'nature,' in the most superficial sense of the word, i.e. as the antithesis of the urban—that realm where people are supposed to be able to breathe freely, stimulated by the presence of plants and animals. This is a vulgar and stereotyped version of the concept of nature that prevailed in nineteenth-century poetry. Music is concocted to go with meretricious lyrics. Particularly landscape shots without action seem to call for musical accompaniment, which then conforms to the stale programmatic patterns. Mountain peaks invariably invoke string tremolos punctuated by a signal-like horn motif. The ranch to which the virile hero has eloped with the sophisticated heroine is accompanied by forest murmurs and a flute melody. A slow waltz goes along with a moonlit scene in which a boat drifts down a river lined with weeping willows.

What is in question here is not the principle of musical illustration. Certainly musical illustration is only one among many dramaturgic resources, but it is so overworked that it deserves a rest, or at least it should be used with the greatest discrimination. This is what is generally lacking in prevailing practice. Music cut to fit the stereotype 'nature' is reduced to the character of a cheap mood-producing gadget, and the associative patterns are so familiar that there is really no illustration of anything, but only the elicitation of the automatic response: 'Aha, nature!'

Illustrative use of music today results in unfortunate duplication. It is uneconomical, except where quite specific effects are intended, or minute interpretation of the action of the picture. The old operas left a certain amount of elbow room in their scenic arrangements for what is vague and indefinite; this could be filled out with tone painting. The music of the Wagnerian era was actually a means of elucidation. But in the cinema, both picture and dialogue are hyperexplicit. Conventional music can add nothing to the explicitness, but instead may detract from it, since even in the worst pictures standardized musical effects fail to keep up with the concrete elaboration of the screen action. But if the elucidating function is given up as superfluous, music should never attempt to accompany precise occurrences in an imprecise manner. It should stick to its task—even if it is only as questionable a one as that of creating a mood—renouncing that of repeating the obvious. Musical illustration should either be hyperexplicit itself—over-illuminating, so to speak, and thereby interpretive—or should be omitted. There is no excuse for flute melodies that force a bird call into a pattern of full ninth chords.

Geography and History

When the scene is laid in a Dutch town, with its canals, windmills, and wooden shoes, the composer is supposed to send over to the studio library for a Dutch folk song in order to use its theme as a working basis. Since it is not easy to recognize a Dutch folk song for what it is, especially when it has been subjected to the whims of an arranger, this procedure seems a dubious one. Here music is used in much the same way as costumes or sets, but without as strong a characterizing effect. A composer can attain something more convincing by writing a tune of his own on the basis of a village dance for little Dutch girls than he can by clinging to the original. Indeed, the current folk music of all countries—apart from that which is basically outside occidental music—tends toward a certain sameness, in contrast to the differentiated art languages. This is because it is grounded on a limited number of elementary rhythmic formulas associated with festivities, communal dances, and the like. It is as difficult to distinguish between the temperamental characters of Polish and Spanish dances, particularly in the conventionalized form they assumed in the nineteenth century, as it is to discern the difference between hill-billy songs and Upper Bavarian *Schnaderhüpferln*. Moreover, ordinary cinematic music has an irresistible urge to follow the pattern of 'just folk music.' Specific national characteristics can be captured musically only if the musical counterpart of beflagging the scene with national emblems like an exhibition is not resorted to. Related to this is the practice of investing costume pictures with music of the corresponding historical period. This recalls concerts in which hoop-skirted elderly ladies play tedious pre-Bach harpsichord pieces by candlelight in baroque palaces. The absurdity of such 'applied art' arrangements is glaring in contrast with the technique of the film, which is of necessity modern. If costume pictures must be, they might be better served by the free use of advanced musical resources.

Stock Music

One of the worst practices is the incessant use of a limited number of worn-out musical pieces that are associated with the given screen situations by reason of their actual or traditional titles. Thus, the scene of a moonlight night is accompanied by the first movement of the *Moonlight Sonata*, orchestrated in a manner that completely contradicts its meaning, because the piano melody—suggested by Beethoven with the utmost discretion—is made obtrusive and is richly underscored by the strings. For thunderstorms, the overture to *William Tell* is used; for weddings, the march from *Lohengrin* or Mendelssohn's wedding march. These practices—incidentally, they are on the wane and are retained only in cheap pictures—correspond to the popularity of trademarked pieces in classical music, such as Beethoven's E-flat Concerto, which has attained an almost fatal popularity under the apocryphal title *The Emperor*, or Schubert's *Unfinished Symphony*. The present vogue of the latter is to some extent connected with the idea that the composer died before it was finished, whereas he simply laid it aside years before his death. The use of trademarks is a nuisance, though it must be acknowledged that childlike faith in the eternal symbolic force of certain classical wedding or funeral marches occasionally has a redeeming aspect, when these are compared with original scores manufactured to order.

Clichés

All these questions are related to a more general state of affairs. Mass production of motion pictures has led to the elaboration of typical situations, ever-recurring emotional crises, and standardized methods of arousing suspense. They correspond to cliché effects in music. But music is often brought into play at the very point where particularly characteristic effects are sought for the sake of 'atmosphere' or suspense. The powerful effect intended does not come off, because the listener has been made familiar with the stimulus by innumerable analogous passages. Psychologically, the whole phenomenon is ambiguous. If the screen shows a peaceful country house while the music produces familiar sinister sounds, the spectator knows at once that something terrible is about to happen, and thus the musical accompaniment both intensifies the suspense and nullifies it by betraying the sequel.

As in many other aspects of contemporary motion pictures, it is not standardization as such that is objectionable here. Pictures that frankly follow an established pattern, such as 'westerns' or gangster and horror pictures, often are in a certain way superior to pretentious grade-A films. What is objectionable is the standardized character of pictures that claim to be unique; or, conversely, the individual disguise of the standardized pattern. This is exactly what happens in music. Thus, for example, throbbing and torrential string arpeggios—which the guides to Wagner once called the 'agitated motif'—are resorted to without rhyme or reason, and nothing can be more laughable to anyone who recognizes them for what they are.

Such musical conventions are all the more dubious because their material is usually taken from the most recently bygone phase of autonomous music, which still passes as 'modern' in motion pictures. Forty years ago, when musical impressionism and exoticism were at their height, the wholetone scale was regarded as a particularly stimulating, unfamiliar, and 'colorful' musical device. Today the whole-tone scale is stuffed into the introduction of every popular hit, yet in motion pictures it continues to be used as if it had just seen the light of day. Thus the means employed and the effect achieved are completely disproportionate. Such a disproportion can have a certain charm when, as in animated cartoons, it serves to stress the absurdity of something impossible, for instance, Pluto galloping over the ice to the ride of the Walkyries. But the whole-tone scale so overworked in the amusement industry can no longer cause anyone really to shudder.

The use of clichés also affects instrumentation. The tremolo on the bridge of the violin, which thirty years ago was intended even in serious music to produce a feeling of uncanny suspense and to express an unreal atmosphere, today has become common currency. Generally, all artistic means that were originally conceived for their stimulating effect rather than for their structural significance grow threadbare and obsolete with extraordinary rapidity. Here, as in many other instances, the motion-picture industry is carrying out a sentence long since pronounced in serious music, and one is justified in ascribing a progressive function to the sound film in so far as it thus has discredited the trashy devices intended merely for effect. These have long since become unbearable both to artists and to the audience, so much so that sooner or later no one will be able to enjoy clichés. When this happens there will be both need and room for other elements of music. The development of *avant-garde* music in the course of the last thirty years has opened up an inexhaustible reservoir of new resources and possibilities that is still practically untouched. There is no objective reason why motion-picture music should not draw upon it.

Standardized Interpretation

The standardization of motion-picture music is particularly apparent in the prevailing style of performance. First of all, there is the element of dynamics, which was at one time limited by the imperfection of the recording and reproduction machinery. Today, this machinery is far better differentiated and affords far greater dynamic possibilities, both as regards the extremes and the transitions; nevertheless, standardization of dynamics still persists. The different degrees of strength are levelled and blurred to a general mezzoforte—incidentally, this practice is quite analogous to the habits of the mixer in radio broadcasting. The main purpose here is the production of a comfortable and polished euphony, which neither startles by its power (fortissimo) nor requires attentive listening because of its weakness (pianissimo). In consequence of this levelling, dynamics as a means of elucidating musical contexts is lost. The lack of a threefold fortissimo and pianissimo reduces the crescendo and decrescendo to too small a range.

In the methods of performance, too, standardization has as its counterpart pseudo-individualization.[4] While everything is more or less adjusted to the mezzoforte ideal, an effort is made, through exaggerated interpretation, to make each musical motif produce the utmost expression, emotion, and suspense. The violins must sob or scintillate, the brasses must crash insolently or bombastically, no moderate expression is tolerated, and the whole method of performance is based on exaggeration. It is characterized by a mania for extremes, such as were reserved in the days of the silent pictures for that type of violinist who led the little moviehouse orchestra. The perpetually used espressivo has become completely worn out. Even effective dramatic incidents are made trite by oversweet accompaniment or offensive overexposition. A 'middle-ground,' objective musical type of interpretation that resorts to the espressivo only where it is really justified could by its economy greatly enhance the effectiveness of motion-picture music.

---

4. 'By pseudo-individualization we mean endowing cultural mass production with the halo of free choice or open market on the basis of standardization itself' (T. W. Adorno, 'On Popular Music,' in *Studies in Philosophy and Social Science*, vol. IX, 1941, p. 25).

27

Frederick W. Sternfeld on Hugo Friedhofer's *Best Years of Our Lives* (1947)

Born and educated in Vienna, the versatile British musicologist F. W. Sternfeld (1914–94) was one of the first writers with a thorough schooling in the classics to write detailed analytical and critical assessments of film music. He had studied at Cambridge and Yale Universities, earning a doctorate at the latter following his emigration to the United States shortly before the outbreak of the Second World War; during the war he taught at a succession of distinguished American universities, but eventually he returned to the United Kingdom to take up a lectureship at Oxford University in 1956. In 1947 and 1951 Sternfeld published two groundbreaking case studies of Hollywood film scores in the *Musical Quarterly* (then published by G. Schirmer, Inc., in New York), which were the first serious and substantial essays on the medium to appear in the pages of a respected academic journal.

Given the author's classical pedigree, the choice of an acclaimed score by Aaron Copland for the second of these articles ("Copland as a Film Composer," *Musical Quarterly*, 37 [1951]: 161–75) was perhaps inevitable; but Sternfeld's first essay was less predictable in focusing on a seminal work by the formerly neglected Hollywood composer Hugo Friedhofer (1902–81). Friedhofer's score to *The Best Years of Our Lives* (1946) had just won him an Academy Award in an overdue vindication of a musician whose skills had previously been diverted into the orchestration of music composed by the likes of Max Steiner and Erich Wolfgang Korngold rather than to original compositions of his own. All but one of Korngold's film scores had been principally orchestrated by Friedhofer, for example,

Source: "Music and the Feature Films," *Musical Quarterly*, 33 (1947): 517–32.

whose handling of the orchestra in many ways came to define a distinctively "Hollywood" sound—including a lush use of ascending harp glissandi that was not to all contemporaneous critics' tastes. Directed by William Wyler, *The Best Years of Our Lives* applied the marked lack of sentimentality already evident in the director's wartime documentaries to a fine drama about the lives of three homecoming U.S. war veterans, and inspired Friedhofer to create a leaner and more distinctively American idiom, strongly indebted to the example of Copland, which (as Friedhofer himself put it) helped him to "weed out the run-of-the-mine schmaltz and aim to do more straightforward and simple, even folklike scoring."

In addition to offering many illuminating insights into the structure of Friedhofer's score, Sternfeld's analysis is particularly stimulating in its identification of the manner in which a film score's characteristically fragmentary development of musical ideas can create the illusion of "an underlying unity," a phenomenon Theodor Adorno and Hanns Eisler failed to grasp when too rigidly comparing film music to opera and other genres in which the music plays continuously and prominently.

There is no denying that the opportunities of hearing genuinely modern music are few. An *avant-garde* manages to keep abreast of contemporary works through the efforts of a few forward-looking schools and certain organizations devoted to contemporary music, but the ordinary citizen takes his musical fare from the standard offerings of concerts, broadcasts, and phonograph recordings. It would be extremely unrealistic to shut our eyes to the conservative hue of this repertory, despite some refreshing exceptions. In fact, so little have the vociferous protests of our distinguished critics and educators changed the general situation that it would offer scarcely any encouragement were it not for relief from quarters little suspected of straying from the hackneyed. To understand this curious phenomenon we must consider the factors that have preserved the anachronistic, 19th-century flavor of our musical life and also what circumstances, if any, might alleviate the rigid control exercised by these factors.

That the taste of our public, largely composed of people who do not make music themselves, is fashioned by hymn tunes and Stephen Foster songs, dance bands and juke boxes, long before the individual becomes a conscious listener, is only too well known. Thus conditioned by the harmonic and melodic idiom of his grandparents the concert-goer, by his acceptance and approval, influences management, to whom the commercial attractiveness of a safe bet, musical performances in an established and successful style, speaks

more persuasively than all the protests or pronunciamentos on behalf of contemporary works. Curiously, and fortunately, the style and idiom of movie
music are not so circumscribed, for the general public does not take *conscious*
notice of the musical commentary attending a picture, however profound its
effect may be. Hindemith's "secundal" counterpoint, presented in Carnegie
Hall as absolute music, receives a cold welcome from a musically unsophisti-
cated audience, but Hindemithian harmonies forming the counterpart of a
duel on the screen, as in *The Bandit of Sherwood Forest* [1946], are absorbed with
keen emotional enjoyment. *Unconsciously*, the public has accepted the dissonances and rhythmic complexities of a modern idiom in expressive and illustrative sequences. In fact, the average listener encounters this idiom so much
more frequently in the cinema than in concert music that, paradoxically, he is
apt to mistake the chicken for the egg. After a performance of a recent symphonic work of one of our distinguished contemporary composers, a layman
was induced to remark that it sounded like the movies.

Ideally, then, a cinematic score may serve a two-fold purpose: to fulfill its
primary function as an important and integral part of a dramatic production, and
to act as a wedge of modernity in our musty concert life. We say ideally for, as in
all walks of life, there is here also too much stereotype and reiteration of formulas
once successful. Every sensitive musician is agonized by the merciless and mo-
notonous repetition of a few clichés and the gruesome habit of "plugging" a tune
in place of organized musical development. One may understand (though not
condone) the excessive redundancy because of the necessity to produce shows the
year round—after all, Italian opera had its clichés and pasticcios. But in the 18th
century the idiom, at least, was contemporaneous. Today, we have fostered, nour-
ished, and brought to near-perfection a new art-form onto which we have grafted
a musical complement that had already run its course by the end of the last century and now lives on in the superannuated romantic tear-jerker, the crash-bang
climax, the standardized "hurry" and "tension" moods. It is the more gratifying,
then, that of the hundreds of shows produced each year on the running band, at
least a handful stand out by their originality and real musical merit.

Those composers who write as they please for this genre, unhampered by
the dissenting musical tastes of producers, directors, and others, seem to fall
into two classes: the famous "outsider," already accepted in the concert hall and
engaged as guest-composer; and the regular Hollywood musician who has
proved his mettle. The latter deserves particular notice because he influences
and molds musical taste more continuously and, therefore, more effectively.
Discriminating observers of the Hollywood musical scene have watched the
work of Hugo Friedhofer with growing interest. He learned his craft the humble
way, accepting as a matter of hard fact the subordinate role of the composer on

the movie lot. With the score for [*The Adventures of*] *Marco Polo* [1938] Fried-hofer gained some general recognition, and in *The Bandit of Sherwood Forest* his score admittedly raised this technicolor Thirteenth Century Western to a degree of distinction it would never have attained otherwise. Having thus proved his adeptness and flexibility, he was given full freedom of expression to write his *chef-d'oeuvre* to date, *The Best Years of Our Lives*.

This film, winner of nine Academy awards, among them one for the best score of the year, is an ambitious undertaking.[1] The unfolding of Robert Sher-wood's script under William Wyler's direction takes almost three hours; a timely subject, discerning photography, and some excellent acting all combine to create absorbing entertainment. It does not always hold that a dramatically superior ve-hicle is accompanied by a worthwhile score, but good music is hardly ever elicited by an otherwise undistinguished film. The breath-taking hunt of *The Informer*, the philosophical smiles and tears of *Our Town*, have inspired gripping music because they are good drama; the truism of the theater that a poor libretto will seldom bring forth a great opera applies *mutatis mutandis* to the screen as well.

The dramatic crux of *The Best Years* is the return of three veterans to ci-vilian life. Separated from each other by branch of service, social background, age, and marital status, they have a common problem in the difficulties of read-justment that they and those dear to them have to surmount. It is fitting, there-fore, that long before it highlights any of the individual protagonists, the music should characterize all three, as a collective hero, so to speak (Ex. 1).

Ex. 1

1. *The Best Years of Our Lives*, Academy Award; Producer, Samuel Goldwyn; Composer, Hugo Friedhofer; Musical Director, Emil Newman.

The very first four notes, the most frequently heard version of the *Best Years* theme, exhibit the simplicity essential to a phrase whose main function is to provide the material for musical and dramatic development. The two notes, G–B-flat, echoed an octave higher in reverse, B-flat–G, produce a melodic profile that is so simple, though at the same time distinctive, that the listener recognizes it even when it is modified. In this initial section the motif occurs, apart from fragmentary allusions, nine times. The characteristic contour, a rise in the lower range answered by a fall in the higher, is unmistakable even though the component intervals are not always the same.

This first subdivision of the musical score, accompanying title, cast, and credits, functions as a prelude and lasts one minute. The theme lends itself equally well to diatonic harmonization by seventh chords or to a linear treatment by having only a few parts, proceeding in similar motion. Either way of statement, reminiscent of both Hindemith and Copland, stays refreshingly clear of the overly lush chromaticism so abundant in lesser scores which proceed from one emotional climax to the next. By his economy Friedhofer insures that the chromaticism used in a few tense scenes is really effective.

A word should be said, perhaps, about the term "*Best Years* theme," since such labelling points to a practice that is widely used in the average film score and is, at the same time, definitely a threat to the spontaneity and variety of both movie and music. Stage commissions, whether for screen, ballet, or theater, provide a dramatic and emotional framework that, by its contemporary quality, has given rise to some of the most distinguished scores of our day. Here are patterns, fluid and flexible, which suggest forms that the composer of the 20th century may evolve for the music of today. For to the modern tone-poet the designs of the 18th and 19th centuries are perfect expressions for those times but, grafted on to the music of the present, they tend to be mere academic exercises devoid of organic meaning. It is the freshness of our best ballet scenarios that has made them such important points of departure for stirring music and, intrinsically, the cinematic script should offer the same advantages. Unfortunately, though, the Hollywood score is so frequently organized by the method of the Wagnerian *Leitmotiv* that a good deal of the spontaneity and modernity of the genre as a whole suffers.

There are obvious conveniences to a system that employs the same succession of notes whenever the same character or situation appears. For copyright reasons new tunes must be tagged, and the trick of using the X theme every time X appears on the screen is facile and produces quick results. The proof of the pudding lies, of course, in the eating. If the technique is applied sparingly and thoughtfully, it will seem appropriate even to the critical observer, besides providing the necessary coherence for the entire fabric. But if used slavishly and mechanically, it will convey a feeling of monotony to the uncritical, while the sensitive listener will be both bored and irritated. On the whole, *The Best Years of Our Lives* uses its *Leitmotive* with discrimination and without damaging the form or spirit of the script by mechanizing it. In fact, it is only where the script itself lags, as in the scenes involving the sailor and his fiancée, that the music, too, loses interest by excessive repetition.

The total running time of *The Best Years* is 170 minutes. Of these about 97 minutes are straight dialogue and about 58 minutes have a full-fledged musical accompaniment, expressive or illustrative. There are about 15 minutes of "stage music," such as the background music in night-club scenes and the piano-playing of Homer and his uncle, where it is part of the action rather than a commentary on or revelation of the plot. Since this portion belongs function-ally to the straight dialogue section, the three hours of the picture's running time divide roughly into two hours of action without and one hour with music. One of the most effective techniques available to a composer of screen music is the judicious non-use of music in places where its absence is a more persuasive agent in enhancing the drama. Novices not familiar with the medium tend to write too much music—that is, to transform a drama with music into a melo-drama. But the seasoned craftsman will use music sparingly and thus make an effective contribution to the over-all result.

The decision to follow the prelude, from which Ex. 1 is taken, with two intro-ductory scenes minus music (minutes 2–11) was a wise one. These first shots of Fred, the handsome air-force captain, of Homer, the sailor who now has hooks instead of hands, of Al, the army sergeant, a successful banker in private life, acquaint us with the protagonists and introduce in the dialogue important ele-ments of the dramatic exposition. But, informative as this initial portion of the dialogue may be, its emotional climate does not require the atmospheric qual-ities of a musical score. As the conversation comes to a temporary stopping-place, we are made increasingly sound-conscious by the hum of the plane engine on the sound track. Now music (minutes 11–17) expresses the intensity of the fears and hopes of these men better than words could do. Without fanfare, it enters quietly and tersely, in a contemporary idiom in which, quite apart from dramatic propriety, the composer shows he has something new and refreshing to offer. The lush strains of 19th-century Romanticism, so often imposed on a helpless audience—however far removed the actual situation from the emotion-alism and exhibitionism of that noble period—are happily absent. A quiet, almost suppressed air surrounds the sparse octave imitation of 1a. When the camera shows a close-up of Homer a statement of 1b is extended into an antici-pation of the theme later associated with Homer's home (Ex. 3). As the camera shoots through the nose of the plane, the music shifts from subdued intensity to the excitement of homecoming, once again strains common to all three heroes. In turn we have the relaxed happy mood (Ex. 2a), succeeded by swifter motion to portray the bustle of the home city (Ex. 2b), and a dignified variation of 2a to express pride. This thematic material is developed again as we view the city a second time from the taxi in which the returning men ride to their families.

Throughout there is little dialogue; photographer and composer convey the sentiments of the heroes. Very telling, for instance, is the use of the bracketed figure from 2b, first in original note-values when the new airport looms through the nose of the plane, then in augmentation when the veterans realize they are looking at a long line of planes good only for scrap. There are also the brief but pathetic statements of 1b and 1d when the sailor waves good-bye to the other two, thus revealing hooks instead of hands to his waiting family and fiancée. Equally brief is the highly suggestive music depicting the excitement of Homer's little sister, again related to the bracketed figure from 2b. However, the characterization of Homer's relatives and neighbors and of his fiancée, by way of Exx. 3 and 4 is anything but succinct nor is it free from sentimentality. One's reaction is that these people are the salt of the earth, all right, but in overly long doses they stall the show dramatically and musically.

The music stops when Homer enters the house and does not return until Al, the army sergeant, ascends the elevator to his apartment (minutes 19–22½ and 27½–30½). His homecoming is from the dramatic standpoint so unlike that of the others that it calls for an entirely different musical treatment. He is neither a physical casualty like the sailor nor a social one like the airforce captain. All the complexities reside in the man's mind; he is nervous with pent-up emotion and self-conscious over the arrival of this moment. The composer has to portray hidden tenderness and potential pitfalls rather than overt crises. This effect is achieved not by presenting the material in self-contained units but by intertwining incomplete statements of motifs and phrases in such a manner that the listener senses an underlying unity and recognizes at the same time that these fragmentary references, suited to the present emotional complexity, are quotations from structural units to appear in complete form later in the film. In itself, the song *Among My*

Ex. 2 A

Ex. 2 B

Ex. 3   Ex. 4

Souvenirs (Ex. 5) has no great distinction, and there is no trick to digging up and quoting a song popular twenty years before. But to combine it with the main themes of the entire drama (1 and 2) in so effortless a manner that it becomes part and parcel of this tragicomedy of postwar adjustment is, indeed, another story. The tune is never given out in the regular four- and eight-bar periods that are typical of the lyric but deadly to thematic development. Rather, it is extended, spun out with some unexpected, Schubertian major-minor touches and, after a fleeting appearance of 1a, almost becomes an ostinato, at which stage it is left in mid-air, as it were (Ex. 6a). But later a development of 1a glides organically back to a snatch of the tune, the very snatch with which the extension started, only to return to 1a after two measures. With the use of the very first notes of 2b, while the wife recovers from her joyful shock, another complex achieves proper dramatic suspense through these fragmentary allusions. Several times the motif is stated incompletely, then sequenced and followed by a series of descending seventh chords. When, at the end of the scene, these first notes reappear, we perceive in tones the "unfinished business" of Millie's happiness and Al's bewilderment.

The ensuing scenes (minutes 22½–50½) can be passed over without comment except to mention the excellent effect that is achieved in the third homecoming—that of Fred, the airforce captain, to the shoddy house of his parents—without music track. His depressing background, in contrast to that of the other two men, is firmly established in a few bare shots. There is also the barroom scene, refreshingly unglamorous in its musical make-up, where a mere piano provides dance music (*Among My Souvenirs*). No fancifully orchestrated playing, here, with camera and soundtrack focused on saxophonist and drummer,

Ex. 5

There's no-thing left for me— of days that used to be— I live in me-mo-ry a-mong my sou-ven-irs

By permission of the copyright owners,
Crawford Music Corporation.

Ex. 6A

Ex 1a

Ex. 6B

Ex 1a   Ex 1a   Ex 1a

but a faithful adherence to dramatic exigence. Actually, the understatement accorded the tune both serves the plot and produces a psychological spotlight on the song with which the audience, from the earlier scene, is already familiar.

But these are slight demands compared with the problems confronting the composer in Fred's nightmare scene. Here the music must reveal the bombardier's real emotional handicap, which is neither his sordid background nor his superficial wife, but the persistence of the fears and shock he experienced in his combat missions. The scene is short (minutes 50½–53½) but intense, and has a companion piece in the bomber scene towards the end of the film (minutes 155–158¼). Both have the same musical climax, a series of descending chords repeated four times. The straightforward repetition of the treble descent, not modified by sequence or variation, has a frightening impact, accentuated, of course, by the chromatically ascending middle parts, because that chromaticism has not been dulled by excessive and inappropriate use. The tonal din becomes a symbol of the mental dread from which its victim has each time to be awakened and rescued by external forces [Ex. 7].

The stages preparatory to this climax, the quadruple statement in quarter-notes, vary. In the earlier scene where Fred is asleep, only four measures elapse before the ominous descent is anticipated in half-notes. These four introductory measures consist of an ascending second-motif followed by the chromatically ascending parallel fourths that then become the middle part of the nightmare motif in the final statement. The half-note version of this descent now appears in full and differs from the quarter-note climax, apart from tempo, by the chromatic ornamentation of the bass line [Ex. 8].

This slower, and therefore less intense, version is now worked upon for half a minute, to be interrupted only when the camera takes us to the adjacent room where the sleeping Peggy is awakened by the stir. As she enters the room

Ex. 7

Ex. 8

and the camera returns to the dreaming, perspiring, and shouting man, the transformation of Ex. 8 into the climax of Ex. 7 takes place.

In the later scene, where the disillusioned soldier finds a dismantled bomber in which to day-dream, the introductory section is greatly extended and the climax—the same quadruple statement—seems terser, since it is not preceded by a slower rendering of the octave descent with its disjointed chromatic harmonization. The dramatic and musical continuity leading up to the nightmare in the empty plane is largely the work of photographer and composer, with a degree of coordination and integration rarely found.

The making of a film is usually completed before the composer is called in. He is obliged to deliver a score to fit the otherwise finished product in four to six weeks. Scenes where the music is recorded first and the actors consciously adjust their timing to that of the score are extremely rare. Whether or not the present sequence is such an exception, it demonstrates Friedhofer's skill and flexibility to the utmost.

When the bomber scene begins Captain Fred Derry is ostensibly not on the screen. As his father reads the Distinguished Flying Cross award the music enters with the ascending second-motif from the earlier scene and continues with a treatment of 1b almost identical with that in the prelude [Ex. 9]. It is given out softly until it reaches, as in the prelude, the heroic chords of 1d. Now the entire passage is played again, continuing as a counterpoint to the actual words of the award. But as citation and dialogue come to an end the sound-mixer increases the volume of the music which now expresses in full-fledged sovereignty, better than words, "the heroism, devotion to duty, professional skill, and coolness under fire displayed by Captain Derry". As the camera shifts to the line of junked planes the ascending second-motif looms more important, the interval finally (after 8 repetitions) being extended to a fourth [Ex. 10].

Now we see the interior of the dismantled bomber, as the ex-captain enters and the music gives us, for the third time in this scene, the half melancholy, half

Ex. 9

Ex. 10

martial treatment of 1b with its heroic conclusion (1d). The obsession of reliving the deadly missions takes hold of the bombardier as we approach the climax, and while trick angles of the camera suggest an imaginary take-off, the progressive diminution of the ascending second-motif symbolizes the warming up of the engine and, more than that, the accelerated heartbeat of a frightened individual. Here, the trumpet statement of 1b against the final diminution of the ascending second reveals, if not the psychological origin of this theme, at least its potential substitute, the signal for taps [Ex. 11]. The tension increases as an inverted pedal on E-flat, sustained for ten measures, accompanies a close-up of the perspiring hero and leads to the quarter-note descent of Ex. 7, in rhythm and pitch (E-flat) a replica of the climax in the earlier scene. The quadruple statement of this simple yet ominous five-note figure that has not been heard for almost two hours has a dreadful suddenness; yet it is nevertheless psychologically prepared.

Taking an over-all view of these two critical scenes that could so easily have been degraded to the superficial sentimentality of the pulp magazines, one admires Friedhofer's economy of means as well as his careful timing of build-up, climax, and tapering off. Moreover, he has taken a perplexing problem of our own time and expressed it in contemporary musical terms. There is nothing self-conscious or recherché about this mode of expression; it is clean, neat, and fits its purpose with a functional smoothness that seems as characteristic of the forties as the various "schools" were of the twenties.

In addition, we perceive a musical pattern of intrinsic merit. For cinematic scores share with works of the concert hall the same elements of balance and contrast that in their organization and integration constitute form. Although musical designs for the screen differ in tempo, dimension, and texture, as well as in other details, they have in common with sonata form one fundamental characteristic: the statement of most of the important matter in an initial section and the following of this exposition with a development. The introduction of novel and spectacular material, long after the main components of the

Ex. 11

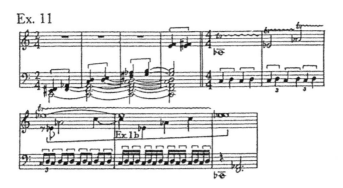

The Best Years of Our Lives (dir. William Wyler, 1946): Fred Derry (Dana Andrews) relives his wartime memories as he climbs aboard a B17 Flying Fortress lying derelict in the USAAF boneyard, a climactic scene that brings Hugo Friedhofer's Oscar-winning music to the fore.

structure have been established, poses a particular problem in either genre. In a film, a new aspect of the plot, expressed by new musical subject matter, like the episode of sonata form, must make its effect by contrast and still be integrated into the work as whole. Here, the inherent laws of an art that lives in time dictate the procedure, for such episodes must be *recreated in time*, in order to become an organic part of the total fabric. Yet, such recapture must not destroy the impress of freshness and novelty on ear and mind. The restatement can succeed only by a rare sense of timing and by the utmost economy. The two enactments of the captain's obsession in plot and music produces in us a delight in *wrought form* akin to that provoked in the opening movement of [Beethoven's] *Eroica* by the reappearance of the episode in the coda or by the unexpected return of the brass fanfare in the slow movement of the [same composer's] Ninth. Here the film gives us truly dramatic music, not the usual cliché of dissonances that so often defeats itself by excessive use.

Since tragedies must have their satyr plays, and nightmares cannot go on forever, we turn next to the musical counterpart of the awakenings of captain and sergeant on the morning after their return (minutes 53½–55½ and 60–62½

Ex. 12

Ex. 13

respectively). The comedy in both scenes is handled with a light touch and in Fred's case the musical fabric is woven of two themes, the homey Ex.2a and a rather saucy, Gershwinesque strain which was first stated in the course of the revelry of the preceding evening.

The contrast of the two themes is amusing in itself and the handling of the material is also not devoid of the comical. As the captain awakes, gradually and painfully, the oboe anticipates Ex.12, never able to complete it, so to speak. In amazement, he watches Peggy enter and leave the room while a series of chords, the treble of which descends in fourths, is sequenced and cleverly gets nowhere; it is followed by Ex.2a which is played slowly, extended, and finally runs out of breath (or at least motion) as the unbelieving captain blows at the dainty ruffles of the canopy. As he gradually gets out of bed Ex.12 is played four times, by the oboe, the clarinet, the trombone, and again the clarinet. At the fourth playing the bracketed interval from Ex. 12 is extended upward from a third to a fifth and ridiculously reflects his groping about the room as it is echoed in the major and twice again echoed in the minor, the last two times in augmentation. The humorous climax is reached as Fred finds the shower; celesta and flute play Ex.2a as a counterpoint to the strings which give forth, unmistakably tongue in cheek, *Home, Sweet Home* [Ex. 13].

The companion skit, the awakening of the sergeant, is largely a portrayal of Al's hangover and his determined eagerness to shed military life. In this scene the thematic material itself is relatively unimportant, but there is the half elegiac, half whimsical mood achieved by thematic variation, a clever travesty of military scoring, and the chromatic frills that conceal an inherently diatonic harmony. As the sergeant gropes for his clothes a wailing figure of two sixteenth-notes creates atmosphere by procedure rather than by substance. When he picks up his army shoes a snare-drum roll ironically points up the incident and the ensuing march makes emphatically yet ridiculously clear their erstwhile institutional significance. These exaggeratedly martial strains, remindful of Prokofiev's March from *The Love of the Three Oranges,* now serve as a counterpoint to *Among My Souvenirs.* The song is played by a muted, distant trumpet, modified by the wailing figure from the preceding measures. Difficult to recognize at a first hearing, it is even so, highly suggestive. As the march peters out it is punctuated by the sound track thud of the shoes, which our sergeant throws out of the window, and the sequence concludes with a harp glissando, synchronized with the falling Venetian blind. This is not a symphonic interlude, which would be quite out of place, but a fleeting sketch that is convincing because its fragmentary character leaves so much to the imagination. Just as camera and sound track rely on only a few elements, so the composer, weaving a brittle and transparent fabric, proceeds swiftly and sparingly. In the making of films, the semantic significance of the terms "movie" and "cinema" is too often overlooked, and long-drawn-out scenes defeat the essence of this novel and fascinating medium both dramatically and musically. *The Best Years,* with but few exceptions, is refreshingly free from this fault.

Both script and score lag whenever Homer, the sailor who has lost his hands, and Wilma, his fiancée, appear. The genuine and deep-felt sympathy that the young couple's difficulties elicit is attacked mercilessly in three scenes of about ten minutes each (minutes 83ff, 138ff, 159ff). Of these, the wedding ceremony has no music track and may, therefore, be dismissed here, but the sequence in which Homer and Wilma decide to marry seems an almost endless series of repetitions of Exx. 1, 3, and 4. One wonders whether the inherently static script failed to inspire the composer. Because in the earlier scene, where the sailor crashes the window, the score certainly takes advantage of the faster tempo of the action as well as of the refreshing contrast offered by the children. The bluntness of these youngsters, mimicking the operation of Homer's hooks and staring with unrestrained curiosity at the couple through the window, is characterized by a traditional song [Ex. 14].

This straightforward and unsentimental tune acts as a counterpoise to the many melancholy statements of 3 and 4, just as dramatically the small fry rescue the scene from immobility. That this children's ditty should become important when the sailor perceives them unexpectedly at the window and in exasperation

Ex. 14

smashes the pane, is an obvious device. However, the slow tapering off of the climax shows an ingenious process of thematic transformation. As piccolo and celesta echo the first phrase of the song in G major, C-sharp minor, and C major successively, the change from the initial minor third to a major one reveals the similarity if not the underlying identity of Exx. 3 and 14, particularly as the succeeding variation of 3 employs the minor third from the children's tune as its first interval. It takes the composer only two more measures to demonstrate that 4, also, by the contour of its first four notes, belongs to this thematic family [Ex. 15]. At the end of the scene, with a close-up of the unhappy, puzzled sailor, the heroic chords of 1d, so prominent in the prelude and in the bomber scene, also enter this web of musical and dramatic relationships [Ex. 16]. To have unravelled the mutual affinities of these ostensibly diverse strains *a posteriori* displays a keen sense of the dramatic. The logical way of procedure would have been the reverse, but with his psychological approach the composer succeeds in injecting variety where it is badly needed and at the same time reveals the underlying unity of the whole complex before its component parts and their interplay are lost sight of.

There are many other aspects of the film that show a real understanding of the limitations and potentialities of dramatic music. There is, for instance, the relationship between the airforce captain and his hard-boiled wife. The complete absence of music at their first meeting is as effective as the "stage music" to which the score is confined in the two following encounters, both of which are introduced by a frivolous dance tune coming from the radio. Later the same song functions as hardly audible background for a nightclub scene that involves our cynical protagonist again. The appearances of the tune are too far apart and too infrequent (minutes 79, 90, and 119) to be noticed at a first hearing; it is a clever manipulation of the *Leitmotiv* technique, for the theme is never predictable because its significance is never *consciously* felt—an illustration of the fact that the truisms of showmanship also apply to dramatic music. For the creator must stimulate the imagination and fancy of his audience but achieve his end without exposing his means. As soon as the listener becomes intellectually cognizant of the effort, the effect vanishes and the subtle and subconscious

Ex. 15

Ex. 16

channels of reaction on which all make-believe depends become clogged. After all, it is only by a thorough awareness of the medium for which they were writing that dramatic composers of any school or century have survived. If those of today are to succeed in making movie music a vehicle that will establish their language as an idiom communicated to and understood by millions, their mastery of tones will have to be paired with the soundness and flexibility that practical considerations make imperative. The commissions of Hollywood resemble in their plenty the conditions that brought forth the incredible abundance of 18th-century opera. The advantages of both systems are manifest, for the continuous box-office demand for novel entertainment provides a sound social basis for the composer who can write and live in and for his time. We must be grateful for a functional framework that offers the industry the opportunities of Maecenas and the musician a challenge he cannot ignore.

28

Aaron Copland in the Film Studio (1949)

Aaron Copland's film work again came to prominence in 1949, when he provided music for highly regarded film versions of John Steinbeck's *The Red Pony* (dir. Lewis Milestone) and Henry James's *Washington Square*; the latter was filmed under the title *The Heiress* (dir. William Wyler), and its score earned Copland an Academy Award. The first article reprinted below incorporates material from Otis L. Guernsey's contemporaneous interview with the composer in which he was asked his views on why a musical score was deemed necessary for a motion picture. Copland's replies develop the theme of modernizing film scoring by leaving romantic models far behind, while noting the need for sensitivity to a film's historical setting.

Along with Bernard Herrmann, David Raksin, and Hanns Eisler, Copland was a relatively rare example of a practicing film composer active in the 1940s whose views on the aesthetics of cinematic music were sufficiently pertinent to be adopted as a benchmark by later critics and commentators. (His earlier views on the subject are reprinted on pp. 83–91.) The second text below was published by Copland shortly after a concert performance of a suite from his score to *The Red Pony* given in October 1949 by the New York Philharmonic. He proposes a categorization of film music into six basic types: creating "atmosphere of time and place," "underlining psychological refinements," functioning as a "neutral background filler," "building a sense of continuity," emphasizing

Sources: (1) Otis L. Guernsey, Jr., "Function of the Movie Musical Score: Try Deleting It and See What Happens to Film's Emotional Impact, Says Aaron Copland, Noted Composer," *New York Herald Tribune*, September 4, 1949; (2) Aaron Copland, "Tip to Moviegoers: Take Off Those Ear-Muffs. There's music on the soundtrack, too, and you're missing too much of it, a film composer advises," *New York Times*, November 6, 1949: 28–32.

dramatic tension, and giving an impression of finality. This approach to under-standing the basic functions of film music was widely cited by later writers until a new generation of scholars and commentators began to reassess the medium in the 1980s.

(1)

It has been said that the best way to hide something is to put it in plain sight, and there is no better living proof of this theory than the motion-picture musical score. Those bassoon arpeggios that hammer at your spine while the hero climbs the fire escape gun in hand are heard by 90,000,000 people every week. These same people, who would run in terror if music materialized in the air of their backyards, will comment on the stark realism of such a scene. The music is not consciously heard, but it registers direct to the brain as an added dimension of emotion and actually helps to heighten the illusion of reality.

The men who work these artistic magic tricks are generally ignored because they are dealing with an auditory art in a visual medium. Yet some of them are giants in their field, and occasionally they receive recognition such as the Pulit-zer Prize which went to Virgil Thomson last year for his score of *Louisiana Story* [1948]. Another noted composer who has done the scores for several pic-tures is Aaron Copland, whose last was for *The Red Pony* and whose next will be heard accompanying the action of Paramount's *The Heiress*. In a discussion of the film last week, Copland was asked: Why is a musical score necessary to a motion picture in the first place?

"There's a good answer to that," he said, "but it can't be expressed in words. Take a scene from a picture and play it, then run it off again without the music, then play it again as it was the first time, with the music. Not only can you sense the difference that way, but you can also detect the exact emotional contribution of the music to that scene."

The composer took as an illustration a scene showing a man walking across a field, a piece of action that might seem long and meaningless without music. Such a scene, he says, is brought to life by music, which suggests with its rhythm the action on the screen and with its mood the thoughts and intentions of the character.

Copland added that though music can carry a scene like this if it is appro-priate, there are examples in which poor artistry will make the score intrusive, or create a score which does not match the style of the action.

Copland's creative system is exemplified in his work on *The Heiress*. He liked the script (he never writes music for something he doesn't like), and he wanted to experiment with love music which, he believes, has been conventionalized since Wagner's *Tristan und Isolde*. Analyzing his problem, he decided that first of all the music should suggest the period, which is the mid-nineteenth century, and the Washington Square setting. Next, he felt, it should play a little bit against the action, particularly in the beginning.

"Everything at first appears to be normal and happy, but my music is a little disharmonious, suggesting that all is not as well as it looks," he explained. "I think this makes an effective contrast and helps to establish the mood."

Some composers write their scores after seeing the picture only three or four times. Copland works in constant association with the film. He will sit down with individual scenes, running them over and over, and they induce musical ideas in him the way an electrified coil induces magnetism in an iron bar.

Once the score is written and orchestrated, the composer faces his most difficult mechanical problem: fitting the harmonies onto the sound track so they won't interfere with the dialogue.

"However carefully you plan and time it, you find that some of it doesn't match," he said. "A simple 'hello' can throw you off. It must be heard, and the music must be phrased to let it come through. From our point of view, there's too much talk in pictures."

All this effort, however successful its outcome, might and indeed usually does go unnoticed in the finished product. But Copland says that certain people with sensitive ears for music are highly susceptible to motion picture scores. He is among them, and he has often been caught grimacing in the wrong place while watching a film, steeling himself against a sequence of notes of which nobody else is aware.

Copland was confronted with the age-old controversy as to whether a symphony orchestra should suddenly appear in the middle of the Sahara Desert. He was asked whether composers ever considered the illogic of music's presence in most movie scenes.

"Mostly the logic is ignored—after all, it's only a question of degree. If the scene takes place in a night club you don't question the presence of music, and you tend to accept it everywhere else too.

"There's just one pet phobia that I have," he added, "I don't like to hear a piano in the music for an outdoor scene. You can stretch the imagination for other instruments, but a piano is such an indoor thing—you can't run along with it or carry it from place to place. I may be the only one who feels this way, but I just cannot connect a piano with the outdoors."

(2)

The next time you settle yourself comfortably into a seat at the neighborhood picture house don't forget to take off your ear-muffs. Most people don't realize they are wearing any—at any rate, that is the impression of composers who write for the movies. Millions of moviegoers take the musical accompaniment to a dramatic film so much for granted that five minutes after the termination of a picture they couldn't tell you whether they had heard music or not.

To ask whether they thought the score exciting or merely adequate or downright awful would be to give them a musical inferiority complex. But, on second thought, and possibly in self-protection, comes the query: "Isn't it true that one isn't supposed to be listening to the music? Isn't it supposed to work on you unconsciously without being listened to directly as you would listen at a concert?"

No discussion of movie music ever gets very far without having to face this problem: Should one hear a movie score? If you are a musician there is no problem because the chances are you can't help but listen. More than once I've had a good picture ruined for me by an inferior score. Have you had the same experience? Yes? Then you may congratulate yourself: you're definitely musical.

But it's the spectator, so absorbed in the dramatic action that he fails to take in the background music, who wants to know whether he is missing anything. The answer is bound up with the degree of your general musical perception. It is the degree to which you are aurally minded that will determine how much pleasure you may derive by absorbing the background musical accompaniment as an integral part of the combined impression made by the film.

One's appreciation of a work of art is partly determined by the amount of preparation one brings to it. The head of the family will probably be less sensitive to the beauty and appropriateness of the gowns worn by the feminine star than his wife will be. It's hopeless to expect the tone-deaf to listen to a musical score. But since the great majority of movie patrons are undoubtedly musical to some degree, they should be encouraged not to ignore the music; on the contrary, I would hope to convince them that by taking it in they will be enriching both their musical and their cinema experience.

Recently I was asked rather timorously whether I liked to write movie music—the implication being that it was possibly degrading for a composer of symphonies to trifle with a commercial product. "Would you do it anyhow, even if it were less well paid?" I think I would, and moreover, I think most composers would, principally because film music constitutes a new musical medium that exerts a fascination of its own. Actually, it is a new form of dramatic music—related to opera, ballet, incidental theatre music—in contradistinction to concert music of the symphonic or chamber music kind. As a new form it opens up unexplored possibilities, or should.

The main complaint about film music as written today in Hollywood is that so much of it is cut and dried, rigidly governed by conventions that have grown up with surprising rapidity in the short period of twenty-odd years since the talkies began. But, leaving the hack composer aside, there is no reason why a serious composer, cooperating with an intelligent producer on a picture of serious artistic pretensions, should not be able to have his movie scores judged by the same standards applied to his concert music. That is certainly the way William Walton in *Henry V* [1944], Serge Prokofieff in *Alexander Nevsky* [1938] or Virgil Thomson in *Louisiana Story* would want to be judged. They did not have to lower their standards because they were writing for a mass audience. Some day the term "movie music" will clearly define a specific musical genre and will not have, as it does have nowadays, a pejorative meaning.

Most people are curious as to just how one goes about putting music to a film. Fortunately, the process is not so complex that it cannot be outlined here.

The first thing one must do, of course, is to see the picture. Almost all musical scores are composed *after* the film itself is completed. The only exception to this is when the script calls for realistic music—that is, music which is visually sung or played or danced to on the screen. In that case the music must be composed before the scene is photographed. It will then be recorded and the scene in question shot to a playback of the recording. Thus, when you see an actor singing or playing or dancing, he is only making believe as far as the sound goes, for the music had previously been put down on film.

The first run-through of the film for the composer is usually a solemn moment. After all, he must live with it for several weeks. The solemnity of the occasion is emphasized by the exclusive audience that views it with him: the producer, the director, the musical head of the studio, the picture editor, the music cutter, the conductor, the orchestrator—in fact, anyone involved in scoring the picture. At that showing it is difficult for the composer to view the photoplay coldly. There is an understandable compulsion to like everything, for he is looking at what must necessarily constitute the source of his future inspiration.

The purpose of the run-through is to decide how much music is needed and where it should be. (In technical jargon this is called "to spot" the picture.)

Since no background score is continuous throughout the full length of a film (that would constitute a motion-picture opera, an unexploited cinema form), the score will normally consist of separate sequences, each lasting from a few seconds to several minutes in duration. A sequence as long as seven minutes would be exceptional. The entire score, made up of perhaps thirty or more such sequences, may add up to from forty to ninety minutes of music.

Much discussion, much give and take may be necessary before final decisions are reached regarding the "spotting" of the picture. In general my impression has been that composers are better able to gauge the over-all effect of a musical accompaniment than the average non-musician. Personally I like to make use of music's power sparingly, saving it for absolutely essential points. A composer knows how to play with silences; knows that to take music out can at times be more effective than any use of it might be. The producer-director, on the other hand, is more prone to think of music in terms of its immediate functional usage. Sometimes he has ulterior motives: anything wrong with a scene—a poor bit of acting, a badly read line, an embarrassing pause—he secretly hopes will be covered up by a clever composer. Producers have been known to hope that an entire picture would be saved by a good score. But the composer is not a magician; he can hardly be expected to do more than to make potent through music the film's dramatic and emotional values.

When well contrived there is no question but that a musical score can be of enormous help to a picture. One can prove that point, laboratory fashion, by showing an audience a climactic scene with the sound turned off and then once again with the sound track turned on. Here briefly is listed a number of ways in which music serves the screen:

1. *Creating a more convincing atmosphere of time and place.* Not all Hollywood composers bother about this nicety. Too often, their scores are inter-changeable; a thirteenth century Gothic drama and a hard-boiled modern battle of the sexes get similar treatment. The lush symphonic texture of late nineteenth century music remains the dominating influence. But there are exceptions. Recently, the higher grade horse-opera has begun to have its own musical flavor, mostly a folksong derivative.

2. *Underlining psychological refinements—the unspoken thoughts of a character or the unseen implications of a situation.* Music can play upon the emotions of the spectator, sometimes counterpointing the thing seen with an aural image that implies the contrary of the thing seen. This is not as subtle as it sounds. A well-placed dissonant chord can stop an audience cold in the middle of a sentimental scene, or a calculated wood-wind passage can turn what appears to be a solemn moment into a belly-laugh.

3. *Serving as a kind of neutral background filler.* This is really the music one isn't supposed to hear, the sort that helps to fill the empty spots between pauses in a conversation. It's the movie composer's most ungrateful task. But at times, though no one else may notice, he will get private satisfaction from the thought that music of little intrinsic value, through professional manipulation, has enlivened and made more human the deathly pallor of a screen shadow. This is hardest to do, as any film composer will attest, when the neutral filler type of music must weave its way underneath dialogue.

4. *Building a sense of continuity.* The picture editor knows better than anyone how serviceable music can be in tieing together a visual medium which is, by its very nature, continually in danger of falling apart. One sees this most obviously in montage scenes where the use of a unifying musical idea may save the quick flashes of disconnected scenes from seeming merely chaotic.

5. *Underpinning the theatrical build-up of a scene, and rounding it off with a sense of finality.* The first instance that comes to mind is the music that blares out at the end of a film. Certain producers have boasted their picture's lack of a musical score, but I never saw or heard of a picture that ended in silence.

We have merely skimmed the surface, without mentioning the innumerable examples of utilitarian music—offstage street bands, the barn dance, merry-go-rounds, circus music, cafe music, the neighbor's girl practicing her piano, etc. All these, and many others, introduced with apparent naturalistic intent, serve to vary subtly the aural interest of the sound track.

Perhaps it is only fair to mention that several of these uses come to the screen by way of the long tradition of incidental music in the legitimate theatre. Most workers in the theatre, and especially our playwrights, would agree that music enhances the glamour and atmosphere of a stage production, any stage production. Formerly it was considered indispensable. But nowadays only musical comedy can afford a considerable-sized orchestra in the pit.

With mounting costs of production it looks as if the serious drama would have to get along with a union minimum of four musicians for some time to come. If there is to be any combining of music and the spoken drama in any but the barest terms, it will have to happen in Hollywood, for the Broadway theatre is practically out of the running.

But now perhaps we had better return to our hypothetical composer. Having determined where the separate musical sequences will begin and end he turns the film over to the music cutter who prepares a so-called cue sheet. The cue sheet provides the composer with a detailed description of the physical action in each sequence, plus the exact timings in thirds of seconds of that action, thereby making it possible for a practiced composer to write an entire score without ever again referring to the picture. Personally I prefer to remain in daily contact with the picture itself, viewing again and again the sequence I happen to be working on.

The layman usually imagines that the most difficult part of the job in composing for the films has to do with the precise "fitting" of the music to the action. Doesn't that kind of timing strait-jacket the composer? The answer is, No, for two reasons: first, having to compose music to accompany specific action is a help rather than a hindrance, since the action itself induces music in a composer of theatrical imagination, whereas he has no such visual stimulus in writing absolute music. Secondly, the timing is mostly a matter of minor adjustments, since the over-all musical fabric is there.

For the composer of concert music, changing to the medium of celluloid does bring certain special pitfalls. For example, melodic invention, highly prized in the concert hall, may at times be distracting in certain film situations. Even phrasing in the concert manner, which would normally emphasize the independence of separate contrapuntal lines, may be distracting when applied to screen accompaniments. In orchestration there are many subtleties of timbre—distinctions meant to be listened to for their own expressive quality in an auditorium—which are completely wasted on sound track.

As compensation for these losses, the composer has other possibilities, some of them tricks, which are unobtainable in Carnegie Hall. In scoring one section of *The Heiress*, for example, I was able to superimpose two orchestras, one upon another. Both recorded the same music at different times, one orchestra consisting of strings alone, the other constituted normally. Later these were combined by simultaneously re-recording the original tracks, thereby producing a highly expressive orchestral texture [see p. 331]. Bernard Herrmann, one of the most ingenious of screen composers, called for (and got) eight celestas—an unheard-of combination of Fifty-seventh Street—to suggest a winter's sleigh ride. Miklos Rozsa's use of the "echo chamber"—a device to give normal tone a ghost-like aura—was widely remarked, and subsequently done to death.

Unusual effects are obtainable through overlapping incoming and outgoing music tracks. Like two trains passing one another, it is possible to bring in and take out at the same time two different musics. *The Red Pony* gave me an opportunity to use this cinema specialty. When the day-dreaming imagination of a little boy turns white chickens into white circus horses the visual image is mirrored in an aural image by having the chicken music transform itself into circus music, a device only obtainable by means of the overlap.

Let us now assume that the musical score has been completed and is ready for recording. The scoring stage is a happy-making place for the composer. Hollywood has gathered to itself some of America's finest performers; the music will be beautifully played and recorded with a technical perfection not to be matched anywhere else.

Most composers like to invite their friends to be present at the recording session of important sequences. The reason is that neither the composer nor his friends are ever again likely to hear the music sound out in concert style. For when it is combined with the picture most of the dynamic levels will be changed. Otherwise the finished product might sound like a concert with pictures. In lowering dynamic levels niceties of shading, some inner voices and bass parts may be lost. Erich Korngold, one of Hollywood's top men, put it well when he said: "A movie composer's immortality lasts from the recording stage to the dubbing room."

The dubbing room is where all the tracks involving sound of any kind, including dialogue, are put through the machines to obtain one master sound track. This is a delicate process as far as the music is concerned, for it is only a hair's breadth that separates the "too loud" from the "too soft." Sound engineers, working the dials that control volume, are not always as musically sensitive as composers would like them to be. What is called for is a new species, a sound mixer who is half musician and half engineer; and even then the mixing of dialogue, music and realistic sounds of all kinds must always remain problematical.

In view of these drawbacks to the full sounding out of his music, it is only natural that the composer often hopes to be able to extract a viable concert suite from his film score. There is a current tendency to believe that movie scores are not proper material for concert music. The argument is that separated from its visual justification the music falls flat.

Personally, I doubt very much that any hard and fast rule can be made that will cover all cases. Each score will have to be judged on its merits and, no doubt, stories that require a more continuous type of musical development in a unified atmosphere will lend themselves better than others to re-working for concert purposes. Rarely is it conceivable that the music of a film might be extracted without much re-working. But I fail to see why, if successful suites like Grieg's *Peer Gynt* can be made from nineteenth century incidental stage music, a twentieth century composer can't be expected to do as well with a film score.

As for the picture score, it is only in the motion picture theatre that the composer for the first time gets the full impact of what he has accomplished, tests the dramatic punch of his favorite musical spot, appreciates the curious importance and unimportance of detail, wishes that he had done certain things differently and is surprised that others came off better than he had hoped. For when all is said and done the art of combining moving pictures with musical tones is still a mysterious art. Not the least mysterious element is the theatregoers' reaction: Millions will be listening but one never knows how many will be really hearing, so the next time you go to the movies remember to be on the composer's side. Remove those ear-muffs.

29

Lawrence Morton: "Composing, Orchestrating, and Criticizing" (1951)

With the exception of George Antheil's column for the journal *Modern Music* (1936–39), the first sustained contribution to the developing field of film-music criticism were the more substantial and wide-ranging essays written for *Hollywood Quarterly* by Lawrence Morton (1904–87). While still a student Morton had provided organ accompaniment to silent films, and after his musical career was interrupted by military service in the Second World War, he began writing criticism for *Modern Music* (in which he inherited Antheil's column) and then *Hollywood Quarterly*, to which he contributed a detailed article on Franz Waxman's scoring techniques ("The Music of 'Objective: Burma,'" *Hollywood Quarterly*, 1/4 [July 1946]: 378–95). In 1948, Morton was given his own regular column in the journal ("Film Music of the Quarter"), which—in a clear sign of changing media dynamics—was renamed *Quarterly of Film, Radio and Television* in 1951; eight years later it changed its name again, becoming *Film Quarterly* (which is still published today). A capable arranger and composer in his own right, Morton enjoyed close personal connections with Copland, Stravinsky, Schoenberg, and Boulez but is perhaps best remembered as an organizer of inspirational concerts. In 1954, he became the first artistic director of California's Ojai Festival; he served sporadically in this capacity until 1984, and from 1965 he was curator of music at the Los Angeles County Museum of Art.

As shown by the article reproduced here, Morton fiercely resented the efforts of some European critics to dismiss Hollywood film music wholesale as worthless, cliché-ridden, and mass-produced. In 1950, the International Film Music

Source: Quarterly of Film, Radio and Television, 6/2 (Winter 1951): 191–206.

Congress had met in Florence, Italy, and the British composer Antony Hopkins and British critic Hans Keller reported on its performances of American film music in the journals *Sight and Sound* (19 [August 1950]: 243–44) and *Music Review* (11/3 [August 1950]: 210–11), respectively. Morton first commented on their remarks in his *Hollywood Quarterly* column the following year (5/3 [Spring 1951]: 282–88), in which he contrasted Hollywood composer Daniele Amfitheatrof's positive account of the proceedings with Keller's description of the exhibition as a "repellant anthology" offered to a gathering of "musicians who could hardly be expected to like the stuff"; the music had been publicly denounced on the following day by the British film composer Benjamin Frankel, who was also attending the conference. In his account of the affair, Hopkins noted that only Copland's music from *The Red Pony* met with warm applause. Morton's first riposte focused on the British commentators' misunderstanding of Hollywood orchestration practices and their elitist bias against the principle of collaborative composing, and concluded: "If future congresses want to find out truly what is wrong with American film music, and resolve resolutions, they would do better to investigate Hollywood studios on the spot instead of waving divining rods in faraway Florence."

Morton's text was subsequently reprinted in the May 1951 issue of *Sight and Sound* along with a reply from Hopkins. Keller responded in his regular film-music column under the title "The Dragon Shows His Teeth" (*Music Review*, 12 [1951]: 221–25), an article in which he confessed "enthusiastically" to his anti-Hollywood bias and described what he termed his own "conscientious study of Hollywood music" as "the most deadening task a contemporary musician can impose upon himself." He continued: "The overwhelming majority of Hollywood scores emit such a stench that one is forced to the conclusion that something is basically wrong with this film industry's musico-sociologico-economical set-up." Adding fuel to the fire, he rigidly stuck to his negative view of American orchestrators and declared that their stereotypical work produced a "sickening effect of empty extravagance." Keller's article was poorly judged, and easily laid itself open to criticism for its obvious prejudices and (in places) downright silliness, notably in his horror that Hollywood scores often do not include second-violin parts. Morton was quick to seize on such ineptitude, and the text below was his response. In his contrastingly level-headed account of Hollywood practices, Morton showed himself to be one of the first serious writers to champion the special merits of music conceived primarily for use in the cinema.

As a postlude to this account of British critics' insularity at the time, it may be noted that in the entry on film music in the fifth edition of the United Kingdom's highly respected reference work, *Grove's Dictionary of Music and Musicians* (ed. Eric Blom [London: Macmillan, 1954]: vol. 13, pp. 93–110), an article of which Keller was coauthor, only two U.S. composers were mentioned by name: Copland

and Herrmann, both of whom could be regarded as "serious" composers, and both of whom entertained strongly negative views on the use of orchestrators.

I am sorely tempted to follow the lead of my two distinguished opponents by devoting a portion of my space to discussing peripheral issues, toying with words, arguing purposely at cross purposes, and striking self-righteous attitudes. I am confident that in these areas I too could score some very unimportant points. But why should I pursue the question of the "strong national passions" aroused at the Florence Congress? If I was in error when I devoted a fraction of a single sentence to this matter, I must attribute the mistake to Mr. Hopkins' reporting. Let Mr. Keller argue this point not with me but with his colleague, whose reply to my article does not disabuse me of the notion I got from the original report. Why should I enter into a discussion of Mr. Keller's racial-cultural background? My own is just as varied as his, just as colorful, just as likely to win a reader's sympathy—and also just as irrelevant. I hope he will not be angry with me if I continue to regard him as an Englishman. Why should I argue about his use of psychological techniques in the criticism of music? I noticed them, to be sure; but I have expressed no objection to them, nor do I now, although I happen not to find them illuminating. They tell me more about Mr. Keller than about the music he discusses, which is the reverse order of my interest.

Or, why should I take time to resent his casting me in the role of Fafner guarding Hollywood's fatal gold since, by so doing, he reveals more about his own attitude than about my personal relationship with the film industry? Both he and Mr. Hopkins appear to be much exercised by the "enormous sums" earned here by composers and orchestrators. I would gladly join in denouncing big salaries if there were any assurance that Hollywood's film music could be improved by the simple expedient of paying less for it, or if there were any likelihood that Stravinsky and Hindemith would work for less money than Steiner and Newman get. Actually, in terms of an average annual wage, the majority of Hollywood musicians just manage to maintain a foothold in the lower middle class. But since Messrs. Keller and Hopkins are evidently misinformed about these matters[1] I shall refrain from giving a name to the sentiments they express.

I must point out to Mr. Hopkins that he is mistaken when he assumes that Hollywood composers have placed no pages "upon the altar of Art rather than on

1. For instance: American film composers, as such, do not yet collect royalties as their British colleagues do through the Performing Rights Society.

the lap of Mammon." The American Society of Music Arrangers, in the now departed days of its prosperity, maintained a rehearsal orchestra which met weekly for the express purpose of reading symphonic scores composed by the men working in the commercial fields. No masterpieces were discovered, but there were no offerings to Mammon. If Mr. Hopkins has not heard of any of this music, it is for the same reason that we have not heard, in this very active musical community, any of his.

Finally, I rejoice that Mr. Keller now takes up the sword of Siegfried and stands in defiance. Without challenging his heroism I must inform him that he comes rather late to the battle. I myself have been in it for a very long time, though I have never fancied myself a hero. Mr. Keller would know this if he had read my articles in this and other magazines during the past dozen years. I mention them only because he and Mr. Hopkins have invited me to delve into their other writings in order to learn about their virtues. I must return the compliment by inviting them to read my complete but still uncollected works. Here they will find that I have not been "shielding" Hollywood composers "out of a mistaken sense of loyalty" but only that I have been careful not to throw the baby out with the bath water.

I think it important to indicate one point where Mr. Keller and I are really in agreement. I define that point in his words: " . . . something is basically wrong with this film industry's musico-sociologico-economical set-up." He presumed, by the way, to "foresee" my answer to this statement. But his foresight is not to be trusted, and I must disappoint him by declining to testify as a defender of the *status quo*. I have condemned mediocrity—which is, I admit, an easy path to virtue. Specifically, I have discussed the unfortunate influence of producers and directors whose semi-cultivated tastes invade and oftentimes rule the music departments, the miscasting of composers and the hiring of them on grounds of personal friendships rather than of ability or style, the distortion of sound by engineers who can't let a piece of music "ride" without fiddling with the controls, the pressure of deadlines, the destruction of musical forms and shapes by injudicious cutting, the overemphasis on showmanship, the prevalence of clichés, the absence of experimentation, and so forth. Mr. Keller cannot now maneuver me into defending these evils.

Nor should he, by using a term like "musico-sociologico-economical," bundle them all into one neat package and leave it on the doorstep of the composer-ar-ranger-orchestrator. He should know about the antimusical forces that are at work everywhere—in concert halls as well as in film studios. My ears tell me from time to time that they are not inactive in Britain. Gerald Cockshott has cited several instances of how British directors have imposed their whims upon film scoring.[2] And what shall be said about the shredding of Rachmaninoff's "Second Concerto"

2. *Incidental Music in the Sound Film* (London: British Film Institute, 1946).

in *Brief Encounter* [1945]? The whole conception of this film score was unmusicianly, and I am unwilling to admit that Muir Mathieson and John Hollingsworth, who are credited with the outrage, actually thought up the scheme. The whole thing smacks of the front office. I mention this not in any attempt to excuse Hollywood for its sins, nor am I suggesting that the British have no right to criticize us because they themselves are open to criticism on the same counts. I mean only to point out that the use of a multiordinal term like "musico-sociologico-economical" does not excuse the critic from distinguishing between what is musical, what is sociological, and what is economic, even while he is being most aware of how these three aspects of the situation react upon one another. Although I do not know the inside story of the scoring of *Brief Encounter*, I would guess that it was found less expensive to record an existing score than to commission a new one; that an executive (Noel Coward?) engineered the project just because he liked the music; that Mr. Mathieson, Mr. Hollingsworth, and Miss [Eileen] Joyce [the pianist] participated in the outrage because there was money to be made and because, in the end, it was their business to give a good performance and not to tell the front office how to run its business; and that every musician concerned in the affair has been "explaining" his part in it for the past six years. I leave it to Mr. Keller to departmentalize the blame and put it where it belongs.

I invite him to exercise his critical powers further by attempting to make some distinctions within that catch-all category that he calls "the overwhelming majority of Hollywood scores." The only distinction he seems so far to have worked out is the one between Aaron Copland and the Hollywood "regulars." This gives him the opportunity to pose as Copland's champion. And so I must digress and point out that again Mr. Keller is late; but I shall not be so immodest as to give the references to my own articles on Copland's film music, written in the early 1940's. Nor need I remind anyone that it was Hollywood, not Mr. Keller, who awarded Copland his Oscar. But I cannot refrain from expressing my astonishment that Mr. Keller took at its face value Dr. Frederick Sternfeld's naïve account of how Copland, in his score for *The Heiress*, combined on a single sound track a string orchestra recording and a full orchestra recording of the same piece of music.[3] This kind of thing is so commonly done in Hollywood that those of us who are close to the scene hardly ever bother to comment on it anymore. It would have been interesting to learn what Mr. Keller thought of this music when he heard it in the theater. I confess, for others of Copland's most faithful fans as well as for myself, that there was nothing extraordinary in the sound that our ears could detect even after several hearings. Dozens of other composers have done far more "monkeying" along these lines than Copland

---

3. "Copland as Film Composer," *Musical Quarterly* (April 1951).

has. That they have not been able to obscure their mediocrity thereby is an argument that I present to Mr. Keller to use against them the next time he is amazed by the use of combined tracks and "sweeteners." In the meantime let us not reduce Copland's stature as a composer by building up his reputation as a dubber. Would Mr. Keller like to be praised for his punctuation?

After this digression I return to the distinctions I would like to see Mr. Keller make within "the overwhelming majority of Hollywood scores." How he has had the time to see any more than a fraction of the 400 to 500 films produced every year is an accomplishment in the management of time that I would fain learn about. For myself, I see no reason to be concerned with any except those that matter (with *Place in the Sun* [1951], for instance, because of the strange mixture of styles that resulted from the replacement of some of Franz Waxman's music, with *Portrait of Jennie* [1948] because of its horrid distortion of Debussy's masterpieces, with *The Day the Earth Stood Still* [1951] because of Bernard Herrmann's use of electronic instruments, with *Thirteenth Letter* [1951] and *Anna Lucasta* [1949] because they were, respectively, the first Hollywood scores by Alex North and David Diamond). I have spies who tell me what scores are worth looking out for. Mr. Keller may be too far from the scene to be able to single these out. Nevertheless I do not understand how he can fail to distinguish between the strongly modal character of much of Friedhofer's music, the chromaticism of Raksin's, the Viennese charm of Hollander's, the aggressiveness of Waxman's, the gaiety of Harline's (when it is not being Hindemithian), the ripe romanticism of Newman's, the extravagant richness of Amfitheatrof's, the theatrical effectiveness of Buttolph's—especially since these qualities must be expressed by sounds combined in particular ways. To assist Mr. Keller in making such distinctions, I quote two themes characteristic of their composers.

Example 1 is from David Raksin's score for *Man with a Cloak* [1951], and the "composer joke" in the theme will doubtless occur to Mr. Keller immediately. In its initial statement, the theme is heard four octaves deep. Raksin used an unusual orchestra for this score: 2 flutes, 1 oboe, 2 clarinets, 1 bass clarinet, 1 bassoon; 1 horn, 1 trumpet, 1 trombone; 1 percussion, and a solo viola d'amore. For a few climactic scenes the orchestra was augmented by a second bassoon, second and third horns, tuba, harp, piano, 6 'cellos, and 1 bass.

Example 2, from Hugo Friedhofer's score for *Edge of Doom* [1950], tells something about the gloomy tragedy and the church setting of the film.

EXAMPLE 1. David Raksin. *Man with a Cloak*. Copyright 1951 by Loew's Incorporated.

Whatever else might be said about these themes, it must be immediately apparent that they are the products of two very different musical minds, and I trust that the differences are not too subtle for Mr. Keller to discover.

I turn now to what is for me Mr. Keller's most important paragraph, wherein he specifies his objections to Hollywood orchestration. "The sickening effect of empty extravagance," he writes, "is not so much due to the strength of the forces employed as to their *disproportion*." There is much of the truth, but certainly not all of it, in this statement. Our studio orchestras are indeed over-brassed, and no one is more keenly aware of this than the musicians. (Some of them have suggested that it is the proper duty of the musician's union to insist that the studios engage enough string players to maintain a symphonic orchestral balance. That the studios would be reluctant to do this may be taken for granted: string sections would have to be increased by twenty to thirty players at a guaranteed minimum wage of about $7,500 each per year. But at least one music executive has spoken out against the inartistic composition of the orchestras.) In a recent forum discussion on film making, in which everyone from producers to costume designers participated, Mr. John Green (head of the M-G-M music department) told a large audience that Hollywood must get over the notion that a microphone can make four fiddles sound like a full section; and that for certain scores he insists on having (and sometimes gets) enough string players to make the music sound as it ought to. Although Mr. Green is a progressive and musically ambitious executive, no one expects that he is going to make heresy orthodox by the day after tomorrow. But his stand gives some insight into the relationship of the musical, social, and economic factors of the setup.

In the meantime composers and orchestrators must do the best they can with the forces available. These, I agree, are disproportionate, but only in relation to the standard symphonic ensemble. There are, however, other ensembles, some of them lacking not only second violins (Mr. Keller's italicized horror of which I find very

EXAMPLE 2. Hugo Friedhofer. *Edge of Doom*. By permission of Samuel Goldwyn Productions, Inc.

amusing), but even wanting first violins, third bassoons, tuba choirs, fipple flutes, and *crwths*. Almost any ensemble can be made to sound good if it is properly composed for. It is under no obligation to sound "normal," as is proved by *Man with a Cloak* as well as Schoenberg's *First Chamber Symphony*. Hollywood's composers and orchestrators can do this. I quote in example 3 one of several settings of a theme from *To the Ends of the Earth* [1948], composed by George Duning and orchestrated by Arthur Morton (who is not to be confused with the present writer). I choose a *tutti* setting so as to illustrate the full deployment of "disproportionate" forces. The orchestra consisted of double woodwinds plus a bass clarinet, triple brass, piano, harp, percussion, 10 violins, 4 violas, 4 'cellos, and 2 basses.

It was the purpose of this theme to express the courage of the Treasury Department officers engaged in tracking down criminals of the international

EXAMPLE 3. George Duning. *To the Ends of the Earth*. By permission of Columbia Pictures Corporation.

narcotics traffic. Its strongly diatonic nature was planned to contrast with the great amount of locale music, mostly oriental, required by the film. I suggest that in this instance a particular piece of music has been made to sound good in one particular performance by one particular orchestra. And that is what the music job in a film studio consists of.

The disproportion of forces does not necessarily result in what Mr. Keller calls "obscene homophony." I take it for granted that he does not mean that homophony is in itself obscene. I know of no better texture for a good melody, nor of a more obscene polyphony than that of a melody swamped in a sea of counterpoint. Homophony is an honorable dramatic device and not to be outlawed even when large orchestral forces are available. In example 4 I quote a passage in which the simple texture of a melody with afterbeats answers the screen's demand for music bordering on hysteria. The string forces were not quite symphonic but still adequate: 10-8-6-6-4.

This melody is only one of several developments of a theme recurring many times throughout the score, mostly in the major mode. The variety of the treatment should convince Mr. Hopkins, when he hears the score, that the development of musical materials is a procedure of which the Hollywood composers are not as innocent as he supposes. I suggest that he listen especially for example 5, which comes almost at the end of the film. Here the melody of example 4 appears in the bass, with two partly imitative voices superimposed upon it, and without accompaniment.

Both of the excerpts from *Carrie* [1952] are quoted exactly as they stand in the composer's sketches. Musicians will see precisely what details were left to the discretion of the orchestrator, Nathan Van Cleave, who also orchestrated *The Heiress* for Copland. He worked out, in example 4, the *divisi* and double-stops of the violas and 'cellos, and the voicing of the horn-trombone chords. But the whole conception of the orchestral color is the composer's. I can understand, although I do not agree with, Mr. Hopkins' opposition to the employment of an orchestrator on the grounds that it relieves the composer of his obligation to make "sacrifices to the Muse." But is it not clear, from the *Carrie* excerpts, that Mr. Raksin *does not need an orchestrator?* It is the studio that needs one, for studios can never wait. It is part of the industrial scheme that while Mr. Van Cleave orchestrates, Mr. Raksin goes on to compose the next scene.

I turn now to Mr. Keller's statement about "the vague fakes and fillers of inner parts." It is sometimes one of the functions of film music to do nothing more than be there, as though it would exist as sound rather than as "constructed" music. Thus, what often seems to be a vague filler is in fact a very conscious dramatic device. Where this is so, Mr. Keller's comment might better be interpreted as a criticism of how a scene has been treated musically, not of how the

EXAMPLE 4. David Raksin. *Carrie*. Copyright 1951 by Famous Music Corporation.

music has been composed. At the beginning of *Broken Arrow* [1950], Hugo Friedhofer underscored a scene where James Stewart rides horseback through the
western desert. Pictorially the setting is spacious, immobile, quiet. The slow amble
of the horse is the only sign of life, and our hero is meditative; a narrator starts the
story on its way. Example 6 is the musical counterpart of this screen situation.

The inner parts here have the maximum interest compatible with the purposes of the scene. Simple as they are, they still make music by themselves.
There is just enough harmony to "bed down" the solo clarinet and keep it from
competing with the narrator's voice, and just enough mobility to counteract the

EXAMPLE 5. David Raksin. *Carrie*. Copyright 1951 by Famous Music Corporation.

monotony of the double pedal. By way of contrast I cite in example 7 a "Narrative Theme" from George Duning's score for *The Family Secret* [1951]. Notewise the inner part here is purposely inexpressive; it is intended principally to carry the *sound* of the vibraphone and harp, and to anchor the solo violin which, by the way, was played with a minimum vibrato in order to avoid the "saccharine" which Mr. Keller is not alone in disliking.

It would not be difficult to give chapter and verse disproving each of the complaints that Mr. Keller has specified. If he thinks that "the brass is used in the most elementarily dialogic, chordal blocks," let him listen for several polyphonic brass passages in *Across the Wide Missouri* [1951], by Raksin. If he wants further evidence on the matter of good part writing, he will find it in almost every Friedhofer score. This composer, almost as though it were ritual, finds at least one opportunity for a passage written in classical four-part style, for strings in *The Lodger* [1944], and for woodwinds in *Broken Arrow*. Such passages are almost like the composer's personal signature to a score. For *fugato* passages, let Mr. Keller listen to some of Waxman's scores, especially *Objective: Burma*

EXAMPLE 6. Hugo Friedhofer. *Broken Arrow*. By permission of Twentieth Century-Fox Film Corporation.

[1945]. For a genuine economy of style I again refer him to Friedhofer, particularly to the scene of the wedding ceremony in *Broken Arrow*. Example 8 shows how it is possible to avoid the pitfall of an Apache *Lohengrin*.

Throughout this article I have quoted music which Messrs. Hopkins and Keller may not regard as typical of Hollywood. This is because I have no time to analyze mediocrity, no intention of wasting my critical powers upon it. Also I have purposely refrained from citing the music of composers who have reputations in the concert hall, such as Rózsa, Antheil, Korngold, Gruenberg, Herrmann, Tedesco. Nor have I cited the "old guard." Raksin, Friedhofer, and Duning are Hollywood "regulars" and they have made their careers almost entirely in the film industry. Also, they had not yet "arrived" when Copland wrote his essay on Hollywood in 1940, which Mr. Keller, always too late, now use against us. Many changes have occurred since that time, and I judge it the duty of criticism to

EXAMPLE 7. George Duning. *The Family Secret*. By permission of Columbia Pictures Corporation.

EXAMPLE 8. Hugo Friedhofer. *Broken Arrow*. By permission of Twentieth Century-Fox Corporation.

notice them. But they will not be noticed by ears that are prejudiced, even though Mr. Keller tries to justify prejudice with an unconvincing *bon mot*. He is more resolved to condemn than prepared to weigh evidence—a strange attitude for a critic. That, I presume, is why he ignored much of the factual material I gave in my previous article. That is why he cannot separate from the "overwhelming majority" of scores those which composers orchestrate themselves. I should have expected him to comment on the sound of Bernard Herrmann's music, since Mr. Herrmann is as opposed as any Briton to the use of orchestrators. Cannot Mr. Keller hear this in a Herrmann score?

Why does not Mr. Keller discriminate between hack work and talent? Certainly he does this at home. For if he didn't, he wouldn't know the difference between the music of Walton and that of, say, the late Hubert Bath. I have at hand some twenty-odd phonograph records of British film music, privately issued by the Rank organization. I do not imagine that they were published as examples of how bad British film music can be. Yet most of them are appalling samples of hack work, the exact counterpart of what our Hollywood hacks produce. And how badly some of them need orchestrators! Ealing and Elstree are, after all, very much like Hollywood. But this is no reflection on the work of Walton and Vaughan Williams and Britten. Unfortunately they do not score *all* the British films. And do their great reputations necessarily assure us that everything they write is automatically a masterpiece? Was Hamlet's "Funeral March," for instance, worthy of Walton, or even worthy of the rest of the *Hamlet* score

[1948]? Its popularity in certain quarters here was damnably unflattering. Yet, on the other hand, was it not the proper obsequy for Olivier's Hamlet, if not for Shakespeare's? Or, what was Lord Berners' music supposed to be doing in *Nicholas Nickleby* [1947]? And did not Sir Arnold Bax's music in *Oliver Twist* [1948] sound as though it had been written less for the film than for an eventual performance at Albert Hall? Some of us, hearing these scores, wonder if, after all, the less-renowned William Alwyn is not a better film composer than his knighted colleagues whose names and works we know from the concert hall.

Because I am so very busy making distinctions of this order—between Louis Levy and Muir Mathieson, between Miklos Rozsa (1940) and Miklos Rozsa (1951), between Adolph Deutsch and Victor Young—I shall have to decline taking time out to do battle with Mr. Keller. Before he girds his loins, sounds his alarms, draws his sword, and rides off simultaneously in all directions, he ought to find out who his enemies are, who are his allies, what and where he is going to attack. He could even enlist my aid, if he would only be a little bit more discerning and not try to swallow the whole musico-socio-economic setup in one gulp. I recommend the strategy of divide and conquer. But let's first divide and divide and divide.

30

Elmer Bernstein: "Film Composers vs. the Studios" (1976)

Like Bernard Herrmann and Jerry Goldsmith, Elmer Bernstein (1922–2004) entered the field of film scoring from a background in radio music. In 1955 he gained some notoriety for his jazz-inflected music for Otto Preminger's controversial drug-addiction movie *The Man with the Golden Arm*, the title theme from which became a best-selling gramophone recording. In the following year he scored Cecil B. DeMille's lavishly extravagant remake of *The Ten Commandments*, a story the director had first told as a silent film in 1923. Bernstein's later film assignments showed him sometimes typecast as a composer of sweeping melody-dominated scores for westerns and action adventures, most famously those for John Sturges's films *The Magnificent Seven* (1960, with a stirring main theme later adopted in Marlboro cigarette commercials) and *The Great Escape* (1963). But he was equally adept at intimate chamber-music cues (*To Kill a Mockingbird*, 1962), a more economical approach that proved influential in the field of television music, and at the end of the 1970s he developed a much-imitated deadpan manner of scoring the emerging genre of spoof comedy (*National Lampoon's Animal House*, 1978; *Airplane!*, 1980).

In addition to his creative work, Bernstein promoted a wider public awareness of film music through his publication *Film Music Notebook* (1974–78) and as a conductor and promoter of recordings. He was notable as a staunch advocate for improvements to film composers' often horrendous working conditions, and he campaigned tirelessly to secure for them the intellectual rights to

Source: Film Music Notebook, 2/1 (1976): 31–39; reprinted in *Elmer Bernstein's Film Music Notebook: A Complete Collection of the Quarterly Journal, 1974–1978* (Sherman Oaks, Calif.: Film Music Society, 2004): 201–9, 203–7.

Elmer Bernstein (far right) in high spirits on the set of Cecil B. DeMille's *The Ten Commandments* in 1956. The use of "authentic" music in historical epics had recently been pioneered by Miklós Rózsa: see pp. 165–71. (Photofest; © Paramount Pictures)

their screen compositions, which he felt were being willfully denied owing to commercial greed on the part of their employers. In 1970, Bernstein succeeded David Raksin as president of the Composers and Lyricists Guild of America, and two years later spearheaded a lawsuit filed by no fewer than seventy-one film composers against leading film studios, television networks, and the Association of Motion Picture and Television Producers, charging them all with violation of antitrust laws and demanding $300 million in compensation. This initiative came on the back of industrial action taken by members of the guild in December 1971, and the plaintiffs' case is set out in the article by Bernstein reproduced here.

A minority of the accused companies preferred to settle privately. After a judicial dismissal of the suit followed by a successful appeal, the case was on the verge of going to court in 1975, when the aggrieved composers had all but exhausted the huge personal funding they had been compelled to spend in order to keep the action alive. A court-ratified agreement was eventually reached in 1979, but under its terms the composers were only awarded limited rights, and their employment prospects in the prevailing freelance climate remained precarious. In 1983, the void left by the now-defunct CLGA was filled by the creation of the Society of Composers and Lyricists (in which Bernstein again played a crucial role), which the National Labor Relations Board refused to recognize as a trade union, deeming its members to be "independent contractors." As film composers bitterly complained, the studios had been happy enough to treat them as "employees" when this enabled the confiscation of their intellectual rights, yet refused to recognize them as such when they presented a united opposition to working conditions they felt were unacceptable. When the SCL reconsidered its status during the 1990s, its members failed to reach an agreement on the best course of action; at the time of writing, however, the organization continues to provide a vital professional and educational service to film composers and remains fully committed to improving their working conditions through constructive dialogue with producers and directors.

There are several factors which require some understanding as a background to the present plight of artists working in commercial areas in music and the pending antitrust suit. First there is the United States Copyright Law itself. A creaky old piece of legislation promulgated by a society that holds commerce in much higher esteem than art. Copyright law does in fact provide that where an Employer-Employee relationship exists, the Employer may indeed construe himself to be the author of the work. It is interesting that a society which looks back in horror at the attempt of a patron to purchase Mozart's *Requiem* and then affix his own name to it as the author, and piously excoriates the Soviet Union for its attitude toward its artists, is perfectly willing to countenance a law which, for a fee, allows a so-called employer to affix his own name as the author of a work composed by another person.

Must we not in fact call into question the whole concept of the use of terms like "Employer and Employee" where art is concerned?

The National Labor Relations Board generally accepts the definition of an employee as a person who works under direction and supervision and whose negiotiative concerns are wages, hours, and working conditions. At some point we must question whether a creative artist can *ever* be construed to be an individual who works under direction and supervision, and whose creativity falls within fixed hours and working conditions. The artist in our society is, in fact, a person producing an art product which another individual can either rent or buy.

Another factor important to the understanding of the background in the antitrust suit is the existence of performance fee societies such as ASCAP,

BMI, SACEM, and PRS. ASCAP was formed by a group of distinguished composers in 1914 in order to insure collection of payments when their works are performed. Its formation was an important step toward economic dignity and self-determination on the part of composers and their publishers. In the beginning the members of these societies were primarily song-writers. With the advent of sound in motion pictures, the art of motion picture scoring was born and a new kind of composer sought membership in these societies. The importance of this art was not immediately recognized and for many years film composers received from ASCAP 1/100th what a songwriter would receive for a work of similar duration. At one point a group of composers formed an organization known as the Screen Composers Organization and through the instrument of this organization and their attorneys, Leonard Zissu and Abraham Marcus, fought for greater economic recognition for composers of motion picture music and in a running battle over the years have succeeded in improving the economic lot of screen composers within performing arts societies very considerably. As ASCAP is a society in which the composers and publishers share equally, any gain for the composer is equal gain for the publisher and it is at this point (the collection of performance royalty monies) that the producers began to have an interest in the acquisition of all rights to such music. It became the practice of motion picture companies to either wholly own, or obtain substantial interests in, music publishing companies. In countries other than the United States,[*] a music performance fee is paid by motion picture theaters for the performance of the music in films they exhibit. On a worldwide basis these fees are substantial. They are collected by the performing arts societies equally by the composer and the publisher of the work. The producer, by virtue of obtaining the publishing rights to the music and by virtue of the onerous contracts quoted above finds himself in the position of amortizing his fees to the composer by simply sitting back and performing no other function on behalf of the music. He rarely performs any of the normal functions of a publisher such as printing sheet music, seeking recordings, etc., etc. He is a publisher only for the purpose of collecting money by forcing the composer into this arrangement or the composer does not work. Obviously the producers' interest in acquiring these rights, ironically, increases with each success the composers have in getting a fairer share of the performing rights distribution.

Another factor in the background of the present situation and a most interesting one has been the formation and existence of the Composers and Lyricists Guild of America. We have been brought up in an era which has recognized

---

[*] The United States is excepted from these payments pursuant to a Lower Court decision in a suit against ASCAP, a decision which is irritating to foreign societies which are thereby prohibited from making such collection in the U.S.

unionism as the most effective tool for the protection of working people from the abuses of employers. The relationship of the artist to such procedures is one that is yet unclear for reasons I have indicated earlier in this article. If in fact it is possible to establish "floors" for fees for artistic endeavors, it is highly questionable whether conditions for direction and supervision, hours and working conditions can be successfully negotiated on an across-the-board basis for an entire group of artists. When a group of composers in the early 50's began to consider the advantages of representing themselves through a Guild, it is interesting to note that the National Labor Relations Board did not consider that composers were employees in their sense of the word. In an opinion reported by 117 NLRB 13 (1957), the Board reviewed the work of the composers applying to them the test of whether they composed words and lyrics under the supervision and direction of the producing companies. The Board concluded that they were not employees. *"Where the person for whom the services are per-formed retains the right to control the manner and means by which the result is to be accomplished, the relationship is one of employment. While on the other hand, where control is reserved only as to the result sought, relationship is that of an independent contractor."* It was apparent to the National Labor Relations Board at that time that the producer had no way of controlling the manner and means by which a music composition is to be accomplished and on that basis the NLRB's opinion was that we were indeed not employees. Its decision not withstanding, and this is most interesting, a Guild was formed as a result of what is known as a consent election. This means that although the producing companies and studios were under no legal obligation under existing labor laws to recognize such a guild or union if formed, they consented to this election of their own free will and as a result of their consent to this procedure, a Guild was indeed formed. Retrospectively, we can now only speculate that as no employer, however good willed, is known for giving things away, there must have been some other motive. Can it be possible that some clever employee of the studios realized that by formalizing an employer-employee relationship through the instrument of negotiating labor problems with a Guild they would also formalize a relationship which accrues such great benefits to the Employer by virtue of the copyright law and at the same time provide themselves with some protection from antitrust prosecution by use of the Clayton Act which protects members of a union acting in concert from antitrust prosecution? The ensuing minimum basic agreement and negotiations would certainly seem to support this speculation, as the wage floors forced upon the young Guild were the lowest for any art or craft in the field of motion pictures and [by] the various procedures through their bargaining agency, the studios consistently showed a lack of interest in the subject of hours and working conditions (those factors so important to the definition of an Employee), but what was clearly spelled out and what the minimum basic agreement shows clearly is that it was intended to be an instrument by which the producers acquired the music rights they so eloquently described in the contracts quoted.

During the period of the 60's, film composers became more and more concerned about two issues. One was the so called "rights" issue which had to do with the stranglehold the studios insisted on having upon the life and future of music far beyond the film for which it was composed. This particular concern was brought into sharp focus as some studios initiated the practice of destroying the scores and parts to their scores as a space-saving measure. It is interesting to note that in practically all cases, the composer was not contacted to find out if he might be interested in storing the scores of his own works. The other issue which became an ever increasing matter of concern for film composers were the intolerable pressures visited upon composers by diabolical schedules. As the composition of a score for a motion picture is the last creative element to be added, and as the composition of the score cannot be undertaken until the picture has been assembled and cut to length, the composer is placed under tremendous time pressure as he becomes the last obstacle to completion. Producers often argue cynically that shorter schedules enable composers to accept more assignments. Bernard Herrmann quite wisely countered that in view of the pressures endured by composers as a result of inadequate scheduling, they should charge twice as much when requested to accomplish the job in half the time it should take. Many composers have caused some of their own problems by agreeing to work under inhuman pressures for fear of losing assignments. This entire problem has been greatly exacerbated by the advent of television. For some reason which is not completely clear, the schedules for the delivery of the segments of a series for the television networks are made with a callous disregard for the physical and mental health of *all* persons involved in their creation. As once again the composer is the last person to make his contribution to the insane timetable, the pressure on him is generally greater as a day or two is usually lost in the editing process. During the autumn of 1971 the members of the Composers & Lyricists Guild of America began to feel that their association in the Guild would have little meaning unless the Guild could help to alleviate the major problems with which they were faced. During the summer of that year, a Negotiating Committee was formed which included Jeff Alexander, Alan Bergman, Benny Carter, Jerry Fielding, Norman Gimbel, Ernest Gold, Jerry Goldsmith, David Grusin, Arthur Hamilton, J. J. Johnson, Quincy Jones, Jay Livingston, Henry Mancini, Larry Orenstein, David Raksin, George Romanis, Leonard Rosenman, Lalo Schifrin, Nathan Scott, Fred Steiner and Guild officers Elmer Bernstein, Richard M. Sherman, Jack Elliott and Lyn Murray. The Negotiating

Committee promulgated the following proposals for discussion with representatives of the producers:

1. A proposal that the composers and lyricists retain the publication rights to their music and lyrics.
2. That the Motion Picture Health and Welfare Fund and the Motion Picture Industry Pension Plan hours be credited on a parity with other guilds and unions in the motion picture industry.
3. A proposal allowing either side to open negotiations at a future date to deal with the problem of future means of exploitation of the use of the music, i.e. video cassettes, etc.
4. In a case where the composer and lyricist of a song are the same person, that the person be paid for both services.
5. To limit the amount of work a composer or lyricist can be required to do within any given week. (Parenthetically, the membership was informed in a memo that this was an old issue but one that we felt we must keep fighting for. The Guild also asked for a 15% raise in the minimum fees paid to composers which I have all ready indicated were the lowest in the motion picture industry.)

One can condense what happened at the negotiations by simply stating that the representatives of the producers refused to discuss any of the proposals. . . .

31

Sidney Lumet: *Making Movies* (1995)

Sidney Lumet (b. 1924) began his directing career in television and first came to prominence as a feature-film director with the tense courtroom drama *12 Angry Men* (1957). From the 1960s onward his films elicited intelligent scores from a clutch of the leading film composers of his generation, and in this chapter from his book on filmmaking he discusses his various collaborations with Rubén Blades (b. 1948), Johnny Mandel (b. 1925), Quincy Jones (b. 1933), Paul Chihara (b. 1938), André Previn (b. 1929), and the British composer Richard Rodney Bennett (b. 1936). Among the films he describes are *Long Day's Journey into Night* (1962), *The Pawnbroker* (1964), *The Deadly Affair* (1966), *Murder on the Orient Express* (1974), *Prince of the City* (1981), *The Verdict* (1982), *Daniel* (1983), and *Q & A* (1990).

Lumet, who here describes the process of soundtrack construction from spotting sessions up to the final music and sound-effects dubbing, had an unusually enlightened attitude toward the musical provision in his films and fully respected the artistry of the composers with whom he worked. Nevertheless, as he recalls, in several films—including *The Hill* (1965), *Dog Day Afternoon* (1975), and *Network* (1976)—he decided to include no music at all in the interests of naturalism, and allowed music onto the soundtrack of *Serpico* (1973) only after a run-in with powerful producer Dino De Laurentiis led to the lucrative involvement of Greek composer Mikis Theodorakis.

Source: Making Movies (London: Bloomsbury, 1995): 170–85.

If the cliché about pictures being made in the cutting room is false, that other cliché, "It'll play better when we add the music," is true. Almost every picture is improved by a good musical score. To start with, music is a quick way to reach people emotionally. Over the years, movie music has developed so many clichés of its own that the audience immediately absorbs the intention of the moment: the music tells them, sometimes even in advance. Generally, that would be the sign of a bad score, but even bad scores work.

When the score is predictable, when it duplicates in melody and arrangement the action up there on the screen, we call it "mickey-mousing." The reference is obviously to cartoon music, which duplicates everything down to Jerry kicking Tom's teeth in. Pictures with scores like that are probably not injured by them. Chances are, the music is not the only cliché in the movie. It's probably loaded with them.

Often it's not even the composer's fault. After the screen-writer, I think movie composers are violated more often than anyone. Everybody thinks he knows something about music and wants to get his two cents in about the score. If the composer comes up with something too original—that is, something the producers or the studio people haven't heard before—the score can get thrown out. I've seen producers make a music editor cut cues, rearrange them, eliminate sections of arrangements, and otherwise tear a score apart until it's unrecognizable. Today, when practically every instrument in the orchestra is recorded separately, it's possible to almost reorchestrate by going back to the original thirty-two-or sixty-four-track recording.

Working in movies is the fatal compromise composers make. In return for very good pay, they go to work writing for a form that can never belong to them. Music, clearly one of our greatest art forms, must be subjugated to the needs of the picture. That's the nature of moviemaking. Even though it may take over completely at certain points, its function is primarily supportive.

The only movie score I've heard that can stand on its own as a piece of music is Prokofiev's "Battle on the Ice" from *Alexander Nevsky* [1938]. I'm told that Eisenstein and Prokofiev talked about it well before shooting began and that some of the composing was started before shooting. Supposedly, Eisenstein even edited some of the sequence to accommodate the score. I have no idea whether these stories are true. Even when I hear the music on a record today, I start remembering the sequence visually. The two, music and picture, are indelibly linked: a great sequence, a great score.

I think that that may be one of the indications of good movie music: the immediate recurrence of the visual elements in the picture that the music supports. But some of the best scores I've heard cannot be remembered at all. I'm thinking of Howard Shore's superb scoring for *The Silence of the Lambs* [1990]. When seeing the movie, I never heard it. But I always felt it. It's the kind of score I try to achieve in most of my movies. With all the Oscar nominations my pictures have gotten in various categories, only Richard Rodney Bennett's score for *Murder on the Orient Express* [1974] received a music nomination. But it was the only picture I've done where I *wanted* the score to shine. As must be clear by now, I feel that the less an audience is aware of how we're achieving an effect, the better the picture will be.

I've sat with my brain trust at Patsy's restaurant, asking them about their feelings after viewing the first cut. Now I will go back into the cutting room and start to reedit. Some of those dialogue lines I didn't like get cut out. Sometimes a whole scene gets removed. Sometimes four, five scenes, a whole reel, get deleted. (It got clear sooner.) Something was dragging in reels 4, 5, 6, 7. Forty minutes of dragging. That's serious. Maybe if we can rearrange some elements, reconstruct a bit. Let this character's story start a little sooner. That helps revive interest. This performance is so good it doesn't *need* that much time. That performance is so bad it *mustn't* have that much time.

In other words, we are editing in the true sense of the word. We are, hopefully, making it better. As I finish the second time around and the third, I screen again. Some of the brain trust may be there, but I widen the audience a little, maybe ten or twelve people. But I pick them carefully, because looking at a picture in this shape isn't easy. The film is scratched, even torn in places. No opticals (dissolves, fade-outs, special effects) have been made. And the audio track particularly is difficult. Dialogue hasn't been equalized, and in some shots you just can't understand what is being said. Since dialogue on exterior locations hasn't been rerecorded (called "looping"), those scenes are especially hard to hear. Sound effects are missing. And of course, the music remains to be scored and placed.

Once we're happy with the cut, I set up two important meetings, one with the composer, the second with the sound-effects editor. The composer was invited to the first screening. The sound effects editor came to the second, and the entire sound effects department (anywhere from six to twenty people, depending on how complicated the job is) came to the third. They're usually a terrible audience. They are listening for sounds only a dog can hear, and they're dreading the amount of work ahead of them.

If the composer was hired before shooting began, perhaps he's attended rushes. He's always invited. But either before shooting or after we have looked at the first cut, we sit and talk in order to decide the critical question: What function should the score serve? How can it contribute to the basic question of "What is the picture about?"

We then adjourn to the cutting room for what we call a "spotting session." We look at the movie reel by reel. I give the composer my feelings about where I think music is necessary, and he does the same. This provides us with a preliminary sketch. Now we review it carefully. Does he have enough room to state the musical ideas clearly? If a musical transition has to take place, have we allowed enough room for it? Very often in melodramas, composers and directors settle for what we call "stings." These are the short, sharp orchestral bursts that accompany the shot of the villain breaking through the door. They last a few seconds. They're supposed to scare the audience. They are such a cliché by now that I don't think they scare anyone. Sometimes music is put in to tide us over a "dissolve," the fading in of a new scene over an old one to show us a change in location or a passage of time. Again, the music will last about twenty seconds. I hate these kinds of cues. I like to make sure that every music cue has enough time to say and do what it's supposed to say and do. We have decided on what we want the music to contribute to the movie. Within the cue itself, there must be enough time to make the idea of the cue work. Short melodramatic bursts or segues from one scene to another simply fill the air with useless sound and therefore reduce the effectiveness of the music when it's really needed.

After the preliminary sketch, we go back over the movie. Now we get very specific about where the music comes in and where it goes out. We time it to the frame. The entry point is particularly critical. The shift of a few frames, or a few feet, can make the difference between whether the cue works or doesn't work. This process takes two or three days. Sometimes if the composer's a really good pianist, as Cy Coleman is, we may bring a small piano into the cutting room and improvise melodies, entrance cues, and general support for the scene.

As I said earlier, I don't want to "mickey-mouse." I want the score to say something that nothing else in the picture is saying.

For instance, in The Verdict [1982], nothing much was ever revealed about Paul Newman's background. At one point there's an indication that he went through a rough divorce and was the fall guy for his father-in-law's shady law firm. But we dealt with nothing in his youth or childhood. I told Johnny Mandel that I wanted the deep, buried sound of a religious childhood: parochial school, children's church choir. He was possibly an acolyte. Since the picture was about this man's resurrection, he had to have been brought up religiously, so he would have somewhere to fall from. The picture could then be about his return to faith. The score's function was to provide the state of grace from which to fall.

The Pawnbroker [1964] had as complex a score as I've ever worked on. In the opening scene, Sol Nazerman, a Jewish refugee from Germany, is sitting in a suburban backyard, soaking up the sun. His sister asks for a loan so she and her family can take a vacation in Europe that summer. To Nazerman, everything about Europe is a cesspool. He says, "Europe? It's rather like a stink, as I remember." The next sequence shows him driving into New York City, to his pawnshop in Harlem. Those two scenes set up the conception of the score. Earlier, I said that *The Pawnbroker* was about how and why we establish our own prisons. At the beginning of the movie, Nazerman is encased in his own coldness. He has tried desperately to feel no emotion, and he has succeeded. The story of the movie is how his life in Harlem breaks down the wall of ice with which he has surrounded himself.

The concept of the score was "Harlem triumphant!"—that the life, pain, and energy of his life there forced him to feel again. I decided I wanted two musical themes: one representing Europe, the other Harlem. The European theme was to be classical in its nature, precise but rather soft, a feeling of something old. The Harlem theme, by contrast, would be percussive, with lots of brass, wild in feeling—containing the most modern jazz sound that could be created.

I started looking for a composer. I first approached John Cage. He had a record out at the time called *Third Stream*, classical music handled with jazz instrumentation and rhythms. He wasn't interested in doing a movie score. Then I met with Gil Evans, the great modern jazz composer and arranger, but found it tough to get through. Next, I approached John Lewis of the Modern Jazz Quartet, but I felt he didn't really like the movie when I showed it to him.

Then someone suggested Quincy Jones. I knew some of his jazz work from records he'd made on a big-band tour of Norway. We met. It was love at first sight. His intelligence and enthusiasm were inspiring. I found out that he'd studied with Nadia Boulanger in Paris, which meant that his classical background was firm. He gave me other records of his, many on obscure labels. He'd never done a movie score, but that made him even more interesting to me. Very often, because of the nature of the work, composers develop their own set of musical clichés when they've done too many pictures. I thought his lack of movie experience would be a plus.

I showed him the movie. He loved it. We went to work. Talking about music is like talking about colors: the same color can mean different things to different people. But Quincy and I found that we were literally talking the same language in music. We laid out a musical plot that was almost mathematical in its precision. Just like the subway-to-railway-car transition, we moved in steps from the European theme to the final total dominance of the Harlem theme. At midpoint in the picture, they were equally balanced.

It was a magnificent score, and the recording sessions were the most exciting I've ever been to. Because it was Quincy's first movie score, the band that turned out for him rivaled Esquire's All-Star Jazz Band. Dizzy Gillespie, John Faddis (a mere child at the time) on trumpet, Elvin Jones on drums, Jerome Richardson on lead sax, George Duvivier on bass . . . the names kept pouring into the recording studio. Dizzy had just come back from Brazil, and for one music cue he suggested a rhythm that none of us, including Quincy, had ever heard before. He had to sing it with clucks, gurgles, and glottal stops until the rhythm section could learn it. Quincy looked as happy as any man I'd ever seen.

Usually, when we finish recording a music cue, we stop and play it back against the picture. But the level of inspired playing from this band was so high that I told Quincy not to interrupt it. We'd play it back at the end of the day. Nobody even asked for the obligatory ten-minute break every hour. We played right through. At the end of five three-hour sessions spread over two days, we played it against the picture. It was immediately apparent: Quincy had made a major contribution to the movie.

As so often happens when you find a kindred spirit, we went on to do three more movies together. Quincy's score for *The Deadly Affair* [1966] was another musical triumph. Based on a John le Carré novella, the movie tells the story of a sad, solitary counterintelligence operator in the British Foreign Office. His wife is constantly betraying him. During the movie, his protégé, whom he trained in espionage during World War II, turns out to betray him both professionally and personally, entering into an affair with his wife.

The two worlds portrayed in the movie, the world of espionage and the almost masochistic love this man feels for his wife, formed the basic concept for the score. But this time, instead of two themes, Quincy created only one: a painfully beautiful love song, sung by Astrud Gilberto. However, as the picture progressed, it slowly turned into one of the most exciting melodramatic scores I'd ever heard. It proved the power and importance of musical arrangements. The theme stayed the same, but its entire dramatic meaning changed as the arrangements changed. Most composers farm out the arrangements. But Quincy did these himself. Again, it was a major contribution.

I've talked about Richard Rodney Bennett's score for *Murder on the Orient Express*. At our first meeting, Richard asked me what sound I heard in my mind for the picture. I said I was thinking of thirties-style Carmen Cavallaro or Eddie Duchin: a really good version of thé dansant, heavy on piano and strings. He not only provided a piano score but also played it himself during the recording session. Richard's a wonderful pianist. He had that Cavallaro style down to perfection. And when I heard the first rehearsal and realized that the train's theme was in waltz tempo, I knew we were on our way to a perfect score.

At one point, Richard suggested underscoring a scene that I felt should have no music. At the recording session, he played it for me. We recorded it and played it back against picture. He was right.

When I haven't been able to find a musical concept that adds to the movie, I haven't used a score. Studios hate the idea of a picture without music. It scares them. But if the first obligation of *Dog Day Afternoon* [1975] was to tell the audience that this event really happened, how could you justify music weaving in and out? *The Hill* [1965] was also done in a naturalistic style, so no score was used. In *Network* [1976], I was afraid that music might interfere with the jokes. As the picture went on, the speeches got longer and longer. It was clear at the first screening that any music would be fighting the enormous amount of dialogue. Again, no score.

Serpico [1973] shouldn't have had a score, but I put in fourteen minutes' worth to protect the picture and myself. The producer was Dino De Laurentiis. Dino is a terrific producer of the old school, wheeling and dealing and somehow always getting pictures financed no matter how wild the idea. His taste, however, tends to be a little operatic, even for me. We argued back and forth. Dino threatened to take the picture to Italy, where I was sure a score would be laid in like wall-to-wall carpeting. I didn't have final cut in those days, and Dino could've done exactly as he wanted.

Fortunately, I'd read in the paper that Mikis Theodorakis, the wonderful Greek composer, had just been released from prison. He had been jailed for left-wing political activities by the ultra-right-wing Greek government. When I reached him in Paris, he'd been out of jail less than twenty-four hours. I explained the situation, telling him about my disagreement with Dino. I said if there was *any* score, I'd prefer that he do it. Happily, he was flying to New York the next day, to see his manager about a concert tour. I told him we'd have a screening room set up so he could come see the picture as soon as he arrived. He drove right from Kennedy to the screening room. His plane was late, and the screening began at one-twenty in the morning.

When the picture ended, he looked at me and said he loved it but it shouldn't have music. I reiterated my problem. I pointed out that Dino would be thrilled to have a composer of Mikis's prestige doing the score, so that we could get away with a minimum amount of music, perhaps only ten minutes. With opening and closing titles consuming about five minutes of music, that would leave very little in the body of the picture. I also pointed out that he could pick up a healthy piece of change. I knew he had to be broke after such a long time in prison. I thought I was being very clever.

Mikis was cleverer still. He pulled from his pocket an audiocassette. He said, "I wrote this little song many years ago. It's a charming folk tune that could work for the movie. Do you think I could get seventy-five thousand dollars for it?" I said I was sure he could. His *Never on Sunday* [1959] score [in fact composed by Manos Hatzidakis] was still being played, by Muzak anyway. He said there was another problem. He would be touring with his orchestra and wouldn't be able to see the picture again or be back for spotting, arrangements, and recording sessions. I told him that I knew a marvelous young arranger named Bob James who would be happy to join him on the road when necessary. I could do the spotting sessions with Bob, who could then arrange the music and conduct the recording sessions. Everybody wound up happy. Dino had his prestigious composer, I wound up with only fourteen minutes of music (including the five minutes of credit music), Bob James got his first movie job, and Mikis took off for his tour a little more solvent than when he had arrived.

Prince of the City [1981] was meant to achieve a sense of tragedy in this story of a man who thought he could control forces that would eventually control him. Again, I chose a composer who hadn't done a movie score before, Paul Chihara. Conceptually, Danny Ciello was to be treated always as one instrument: saxophone. Over the body of the picture, his sound was to become more and more isolated, until finally three notes of the original theme, played on sax, was all that remained of the music.

American musicians were on strike, so I was forced to go to Paris to record the music. I bore up as best I could. But poor Paul wasn't even allowed to step into the recording studio. If word got back to New York, he would've been thrown out of the union immediately. They were watching the recording studios in London and Paris particularly. Paul was terrified. He had had a long struggle. Tony Walton had recommended him, and I'd admired his score for *The Tempest*, written for the San Francisco Ballet. Here he was on his first movie, riding with me to the recording studio but not coming in. During lunch, I'd see him across the street, gazing at us like a starving man in front of a bakery window. Every night I brought him a cassette of the day's work. Fortunately, Georges Delerue was conducting. He knew and loved Paul's classical work. No composer ever had a more devoted interpreter.

What makes my work so endlessly interesting is that every picture requires its own specific approach. *Prince of the City* had close to fifty minutes of music. For a picture of mine, that's a lot of scoring. *Long Day's Journey Into Night* [1962] was also a picture that I hope achieved tragic dimensions. The musical approach was exactly the opposite. André Previn wrote a simple, slightly discordant piano score, which was used very sparingly. At the end of the movie, Mary Tyrone, thoroughly drugged out, wanders into the parlor, opens an ancient upright, and painfully, with arthritic fingers, stumbles through a piano piece. At first it sounds like a typical piano étude. Then we recognize it as the bare, sparse piano piece that Previn had written and been playing intermittently through the movie. I don't think there was more than ten minutes of music in a picture that ran over three hours.

Two other scores are worth mentioning. Like everything about *Daniel* [1983], the score was easy to conceive and hard to execute. For the only time in one of my pictures, I used music that already existed. I knew from the beginning that I wanted to use Paul Robeson recordings. He was perfect for the period. He was right politically, since it is at a Robeson concert in Peekskill, New York, that one of the leading characters has a traumatic experience. But which songs, and where to spot them? Through trial and error, the score shaped itself. The first song, "This Little Light of Mine," didn't occur until halfway through the picture. It was reprised at the end, when Daniel, restored to life, attends an enormous antiwar rally in Central Park. Only this time around, it was played and sung in a more modern, Joan Baez arrangement. For his sister's funeral, "There's a Man Going Round, Taking Names" worked wonderfully. Editing had to be changed to accommodate the already finished recordings, since the changes we were allowed to make in them were very limited. We could cut a chorus, but that was about it. Two other Robeson recordings were used, including his magnificent "Jacob's Ladder."

For *Q & A* [1990], which took place largely in Spanish Harlem, with the climax in Puerto Rico, I asked Rubén Blades to do the score. He had made a recording of a song he wrote called "The Hit." It fit perfectly into the spirit and the meaning of the picture. Here was a movie about the racism, conscious and subconscious, that governs so much of our behavior. Rubén recorded the song anew, matching the performance to the intensity of the movie. Then he built a full-fledged score based on the song's melody.

The other vital component in the audio power of a movie is sound effects. I'm not talking about the car crashes and explosions of a Stallone or Schwarzenegger epic. I'm talking about the brilliant use of sound in, for example, *Apocalypse Now* [1979], which has the most imaginative and dramatic use of sound effects of any movie I've seen. A close second is *Schindler's List* [1993]. I've never done a movie that required such elaborate sound effects. This is partly because many of my pictures have a great deal of dialogue, which forces you to keep sound effects to a minimum.

Immediately after the spotting session with the composer, I have my second meeting, a session with the sound editor and his entire department. If possible, we try to come up with a concept for the sound effects. I don't know what was discussed on *Apocalypse Now*, but a concept was clearly at work: to create an unearthly experience in sound, emerging from the realism of the sounds of battle. On *Prince of the City*, we simply started with as much sound as possible, then kept reducing it as the picture went on. On location interiors, there is always an exterior ambience that comes into the set. We added exterior sounds to interior locations (pile drivers, buses, auto horns) at the beginning of the movie. Then we slowly kept reducing those sounds until we played the final interiors, with the least exterior sound possible.

Sometimes a sound can carry a subtle dramatic effect. In *Serpico*, as Pacino tiptoed onto the landing near the door of a drug dealer he was about to arrest, a dog in a nearby apartment barked. If the dog heard him there, could the dealer hear him also?

We again go through the picture, reel by reel, foot by foot. Much of the work is sheerly technical. Because so much work, both interior and exterior, is done on location, we use highly directional microphones. Their spread is about seven to fifteen degrees. The reason is that we want to pick up dialogue with as little background sound as possible. When we go into the studio, we stay with the same mikes, because the quality of the sound would change too drastically if we switched to normal studio mikes. That would create a lot of extra work later on, because we'd have to equalize the two different types of microphones. So a great deal of the discussion is about adding foot-steps, or the sound of someone sitting down on a couch, or the scrape of a chair as someone gets up, and so forth—sounds that are lost because of the highly directional mikes. All of this added sound has to be done anyway, in preparation for the foreign versions of the movie. Dialogue will be dubbed by the various foreign distributors, but we are obligated to provide all background sound effects and music.

The sound editor splits the reels among the people in the sound department. This group takes reels 1 to 3, that group reels 4 to 6, and so on. Each group usually consists of an editor, an assistant editor, and an apprentice. But the sound editor is responsible for the overall supervision. A normal sound job takes six to eight weeks. Obviously, bigger pictures need more personnel and time.

Even if no overall concept has been articulated, I like effects that enhance the dramatic value of a scene. In *The Pawnbroker*, Sol visits a woman he has consistently rejected. It is the actual anniversary of the day he and his family were loaded into cattle cars to be taken away to the camps. She lives in a modern complex of buildings that overlook a railroad yard in the distance. On location one could see the railroad yards. We put in the sounds of a railway switching yard, the sounds of engines, of cars being shunted and bumping into one another. Sound loses its distinctiveness when it continues for any length of time.

Used behind the whole scene and played at a very low level, it is barely distinguishable. But it's there. And I think it adds to the scene.

On *The Hill*, I asked the sound editor to play one scene in complete silence. When he played it back for me, I heard the buzz of a fly. "I thought we'd agreed that this scene was silent," I said. He replied, "Sidney, if you can hear a fly, then the place is *really* quiet." A good lesson.

The sound editor on *Murder on the Orient Express* hired the "world's greatest authority" on train sounds. He brought me the *authentic* sounds of not only the Orient Express but the Flying Scotsman, the Twentieth Century Limited, every train that had ever achieved any reputation. He worked for six *weeks* on train sounds only. His greatest moment occurred when, at the beginning of the picture, the train left the station at Istanbul. We had the steam, the bell, the wheels, and he even included an almost inaudible click when the train's headlight went on. He swore that all the effects were authentic. When we got to the mix (the point at which we put *all* the sound tracks together), he was bursting with anticipation. For the first time, I heard what an incredible job he'd done. But I had also heard Richard Rodney Bennett's magnificent music score for the same scene. I knew one would have to go. They couldn't work together. I turned to Simon. He knew. I said, "Simon, it's a great job. But, finally, we've heard a train leave the station. We've never heard a train leave the station in three-quarter time." He walked out, and we never saw him again. I bring this up to show how delicate the balance is between effects and music. Generally, I like one or the other to do the job. Sometimes one augments the other. Sometimes, as here, not.

Sound effects have also developed their own clichés over the years. Can there be a country night scene without crickets? A dog barking in the distance? How about a pile driver in a tense urban scene? Slowly, progress is taking some of the clichés away. Phones in an office no longer ring, they purr. Computers have replaced typewriters, fax machines for teletypes. Everything grows quieter and colorless. Car alarms are a great help, but they're just as annoying on-screen as they are off.

Everything becomes creative if the person doing the job is. It's true as well for something that seems as mechanical as sound effects.

Acknowledgments

This book would not have come into being without the enthusiasm, energy, and vision of my editor, Norm Hirschy at Oxford University Press, with whom it has been a constant pleasure to work, and whose patience and sustained moral support have been much valued at all stages in the volume's planning and preparation. I am also grateful to production editor Christine Dahlin and copy editor Christi Stanforth for their sterling work on the project. For their valuable input in the book's planning stages, I am indebted to David Cooper, Annette Davison, Peter Franklin, and Raymond Knapp. Both editor and publisher extend grateful thanks to the University of Nottingham's School of Humanities for its generous contribution toward the cost of securing permissions to reprint copyright material and photographs, and to those individual rights holders who have been happy for their texts and images to be reproduced free of charge.

While formal credits for permission to reproduce the texts in our selection follow here, I should like to take the additional opportunity to thank those many individuals and institutions who were unfailingly helpful in offering assistance to track down both the original sources and in some cases the identity and whereabouts of the rights holders themselves. For their encouragement I am especially grateful to André Previn, John Williams, and Olivia Tiomkin Douglas, and to their respective assistants Tanja Dorn (IMG Artists), Jamie Richardson, and Suzie Weston. The support of Mike Barrier, Marilee Bradford (Film Music Society), Roy Frumkes (*Films in Review*), Gene Lees, and Michael Schelle has been most valuable. Literary executors who deserve particular thanks include Charles Amirkhanian (on behalf of Peter Antheil) and Anthony Linick (on behalf of Ingolf Dahl), and I am also indebted to Steve Ashford and Polly-anna Gunning (Sony Music); Craig L. Byrd; Alfred W. Cochran (Kansas State University); Lee Dion (Copyright Clearance Center); John Fitzpatrick (Rózsa Society); Sarah Garcia, Laura Muhlhammer, and Carol Roeder (Lucasfilm); Cynthia Harris (Hale Library, Kansas State University); Lukas Kendall (*Film Score Monthly*); Edward R. Leydon (Reichhold, Inc.); Richard Lonsdorf (Columbia Artists Management); Gabriel Nordyke (Insights Design); Jessica Rauch (Aaron Copland Fund for Music, Inc.); Patrick Russ; and Yuval Taylor (A Cappella Books). For their helpfulness in acting on behalf of various publishers I am grateful to Christina Bauer (Taylor & Francis), Elizabeth Clementson (W. W. Norton), Nicci Cloke (Faber and Faber), Katy DiSavino (Samuel French, Inc.), Jonathan Eyers (Bloomsbury), Marta Granatowska and Adele Hutchinson (Sage), Michael Hopkins and Yan Wu (PARS International, on behalf of *New York Times*), Ben Kennedy (OUP journals), Ebony Lane (McGraw-Hill Education), Jennifer C. Rowley (Random House, Inc.), Gabrielle White (Random House UK), Janet Wilkin (Pearson Education), Kelly Wilson (Chicago Review Press), and Patricia Zline (Rowman & Littlefield). For their help on various matters I am indebted to Jonathan Branfield and Fiona Ford at the University of Nottingham.

The resources and staff of a number of academic institutions and libraries have been of considerable assistance, and thanks are due in particular to the Hallward Library at the University of Nottingham, and especially to its staff members Kenneth Robinson and Alison Stevens. For their invaluable participation in interlibrary loan services I am grateful to the Bodleian Library, University of Oxford; the British Library, London; Cambridge University Library; Durham University Library; Mortensen Library, University of Hartford, Connecticut; Leeds University Library; Library of Congress, Washington, D.C.; John Rylands Library, University of Manchester; University of Miami Libraries; Nottingham County Libraries; Princeton University Library; Sheffield University Library; Warwick University Library; and Yale University Library. For helping me trace a number of rights holders I am indebted to Ned Comstock (Cinematic Arts Library, University of Southern California), David Seubert (Davidson Library, University of California at Santa Barbara), and Claude Zachary (Doheny Memorial Library, University of Southern California).

Lastly, and most importantly, my love and gratitude to one who never expects to be thanked for all her many kindnesses: my wife, Sally, whose friendship and decency illuminate the lives of all those fortunate enough to be close to her.

Credits

The following publishers, organizations, and individuals have generously given permission to reprint articles and excerpts from longer works:

"The Origin of Film Music," by Max Winkler. First published in *Films in Review*, 2/10 (December 1951): 34–42. Copyright © 1951 by *Films in Review*. Used by permission of Roy Frumkes (editor).

Excerpt from "An Interview with Gaylord Carter, 'Dean of Theater Organists,'" by Rudy Behlmer. From Clifford McCarty, ed., *Film Music I* (New York: Garland, 1989). Copyright © 1989 by The Society for the Preservation of Film Music. Used by permission of Taylor & Francis Group LLC.

"Scoring the Film," by Max Steiner. From *We Make the Movies*, edited by Nancy Naumburg. Copyright © 1937 by W. W. Norton & Company, Inc. Used by permission of W. W. Norton & Company, Inc.

"Life with Charlie," by David Raksin. First published in *Quarterly Journal of the Library of Congress*, 40/3 (1983): 234–53. Used by permission of The Library of Congress.

Excerpt from *Our New Music: Leading Composers in Europe and America*, by Aaron Copland. Copyright © 1941 by the McGraw-Hill Book Company, Inc. Used by permission of The McGraw-Hill Companies.

"Notes on Cartoon Music," by Ingolf Dahl. First published in *Film Music Notes*, 8/5 (May/June 1949): 3–13. Copyright © 1949 by Ingolf Dahl. Used by permission of Dr. Anthony Linick.

"Personality on the Soundtrack: A Glimpse Behind the Scenes and Sequences in Filmland," by Scott Bradley. First published in *Music Educators*

Journal, 33/3 (January 1947): 28–29. Copyright © 1947 by Music Educators National Conference. Used by permission of Sage Publications Inc. (Journals).

"Conversations with Carl Stalling," by Michael Barrier. First published as "An Interview with Carl Stalling," *Funnyworld*, 13 (Spring 1971): 21–27; reprinted in Daniel Goldmark and Yuval Taylor, eds., *The Cartoon Music Book* (Chicago: A Cappella, 2002): 37–60. Copyright © 1971 by Michael Barrier. Used by permission of Michael Barrier.

Excerpts from *Please Don't Hate Me!* by Dimitri Tiomkin and Prosper Buranelli. Copyright © 1959 by Dimitri Tiomkin and Prosper Buranelli. Used by permission of Mrs. Olivia Tiomkin Douglas and Volta Music Corporation.

"Music in Documentary Films," by Gail Kubik. First published in *Music Publishers' Journal*, 3/5 (September–October 1945): 13, 54–56. Copyright © by the Estate of Gail Kubik.

"*Quo Vadis*," by Miklós Rózsa. First published in *Film/TV Music*, 11/4 (November–December 1951); reprinted in James L. Limbacher, ed., *Film Music: From Violins to Video* (Metuchen, N.J.: Scarecrow Press, 1974): 147–53. Used by permission of Scarecrow Press, Inc.

Excerpts from *No Minor Chords*, by André Previn. Copyright © 1991 by André Previn. Used by permission of André Previn and The Random House Group Ltd.

Excerpts from *Did They Mention the Music?* by Henry Mancini and Gene Lees. Copyright © 1989 by Henry Mancini and Gene Lees. Used by permission of Gene Lees.

Excerpt from "Bernard Herrmann, Film Composer." First published in Evan William Cameron, ed., assisted by William F. Wilbert and Joan Evans-Cameron, *Sound and the Cinema: The Coming of Sound to American Film* (Pleasantville, N.Y.: Redgrave Publishing, 1980): 117–35. Copyright © 1980 by Redgrave Publishing. Used by permission of Taylor & Francis Group LLC.

"A Conversation with Jerry Goldsmith." First published in *Film Music Notebook*, 3/2 (1977): 18–31; reprinted in *Elmer Bernstein's Film Music Notebook: A Complete Collection of the Quarterly Journal, 1974–1978* (Sherman Oaks, Calif.: Film Music Society, 2004). Copyright © 2004 by The Film Music Society. Used by permission of The Film Music Society.

"The Star Wars Interview: John Williams," by Craig L. Byrd. First published in *Film Score Monthly*, 2/1 (1997): 18–21. Used by permission of John Williams and Lucasfilm Ltd.

"Thomas Newman on His Film Music." First published in Michael Schelle, *The Score: Interviews with Film Composers* (Beverly Hills: Silman-James Press, 1999): 269–92. Copyright © 1999 by Michael Schelle. Used by permission of Michael Schelle.

Index

CPSIA information can be obtained
at www.ICGtesting.com
Printed in the USA
BVOW06s1654160117
473604BV00001B/1/P